PSYCHOLOGY IN PRACTICE

PERSPECTIVES ON PROFESSIONAL PSYCHOLOGY

PSYCHOLOGY IN PRACTICE

PERSPECTIVES ON PROFESSIONAL PSYCHOLOGY

Edited by

Sandra Canter

and

David Canter

University of Surrey

1807 1982

JOHN WILEY & SONS

Chichester · New York · Brisbane · Toronto · Singapore

Library of Congress Cataloging in Publication Data:
Main entry under title:

Psychology in practice.

 Includes indexes.
  1. Psychology — Vocational guidance — Addresses, essays,
Lectures. 2. Psychology, Applied — Vocational guidance —
Addresses, essays, lectures. I. Canter, Sandra.
II. Canter, David V.
BF76.P78 1983   150′.23   82-2733
ISBN 0 471 10411 6

British Library Cataloguing in Publication Data:
Psychology in practice
  1. Psychology, Applied — Addresses, essays,
  lectures
  I. Canter, Sandra   II. Canter, David
  158   BF636

 ISBN 0 471 10411 6

Phototypeset by Dobbie Typesetting Service, Plymouth, Devon, England
and printed by the Pitman Press Ltd., Bath, Avon.

CONTENTS

LIST OF CONTRIBUTORS.................................... vii

1 PROFESSIONAL PSYCHOLOGY
Sandra and David Canter....................................... 1

2 CLINICAL PSYCHOLOGY IN PRACTICE
William Reavley 23

3 PSYCHOLOGY IN MEDICINE
Philip Ley 41

4 PSYCHOLOGY AND MENTAL HANDICAP
Jeanne Males... 63

5 FORENSIC PSYCHOLOGY
Lionel Haward 89

6 PSYCHOLOGISTS IN THE PRISON DEPARTMENT
Bernard Marcus 105

7 PSYCHOLOGY AT WORK IN EDUCATION
Keith Topping... 125

8 PSYCHOLOGY AND ADULT EDUCATION
Athalinda McIntosh....................................... 151

9 PSYCHOLOGY AND WORK: THE GROWTH
OF A DISCIPLINE
Pat Shipley... 165

10 THE OCCUPATIONAL PSYCHOLOGIST
Andrew Stewart 177

11 ORGANIZATIONAL PSYCHOLOGY
Frank Blackler.. 203

12 PSYCHOLOGY AND AVIATION
V. David Hopkin 233

13 CONSUMER PSYCHOLOGY
Alan Frost and David Canter 249

14 PSYCHOLOGY AND COMMUNICATION TECHNOLOGY
    Bruce Christie 271

15 PSYCHOLOGY AND ENVIRONMENTAL DESIGN
    David Canter 289

16 PSYCHOLOGY AND WRITTEN INSTRUCTION
    James Hartley 311

17 CAN EXPERIMENTAL PSYCHOLOGY BE
    APPLIED PSYCHOLOGY?
    Ray Bull 335

    SUBJECT INDEX 347

LIST OF CONTRIBUTORS

Frank Blackler
Lecturer and Head of Department, Behaviour in Organizations, University of Lancaster, Lancaster

Ray Bull
Senior Lecturer, Department of Psychology, North East London Polytechnic, London

David V. Canter
Reader in Psychology, Department of Psychology, University of Surrey, Guildford, Surrey

Sandra L. Canter
Lecturer in Clinical Psychology, Department of Psychology, University of Surrey, Guildford, Surrey

Bruce Christie
Manager, Systems Psychology, ITT Europe, Great Eastern House, Edinburgh Way, Harlow, Essex

Alan Frost
Alan Frost Associates, 1 Pond Street, London

Lionel R. C. Haward
Professor of Clinical Psychology, University of Surrey, Guildford, Surrey

V. David Hopkin
Senior Principal Psychologist, Royal Air Force Institute of Aviation Medicine, Farnborough, Hampshire

James Hartley
Reader in Psychology and Head of Department, The University of Keele, Staffordshire

Philip Ley
Professor of Clinical Psychology, Department of Psychology, Clinical Psychology Unit, The University of Sydney, New South Wales, Australia

Athalinda J. McIntosh
Lecturer in Educational Studies, Department of Educational Studies, University of Surrey, Guildford, Surrey

Jeanne Males
Principal Clinical Psychologist, St Lawrence Hospital, Caterham, Surrey

Bernard Marcus
Principal Psychologist, HM Prison Grendon, Aylesbury, Bucks

William Reavley
Principal Clinical Psychologist, Graylingwell Hospital, Chichester, Sussex

Pat Shipley
Lecturer in Psychology, Department of Occupational Psychology, Birkbeck College, London

Andrew M. Stewart
Consultant Industrial Psychologist, Macmillan Stewart and Partners, Heather Ridge, Thursley Road, Elstead, Godalming, Surrey

Keith Topping
Educational Psychologist, Calderdale Psychological Service, Halifax, West Yorkshire

CHAPTER 1

PROFESSIONAL PSYCHOLOGY

Sandra Canter and **David Canter**
Lecturer in Clinical Psychology and Reader in Psychology
University of Surrey

The present book evolved from a symposium we organized, a few years ago, under the title of 'The Uses and Abuses of Psychology in Practice'. We considered that there was a need for such a symposium, because of two separate developments. The first is the growing gap between, on the one hand, what students (and many of their lecturers) think that psychologists do in practice, beyond the walls of universities, and on the other hand what professional, practising psychologists actually do in their day-to-day working lives. The second development is the growing recognition by practitioners themselves of the similarities which they share with each other across the many fields of psychological application. These similarities in the activities of professional psychologists, the way those activities are changing and the consequent skills and knowledge on which they must draw are seen by many now to be greater than the differences implied by the existence of distinct training courses, sections of professional bodies, and specialist journals.

During the symposium and the lengthy discussions and correspondence which followed, it emerged that our focus on 'uses and abuses' was far too restrictive. We found that we were witnessing a broadening and deepening of professional psychology which went a long way beyond that presented in a great many undergraduate courses. We decided, as a consequence, that we should bring together a wider range of contributions than was possible in a symposium, in order to present a reflection of current developments in the applications of psychology, whilst still keeping our initial aim of giving an account of what the practitioners actually do in their professional work and the perspectives from which they approach it.

One further reason for this book was that we knew, as admissions officers for post-graduate courses in clinical and environmental psychology, that the horizons of many psychology graduates are limited and their understanding of the work opportunities available to them frequently very restricted. Why is it that there are perhaps as many as twenty well-qualified applicants for every place on post-graduate clinical psychology courses while some courses in other areas of applied psychology may have as few as two or three after each place?

For many applicants it is possible that the attraction to clinical psychology goes beyond the pragmatic quest for a training in a field where there are likely to be jobs and where there is a clear professional structure, and relates to the desire of students to 'work with individuals' or 'help others'. Indeed this probably weights the balance towards clinical psychology as much in other countries without National Health Services, such as the USA and Germany, as it does in Britain. But this is where ignorance is so misleading. As will be stated from various perspectives, time and again in later chapters, not only are clinical psychologists no longer content to expend all their efforts on individual clients (they are increasingly working with groups and organizations and attempting to influence policy formulation), but those psychologists working in the context of industry are frequently involved in activities, such as for example counselling and anxiety management, which might, naïvely, be considered the sole province of the clinical psychologist.

Indeed, even the distinction between the clinical, or for that matter the welfare context and the industrial or management context is becoming a distinction which it is increasingly hard to defend. We realized this problem acutely when trying to find a logical order and structure to the book. In the same way that marital harmony may be stretched by attempting to wallpaper a room together, or when one spouse teaches the other to drive, it was stretched when we attempted to agree on a way of structuring the contents of this book. One issue we discussed, for example, was where to put prison psychologists. They may often be attempting to change an organization so that many individual prisoners will benefit, yet some may well be giving therapy. Consider organizational psychologists. When advising on the introduction of new office technologies, for example, they may often find themselves helping individuals to adjust to their changing work situations. What of educational psychologists? Are they mainly concerned with the welfare of individuals? Surely, more than any other area of psychology this is one in which professional psychologists have influenced central and local government policy?

When the actual activities of professional psychologists and the perspectives the practitioners themselves have of those activities are taken as the focus, rather than academic discussions of 'applied psychology', it becomes clear that the old demarcations are decaying in practice far more quickly than the institutional paraphernalia which supports them. What we are being left with are various focii for professional activity each with its own emphasis and context yet all being carried out against the backdrop of professional psychology as a unitary endeavour. We shall turn later to our attempt at specifying what characterizes this endeavour and the implications we believe it has for under-graduate and post-graduate training.

One further reason why a book which overviews professional opportunities in psychology is now necessary is that the career routes which were attractive and available for many well-qualified graduates in the universities are now being cut off as the drastic reduction in university expenditure continues. More and more of the best psychology graduates, who in the past would have found their way into university lectureships, must now find opportunities outside the sheltered university cloisters. They therefore need to be made aware of the other possibilities open to them which may still be expanding.

Bringing together an overview of what psychologists actually do proved a more difficult task than we had anticipated. We began to understand why no one else had accomplished this task before. These difficulties were not just those associated with locating a broad spectrum of practitioners who were prepared to take time off to write about their work but the more fundamental problem, with which all our contributors have had to grapple, of how to write about activities. Obviously, spending a day watching what a psychologist is doing would reveal far more of the essence of his activities and the skills and stresses associated with it, than can ever be gained from a book. However, the generality and the ready availability of the written word commends it at least as an initial stage in the teaching process.

It is because of this difficulty of capturing on paper the actions and experiences of a great many different practitioners that we decided to produce a book which focuses on 'perspectives'. We decided against the 'day in the life of' approach or other forms of documentary or anecdotal styles because we thought they would lose so much of the more fundamental themes that are emerging across professional practice. The strictly academic review of the literature was also not encouraged, because that would defeat our purpose of providing an account from within the practitioner's experience. Instead we aimed at a balance (some would call it a compromise) between the 'folksy' at one end and the 'learned' at the other. Our intention was to get the viewpoint of practitioners on what their work is about, the experiences which characterize it, and the skills which they draw upon, illustrated fully with actual examples of their work. In short we have tried to bring together a variety of *perspectives* on professional psychology.

Different authors, according to their predilections and their context, have struck a balance at different points. Some of the contributors are firmly based in the field, grappling daily with professional issues. Others are based within universities, foraying out into the world beyond their ivory towers in order to practise their profession. Furthermore, we also recognize that no such collection as the present one can be comprehensive. It is in the nature of the presentation of a perspective that it is personal to the individual who has it, as most of the contributors to this volume have been at pains to point out. Other contributors from the same areas of application could well express quite different emphases. This book, then, should be read as a number of sample drillings in different fields of psychology. The overall map which emerges will be accurate enough for a general picture, but before detailed decisions are made on any particular site the reader would be well advised to explore the chosen field in much more detail.

It should also be recognized that within the time and resources available a completely all-inclusive set of contributions could not be collected together, assuming that any one (or two) individuals could ever formulate a view of what the totality of professional psychology was. We are aware of a number of areas of professional psychological activity which are not covered in this book. For example the involvement of psychologists with the armed forces, reviewed so fully in Watson's (1978) book *War on the Mind*, is barely mentioned in this volume. An omission which contrasts with this military work is the increasing involvement of psychologists in the area of tourism, discussed by Mayo and Jarvis in their (1981) book *The Psychology of Leisure Travel*.

Psychology now covers such a wide variety of activities that there is hardly an area of human experience which is not touched. Disaster victims (Cohen and Ahearn, 1981), energy conservation (Baum and Singer, 1981) and football violence (Marsh *et al.*, 1978) have all come under psychological scrutiny. Thus the psychological practitioner can be found in relation to just about any human endeavour (and a number of non-human ones too). However, despite this variety we are confident that there are a number of common threads which tie these professional activities together, and that the articles included here reflect the changes and current status of the professional field in general.

CHANGES IN THE PRACTICE OF PSYCHOLOGY

The use of the form 'professional' psychologist in the title of this book is meant to reflect what we see as the changes which are taking place both in attitudes to the practice of psychology and in the activities of psychologists. Even a cursory look at the British Psychological Society's monthly Bulletin indicates that a lively debate over the issue of professionalization has been pursued over the last few years, culminating in the recent vote by British Psychological Society members for the registration of psychologists. This, surely, is an important stage in the process of increasing professionalism. Concurrent with the debate on registration there continue to be attempts to improve and regulate training of psychologists both at undergraduate and post-graduate levels. It is clear that this has been pursued more vigorously in some areas than in others, but there does seem a genuine move toward making all training of psychologists more relevant to the demands of professional life.

As a group of practitioners, in all areas of activity, we have become more client-centred than psychology-centred. Where once we were content to dream up our own problems for investigation and test the adequacy of our work by the reactions of members of our own small group, we have become much more concerned with responding to the problems posed by our clients. We are less concerned with scientific respectability for its own sake and more concerned with doing a worthwhile job, judging our success, in part at least, by the satisfaction of our client and recognition from other professional groups that we have contributed effectively and responsibly to the task in hand.

As is reflected in all of the chapters in this book there has been a change in our views of our role from that of diagnostician, putting labels on problems, to that of active problem-solver. At one time the tools of our trade and the level of our courage were such that we were content to be diagnosticians often working towards objectives specified by others. We were largely concerned with clarifying problems, either in the form of testing to confirm diagnoses, as in the educational or clinical field for example, or as an industrial context, by developing selection procedures or measures of morale. The fruits of our efforts were usually passed on to others and our recommendations, if any, were rarely implemented. A situation in which we felt more frustration than responsibility! Such a narrow role is now being relinquished in all fields of endeavour and there is increasing involvement in practical intervention.

As professional psychologists we have become problem-solvers and see assessment activities as only one stage in the process with which we wish to be concerned. Our role is not simply to identify the problem but to offer solutions and to evaluate their consequences. This emphasis on intervention and problem-solving means that we can no longer retain a position of passive researcher content to study the effects of other people's work and to reflect passively the state of our client, group, organization, or society. We are becoming actively involved in shaping events with a desire to take part and be responsible for the implementation of change. As a consequence we are having to confront the moral issues that are an inevitable part of working within society.

As our confidence as practitioners grows we have paradoxically become more modest in our aspirations. There seems to be a move away from characterizing ourselves as experts and an increasing use of terms such as 'consultant', 'adviser', and 'specialist helper'. By removing our expert status we have removed the burden to produce expert solutions. Previously our scientific training was such that we expected to be able to predict future events with a high degree of certainty or we would dismiss the theory on which those predictions were based. This led to a reduction of the real, complex problems (which usually initiated the enquiry) to such a simplistic level that they were seen to be banal and the results unconvincing to non-psychologists. By increasing our range of activity we find the need to acknowledge the complexity of the problems to which we are asked to contribute and consequently have ceased to look for or to find perfect solutions to difficult problems. Rather as Blackler (Chapter 11) points out we are content to nibble away at the edges and with highly complex issues expect to implement change slowly. We have become pragmatist rather than rationalist! With this it would seem that many practitioners are putting less emphasis on psychological knowledge as such and more on the approaches toward and methods used to obtain information.

Within the more long-standing fields of industrial, clinical, and educational psychology there was a bias towards concern with specific problems and in many instances with specific individuals. Though this type of activity, as is well-illustrated in later chapters, is still an important aspect of the work of the professional psychologist there is a definite move towards more involvement at the organizational level. This may be in the sense of greater involvement in management or at the level of obtaining policy changes such as changes in the law, industrial policy, or allocation of health service resources. As yet there are still great gains to be made in this area but it is encouraging that the proposals of Tizard in his presidential address of 1976 are beginning to find a response in the profession at large.

CURRENT EMPHASES IN PROFESSIONAL PSYCHOLOGY

Broadening activities and roles

It is clear from the accounts in this book that psychology is continuing to thrive within the well-established fields of industry, health, and education and at the same time that psychologists are taking their skills into new territories such as design, the law, and communication, both written and technological. It looks as if psychologists are beginning to infiltrate into every aspect of life. We are no longer simply patching holes in the fabric of society but shaping that society in providing for a better quality of life. As yet the consequences of many of these activities are potential rather than actual, but there is a growing awareness of the possible contributions which can be made and, more importantly, what needs to be done in order to make them. This is taking us beyond the development of our own knowledge and skills to the broader and more difficult realms of communicating with and relating to other professionals and the public at large.

Although the contexts in which psychologists are working now vary enormously a number of aspirations can be discerned to be common to many practitioners, not least the professional psychologist's active determination to expand and develop his role. Even within the traditional roles of assessment and research the activities in which psychologists engage are expanding. No longer is an occupational psychologist content only to do vocational testing, now he will recognize the counselling component of his work. He has become more concerned with the whole person and the life decisions that person has to make.

It is clear from the many examples given in this book that the research role of the professional psychologist is considered an important one, not so much from the point of view of developing psychological knowledge *per se* but in providing information to aid decision-making and policy formulation. There are numerous examples cited here, ranging from providing research evidence to help a client contest a court case (Chapter 5), or avert a porters' strike (Chapter 2); evaluating and monitoring programmes for prisons (Chapter 6); investigations of organizational events to help management decision-making, (Chapter 11); or changing policy on fire regulations (Chapter 15).

As we have noted, the psychologist has moved from the role of diagnostician to that of problem-solver and change agent. From the research viewpoint this leads to a concern not only to assess an individual's problems but to identify ways of intervening and implementing change. One consequence of this is to involve the researcher in issues far outside the specific case he is studying. His research role can thus easily broaden to the provision of advice on policy and to giving assistance to bring about necessary changes, as well as introducing new systems for educating and aiding people's adjustments to those changes.

Beyond the broadening research role, and partly as a result of a scarcity of psychologists in Britain, psychologists are spending more of their time in the role of educator and trainer. In the health and welfare fields in particular and to a growing extent in industry and the law, we are involved in the training of direct-care staff, prison officers, management and other groups whose daily work involves close links with other people. The objective of this is not only to help those people to provide a better service but also to help their activities become more satisfying. That psychological ideas are more easily assimilated and that psychology will have more involvement in policy-making as a consequence of a fuller understanding of its contribution by the population at large, is a further longer term objective of education and training.

The emphasis on involvement in management when working within organizations is a common theme of many of the following chapters. There appear to be two types of involvement emerging; firstly in providing information for management to enable them to make more appropriate decisions, and secondly in the sense of being a part of management and being responsible for decisions outside the reach of psychology, for example Reavley's illustration of influencing the planning of health care provision in general (Chapter 2).

Underlying many of these activities is the notion of the psychologist as a consultant, a resource on which others can draw for information, advice, practical and research skills.

Communicating psychology and interprofessional relationships

Without exception all the professional psychologists contributing to this book are in continuous contact during the course of their work with other professionals who are not psychologists and all recognize the importance of co-operation and understanding between the various disciplines. In some instances, as cited by Blackler (Chapter 11) in the case of organizational psychology, or Canter (Chapter 15) dealing with architects, there will be an overlap in the contributions of psychologists and other professional. Yet it is important for psychologists, if we are to be effective, to recognize that our contributions may not be unique. In other instances it may be essential for the psychologist to work closely with someone in another profession, often for a third person who is the client. In such cases it is essential that we are to some extent familiar with the discipline with which we must interact so that, as much as anything else, we can understand and take account of the practical constraints and stresses of our colleagues' work and increase the chance that the psychological contribution be a meaningful one. This is nicely illustrated in the work of Hartley (Chapter 16) who, by working closely with a printer, has been able to make much of his work highly relevant to everyday life. This may, as illustrated for instance by Canter (Chapter 15), not only involve convincing the other professional of the relevance of his (the psychologist's) contribution but also convincing the client that the various professions involved should work together.

Hopkin gives an example (Chapter 12), when describing his work on the design of aviation maps, of how the psychologist acted as a link between two other groups, in this case the pilots who read the maps and the cartographers who make them. In this instance some knowledge about aviation and cartography was necessary in order to facilitate the process of designing better maps. All chapters reveal psychologists who have come out of their isolation and expect to have to develop working relationships with others. Of course, this has developed to a greater extent in some fields than others. Indeed Haward (Chapter 5) concludes his article on forensic psychology with the caveat that while psychologists have contributed to the individual case they have made little contribution to legal reform, partly because they have little knowledge of the priorities and problems that lawyers have. He insists that improvement of communication between professions is a major priority.

Psychologists are recognizing that psychological activity should be tailored to meet the particular demands of other professions and be communicated in a way that specific practitioners can grasp. This requires us to talk in a language that others can understand. Having an understanding of the frame of reference of those with whom we are communicating, as any undergraduate psychologist will know, can facilitate this process. We are having to sell our ideas to others and to do this we must first of all acknowledge their needs. Ray Bull (Chapter 17) points out that both the other professionals with whom we interact and the public make little distinction between applied and pure psychology, indeed many still see little distinction between psychoanalysis and psychology. There has been rapid growth in the attempts to educate the public, including other professionals, about psychology but there is still a long way to go.

The teaching of psychology in schools and, as McIntosh illustrates in Chapter 8, its expansion in adult education classes has gone some way toward this wider education. Many psychologists, such as those involved in the prison service (Chapter 6) are now involved in the teaching and training of other professionals. Some see the education of the public as a direct part of their role in order to change attitudes toward the field in which they work, such as Males in Chapter 4, or see the education of their client as an integral part of the service they have to offer (for example Frost and Canter in Chapter 13). As part of this process of taking psychology to non-psychologists, we are beginning to lose our fear of the media. An increasing number and variety of psychologists are appearing on radio and TV and are writing for (or being written about in) the popular press.

GROWTH OF PROFESSIONAL PSYCHOLOGY

Beyond the consideration of the changes in the practice of psychology and the emphases which are emerging it is instructive to consider the actual numbers of people in Britain who are going into different areas of professional psychology, as recorded in the admittedly limited published figures available. Although the figures do not tell the whole story they help to clarify some of the trends we have been discussing and provide further evidence of how professional psychology is developing. However, it is important to note that the figures available are always a few years out of date and in the last year or two the economic climate in Britain is likely to have had a dramatic effect on all trends. Looking at the available figures also gives us an opportunity to consider briefly some of the more institutional aspects of professional psychology, notably the way in which the British Psychological Society is responding to the developments encompassed by the present book.

There are two distinct sources of information about the numbers of psychologists emerging in Britain. One is the number of people who belong to the British Psychological Society as announced in the Society's annual reports. The other is the number of graduates in psychology declared in the government statistics (HMSO, 1967, 1972, 1980). Figure 1 shows the number of graduates in psychology from 1970 to 1979 and the increase in membership of the BPS for each of those years. The number of new members each year has been very erratic and all that can be said of any trends within it is that although the membership of the BPS has been growing throughout the 1970s it has not paralleled the steady increase in the number of people graduating in psychology over the same period.

Clearly it should not be expected that all graduates would immediately become members of the society, a time lag while they obtain higher degrees and establish themselves as psychologists would be expected. It is also the case that not all practising psychologists consider that membership of the BPS is essential. Certainly many employers do not give any weight to membership of the society. But if we were looking at the growth of a professional discipline we might expect that an increasing number of the graduates in that discipline were joining the only professional body existing in the country. Yet the figures do not show this trend. Although the number of graduates each year tends to increase, the number of new members of the BPS, although very variable in the mid 1970s, has stayed around a similar level throughout the decade. This certainly raises the question as to whether the BPS really does provide a society for graduates in psychology in general.

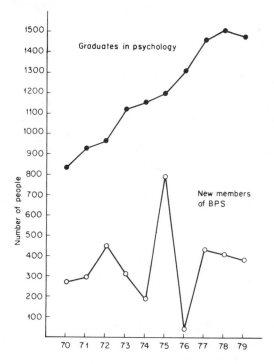

Figure 1 Numbers entering psychology

This is probably not the context to explore the role of a learned society in the development of a professional body. But it is instructive to note both from the figures above and from the various discussions on the role of the society that there is a recognition within this institution that the nature of psychology and what psychologists do is changing and that it is necessary to find some way for the BPS to respond to this. We have already made reference to the debate within that society on the registration of psychologists and we have pointed to the fact that past presidents of the BPS, such as Tizard, have been at pains to highlight the nature of psychology's contribution to society. Other presidential addresses such as Davidson's (1978) and Connolly's (1981) have also stressed the social values of psychology. In recent years the BPS has also set up a professional affairs board which is directly concerned with the standards, education, and efficiency of psychologists in their professional work.

The exact role of the professional affairs board is a frequent source for discussion within the BPS, as is shown by the annual reports and the documents produced by the board. As might be expected, it is continually exploring which role can most appropriately respond to the changing activities of psychologists. For example, it was the professional affairs board which initiated the discussion of the registration of psychologists, and it is this board which frequently provides reports for government departments in response to consultative papers. However, in the light of our earlier discussion of the overlap between the various areas of psychological application it is interesting to see that when the board itself commented on its terms of reference it mentioned first its value in providing a forum by means of which psychologists from different areas of professional activities 'can discover areas of mutual interest'.

Turning to graduate employment drawn from government figures some similar questions are raised about career consequences of a degree in psychology. In 1966 almost as many graduates in psychology went into research or academic study as went into permanent employment (101 and 161 respectively). By 1979 the pattern had changed dramatically. The number going into research or academic study had crept up to 192 but the number going into permanent employment was now 485. As we mentioned earlier, the career route for psychologists through university posts has not kept up at all with the increase in the number of graduates. When we look at the detailed figures for the employment of psychology graduates the picture becomes even clearer. From 1966 to 1979 the numbers going into all forms of educational employment actually dropped from 75 to 51. Those going into 'local government and hospital service' rose from 43 to 172 and those gaining employment in industrial and commercial contexts grew from 55 to 253. These figures are also intriguingly paralleled in the membership of the three largest professional divisions of the BPS as shown in Figure 2. Whilst the membership of the division of educational and child psychology has stayed moderately constant, increasing only slowly during the 1970s, the membership of the division of clinical psychology has grown very steadily during this period, reflecting the increasing number of psychologists practising in this area.

The figures for the occupational psychology division are surprisingly low given the number of graduates going into industrial and commercial contexts, even though they do indicate a relatively larger increase than for other divisions. However, these figures are possibly masked because of the existence of a more general occupational psychology 'section' within the BPS. The sections are less restricted in who can join and thus function less as professional bodies within

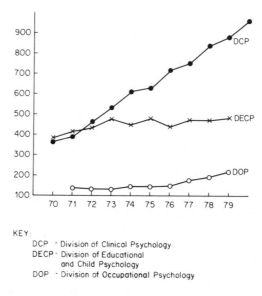

KEY:

DCP - Division of Clinical Psychology
DECP- Division of Educational
        and Child Psychology
DOP - Division of Occupational Psychology

Figure 2 Membership of divisions

the society than do the divisions. They reflect interest groups rather than professional groups *per se*. Figure 3 shows the membership for the four largest sections. Here the growth in interest in occupational psychology can be much more clearly seen together with the decrease in numbers for both the educational and medical sections. The increasing membership of the social psychology section is also worth noting and is a point to which we shall return.

What then, if anything, can we deduce from these rather bald figures? To us the most intriguing thing about them is the way they provide further evidence for the general trends which we have discussed in this chapter and which we discern throughout the contributions to this book. In summary, the activities of psychologists are moving away from the university base. They are penetrating more broadly into a range of activities within the community and industry.

We are certainly not witnessing a revolution or crisis in psychology but what might be considered to be a natural stage in the process of evolution of a discipline from an academic to a professional framework. However, what is of great importance in such a process is that it is in the nature of such developments that those least in contact with the changes, people within university departments, are those who are in the best situation to help the evolution to be a productive and effective one through the processes of education and training. We now turn, then, to consider the consequences for courses of the changing perspective we perceive and the implications these consequences have for the relationship between professional and academic activity.

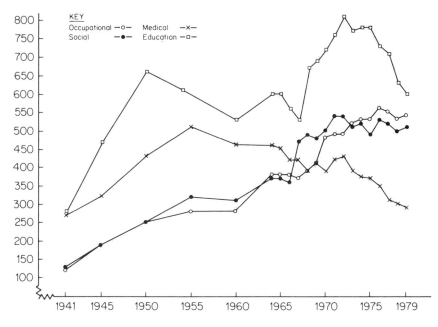

Figure 3 Membership of sections

TRAINING FOR PROFESSIONAL PSYCHOLOGY

It is apparent in the chapters that follow and from those recurrent themes which we have already highlighted that much of the training available for psychologists is not as relevant as it could be. Both the content and the structure of university education in psychology are in need of reconsideration. The content areas covered in most undergraduate courses have emphases which are not in keeping with what is required in practice. A fully integrated structure to professional training, which links different areas of application as well as the undergradute and post-graduate components has still to emerge.

Of course, the training of a professional psychologist, as is clearly seen for clinical and educational psychology, requires six or seven years. But in order to make a clearer link between the undergraduate and post-graduate components than exists at present, and to prepare students more effectively for later professional practice, it is necessary to make a change in both emphasis and approach to undergraduate teaching. The nature of undergraduate teaching has come in for quite regular criticism in the pages of the *BPS Bulletin* (Mack, 1977; Vine, 1977; Stone, 1980; Davies and Bennett, 1981). In general, the critics are all making a plea for an increase in links between what is taught and the experiences of the student, at the time of the course as well as in later professional life.

The debate on university education has also encompassed serious questioning of the value of PhD training (Bailey, 1977; Baddeley, 1979). It is argued that not only is a PhD training lacking in the development of many professional skills, but that the leisurely style in which it is conducted may actually be counter-productive in the professional world. Even the substance of PhD research, by virtue of the nature of the training, typically contributes little to the body of psychological knowledge. Furthermore, the intensive focusing on a limited area of psychology, characteristic of PhD study, also does little to answer the consideration that we have already had cause to mention, that there is considerable overlap between various branches of professional psychology. Thus the PhD neither contributes to the emergence of a body of professional wisdom, nor provides PhD students with an understanding of the range and concerns of applied psychology, even though people who achieve this qualification will form the bulk of university lecturers and thus be in a crucial position for passing on perspectives of the uses of psychology to students who may well go further into the professional applications of psychology than their lecturers.

These considerations show that there is an important need for a much fuller debate about psychological training. But in order for this debate to be of some positive value it is essential to go beyond the very broad issues outlined and to identify some of the common areas of psychology which should now be part of undergraduate training in order to provide a firm basis for later professional development, be it within the academic or practical spheres or even beyond the boundaries of professional psychology as such.

The content of undergraduate psychology

Towards the social

Probably the most heretical statement to be made about undergraduate teaching, but one that is echoed again and again in later chapters, is that the current focus which can be perceived from the syllabi of many departments (as shown for example in Vine's 1977 discussion of a survey of examination questions) misses the centre of psychology as it is practised. There still appears to be a belief, which is reflected in introductory textbooks as much as in course descriptions, that central to psychological activity are the issues of perception and cognition, learning and memory as derived from the laboratory, experimental traditions enshrined in such texts as Woodworth and Schlosberg (1938) or even the more recent 'cognitive' information-processing orientation as in Lindsay and Norman's (1977) text. Only a small minority of contributions to the present volume draw in any direct way on this area of undergraduate psychology. Time and again contributors refer to the social and organizational psychology literature as the main impetus for their activities. Even the work in aviation psychology, consumer psychology, communication technology, and environmental psychology (all areas where it might be assumed that the study of perception, cognition, and memory were paramount) draw heavily on concepts and methods from social, organizational, and clinical psychology.

Together with the blurring of professional boundaries has gone the cross-fertilization of different areas of academic psychology. The evolution of a cognitive perspective in what used to be known as experimental psychology has opened the way for the study of much more complex stimulus sets than the illusions and random numbers of which experimental psychologists were once so fond. This has enabled social psychologists to draw on the models of the cognitive psychologists, and for it to become increasingly difficult to say of the best work in these border areas whether it is cognitive, social or even organizational, as for example in the Nobel-prize-winning work of Simon (1969) or the recent work of Broadbent (1981). Nonetheless, whatever your particular perspective on these developments it is clear that the traditional partitions of undergraduate courses, with their emphases on experimental/cognitive psychology, are now open to question as a basis for the training of professional psychologists.

A clinical orientation

The proverbial layman, who has always had trouble distinguishing between psychology and psychoanalysis, and more recently has been confused by the notion of a psychotherapist and the distinction of all these from psychiatry, would probably be even more confused when reading many of the contributions to this book. Certainly the educational, occupational, prison, forensic, and consumer psychologists, as well as the psychologist working in adult education, all make explicit reference to the contribution to their own activity of concepts, methods, and skills drawn from clinical psychology. Most of the other contributors implicitly acknowledge this contribution. It is no accident that, even though we trawled for contributors from as many and various areas of applications as we could identify, we ended up with seven out of seventeen contributors whose post-graduate training was in clinical psychology.

As clinical psychology has broadened its sphere of activity so the other fields have found it of value to draw upon this area to answer their own problems. It should also be noted that the impact of clinical psychology is not only due to the development of behavioural approaches and the great theorists who wrote from a clinical perspective, such as Sigmund Freud, Carl Rogers, and George Kelly, but it is also the fact that as professionals clinical psychologists have organized themselves more systematically and articulated their perspective more effectively than any other group. This is possibly because of the power of the medical profession with whom they have had to find a rapprochement and whose own tight professional structure they could use more clearly as a model.

But whatever the causes it is becoming apparent that in order to perform effectively as a professional psychologist some ability is necessary in those areas usually recognized as in the provenance of the clinician.

Into the field

Besides the shifting focus from intraindividual to interpersonal and group processes and the emergence of the clinical perspective as a central one, the other major change in emphasis which can be seen in all the contributions to this book is the move away from laboratory-based procedures for solving problems to those which are especially suited to studies 'in the field'. Any comparison of the form of studies reported in learned journals with the projects and assignments discussed in the following chapter will show that the change taking place here is a rather profound one, which must eventually leave its mark on academic research as well. For with the desire to resolve the problems of the client in a way which will provide guidance for action the whole fabric of scientific psychology, as it is taught to undergraduates, is called into question. For example, as Bull discusses in the last chapter of this book, the paradigm of the laboratory experiment, whereby even field studies are described as forms of 'experiment' ('quasi-experiments' as Campbell and Stanley, 1966, call them), is no longer universally accepted.

What is happening is that people have found the language and vocabulary of the experiment to be inappropriate as well as the way experimental results may be statistically significant but practically useless. Thus the testing of hypotheses is becoming less important than the clarification of the options for action available, and the degree of control over experimental conditions is given less weight than the precision with which the situation being studied is described. As a consequence new procedures and a new vocabulary for describing their use are slowly emerging.

These developments of the strategies of research include, for example, detailed studies of individual cases, in which there is no pretence that an 'experiment' with an $N = 1$ is being carried out, but in which as full an understanding as possible of the activities and experiences of particular individuals will provide a key to the problem in question. The influence of Kelly's Personal Construct Theory and more recently Harre's ethogenic approach can be seen here. Another aspect of these same developments, perhaps paradoxically, is the embracing of sophisticated multivariate analysis procedures. The widespread availability of powerful computers has meant that very large and involved sets of data, derived from one or many individuals, can now be handled with relative ease.

Problem definition

It is important to emphasize that the above developments are not leading to an applied psychology which is atheoretical. Throughout the contributions to this book it will be seen that theoretical stances are interwoven with the perspectives on professional activity. What seems to be happening is that we are recognizing that theories are not enough. Increasingly practitioners are realizing that theoretical frameworks must be harnessed to help problem definition, as the client sees it. Students as a consequence need to be given the skills to help them formulate clearly an account of the problems the client is facing. The formulation of 'testable hypotheses' within the language of a particular theory loses more clients than it helps. On the other hand, if the same issues can be phrased as action possibilities the value of which can be tested within the client's own context, then not only are the rigours of scientific endeavour maintained but the problems which the client recognizes can be solved.

Skills transmission

The majority of contributors to this book have implicitly or explicitly expressed the need for a variety of professional and social skills which go beyond an access to psychological knowledge or research methodologies. The transmission of these skills to undergraduates as a direct part of their training would be of value whatever their later professional life. Some of the skills to which a number of contributors to this volume refer can be summarized.

(1) Communication and interpersonal skills. The ability to understand what others have to say and to express oneself clearly in writing and speech are prerequisites for the professional psychologist. The cut and thrust of learned debate and the dressing-up of simple ideas in confusing technicalities are no part of this requirement to be able to communicate intelligently with people who have a diverse set of backgrounds. Interpersonal communication is not only the communication of ideas as such but includes all those related skills to do with working with other people, appreciating their perspective and being able to provide them with the appropriate emotional as well as intellectual response.

(2) Management skills. This includes peoples' ability to manage themselves, programme their work, plan for their use of time and other resources and their ability to manage others whether it be in an executive or a consultancy capacity. The leisurely PhD completed over three or more years is certainly no training for the time-keeping and responsiveness to deadlines which are essential to the professional.

(3) Interdisciplinary skills. The ability to move with intelligence and confidence between a variety of disciplines outside psychology is also a skill which is essential to the practitioner. This does not mean solely or necessarily a

knowledge of other disciplines but rather a perspective on the relationship of the psychologist's contribution to that of others. This requires an informed humility combined with the flexibility to reconsider the nature of the psychologist's role for any given problem.

When the emphases of psychological training are outlined, as they are here, in relation to the later employment of graduates, it is curious to note how close they come to the demands frequently expressed by students. For underlying all the shifts in focus we have described is the linking of psychological teaching and training to what is often called 'the real world'. This has one further, almost paradoxical, consequence. The real world is actually closer to the student's own personal experiences and the problems with which they have to cope themselves than are the abstruse contents of so many psychological texts.

Approaches to undergraduate teaching

The developments necessary in the content of psychology courses pose problems for the educator. The great advantage of the laboratory study which tests hypotheses derived from a 'literature' is that such studies are readily manageable within the walls of an educational establishment. Many such studies can be experienced during a conventional course and the lecturer and student together can hope to have reasonable control over the programme of activity and its consequences. As such the laboratory study commends itself as an efficient training procedure to teach the skills of systematic, scientific enquiry, and is one of the reasons why the laboratory study is so generally agreed to be an essential part of undergraduate training (Davies and Bennett, 1981). Once, however, the concerns of the world are brought to bear the enquiry inevitably becomes more time-consuming and complex. Where a student doing a laboratory study can aspire to make a contribution to the literature within the resources available to him, the student who wishes to gain experience of real problem-solving will find the need to compromise at every stage unless he or she is lucky enough to find a particularly conducive context.

Because of the dilemma of resources whereby a field study of any substance is likely to be so much more demanding than a laboratory study, especially if it aspires to provide an understanding of problem-solving skills and other content areas discussed above, it is essential for us to develop new approaches to teaching psychology. As long ago as 1973 Hartley showed from a survey of British universities how conservative teaching methods were. There is little evidence that the changes we have noted in the practice of psychology with their implications for university education have found any response in teaching approaches since Hartley's study.

Yet other professional disciplines have solved the dilemma of resources in many different ways, for example through various forms of role-playing and the use of case studies. A surgeon does not perform an operation until he has practised on cadavers and watched many similar operations being performed. An architecture student does not expect the buildings he designs as part of his studies to be built. He also accepts that the person who plays the role of a client for his design will not expect to see the plans and elevations rise from the ground. Trainee lawyers and business students study many exemplary cases and may even play out the role of the participants in 'decision games'. Yet in both undergraduate and post-graduate training in psychology it is fruitless to search for more than a handful of parallels. The lecture and seminar backed up by 'laboratory classes' are the stock in trade. The discipline of psychology is taught throughout as an academic, essentially bookish enterprise. Even handbooks of 'what to do when . . .' (such as Wilkinson and Canter, 1982) are rare. However, if the training of psychologists were to become less conventionally academic the value of the training would go beyond the student's later role as a psychologist; it would contribute considerably to his day-to-day effectiveness in all his activities. In other words, the new emphases necessary for the content of psychology teaching point to the need to organize courses so that students are given what have been widely labelled as social and professional skills as well as providing them with an understanding of their chosen discipline.

THE FUTURE OF PROFESSIONAL PSYCHOLOGY

In his 1976 Presidential address Tizard (Tizard, 1976) made a plea for a greater contribution from psychologists to social policy and affairs of everyday life. The chapters in this book suggest that professional psychologists are moving some way to achieving such contributions albeit within relatively circumscribed areas. Certainly all see the necessity of involvement in policy formulation at local and national levels, since the pay-offs are so much larger than a preoccupation with individual cases. Moreover, working with individual people or problems is often thwarted because of the systems in which they are embedded. Topping, in Chapter 7, lists a number of ways educational psychologists have contributed to policy but he cautions against simple, overall criticism of 'systems' when a case is being made for a particular child. However, contributions at national level still have little influence despite the increasing efforts of the scientific and the professional affairs boards of the British Psychological Society. Yet there is a hope that as we begin to become more public and achieve success in contributing to the problems of society our voice will grow to the extent of being heard in the corridors of power.

This book and the contributions to it are unashamedly British. We are certain that the context of professional activity, as created by a given society and the institutions of which it is a part, has an all-pervading influence over the nature and development of that activity. This does not mean, of course, that professional groups in different countries have nothing to learn from each other. For example, the American Psychological Association with its more than 50,000 members and over 30 divisions provides many interesting examples of how a professional body can develop. But such comparisons also serve to show how much British professional psychology gains its structure from the centralized nature of our government and the existence of such monolithic institutions as the National Health Service and the Home Office.

In an interesting US parallel to the present volume Platt and Wicks (1979) provide an overview of 'The Psychological Consultant'. It is clear there that the private-enterprise, federal structure provides an opportunity for what might be called the free-market psychologist which does not exist to at all the same extent in Britain. They discuss consultation with schools, welfare agencies, the federal government, the courts and 'correctional agencies' (prisons) as an essentially freelance activity. This has its obvious strengths but also the weaknesses that each individual must break his own new ground and the potential for the growth of a professional discipline is more difficult to achieve. Nonetheless the consultants who contribute to that volume emphasize many of the points raised here, especially the need for the consultant to devote professional time and effort to the evaluation of his activities.

Platt and Wicks also draw attention to many of the issues which we have still to face up to on this side of the Atlantic. Most notably they draw attention to the need to demonstrate the value of any psychological intervention. They argue that evaluation should be an integral part of the professional activity, thus building up an account of the costs and benefits to society of the psychologist's activities. This really opens up the many moral and ethical questions. As many of our authors here recognize, professional psychology cannot be value-free once psychologists can actually make a contribution. The APA regularly publishes a great many detailed ethical 'codes of practice' (see for example *American Psychologist*, June 1981). But built into these guidelines are many more fundamental questions which most psychologists must answer for themselves in each particular situation. We can list these questions in the hope that there will be more general discussion of them than is apparent at present.

(1) Under what conditions should psychological services be refused?
(2) Who can be identified as the responsible party for any given professional activity?
(3) Who owns the results of any psychological investigation and who has the right of access to them?
(4) In general, what are the rights of the client who requests psychological services?
(5) How is the activity of professional psychologists to be regulated?
(6) How are psychologists to be accountable for their activities, and to whom?

(7) What are the rights and obligations of the psychologist when providing services?

These are some of the questions which come with the responsibilities of the professional role. They reflect the way in which the maturation of psychology as a profession brings with it a wave of issues not considered when psychologists could content themselves with being merely academics.

REFERENCES

Baddeley, A. (1979). 'Is the British PhD system obsolete?' *Bulletin of the British Psychological Society*, **32**, 129-131.

Bailey, L. F. (1977). 'Unlearning for a PhD', *Bulletin of the British Psychological Society*, **30**, 15-16.

Baum, A. and Singer, J. E. (1981). *Energy Conservation: Psychological Perspectives*, New Jersey: Lawrence Erlbaum.

Broadbent, D. (1981). 'Human action in dynamic situations', *Bulletin of the British Psychological Society*, **34**, 182 (abstract).

Campbell, D. T. and Stanley, J. C. (1966). *Experimental and Quasi-Experimental Designs for Research*, Chicago: Rand McNally.

Cohen, R. E. and Ahearn, F. L. (1981). *Handbook for Mental Health Care of Disaster Victims*, Baltimore: Johns Hopkins.

Connolly, K. (1982). "Psychology and poverty", *Bulletin of the British Psychological Society*, **35**, 1-9.

Davidson, M. (1977). 'The scientific/applied debate in psychology: a contribution', *Bulletin of the British Psychological Society*, **30**, 273-278.

Davies, P. and Bennett, S. (1981). 'Laboratory classes: education or initiation', *Bulletin of the British Psychological Society*, **34**, 312-313.

Hartley, J. (1973). 'New approaches to the teaching of psychology in the United Kingdom', *Bulletin of the British Psychological Society*, **26**, 87-94.

HMSO, University Grants Committee (1967). *First Employment of University Graduates 1965-1966*, London: HMSO.

HMSO, University Grants Committee (1972). *First Employment of University Graduates 1970-1971*, London: HMSO.

HMSO, University Grants Committee (1980). *Details of First Destinations of University Graduates 1978-1979*, London: HMSO.

Lindsay, P. H. and Norman, D. A. (1977). *Human Information Processing: An introduction to psychology*, London: Academic Press.

Mack, D. (1977). 'Personalizing learning in the introductory psychology course', *Bulletin of the British Psychological Society*, **30**, 312-314.

Marsh, P., Rosser, E., and Harre, R. (1978). *The Rules of Disorder*, London: Routledge & Kegan Paul.

Mayo, E. J. and Jarvis, L. P. (1981). *The Psychology of Leisure Travel*, Boston: CBI Publishing.

Platt, J. J. and Wicks, R. J. (1979). *The Psychological Consultant*, New York: Grune & Stratton.

Simon, H. A. (1969). *The Sciences of the Artificial*, London: MIT Press.

Stone, V. (1980). 'University reform', *Bulletin of the British Psychological Society*, **33**, 15-16.

Tizard, J. (1976). 'Psychology and social policy', *Bulletin of the British Psychological Society*, **29**, 225–234.

Vine, I. (1977). 'What we teach—and don't teach—to psychology students', *Bulletin of the British Psychological Society*, **30**, 376–377.

Watson, P. (1978). *War on the Mind: The military uses and abuses of psychology*, London: Hutchinson.

Wilkinson, J. and Canter, S. (1982). *Social Skills Training Manual*, Chichester: Wiley.

Woodworth, R. S. and Shlosberg, H. (1938). *Experimental Psychology*, London: Methuen.

Psychology in Practice
Edited by S. Canter and D. Canter
© 1982, John Wiley & Sons, Ltd.

CHAPTER 2

CLINICAL PSYCHOLOGY IN PRACTICE

William Reavley
Principal Psychologist
Graylingwell Hospital, Chichester, Sussex

Along any dimension you care to use the role of the clinical psychologist, as defined by what he does, to whom he does it, at whose request and where, has radically altered over the past fifteen years. For a comprehensive overview of the activities of clinical psychologists in the National Health Service the reader is referred to the Trethowan Report (DHSS, 1977) *The Role of Psychologists in the Health Service*. On occasion references will be made to the Trethowan Report but this chapter does not aim to be an appraisal of the current status of clinical psychology in the National Health Service. What follows is a personal view of changes and developments in clinical psychology and as such draws largely on first-hand experience for illustration.

THE STRUCTURE AND ORGANIZATION OF THE PROFESSION

Before we look in detail at what a clinical psychologist does and the kinds of services he provides we need some idea of what he is and how he fits into the National Health Service.

Despite a growth rate of 8 per cent per annum between 1957 and 1978 there are still only 1109 clinical psychologists working in the National Health Service in England and Scotland (Barden, 1979). We are a very small profession compared with our medical, nursing, and social worker colleagues, and despite the growth rate (even if it should continue) we will be a small profession for a considerable time. How does an aspiring Honours Psychology graduate join this élite group?

The conditions for employment are laid down by the DHSS. To be eligible for employment as a qualified clinical psychologist in the National Health Service the applicant must fulfil one of the following conditions.

(1) Shall have satisfactorily completed a recognised post-graduate training in clinical psychology at a university or polytechnic in the United Kingdom.*

(2) Shall hold the Diploma in clinical psychology of the British Psychological Society.

The career structure and details of eligibility for promotion are to be found in DHSS Circular PTA 148 but in brief the progression is: Probationer (while satisfying conditions 1, 2, or 3), Basic Grade, Senior, Principal, and Top Grade Principal. Although qualified, the psychologist working at Basic Grade is still considered to be in training. It is at Senior Grade that the clinical psychologist can supervise the training of probationers.

The Trethowan Report advised on the orgnization of clinical psychology services and provoked a great deal of self-examination on the part of clinical psychologists. In a paper on the organization of clinical psychology services Kat and Thomas (1978) distinguish five levels of service which a clinical psychologist might operate, as shown in Table 1.

The level the clinical psychologist will work at will vary between situations. The same person may well work at levels 2, 3, and 4 at different times in the same week. As a member of a ward team he may well offer social skills training as part of a treatment programme for a patient. In another context the clinical psychologist may well be in charge of the overall management of a therapy programme and be responsible for the co-ordination of the efforts of other professionals. An example of this level 3 work might be found in working with general practitioners, health visitors, and social workers in the field of child abuse. In practice a Basic Grade psychologist might be working at level 3 a little of the time but it would be more usual to expect a Senior or Principal Grade to be operating at this level.

It is only recently, since the 1974 reorganization of the National Health Service, that clinical psychologists have had the opportunity to work at levels 4 and 5 and activities at these levels would be carried out by Heads of Department, usually Principal Grade. At level 4 the clinical psychologist would be involved in 'identifying' the needs of a community and planning and developing psychological services to meet these needs.

In the late 1950s many clinical psychologists of all grades were working at level 1. They were administering psychological tests often routinely, to patients referred by consultant psychiatrists. The work consisted largely of providing a response to a request no more detailed than 'IQ and Personality Assessment please'. Once the report was written and sent off the psychologist had no further responsibilities or influence. The amount of professional judgement

*A list of approved post-graduate training courses can be obtained from the British Psychological Society.

Table 1 Levels of service in clinical psychology

Level	Description of work	Some examples in clinical psychology
5	Comprehensive field coverage — making comprehensive provision of services within some general field of need throughout some given territorial or organizational society	(i) Psychologist regularly involved in decisions of DMT providing expertise concerning the psychological aspects of health care generally (ii) Psychologist devises and negotiates strategic plan for improving psychological aspects of health care in district
4	Comprehensive service provision — making comprehensive provision of services of some given kinds according to the total and continuing needs for them throughout some given territorial or organizational society	(i) Psychologist conceptualizes, plans, and organizes a conventional range of psychology services (ii) Psychologist takes a lead role in a health-care planning team for the elderly
3	Systematic service provision — making systematic provision of services of some given kinds shaped to the needs of continuous sequence of concrete situations which present themselves	(i) Psychologist has a continuing responsibility to provide and develop psychological services in a programme, making a personal assessment of whether and how to intervene in particular cases. May take on team-co-ordinating responsibilities (ii) Psychologist working in a health centre, sees need for receptionist training and designs and implements a programme
2	Situational response — carrying out work where the precise objectives to be pursued have to be judged according to the needs of each specific concrete situation which presents itself	(i) Psychologist assesses a patient's suitability for rehabilitation, the nature of the assessment being chosen by the psychologist (ii) Psychologist selects and undertakes an appropriate form of behaviour therapy with a patient, the policy for the case being determined by a more experienced psychologist or a medical consultant.
1	Prescribed output — working towards objectives which can be completely specified (as far as is significant) beforehand according to defined circumstances which may present themselves	(i) Psychologist administers a pre-determined intelligence test or carries out a specific request concerning a patient (ii) Psychologist collects research data, the research strategy and techniques being determined by others

For further details see Rowbottom and Billis (1978)

given him to exercise by his colleagues was limited to the choice of tests and in some cases not even that. This would be working at level 1. Working at this level is unlikely to satisfy a Probationer clinical psychologist today.

Most psychologists of all grades are working at level 2. As members of multidisciplinary teams, which may include in their numbers members of medical, nursing, and social work professions, the psychologist may well be asked to make a contribution to the treatment and care of a patient in the context of an overall treatment programme.

Although a district-based Clinical Psychology Department may provide a wide range of psychology services it is likely that their base will be in a psychiatric hospital and the majority of their work will be with psychiatric patients.

It is not uncommon to find the Head of the Psychology Department as a member of the Sector Management Team of the psychiatric hospital in which he is based. The Sector Management Teams are the bodies responsible for the management of the psychiatric hospital and thus the provision of psychiatric services to their catchment area. Thus in addition to managing their own services the clinical psychologists may well make significant contributions in the management of the services of which they are part.

It is quite a big leap from providing IQs and personality profiles, level 1, to working with the autonomy associated with level 3, and being a practitioner with recognized areas of expertise who contributes to the development of health care services and innovates new schemes for the organization and delivery of his own and other professional services. How have these changes come about?

THE VALUE OF BEHAVIOUR THERAPY
TO CLINICAL PSYCHOLOGY

Many factors have influenced the changes noted above but most clinical psychologists who have worked in the National Health Service through the period agree that the development of clinical psychology is inextricably and reciprocally linked with the growth and popularization of approaches to clinical activity falling under the heading 'behaviour therapy'.

Clinical psychologists eagerly embraced behaviour therapy and have been in the vanguard of researchers and popularizers of behavioural treatments. In the early days behaviour therapy concerned itself exclusively with overt behaviour and drew upon the principles of conditioning for explanations of 'maladaptive behaviour'. Therapies involving 'speech' were seen as the province of psychoanalysts (Eysenck, 1959). However, the emphasis on learning theories gave clinical psychologists the opportunity of staking a claim to behaviour therapy.

Over the last twenty years, the content and range of behaviour therapy has changed considerably. From being ignored as irrelevant, internal events such as beliefs, attitudes, and cognitions have been incorporated, not without difficulties, into the mainstream of behaviour therapy. As an approach to treatment behaviour therapy carries within it the principles of experimental psychology and it has been argued (Lazarus, 1973) that behaviour therapy can draw upon techniques from other therapeutic approaches and still be behaviour therapy as long as the following conditions are met:

(1) specification of goals and problems;
(2) specification of treatment techniques to achieve these goals and remedy these problems;
(3) systemic measurement of the relative success of these techniques.

When these guidelines are accepted then a wide variety of therapeutic activities, including the manipulation of cognitions and beliefs, become an accepted part of behavioural psychotherapy. Most practitioners of behaviour therapy would accept the statement of Ledwidge (1978): 'There are no therapies that are purely behavioural and there are no therapies that are purely cognitive because we do not treat behaviours or cognitions, we treat people'.

Evidence of the effectiveness of behavioural interventions continues to accumulate and behaviour therapy is the treatment of choice with phobic disorders, obsessive compulsive behaviour, and social anxieties (Marks, 1976). It has also been shown to be of great help with sexual dysfunction, sexual deviation, and habit disorders (Chesser, 1976). The favourable response to behaviour therapy by many patients, those with previously intractable problems (such as those patients with obsessive-compulsive behaviour: Rachman, 1973), speeded up the development of clinical psychology. Psychologists became recognized as therapists with special skills and expertise. Patients were referred to them for therapy and the psychologist decided upon the patients' suitability for his treatment approaches and what the treatment should be. Thus the clinical psychologist found himself working at level 3. Many clinical psychologists had been dissatisfied with their professional relationships with medical colleagues and had been working towards clinical independence with some acrimony and little success.

One of the major issues discussed in the Trethowan Report is the question of the problems of doctor/psychologist relationships hingeing around the questions of 'medical' and 'clinical' responsibility. At Graylingwell any difficulties there might have been on this topic were solved by the introduction of a course, run under the auspices of the Joint Board of Clinical Nursing Studies, Course 650, the aim of which is to '. . . train a nurse to be competent to treat a wide variety of clinical problems as the main therapist by behavioural psychotherapy'.

In order for the course to begin the consultant psychiatrists, whose patients were to be treated by the trainee course members, needed to agree to those course members being supervised and monitored by the clinical psychologists doing the training. In our case referring doctors retain medical responsibility but clinical responsibility rests with the therapist and their supervisor.

WHAT DO CLINICAL PSYCHOLOGISTS DO?

Traditionally the work of the clinical psychologist has been described as falling under the headings of assessment, teaching, therapy, and research (Shapiro, 1967). While these headings can still be used to describe the work of the clinical psychologist the content of each has changed over the years due to altered 'levels of work'. It is not always easy to compartmentalize the activities of the clinical psychologist. The boundaries between assessment, therapy, teaching, and research have blurred, and other descriptive headings have emerged. What the clinical psychologist actually does now, whether it be assessment or falls under one of the other headings, often carries with it the role of 'consultant'.

The clinical psychologist has always been consulted by his colleagues but we have seen how this consultation has altered from being asked to provide an IQ to being asked to assess the needs of a patient and design and carry out and manage treatment programmes. The role of consultant is expanding in all of the traditional areas of clinical psychological activities of assessment, therapy, teaching, and research and will be discussed more fully below.

Assessment

Assessment covers a wide range of activities which can include the administration and interpretation of standardized psychological tests, rating scales, and the use of laboratory-based experimental measures (Mittler, 1970). In order to give priority to the activity the clinical psychologist needs to see the assessment as being related to well-defined goals. The referral request of 'IQ and Personality Assessment please' is not seen as appropriate information to provide without it being given a context or aim. The psychological assessment will be directly relevant to decisions that are being taken about a patient.

The proportion of his time spent in assessment has been estimated as 10 per cent (British Psychological Society evidence to the Trethowan Committee) but there is a wide degree of variation depending upon the setting in which the clinical psychologist is working, his particular skills and interests, and the kinds of assessmen made. At Graylingwell less than 10 per cent of time is spent on formal psychological testing of patients. However, other aspects of assessment such as assessing the person's suitability for and responsiveness to therapy occupy about 20 per cent of our time.

As well as using established assessment instruments clinical psychologists may well modify existing assessment methods and develop their own instruments where no suitable techniques are at hand. The psychologist will then proceed experimentally to assess the reliability, validity, and utility of these instruments. Such an exercise has been started by one of our psychologists in association with the staff of the rehabilitation wards of the hospital. Using a format suggested by the Progress Assessment Chart (Gunzberg, 1969) the team, under the chairmanship of the clinical psychologist, developed an assessment schedule with the aims of obtaining information on a particular patient about:

(1) those basic capabilities which will enable a patient to look after himself and get along with others in the community;
(2) those areas in which a patient could benefit from training or help.

The assessment schedule is divided into five main sections: (i) self-care; (ii) home management; (iii) communication; (iv) occupation; (v) social skills. Within each of these major sections is listed a number of skills which are in turn analysed into subskills. For example, under the heading Mobility we find
(1) Can walk in town unaided:
  (a) can find route into town;
  (b) can cross the roads without causing danger to himself or others;
  (c) understands and can make use of a Pelican Crossing.
(2) Can make short journeys by both bus and rail:
  (a) can find own way to bus stops and bus/train stations;
  (b) knows the procedure for purchasing tickets;
  (c) can ensure getting on and off buses and trains at correct places;
  (d) knows how to find bus/train service times.
(3) Can read and understand public signs:
  (a) can read and understand several essential public signs, such as entrance, exit, subway, etc.

Instructions for using this inventory are very detailed and work is proceeding to assess the instrument in terms of reliability and validitiy. In this case the assessment procedure allows the staff to identify the range of abilities and skills of their patient. It indicates areas for therapy and is also the means of assessing the effectiveness of that therapy. Readministration of the assessment at regular intervals provides information with which to chart the patient's progress and evaluate the effectiveness of training programmes.

At Graylingwell the source of our formal psychological testing referrals has changed as has the kind of information asked for. In 1973 the majority of our psychological testing referrals came from psychiatrists and asked for help in locating an hypothesized lesion. Currently almost all of our referrals of this type come from neurologists and ask different questions. Due to improved medical technology the site of the lesion is often known and the doctor is interested in knowing the answer to questions like 'Does this man have the intellectual capacity and functioning to benefit from retraining?' — a question clearly related to decisions to be taken about the patient's rehabilitation. So rather than wanting to know if there is or is not evidence of brain damage and if so the location, there is more interest in knowing what psychological functions, for example memory or perception, are affected, in what ways, and how the person's overall functioning is affected.

Teaching

In the 1950s and 1960s the teaching commitment of clinical psychologists was usually limited to a series of lectures on 'Psychological Concepts' to student psychiatric nurses, and 'Mental Testing' to psychiatrists in training. The range of topics taught has broadened (General Nursing Council Syllabus, 1974) but more importantly the aim of the teaching has changed from the simple transmission of information about individual differences or aspects of group behaviour, to the training in the use of skills that the clinical psychologist has developed. Mention has already been made of the Joint Board of Clinical Nursing Studies Course 650. There are currently three courses of this type recognized by the Joint Board. They are based at the Maudsley, Moorhaven, and Graylingwell Hospitals. The latter two courses are centred in Psychology Departments. Clinical psychologists take part in planning the syllabus of, and indeed they play a part in the overall activities of, the Joint Board of Clinical Nursing Studies (Hall, 1978).

In addition to the behavioural psychotherapy course for nurses we also run social skills groups for trained staff. The staff requested the training themselves and this reflects the move away from the medical model in psychiatry towards a more problem-oriented approach. The aims are that after the course the participants will be able to play a major part in:

(1) identifying the social skills deficits of the patient in their care;
(2) being able to be an active co-therapist in social skills training.

The training is very practical, the participants learn about social skills training by the active experience of participating in a social skills group.

A considerable amount of our time at Graylingwell is taken up with the Nurse Behaviour Therapy Course and we also accept social workers (Reavley and Griffiths, 1981) on secondment to gain experience in behaviour therapy. Many other Psychology Departments offer similar training facilities which have proved very popular. About half the membership of the British Association of Behavioural Psychotherapy is made up of non-psychologists. This popularization of behaviour therapy has been viewed with concern by some clinical psychologists who had perhaps begun to see the terms clinical psychology and behaviour therapy as synonymous.

Their alarm was probably increased by the finding that registered mental nurses with a comprehensive training in behaviour therapy (a Joint Board of Clinical Nursing Studies Course) were as effective therapists as psychiatrists or clinical psychologists (Marks *et al.*, 1975). There is certainly enough psychopathology and suffering around to take up the energies of many more therapists than are available now.

An important role for clinical psychologists is to provide supervised training experiences for carefully selected members of other professions and to act as a consultant to them when they begin independent therapy.

Therapy

Attention has been drawn to the effect behaviour therapy has had on the development of clinical psychology. The list of problems to which the approach is being applied is increasing. We are interested in the behavioural analysis and treatment of child abuse (Reavley, *et al.*, 1978). There is an increasing literature on behaviour treatments used with parents who abuse their children (Hutchings, 1981) but it is very difficult to use conventional experimental designs to examine the efficacy of the treatment approaches and to attempt to tease out which elements of therapy are effective and which are not. We do not think it appropriate to allocate clients randomly to different therapy groups to satisfy the demands of an experimental design with child abuse. Our style of behaviour therapy is to allow the behavioural analysis of the clients' problems to indicate where and how the therapy intervention should be made.

Our conceptualizations and treatments of child abuse have altered and are still altering. We are coming to the conclusion that in many cases, although 'excess' behaviours like shouting need to lessen in frequency, it is equally, if not more, important to increase the frequency of those behaviours (deficits) that both the parent and the therapist see as desirable. Therapy is often directed towards encouraging the parent to produce more of these behaviours which are lacking and this may lead to the additional benefit of reducing the frequency of behavioural excesses (Reavley and Gilbert, 1979a).

We have found that in those cases where marital disharmony is present, it is not only contributing to the problems but it maintains the child abuse behaviour. If the quality of the marital relationship does not improve during therapy the progress made by the parents in the handling of their children is unlikely to be maintained (Reavley and Gilbert, 1979b).

So far behaviour therapy has received a great deal of attention but it would be misleading to give the impression that it was the only therapy approach used by clinical psychologists. Other forms of therapy are practised to a greater or lesser degree by clinical psychologists and include varieties of psychodynamic therapy and different connecting approaches. Some clinical psychologists adopt an eclectic approach and vary their therapeutic approaches to suit their perception of the needs of their patients.

Research

The term 'research' covers a wide range of activities for the clinical psychologist. He is in a unique position in the National Health Service being a clinician who is also a trained researcher. This allows him to carry out formal research into psychological and psychiatric phenomena and because of his training he will be able to advise his colleagues in other disciplines on research methodology appropriate to the problem they wish to investigate.

A review of the empirical researches carried out by clinical psychologists is beyond the scope of this chapter but the reader can gain an appreciation of these by examining the *British Journal of Social and Clinical Psychology*. It is other, less formal aspects of the clinical psychologists' research contribution I wish to describe.

Because of his training the clinical psychologist is able to introduce into the National Health Service information and methods from the science of psychology. Indeed this has been described as his essential function (Shapiro, 1967). As an undergraduate the clinical psychologist is trained in scientific methodology and statistics. The application of this knowledge to clinical issues and problems figures largely in his post-graduate training. Through this training and knowledge of and access to the psychological literature the clinical psychologist has an important research contribution to make in addition to formal research into psychiatric phenomena. This role of applied researcher I have rather grandiosely described as 'The Voice of Reason'. By this term is meant the application of scientific methodology to the definition of problems and experimental manipulations to test hypotheses about possible solutions.

The following examples illustrate that the clinical psychologist will often need to draw upon the research finding of 'general psychology' and incorporate this information into his experimental and clinical work. The first example illustrates how something basic to any applied science, systematic data gathering, can be an innovative and very useful contribution towards a solution of a difficult clinical and managerial problem.

Self-referring patients

In 1974 the hospital porters at Graylingwell Hospital expressed serious concern that they were being asked to turn away self-referring patients who turned up at the front entrance. The duty doctor was not always available and their instructions were to direct these people to the Accident and Emergency Department of a nearby general hospital. The porters were not happy with this procedure. Although they were reassured by the administration that they were 'covered' the porters were worried in case something untoward happened to the patients between Graylingwell and the Accident and Emergency Department. The problem was gradually escalating towards a possible industrial dispute. At a Psychiatric Division meeting it became clear that although no-one knew how many self-referring patients there were or indeed who they were the members of the meeting were attempting to offer solutions to the problem. The services of the Psychology Department were offered to look at the problem, so that with the benefit of some data a more rational discussion might occur. The project was carried out by Brenda Roberts as the research component of the MSc at the University of Surrey.

Many different 'tribes', including nursing, medical, and porters, were involved in meeting some but not all of the self-referring patients so the first step was to organize a communication system which would allow the collection of information and prevent duplication so that the same patient, meeting members of the different 'tribes', would be readily identifiable. A number of 8 inch × 5 inch cards were printed with various questions thought relevant to the problem of finding out who self-referred patients were, where they came from, and what happened to them. These cards were given to those members of staff who were likely to be contacted by such patients. They were asked to fill out a card for every request for emergency psychiatric assistance which did not come through the hospital's acceptable channels of a general practitioner's request for a domiciliary visit or out-patient appointment, a social services request for a domiciliary visit, an admission request falling within the Mental Health Act of 1959 (for example police), or a current patient asking for an emergency consultation with his own psychiatrist during normal working hours.

Over a six-week period it transpired that twenty-one patients self-referred themselves to the hospital. Contrary to popular opinion they were not drifters temporarily in the area as holiday camp workers drawn to the hospital in search of drugs. Nearly all of them were past patients of the hospital who had identified themselves as in need of further treatment. Only three had never been in the care of the hospital, and of these only one was not resident in the catchment area. This information gave some meaning to the discussions between the psychiatrists, porters, and administration. There is a local ruling at Graylingwell Hospital that it should not be the decision of a non-medical member of staff to turn a potential patient away from the hospital.

The Graylingwell booklet

In the report 'Communications between Doctors, Nurses and Patients' (1963) hospitals were advised to provide patients with booklets containing information to '. . . ease the sudden transition to in-patient life'. Most hospitals provide these and patients are said to find them useful. With the National Health Service reorganization and changes in hospital administrative and clinical facilities the Graylingwell booklet was out of date and it was likely that a new booklet would be written. Some reservations had been expressed about how well information had been communicated in the old booklet so it seemed like a good opportunity to (i) assess how well information was already being communicated, and (ii) advise on the rewriting of the booklet.

The study was undertaken by Lynne Stock as part of the requirement for her MSc in clinical psychology at the University of Surrey. In the first part of the study the booklet was analysed in terms of its comprehensibility and its readability (as discussed by Hartley in Chapter 16). Several indices were used, the Flesch Reading Ease formula (Flesch, 1948; Ley, 1973) the SMOG grading (McLaughlin, 1969), and the Fry Readability Chart (Fry, 1968). On all of these measures the Graylingwell booklet failed to reach satisfactory levels of 'communicability'; for example applying the Flesch formula to four randomly chosen paragraphs showed that only 24 per cent of the population would understand and the SMOG index revealed that for complete comprehension of the booklet a college education would be needed. The same four paragraphs were rewritten in order to make them more readable, using the analysis criteria as guidelines, that is, shorter sentences, few polysyllabic words. A reanalysis of the paragraphs showed an increase in comprehensibility to 80 per cent on the Flesch formula and a reading age level of 'low age 12' on the Fry scale.

Having shown that the booklet could be rewritten to be statistically more comprehensible the next stage was to see if patients could recall more information from the new than the old booklet. The patients were given one of the booklets to read. They then took part in a standard distraction task (Koh's blocks) after which they answered questions based upon information to be found in the Graylingwell booklet. The results showed that significantly more information was recalled from the rewritten booklet (p 0.01). These findings were made available to the administration who were concerned with rewriting the booklet.

The overlap between categories of research, clinical work, knowledge of teaching techniques and the management/consultant role is further illustrated by the next example.

For the foreseeable future there will be little or no funds available for expansion of health care services. This means that how resources are deployed needs to be carefully examined and assessed. The managers of the National Health Service are slow to lead in this area and most of the drive critically to examine the services provided comes from the clinicians involved in the provision of those services. This is an appropriate area for the clinical psychologist to develop his role as an applied scientist. The work described below is closer to the popular idea of what 'research' should be but I include it as a further example of the 'Voice of Reason' role.

For some time we had been interested in becoming more closely involved with patients at a primary care level. This move towards working with general practitioners is an identifiable trend in clinical psychology but more of this later. Through working with cases of non-accidental injury to children I had met several health visitors and their Nursing Officer. We had worked together on several cases and it became clear that the practical and direct intervention methods of behaviour therapy fitted very well with the practical approaches favoured by the health visitors. The outcome of working together with individual cases led to a joint clinic being set up in March 1979 (Reavley, 1981). It was at one of the regular pre-clinic discussions that the idea of looking critically at the parentcraft classes taught by the health visitors was raised. The aim of these classes is to prepare expecting parents for the birth of their child and the effect upon their lives of having a child. The health visitors who taught the parentcraft classes expressed their reservations about both the content and style of presentation of the classes and were already looking at ways of improving them. The psychologist's advice was sought. It was agreed that before contemplating changes it was important that we examine the style, content, and effectiveness of the classes as they were already being taught. The research had two aims:

(1) to assess the impact of each class, that is, how effective was the teaching; and
(2) to identify which parts of the course the parents found the most valuable.

A health visitor volunteered her class for study and questionnnaires, both factual (adapted from the Open University 'First Years of Life' course) and self-report were constructed. The self-report questionnaire was completed weekly by every member after each class. To help respondents structure their replies rating scales favoured in behavioural research were used. Also an interview schedule was prepared for use with members of the class after the birth of their child.

A detailed discussion of the findings is not possible here but recommendations were made about the style of presentation. The health visitors made use of handouts but usually gave them to the class of the night on the night of the topic to which they referred. They were advised to issue handouts for the following week at the end of each class. This was so that the parents-to-be would have a frame of reference into which to fit the information they would be given in the class itself. Also they would not be distracted from the presentation itself by leafing through the handout given that evening. Research by Bandura (1977) has shown that while modelling is a very powerful teaching method participant modelling is even more effective. Thus the health visitors were advised to include as much class participation and practice as possible rather than relying upon demonstration. The weekly self-report questionnaire indicated that changes in the order of presentation of the topics would increase the interest and participation of the men in the class.

The questionnaires also highlighted the problem some class members had about asking questions due to their shyness or the perceived intimacy of the questions. Recommendations were made about the planning of the evening to overcome the barriers.

The mothers-to-be ratings showed that they did not see themselves as increasing in their capacity to relax beyond the third training session. Learning to use relaxation was seen as a very important function of the classes (about half of each of the sessions was devoted to this). From talking with the mothers it seemed likely that lack of practice between sessions accounted for their lack of improvement. The self-report data suggested that we might be able to increase the amount of between-class practice of relaxation if the husbands were more actively involved in the teaching of relaxation. We plan to test this out.

This example illustrated the blurring of lines between assessment, teaching and research. The psychologist worked as a consultant and offered advice, based upon observation and assessment of the classes, on how they might be made more effective.

FUTURE DEVELOPMENTS

In the 1960s clinical psychologists were based exclusively in psychiatric hospitals and gained almost all of their referrals from consultant psychiatrists. But just as there have been changes in level and content of work so there have been changes in the patient population clinical psychologists have worked with. Many clinical psychologists now work outside the mental hospitals in which they are based. Since 1973 the proportion of in-patients to out-patients referred to the Psychology Department at Graylingwell Hospital has changed. At that time approximately three out-patients were seen for every two in-patients. Now the proportions are of the order of eight to one in favour of out-patients and only half of our referrals come from hospital doctors. The others are referred by general practitioners, social workers, and health visitors with the occasional self-referral.

The Trethowan Report (1977) suggested that clinical psychologists had much to contribute to diagnosis and treatment in general medical practice. Several descriptions of clinical psychologists' work at primary care level have been published (McAllister and Phillips, 1975; Kincey, 1974; Kat and Thomas,

1978) and these have encouraged others to venture out of the institution into a health centre. But this move has not been universally welcomed. Although it has been shown that clinical psychologists' intervention at primary care level can reduce demands for general practitioner time and amounts of psychotropic medication (Koch, 1979) it has yet to be demonstrated that the need for clinical psychology services can be most efficiently provided by someone working at a primary care level (Hood, 1979).

The overall gains to be made, in terms of efficient and effective use of clinical psychologists' time, are likely to be trifling if all one is doing is seeing the same sexual dysfunction cases in a health centre rather than at the Out-Patient Department of a general hospital.

One of the criteria which has been used to evaluate working at a primary care level has been changes in referral rate. A common finding is that referrals from general practitioners will double (Bhagat et al., 1979). But, as has already been mentioned, we are a very small profession and there is a real danger that we could create a market for our services which we could not begin to satisfy. It is important that we continue to explore new areas of work but this could well create more dilemmas for us. While we were carrying out prescribed work arguments about where we should direct our activities and to whom were largely academic. However, now that most clinical psychology departments are in a position of having to provide a comprehensive psychological service for their health district we have to allocate priorities to our work. In practical terms this means that some areas which could benefit from our intervention will be neglected.

Whenever the clinical psychologist has branched out into new territory, such as primary care, he has been enthusiastically welcomed. Some social service departments now employ clinical psychologists and many others refer patients to them. It is very encouraging to find care-givers, other than psychiatrists and psychiatric nurses, are eager for clinical psychology services. From the examples given above it can be seen that quite a low level input from general psychology can be very useful. A frontier is an exciting and seductive place to work and it can be argued that clinical psychologists have an obligation to make their services available to as wide a range of people as possible. However, the need for caution and careful evaluation of our contribution to these frontier areas must be emphasized. We must remind ourselves that there is a considerable amount of work for us to be doing inside the institutions, which show every sign of continuing, before we too quickly leave them.

One possible solution to our dilemmas has already been mentioned. From working in direct contact with our patients we can, when appropriate, move into the area of skills transmission. This can take the form of training other professionals to do what we have been doing. In our case at Graylingwell this has taken the form of teaching nurses and social workers to carry out behaviour therapy but this is not the only possibility. In the case of working as members of the primary health care team it can take the form of helping team members enhance their psychological skills for the benefit of all patients in the practice (Bhagat *et al.*, 1979) rather than only treating a small carefully selected group of patients.

CONCLUSIONS

Over the last ten years several themes in the work of clinical psychologists have emerged. There have been changes in their level of work which have been accompanied by changes in the content of the work itself. From occupying a rather solitary role with the bulk of his work based in the setting of a psychiatric hospital the clinical psychologist now works with, and often through, other care-givers both inside and outside the hospital.

Through requests for the services associated with him, such as behaviour therapy, the clinical psychologist is in demand to teach others these skills. It has been argued that clinical psychologists should become involved more in skills transmission.

The services clinical psychology departments offer will always differ in emphasis. This will depend in part upon the needs of the district and partly upon their own special interests but of their several roles; therapist, teacher, researcher, the foremost role should be that of applied scientist making available to his colleagues the fruits of his specialist knowledge and training.

REFERENCES

Bandura, A. (1977). 'Self efficacy: towards a unifying theory of behavioural change', *Psychological Review*, **84**, 191–215.

Barden, V. E. (1979). 'Basic data for manpower planning in clinical psychology', *Bulletin of the British Psychological Society*, **32**, 12–16.

Bhagat, M., Lewis, A. P., and Shillitoe, R. W. (1979). 'Clinical psychologists and the primary health care team', *Updata*, 479–488.

Central Health Services Council (1963). 'Communication between doctors, nurses and patients', London: HMSO.

Chesser, E. S. (1976). 'Behaviour therapy: recent trends and current practice', *British Journal of Psychiatry*, **129**, 289–307.

DHSS (1977). *The Role of Psychologists in the Health Services* (The Trethowan Report), London: HMSO.

Eysenck, H. J. (1959). 'Learning theory and behaviour therapy', *Journal of Mental Science*, **105**, 61–75.

Flesch, R. (1948). 'A new readability yardstick', *Journal of Applied Psychology*, **32**, 221–233.

Fry, E. (1968). 'A readability formula that saves time', *Journal of Reading*, **21**, 513–516.

General Nursing Council Syllabus (1974). Syllabus to the registered mental nurse training course, General Nursing Council.

Gunzberg, H. C. (1969). *The PAC Manual*, London: National Society for Mentally Handicapped Children.

Hall, J. (1978). 'Clinical psychologists and the JBCNS', *Division of Clinical Psychology Newsletter*, October, 15-17.

Hood, J. E. (1979). 'Clinical Psychology and Primary Care: A Plea for restraint', *Bulletin of the British Psychological Society*, **32**, 422-426.

Hutchings, J. (1981). 'The behavioural approach to child abuse', in *Psychological Approaches to Child Abuse* N. Frude (ed.)., London: Batsford.

Kat, B. and Thomas, D. (1978). 'The organisation of clinical psychology: beyond Trethowan', *Division of Clinical Psychology Newslatter*, October, 19-25.

Kincey, J. A. (1974). 'General practice and clinical psychology: some arguments for a closer liaison', *Journal of the Royal College of General Practitioners*, **24**, 882-888.

Koch, H. C. H. (1979). 'Evaluation of behaviour therapy intervention in general practice', *Journal of the Royal College of General Practitioners*, **29**, 337-340.

Lazarus, A. A. (1973). 'Multimodal behaviour therapy: treating the BASIC ID', *Journal of Nervous and Mental Disease*, **156**, 404-411.

Ledwidge, B. (1978). 'Cognitive behaviour modification: a step in the wrong direction', *Psychological Bulletin*, **85**, 353-376.

Ley, P. (1973). 'The Journal of comprehensibility' *Journal of the Institute of Health Education*, **11**, 17-20.

Marks, I. M. (1976). 'The current status of behavioural psychotherapy: theory and practice', *American Journal of Psychiatry*, **133**, 253-261.

Marks, I. M., Hodgson, R., and Rachman, S. (1975). 'Treatment of chronic obsessive compulsive neurosis by *in vivo* exposure', *British Journal of Psychiatry*, **127**, 349-364.

Marks, I. M., Hallam, R. S., and Philpott, R. (1975). 'Nurse therapists in behavioural psychotherapy', *British Medical Journal*, **3**, 144-148.

McAlister, T. A. and Phillips, A. E. (1975). 'The clinical psychologist in a health centre: one year's work', *British Medical Journal*, **4**, 513-514.

McLaughlin, G. H. (1969). 'SMOG grading — a new readability formula', *Journal of Reading*, **22**, 639-646.

Mittler, L. (1970). *The Psychological Assessment of Mental and Physical Handicap*, London: Methuen.

Rachman, S., Hodgson, R. W., and Marks, I. M. (1973). 'The treatment of obsessive compulsive neurosis by modelling and flooding *in vivo*' *Behaviour Research and Therapy*, **11**, 463-471.

Reavley, W., Gilbert, M. T., and Carver, V. (1978). 'The behavioural approach to child abuse', in *Child Abuse: A study text*, V. Carver (ed.), Milton Keynes: The Open University Press.

Reavley, W. and Gilbert, M. T. (1979a). 'The analysis and treatment of child abuse', *Child Abuse and Neglect*, **3**, 509-514.

Reavley, W. and Gilbert, M. T. (1979b). *Behavioural psychotherapy with child abuse. Outcome on follow-up of four and a half years of clinical work.* Paper presented at European Association of Behaviour Therapy Conference, Paris.

Reavley, W. and Griffiths, G. (1981). 'Training social workers to use behaviour therapy with abusing parents', in *Psychological Approaches to Child Abuse* N. Frude (ed.), London: Batsford.

Reavley, W. (1981). 'The setting up of a joint clinic between health visitors and a clinical psychologist', *Midwife, Health Visitor and Community Nurse*, **17** (8), August.

Roberts, B. (1975). *Self-referring Psychiatric Emergencies*. Unpublished dissertation for MSc, University of Surrey.

Rowbottom, R. W. and Billis, D. (1978). 'The stratification of work and organizational design', in Jacques, E., *Health Services*, London: Heineman.
Shapiro, M. B. (1967). 'Clinical psychology as an applied science', *British Journal of Psychology*, **113**, 1039–1042.
Stock, L. (1975). *The Comprehensibility of Written Material in Staff-Patient Communication*. Unpublished Dissertation for MSc, University of Surrey.

Psychology in Practice
Edited by S. Canter and D. Canter
© 1982, John Wiley & Sons, Ltd.

CHAPTER 3

PSYCHOLOGY IN MEDICINE

Philip Ley
Professor of Clinical Psychology
University of Sydney

INTRODUCTION

This chapter describes some of the applications of psychology to medicine. In many general hospitals it will be possible to find a psychologist using repertory grid techniques to explore a depressed person's construct systems, while within yards of that psychologist a variety of problems which psychology could help with are being ignored. Frightened children will be being admitted without either they or their parents being adequately prepared. Patients at risk for coronary attacks will be being discharged without any training in stress management techniques. The hospital pharmacy will be providing medication for patients, half of whom will not take it properly if at all. Doctors will be having difficulty deciding on whether and how to tell patients that they are dying. These are only a small sample of the problems with which psychology could help and which the rapidly growing field of medical psychology is beginning to tackle.

An outline diagram of the possible activities in which psychologists could apply their subject to the field of health care is shown in Table 1. The basic dimensions of the diagram can be seen to be:

(1) whether the problem tackled is traditional or non-traditional (medical or non-medical);
(2) whether the emphasis is on prevention or remediation;
(3) whether the method used to deal with the problems is a traditional clinical one, for example application of treatment methods to single patients or a small group of patients, or a non-clinical method, for example organizational change, social action, or changing the health care personnel rather than the patients. These are of course not the only possible dimensions, and some may feel that others are more important, but they will serve for present purposes.

Table 1 A schematic outline of possible categories of the application of psychology to health care, with examples, and comments on the state of the art in each category

Target clients	Aim	Method	
		Clinical	Non-clinical
Traditional-psychiatric, mentally handicapped, etc.	Prevention	Growing, e.g. crisis intervention; suicide night line; community psychology	Virtually non-existent
	Remediation	Healthy, e.g. Psychotherapy; behaviour modification; rehabilitation	Little psychologist involvement, e.g. hostel and workshop management, environmental design
Non-traditional (a) Medical	Prevention	Growing, e.g. altering Type-A behaviour by behaviour modification; stress management techniques	Little psychologist involvement, e.g. health education, lifestyle development, preparation for hospitalization
	Remediation	Healthy, e.g. biofeedback, pain management behavioural medicine	Little psychologist involvement, e.g. patient non-compliance, clinical decision-making, organizational change
(b) Non-medical	Prevention	Little psychologist involvement, e.g. pre-retirement and pre-marriage counselling	Little psychologist involvement, e.g. health and sex education programmes
	Remediation	Healthy, e.g. smoking, obesity, sexual problems	Little psychologist involvement, e.g. consulting to self-help groups

In terms of this classification it is clear that there has been relative neglect by psychologists of the use of non-clinical methods, and lack of concern with prevention. This last neglect can be explained in the field of psychiatry, by the sheer lack of knowledge about what can be done to reduce the frequency of disorders. Indeed, perhaps slightly paradoxically, some of the possibilities for prevention seem clearer in the area of physical medicine (see below for further discussion).

Non-clinical methods which could be used in remediation include:

(1) changing the behaviour of patients in ways conducive to more effective care;
(2) changing the behaviour of professionals so as to promote more efficient care;
(3) changing the organizational climate in which health care takes place;
(4) changing the physical environment in which health care takes place.

In addition, there are problems which arise in health care which do not necessarily have implications for recovery. An example of this is the problem of 'informed consent' — a legal and moral problem really but, nevertheless, one to which psychologists can contribute. If patients are to give genuine, informed consent to treatments, then they must be fully informed about those treatments. This, of course, yields a variety of psychological problems concerned with how to get the information across, and what side-effects, if any, the provision of such information might have.

To provide examples of psychological factors in all of these types of problems, it is proposed to look in some detail at:

(1) the more efficient use of medication by increasing patients' compliance with treatment regimens;
(2) the problem of making a reality of informed consent procedures;
(3) the problem of non-compliance by health care professionals;
(4) ways in which patients' post-operative recovery could be speeded up, and hospital stay reduced.

These are only some of the problems which might have been chosen. Others include the motivation of blood and organ donors (Ostwalt, 1979); the improvement of decision-making (Schwartz and Wiedel, 1979; Triggs and Bennett, 1979); and programmes for the preparation of children for hospitalization and surgery (Melamed, 1977). For reviews of these and other areas of interest, see the volumes edited by Rachman (1977, 1980); Oborne *et al.* (1979); and Eiser (1981).

PATIENTS' NON-COMPLIANCE WITH ADVICE

Patients' non-compliance with advice is now a well-documented phenomenon (Haynes *et al.*, 1979). As an example of the magnitude of the problem, Table 2 summarizes the results of three surveys of the extent to which patients fail to comply with advice about medication.

Table 2   The frequency with which patients fail to take their medication properly

Type of medication	Ley (1977)	Per cent of patients non-compliant Food and Drug Administration (1979)	Barofsky (1980)
Antibiotics	49	48	52
Psychiatric	39	42	42
Anti-hypertensive	—	43	61
Anti-tuberculosis	38	42	43
Other medications	48	54	46

Of course, it could be possible that non-compliance with medication, and other regimens, does not really matter in that it produces no measurable ill-effects. Unfortunately, there is evidence to show that this rosy view is incorrect. For example, Ausburn (1980) reported that approximately one-third of the medical in-patients she studied had had to be hospitalized as a result of non-compliance. In addition, the Food and Drug Administration (1980) has produced estimates of the health costs of non-compliance.

These are based on the assumptions (i) that the non-compliance rate is about 40 per cent; (ii) that in the USA there are 75 million prescriptions per year for drugs for which non-compliance would cause problems; and (iii) that the cost, on 1978 figures, of a lost workday, a hospital day, a revisit to the physician, and an extra prescription are, respectively, 45, 250, 15, and 7 dollars. The estimated costs are shown in Table 3.

It can be seen from these estimates that the economic costs of non-compliance are not trivial, and that small reductions in non-compliance could lead to the saving of large sums of money. Thus, a 10 per cent reduction in non-compliance could save 40,000,000 and 80,000,000 dollars.

In view of this, it is important to consider whether it is possible to reduce non-compliance, and here there are grounds for reasonable optimism. The manipulation of cognitive and social variables (Ley, 1979b), the provision of leaflets about medication (Morris and Halperin, 1979) and the use of behaviour modification techniques (Dunbar *et al.*, 1979), have all shown at least partial success in reducing non-compliance. Some of these techniques are, of course, more expensive than others, and any intensive behavioural programme might well generate costs as great as the likely savings. From this

Table 3   Estimates of costs of non-compliance provided by the US Food and Drug
Administration

Adverse outcome of non-compliance	Estimated incidence (per cent) of adverse outcome	Estimated costs (millions of US dollars)
Unnecessary prescription refills	10–20	21–42
Additional visit to physician	5–10	22.5–45
Additional workday lost	5–10	67.5–135
Two additional workdays lost	5–10	135–270
Hospitalization:	1–2	
one day	0.25–0.5	16.75–37.5
two days	0.5–1.0	75–150
three days	0.25–0.5	56.25–112.5
Total		394.0–792.0

purely economic perspective, it is, therefore, of interest that written leaflets for
patients are often effective. For example, Ley *et al.*, (1975) found that
medication errors were reduced by 60 per cent or more by the provision of an
appropriate leaflet. Not all investigations report such successful results
(Morris and Halperin, 1979). This is probably in part due to the currently
inefficient psychological packaging of the information. For example, Ley

Table 4   Understandability of health-related written information as assessed by readability
formulae

Material	Numbers of leaflets likely to be understood by stated percentage of population			
	25% or less	26–40%	41–74%	75% or more
X-ray leaflets (Ley *et al.*, 1972)	—	2	—	3
Dental leaflets (Ley, 1974)	1	1	—	3
OTC drug leaflets (Pyrczak and Roth, 1976)	6	3	—	1
Prescription drug leaflets (Liguori, 1978)	—	2	—	2
Opticians' leaflets (French *et al.*, 1978)	7	20	9	2
Pamphlets about cancer (Dept. of Health, Education & Welfare, 1979)	6	2	—	—
Health Education leaflets (Cole, 1979)	4	4	0	7
Total n =	24	34	9	18
% =	(28)	(40)	(11)	(21)

(1980) has reviewed investigations reporting the understandability of written information for patients, with the results summarized in Table 4.

These results show that much of the written information provided is much too difficult for its intended audience. Over two-thirds of the documents and leaflets assessed would be understood by 40 per cent or less of their intended audiences. The vast majority of people would find the information too difficult to comprehend.

In addition, physical packaging of the information shows little evidence of being informed by current psychological knowledge of how to present information (see Wright, 1977; Hartley, this volume). There is therefore a great deal of scope for psychologists to conduct research into the improvement of such documents.

As well as these factors, there are, of course, many others which have been shown to affect compliance with advice; and most of these have a strong psychological component (Ley, 1979b). They include such factors as the patient's perception of the seriousness of the illness and the perceived efficacy of treatment; the presence or absence of social support; and whether the patient feels satisfied with the consultation. But is it ethical to attempt to increase compliance with advice?

INFORMED CONSENT AND THE ETHICS OF COMPLIANCE INDUCTION ATTEMPTS

The problem of whether or not it is proper to attempt to apply psychology to increase the probability that a patient will follow advice has been raised by Stimson (1974) and Jonsen (1979), amongst others. To these authors, the term 'compliance' is, itself, objectionable, smacking, as it does, of subordinate persons complying with the requests of their superiors. Further, there is to some a nasty taste of manipulation about the whole enterprise.

However, it is probably true that most of the ethical problems would be overcome if, before any attempt at compliance induction, the patient:

(1) is fully informed about the suggested treatment, alternative treatments, and the consequences of not having any treatment at all;
(2) then makes a decision to accept one or none of the treatments;
(3) then, if treatment is accepted, is given frequent opportunities to change this decision.

If it is accepted that a scheme such as this is desirable, then two major problems present themselves. The first is the problem of effectively informing the patient. The second lies in the possibility that effective communication might have adverse effects.

The problem of successfully presenting information is a major one. It has already been shown that in the case of written information, there is reason to doubt that success is always achieved. Even if the information is efficiently transmitted, it is highly likely that much of it will be forgotten. Ley (1979a), reviewing studies of patients' forgetting of medical information, has shown that between a third and a half of what the doctor says is forgotten within minutes of the patient hearing it. A summary of investigations of patients forgetting, including those reviewed by Ley (1979a), is given in Table 5.

Table 5   Patient's forgetting of what their doctors have told them

		Type of patients	% forgotten
1.	*General Practice*		
	Ley *et al.* (1973)	Mixed	50
	Ley *et al.* (1976)	Mixed	44
	Bertakis (1977)	Mixed	38
2.	*Medical Out-patients*		
	Ley and Spelman (1965)	Mixed	37
	Ley and Spelman (1967)	Mixed	39
		Mixed	41
	Joyce *et al.* (1969)	Rheumatological	52
		Rheumatological	54
	Anderson (1979)	Rheumatological	60
	Bergler *et al.* (1980)	Hypertensive	28
3.	*Mixed Out-patients*		
	Cassileth *et al.* (1980)	Cancer	31
4.	*Surgical In-patients and Out-patients*		
	Robinson and Merav (1976)	Cardiac surgery	71
	Priluck *et al.* (1979)	Detached retina	43

It is obvious that before genuine informed consent will be obtainable, problems of patients' understanding and recall will need to be overcome. Some methods for achieving this goal are already available and include simplification, repetition, explicit categorization, use of specific instructional statements, and use of primacy and importance effects. Results of a number of investigations which have tried to improve memory for clinical information are shown in Table 6.

Despite these successes, there is still a substantial amount of research to be conducted before psychologists will be able confidently to advise clinicians on methods for better information transmission, and for increasing patients' recall.

Some clinicians have been concerned about the effects of presenting full information about illness and treatment. This is because there would necessarily have to be potentially frightening information presented. Virtually no treatment is without its hazards, and most illnesses can have serious complica-

Table 6   Effects of memory-enhancing techniques on recall of medical information

Investigation	Material	Method	Improvement in recall	P
Ley *et al.* (1972)	X-ray leaflets	Simplification	(a) —6	NS
Bradshaw *et al.*	Slimming advice	Simplification	(b) + 34	<0.01
Bradshaw *et al.* (1975)	Slimming advice	Simplification	(a) + 29	NS
			(b) + 72	<0.05
			(c) + 48	<0.01
Ley *et al.* (1979)	Menopause booklet	Simplification	+ 27	<0.05
Kupst *et al.* (1975)	Doctors' statements	Repetition	(a) + 20[1]	<0.01
			(b) + 20[2]	<0.01
Ley (1979a)	Medical statements	Repetition (6 analogue studies)	+ 31	<0.01
Ley *et al.* (1973)	Doctors' statements	Explicit categorization	(a) + 42	<0.01
			(b) + 24	<0.01
Ley (1979a)	Medical statements	Explicit categorization (7 analogue studies)	+ 31	<0.01
Bradshaw *et al.* (1975)	Slimming advice	Use of specific advice statements	(a) + 350	<0.001
			(b) + 158	<0.001
			(c) + 219	<0.001
Ley (1972)	Doctor's advice	(a) Primacy	+ 74	<0.01
		(b) Stressing importance	+ 38	<0.06
Ley *et al.* (1973)	Contraception booklet	Mixture of techniques	—6	NS

[1]by clinician
[2]by patient

tions. It is, therefore, possible to imagine a scenario in which informed patients refuse treatment and, in consequence, cure rates drop.

There is very little known, theoretically or practically, about the effects of presenting frightening information. The available evidence is conflicting, and direct studies of what happens when doctors present such information to patients are a little thin on the ground. Some of these have been reviewed by Ley (1981a) and a summary of them is provided in Table 7. Yet again, an aspect of medical care proves to have major psychological aspects, and is relatively ignored by psychologists.

NON-COMPLIANCE BY HEALTH CARE PROFESSIONALS

It has been shown earlier that patients are often non-compliant with the advice given to them. However, in health care systems it is not only the consumers

Table 7   Effects of giving patients potentially frightening information

Topic	Investigations	Outcome
Telling patients that they have cancer	1, 2, 3, 4	11–34% disapproved of doctors telling
Fuller information on other illnesses	5, 6, 7, 8	4–14% would have preferred not to know
Informing patients of side-effects of drugs	10, 11, 12, 13, 14, 15	No study showed reduced compliance One study showed more frequent side-effects

1. Kelly and Friesen (1950)
2. Aitken-Swan *et al.* (1959)
3. Gerle *et al.* (1960)
4. Gilbertson and Wangensteen (1962)
5. Alfidi (1971)
6. Greenwood (1973)
7. Golodetz *et al.* (1976)
8. Stevens *et al.* (1977)

9. Myers and Calvert (1973)
10. Myers and Calvert (1978)
11. Newcomer and Anderson (1974)
12. Elkund and Wessling (1976)
13. Paulson *et al.* (1976)
14. Suveges (1977)
15. Weibert (1977)

are given advice. The providers are also provided with rules and advice about standards of good care. While it is usually assumed that the majority of health care professionals do adhere to these standards, there is, at least, some evidence to make one question this assumption.

Ley (1981b) has reviewed investigations involving psychologists, pharmacists, nurses, and doctors and has reported that levels of non-compliance with officially approved standards and methods of care are running at an alarmingly high level. The results of his survey are summarized in Table 8. If these investigations reveal typical standards of practice, it will be important to find out why such high levels of non-compliance exist. Possible reasons include:

(1) lack of appropriate knowledge;
(2) disagreement with the rule or with the principle of issuing rules;
(3) social pressures leading to the ignoring of the rule.

Each of these has some validity. For example, Watkins and Norwood (1978) have shown that the less a pharmacist knows about the medication he is prescribing, the less likely is he to provide essential information. With regard to disagreement with recommendations, Melville (1979) found that British general practitioners, who continued (against official advice) to prescribe barbiturates, tended to score highly on a scale measuring autonomy of prescribing habits. A possible interpretation of this correlation is that their desire for autonomy made them feel that it was inappropriate for their

Table 8   Non-compliance with rules of good practice by health care professionals

Investigation	Topic		% not complying
Miller *et al.* (1970)	Correct scoring of tests		94
Miller and Chansky (1972)	Correct scoring of tests		84
Knapp *et al.* (1969)	Warning of potentially	(a)	83
	dangerous drug interactions	(b)	92
Campbell and Grisafe (1975)	or drug danger		91
Wertheimer *et al.* (1973)			64
Wertheimer *et al.* (1973)	Adequate labelling		81
Rowles *et al.* (1974)	and counselling about		80
Campbell and Grisafe (1975)	medicine use		53
Gordis *et al.* (1976)	Appropriate antibiotic	(a)	21
	prescription	(b)	76
		(c)	12
		(d)	59
Hofling *et al.* (1966)	Observing rules about issuing medicine		95
			% of patients not receiving
Scheckler and Bennett (1970)	Appropriate antibiotic therapy		62
Roberts and Visconti (1972)	Appropriate antibiotic therapy		66
Kunin *et al.* (1973)	Appropriate antibiotic therapy		51
Svarstad (1974)	Adequate information about		66
Webb (1976)	medication		100

prescribing to be restrained. Finally, a good example of the effects of social pressures has been provided by Hofling *et al.* (1966). In this investigation nurses who knew that they should not be issuing a particular drug to patients, did so when instructed by an unknown doctor who transmitted the order by telephone. To accept such an instruction infringed several rules governing the conditions under which the drug should have been issued. It seems to be very hard for nurses to resist a doctor's orders even when the situation demands that they should.

A reduction in non-compliance by health care professionals would probably lead to better patient outcomes and reduced levels of iatrogenic disease. Psychologists have a clear role in this endeavour as they are qualified to investigate the educational, organizational, and interpersonal factors which lead to such non-compliance.

SHORTENING PATIENTS' STAY IN HOSPITAL BY SPEEDING RECOVERY

It would seem to be possible to speed recovery amongst patients who have undergone surgery. To date, two non-clinical methods would seem to achieve this end. It would appear that patients' pain (as measured by their analgesic requests), and their length of stay in hospital, can be reduced by a variety of pre-operative communications. Ley (1977) has classified these as:

(1) information giving, that is telling the patient what to expect, what is going to happen, etc.;
(2) technical advice, that is telling patients how to cough, how to turn in bed, how to use a trapeze, etc.;
(3) quasi-psychotherapeutic, dealing with the patients' fears and worries.

All these methods seem to be successful in achieving faster post-operative recovery. The results of the studies, reviewed by Ley (1977), are summarized in Table 9. More recent investigations by Leventhal and his associates confirm this result (Leventhal et al., 1979). The savings, in length of time in hospital, are approximately two days on average.

Table 9   Effects of pre-operative communication on progress after surgery

Type of communication	Patients	Required fewer analgesics	Discharged sooner?
Instruction	1. Mixed surgical	Yes	Yes
	2. Mixed surgical	No	Yes
Information	1. Mainly hernia	Yes	Yes
	2. Hernia	Yes	Yes
	3. Peptic ulcer	—	Yes
	4. Mixed surgical	No	No
Counselling	1. Peptic ulcer	—	Yes
	2. Hernia	Yes	Yes
Information + counselling	1. Abdominal surgery	Yes	Yes
Information + counselling instruction	1. Abdominal surgery	—	Yes
	2. Mixed surgical	Yes	Yes

Why these disparate techniques should all be effective is not clear, and research is needed to discover whether they are due to placebo effect or a particular psychological component, such as directing attention to the sensations arising from the injured part (Leventhal and Everhart, 1979). Another possible way of reducing patient stay might be to bring about the organizational and attitudinal changes suggested by the investigations of Revans (1964). This research found that length of hospital stay, of both medical and surgical patients, was correlated with attitudes which affected ease of upward communication (nurse–sister–consultant). In hospitals where such communication was not easily achieved, patient stay was longer than in hospitals with free upward communication. It was also found that hospitals, characterized by those attitudes associated with greater patient stay, were also more prone to losing their staff, and that nursing staff in them tended to experience more frequent and longer illnesses. These findings deserve much more attention than they have received from psychologists. If they are generally valid, then attitudinal and organizational change could benefit both staff and patients, and save considerable amounts of money by reducing the numbers of nursing students leaving before they are trained, staff illnesses, and duration of patient stay. Evidence from the UK Hospital Internal Communications Project (Wieland and Leigh, 1971) shows that it is difficult to change such attitude and communication patterns, but it would be a pity if Revan's findings were forgotten because of the relative failure of this project. Once more, there are problems of both theoretical and practical interest for psychologists.

PREVENTION

Relatively little is known about way in which mental disorder can be prevented. Some would say that the only hope lies in good genetic counselling services, but others feel that better preparation for parenting, improvement of the material environment, and teaching stress management techniques would be of value. No doubt, continued research will lead to surer knowledge of what factors can be modified so as to reduce mental disorder.

As examples of the current lack of knowledge, it is worth considering the success rate of phone-in services for those considering suicide. These services are usually staffed by volunteer helpers supervised by professionals, and their aim is to provide, not only friendly and empathic understanding, but also information about facilities for help and, where possible, an agreement from the caller to take specific steps to seek further help, if it is needed. The provision of such services is expanding rapidly, and it would, perhaps, be expected that this would lead to fewer suicides. Unfortunately, there appears to be little evidence that this is the case. Cities and towns with such services do not have lower suicide rates than towns without them (Weiner, 1969; Lester, 1972), and even massive increases in lay and professional help for potential suicides can lead to an increase in the suicide rate (Nielsen and Videbech, 1973). Indeed, Ullman and Krasner (1975) conclude that the services fail in that they do not usually reach the high-risk person and might even possibly increase the risks amongst low-risk individuals who do contact them.

Paradoxically, if prevention of mental disorder remains a mystery, there appear to be clear ways in which psychology might contribute to the prevention of some major physical disorders. There appears to be fairly general agreement that, at least, in the cases of cardiovascular disorders, some cancers, bronchitis and emphysema, cirrhosis of the liver, there is reason to suppose that faulty behaviour is involved (Turner and Ball, 1973; Louria *et al.*, 1976; Haggerty, 1977). To some extent, these disorders are caused or aggravated by: (i) faulty eating habits, (ii) smoking, (iii) insufficient exercise and possibly, in the case of coronary heart disease, by patterns of behaviour characterized by impatience, hostility, and striving for achievement. In addition, there are those specific behaviours related to particular health outcomes, for example wearing safety belts, and the risk of serious injury or death in car crashes; or the effects of eating sweets on the probability of developing dental caries.

Basically, there are three main ways in which these undesirable behaviours could be prevented. These are: legislation which is not conducive to them; health educational programmes; and product changes. Thus, for example, laws can be passed which make the non-wearing of seat belts illegal, health educational campaigns about the beneficial effects of exercise can be conducted; cars can be designed with built-in safety features; foods with low sugar levels encouraged, and so on. In addition, organizational and ideological barriers to the achievement of healthy lifestyles can be reduced. For example, it is likely that current school games and physical education are aversive to many children and, in any case, not the types of activity which can be carried into adult life. A switch to an ideology that saw such activities as being an opportunity to develop lifelong exercise habits might make a major contribution to health.

Of these methods of changing lifestyles, that to which psychologists could make the greatest contribution is probably health education. Currently, views as to the effectiveness of health education are divided. Gatherer *et al.* (1979) provided an annotated bibliography of studies of health education, and the summary shown in Table 10. Critics of health education, e.g. Cohen and Cohen (1978), would probably say that these results paint far too good a picture, and point out the methodological and other inadequacies of the investigations summarized. indeed, these are pointed out by Gatherer *et al.* themselves. These methodological inadequacies are a major argument for the involvement of psychologists in this field. Their training should have given them the appropriate methodological expertise.

Secondly, psychologists should be able to make a major contribution in terms of improving the effectiveness of the content and presentation of health educational messages.

Thirdly, they should be able to make a contribution to the understanding of why health education sometimes produces adverse effects. A classic example of the production of adverse effects can be found in the investigation by Stuart (1973). In a well-designed study with appropriate controls, it was found that the experimental groups who received the health educational messages about the dangers of taking drugs were *more* likely to use drugs than controls.

Table 10   Effects of health education programmes (after Gatherer *et al.* 1979)

	Number of studies showing: Effect	No effect	% showing effect
(a) Method of Education			
Mass media	35	14	71.4
Group method	74	29	71.8
Individual method	41	4	91.1
(b) Outcome Variable			
Increased knowledge	42	7	85.7
Changed attitude	23	11	67.6
Changed behaviour	85	29	74.6

However, despite the occasional disaster, such as that found in Stuart's investigation, there is some strongly suggestive evidence that health educational programmes can produce lifestyle change. Examples of this are the Finnish North Karelia Project (Koskela, 1976) which involved mass media, written and individual education attempting to reduce smoking and the use of high-fat foods, and increased monitoring of blood pressure. Some of the results of this investigation are shown in Table 11.

Table 11   Effects of the North Karelia educational campaign

Health-relevant behaviour	Per cent of participants showing behaviour at: Base-line	Last follow-up	% Change
Smoking { men	54	42	(−22)
women	12	12	(0)
Use of low-fat milk	17	41	(+141)
Use of butter	86	72	(−16)
Blood pressure measured in last 3 months	28	56	(+100)

An even better known investigation is that reported by Farquhar *et al.* (1977) and Maccoby and Alexander (1980). In this study, an attempt was made to reduce risk factors associated with coronary heart disease. Three communities in California were chosen for the experiment. Two towns received media education about risk factors and what to do about them. In addition, in one of these towns, two-thirds of high-risk individuals were given face-to-face education as well. The third town served as a control. The programme was successful in increasing knowledge of risks and in reducing overall risk of coronary heart disease, the reduction in risk being estimated by Stunkard (1979) as equivalent to a gain of five years in life for a 45-year-old man. However, it was less successful in obtaining worthwhile reductions in cigarette smoking and blood-pressure levels. Results of both this study and the Finnish one are encouraging, and it is likely that even better results could be obtained if more research effort went into this area. Lest this should sound like a mere platitude, it is worth considering the research into the use of media campaigns to increase the use of car seat belts described by Kelley (1979). Current lack of adequate knowledge is emphasized by the fact that, although the advertisements used in this investigation were judged by experts as excellent (they even won an award), they had no effect on the probability that seat belts would be worn. This result was consistent with the findings of other research reviewed by Kelley. The present state of knowledge is such that it is not possible to predict what sort of media campaign will have what sort of result for any health topic. The area is, therefore, of great theoretical and practical importance.

For the sake of completeness, brief reference should also be made to the use of clinical methods in the changing of lifestyle. The main effort has, of course, been in the fields of smoking and obesity, but recently there have been attempts to change behaviour associated with coronary heart disease. These behaviours (Type-A behaviours) include striving for achievement, sense of time pressure, and hostility. There is evidence to suggest that coronary heart disease is more common in men exhibiting these behaviours. (For reviews, see Glass, 1977; Roskies, 1979, 1980). Research by Suinn et al. (1975), Suinn and Bloom (1978), and Roskies et al. (1978) has shown that both behaviour modification and psychotherapeutic methods might be capable of reducing Type-A behaviour. Related research, not based on the Type-A theory, is also suggestive of a role for behaviour modification methods in reducing risks of heart disease, e.g. Meyer and Henderson (1974), Pomerleau (1979).

Lifestyle change clearly poses formidable problems. It will be interesting to see the extent to which psychology can overcome them. Sometimes it will probably emerge that legislation or product alteration will be the better alternatives. Consider the comparative effectiveness of pasteurizing milk before bottling, as opposed to using psychological principles and methods to induce housewives to heat all the milk delivered to them to the required temperature before using it (Kelley, 1979).

CONCLUSIONS

The main conclusion to be drawn from this chapter is that psychologists in the field of medicine have been guilty of few sins of commission, but many of omission. There has been excessive concentration on remediation of problems using intensive clinical methods. This has taken place in the context of a relative neglect of the possibilities of prevention, and a relative neglect of non-clinical strategies for solving problems of health care. These last include manipulation of the organizational and physical environments in which health care takes place, and the alteration of patient and clinician behaviour to make health care more effective and efficient.

The encouraging signs include the rapidity with which new target groups have been incorporated into the population to which clinical methods have been applied, the beginning of interest in less clinical methods and, above all, the increasing emphasis on evaluation of effectiveness. This last has still a long way to go, and many clinicians remain content with techniques of unknown usefulness. An impressive example of the emphasis on evaluation can be found in the research into the usefulness of biofeedback techniques for hypertension and other physical maladies (Blanchard and Epstein, 1977; Gatchel and Price, 1979). Although the results have been disappointing in many respects, it is a sign of the increasing maturity of psychology that the relative inefficiency of these techniques has been so quickly demonstrated.

Mention of economic factors has been made from time to time in this chapter, and it is encouraging to see that substantial savings in costs of health care can be made by the application of psychology to problems of patients' non-compliance, and the use of pre-operative counselling to shorten lengths of hospital stay. In health services short of resources, these might be very important contributions.

Finally, it will be necessary for psychologists in the health field not only to consider the cost-effectiveness of their actions, but also some of the wider societal implications of what they are undertaking. Thus, a totally effective anti-smoking programme would leave a large gap in tax revenue. A totally effective programme for eliminating Type-A behaviour might leave society short of its innovative and hard-working executives. Early detection of symptoms, in the absence of guaranteed cures, could lead to greater anxiety and distress than later detection of illness. These are only a few of the possible examples, but they are worth pondering.

REFERENCES

Aitken-Swan, J. and Easson, E. C. (1959). 'Reactions of cancer patients on being told their diagnosis', *British Medical Journal*, **1**, 779–783.

Alfidi, R. J. (1971). 'Informed consent. A study of patient reactions', *Journal of The American Medical Association*, **216**, 1325–1329.

Anderson, J. L. (1979). 'Patients' recall of information and its relation to the nature of the consultation', in D. Osborne, M. M. Gruneberg, and J. R. Eiser (eds), *Research in Psychology and Medicine*, London: Academic Press.

Ausburn, L. (1980). 'Patient compliance with medication regimes', in J. Sheppard (ed.), *Advances in Behavioural Medicine*, Vol. 1, Lidcombe, NSW: Cumberland College of Health Sciences.

Barofsky, I. (1980). *The Chronic Psychiatric Patient in the Community*, New York: Plenum Press.

Bergler, J. H., Pennington, A. C., Metcalfe, M., and Freis, E. D. (1980). 'Informed consent: how much does the patient understand?', *Clinical Pharmacology and Therapeutics*, **27**, 535-440.

Bertakis, K. D. (1977). 'The communication of information from physician to patient: a method for increasing retention and satisfaction', *Journal of Family Practice*, **5**, 217-222.

Bradshaw, P. W., Ley, P., Kincey, J. A., and Bradshaw, J. (1975). 'Recall of medical advice: comprehensibility and specificity', *British Journal of Social and Clinical Psychology*, **14**, 55-62.

Campbell, R. K. and Grisafe, J. A. (1975). 'Compliance with the Washington State patient information regulations', *Journal of the American Pharmaceutical Association*, **15**, 494-495, 528.

Cassileth, B. R., Zupkis, R. V., Sutton-Smith, K., and March, V. (1980). 'Informed consent — why are its goals imperfectly realised?', *New England Journal of Medicine*, **302**, 896-900.

Cohen, C. I. and Cohen, E. J. (1978). 'Health Education: panacea, pernicious or pointless?', *New England Journal of Medicine*, **299**, 718-720.

Cole, R. (1979). 'The understanding of medical terminology used in printed health educational materials', *Health Education Journal*, **38**, 111-121.

Department of Health and Welfare (1979). *Readability testing in cancer communication*, Washington DC, DHEW Publication No. (NIH) 79-1689.

Dunbar, J. M., Marshall, G. D., and Hovell, M. F. (1979). 'Behavioural strategies for improving compliance', in R. D. Haynes, W. D. Taylor, and D. O. Sackett (eds), *Compliance in Health Care*, Baltimore: Johns Hopkins University Press.

Eiser, J. R. (1981). *Social Psychology and Behavioural Medicine*, Chichester: Wiley.

Elkund, L. H. and Wessling, A. (1976). 'Evaluation of package enclosures for drug packages', *Lakaridningen*, **73**, 2319-2320.

Farquhar, J. W., Maccoby, N., Wood, P. D., Alexander, J. K., Beitrose, H., Brown, B. W., Haskell, W. L., MacAlister, A. L., Meyer, A. J., Nash, J. D., and Stern, M. P. (1977). 'Community education for cardiovascular health', *Lancet*, **1**, 1192-1195.

Flesch, R. (1948). 'A new readability yardstick', *Journal of Applied Psychology*, **32**, 221-233.

Food and Drug Administration (1979). 'Prescription drug products: patient labelling requirements', *Federal Register*, **44**, 40016-40041.

Food and Drug Administration (1980). 'Prescription drug products: patient package insert requirements', *Federal Register*, **45**, (179), 60754-60780.

Gatchel, R. J. and Price, K. P. (1979). *Clinical Applications of Bio-Feedback: Appraisal and Status*, New York: Pergamon Press.

Gatherer, A., Parfit, J., Porter, E., and Vessey, M. (1979). *Is Health Education Effective?*, London: Health Education Council Monograph Series (No.2).

Gerle, B., Lunden, G., and Sandblom, P. (1960). 'The patient with inoperable cancer from the psychiatric and social standpoints', *Cancer*, **13**, 1206-1217.

Gillertsen, V. A. and Wangensteen, O. H., (1962). 'Should the doctor tell the patient that the disease is cancer?', *Cancer*, **12**, 82-86.

Glass, D. C. (1977). 'Stress behaviour patterns and coronary disease', *American Scientist*, **65**, 177-187.

Golodetz, A., Reuss, J., and Milhous, R. L. 'The right to know: giving the patient his medical recort', *Arch. Phys. Med. Rehabil.*, **57** (2), 78-81.

Gordis, L., Desi, L., and Schmerler, H. R. (1976). 'Treatment of acute sore throats: a comparison of pediatricians and general physicians', *Pediatrics*, **57**, 422-424.

Greenwood, R. D. (1973). 'Should parents be informed of innocent murmurs? Some consequences of routine disclosure and some suggestions for transmitting the information', *Clinical Pediatrics (Philadelphia)*, (1976). **12**, 468–476.

Haggerty, R. J. (1977). 'Changing lifestyles to improve health', *Preventive Medicine*, **6**, 276–289.

Haynes, R. G., Taylor, D. W., and Sackett, D. L. (1979). *Compliance in Health Care*, Baltimore: Johns Hopkins University Press.

Hofling, C. K., Brotzman, E., Dalrymple, S., Graves, N., and Pierce, C. M., (1966). 'An experimental study in nurse–physician relationships', *Journal of Nervous and Mental Diseases*, **143**, 171–180.

Jonsen, A. R. (1979). 'Ethical issues in compliance', in R. B. Haynes, D. W. Taylor, and D. L. Sackett (eds), *Compliance in Health Care*, Baltimore: Johns Hopkins University Press.

Joyce, C. R. B., Caple, G., Mason, M., Reynolds, E., and Mathews, J. A. (1969). 'Quantitative study of doctor–patient communication', *Quarterly Journal of Medicine*, **38**, 183–194.

Kazdin, A. E. (1977). 'Extension of reinforcement techniques to socially and environmentally relevant behaviour', *Progress in Behaviour Modification*, Vol. 4, New York: Academic Press.

Kelley, A. B. (1979). 'A media role for public health compliance?', in R. B. Haynes, D. W. Taylor, and D. L. Sackett (eds), *Compliance in Health Care*, Baltimore: Johns Hopkins University Press.

Kelly, W. P. and Friesen, S. (1950). 'Do cancer patients want to be told?', *Surgery*, **27**, 822–826.

Knapp, D. A., Wolff, H. H., Knapp, D. E., and Rudy, T. A. (1969). 'The pharmacist as drug advisor', *Journal of the American Pharmaceutical Association*, **9**, 502–505, 543.

Koskela, K. (1976). 'The North Karelia Project: a first evaluation', *International Journal of Health Education* **19**, 59–56.

Kunin, C. M., Tupasi, T., and Craig, W. (1973). 'Use of antibiotics', *Annals of Internal Medicine*, **79**, 555–560.

Kupst, M. J., Dresser, K., Schuman, J. L., and Paul, M. H. (1975). 'Evaluation of methods to improve doctor–patient communication', *American Journal of Orthopsychiatry*, **45**, 420–429.

Leventhal, H., Brown, D., Schacham, S., and Engquist, G. (1979). 'Effects of preparatory information about sensations, threat of pain and attention on cold pressor distress', *Journal of Personality and Social Psychology*, **37** (5), 688–714.

Ley, P. (1972). 'Primacy, rated importance and the recall of medical information', *Journal of Health and Social Behaviour*, **13**, 311–317.

Ley, P. (1974). 'Communication in the clinical setting', *British Journal of Orthodontics*, **1**, 173–177.

Ley, P. (1977). 'Psychological studies of doctor-patient communication', in S. Rachman (ed.) *Contribution to Medical Psychology*, vol. 1, Oxford: Pergamon Press.

Ley, P. (1979a). 'Memory for medical information', *British Journal of Social and Clinical Psychology*, **18**, 245–255.

Ley, P. (1979b). 'Psychology of compliance', in D. Osborne, M. M. Gruneberg, and J. R. Eiser (eds), *Research in Psychology and Medicine*, London: Academic Press.

Ley, P. (1980). 'Practical methods for improving communication', in L. Morris, M. Mazis, and I. Barofsky (eds), *Product Labelling and Health Risks*, Cold Spring Harbor, New York: Banbury Reports.

Ley, P. (1981a). 'Giving information to patients', in J. R. Eiser (ed.), *Social Psychology and Behavioural Medicine*, New York: Wiley.

Ley, P. (1981b). 'Professional non-compliance: a neglected problem', *British Journal of Clinical Psychology*, **20**, 151–154.

Ley, P. and Spelman, M. S. (1965). 'Communications in an out-patient setting', *British Journal of Social and Clinical Psychology*, **4**, 114–116.

Ley, P. and Spelman, M. S. (1967). *Communicating with the Patient*, London: Staples Press.

Ley, P., Goldman, M., Bradshaw, P. W., Kincey, J. A., and Walker, C. M. (1972). 'The comprehensibility of some X-ray leaflets', *Journal of the Institute of Health Education*, **10**, 47–55.

Ley, P., Bradshaw, P. W., Eaves, D. E., and Alker, C. M. (1973). 'A method for increasing patients' recall of information presented to them', *Psychology Medicine*, **3**, 217–220.

Ley, P., Jain, V. K., and Skilbeck, C. S. (1975). 'A method for decreasing patients' medication errors', *Psychological Medicine*, **6**, 599–601.

Ley, P., Whitworth, M. A., Skilbeck, C. E., Woodward, R., Pinsent, R. J. F. H., Pike, L. A., Clarkson, M. E., and Clark, P. B. (1976). 'Improving doctor patient communication in general practice', *Journal of the Royal College of General Practitioners*, **26**, 720–724.

Ley, P., Pike, L. A., Whitworth, M. A., and Woodward, R. (1979). 'Effects of source, context of communication and difficulty level on the success of health educational communications', *Health Education Journal*, **38**, 47–52.

Ligurori, S. (1978). 'A quantitative assessment of the readability of PPIS', *Drug Intelligence and Clinical Pharmacy*, **12**, 712–716.

Louria, D. B., Kidwell, A. P., Levenhar, M. A., Thind, I. S., and Najem, R. G. (1976). 'Primary and secondary prevention among adults: and analysis with comments on screening and health education', *Preventive Medicine*, **5**, 549–572.

Maccoby, N. and Alexander, J. (1980). 'Use of media in lifestyle programs', in P. O. Davidson and S. M. Davidson (eds), *Behavioural Medicine*, New York: Brunner-Mazel.

Melamed, B. G. (1977). 'Psychological preparation for hospitalisation', in S. Rachman (ed.), *Contribution to Medical Psychology*, Vol. 1, Oxford: Pergamon Press.

Melville, K. A. (1979). 'The influence of general practitioners' attitudes on their prescribing', in D. J. Oborne, M. M. Gruneberg, and J. R. Eiser (eds), *Research in Psychology and Medicine*, London: Academic Press.

Meyer, A. J. and Henderson, J. B. (1974). 'Multiple risk factor reduction in the prevention of cardiovascular disease', *Preventive Medicine*, **3**, 225–236.

Miller, C. K., Chansky, N. M., and Gredler, G. R. (1970). 'Rater agreement on WISC protocols', *Psychology in the Schools*, **7**, 190–193.

Miller, C. K. and Chansky, N. D. (1972). 'Psychologists scoring of WISC protocols: *Psychology in the Schools*, **9**, 144–152.

Miller, E. (1972). *Clinical Neuropsychology*, Harmondsworth: Penguin Books.

Morris, L. A. and Halperin, J. (1979). 'Effects of written drug information on patient knowledge and compliance: a literature review', *American Journal of Public Health*, **69**, 47–52.

Myers, E. D. and Calvert, E. J. (1973). 'Effects of forewarning on the occurrence of side-effects and discontinuation of medication in patients on amitryptiline', *British Journal of Psychiatry*, **122**, 461–464.

Myers, E. D. and Calvert, E. J. (1978). 'Knowledge of side-effects and perseverance with medication', *British Journal of Psychiatry*, **132**, 526–527.

Newcomer, D. R. and Anderson, R. W. (1974). 'Effectiveness of a combined drug self-administration and patient teaching program', *Drug Intelligence and Clinical Pharmacy*, **8**, 374–381.

Nielson, J. and Videbech, T. (1973). 'Suicide frequency and after, introduction of Community psychiatry on a Danish Island', *British Journal of Psychiatry*, **123**, 35–39.

Oborne, D., Gruneberg, M. M., and Eiser, J. R. (1979). *Research in Psychology and Medicine*, London: Academic Press.

Ostwalt, R. M. (1979). 'A review of the experimental manipulation of blood donor motivation', in D. Oborne, M. M. Gruneberg, and J. R. Eiser (eds), *Research in Psychology and Medicine*, London: Academic Press.

Paulson, P. T., Bauch, R., Paulson, M. L., and Zilz, D. A. (1976). 'Medication data sheets — an aid to patient education', *Drug Intelligence and Clinical Pharmacy*, **10**, 448–453.

Pomerleau, O. F. (1979). 'Behavioural medicine', *American Psychologist*, **34**, 654–663.

Priluck, I. A., Robertson, D. M., and Buettner, H. (1979). 'What patients recall of the pre-operative discussion after retinal detachment surgery', *American Journal of Ophthalmology*, **87**, 620–623.

Pyrczak, R. and Roth, D. H. (1976). 'The readability of directions on non-prescription drugs', *Journal of the American Pharmaceutical Association*, **16**, 242–244.

Rachman, S. (1977). *Contribution to Medical Psychology*, Vol. 1, Oxford: Pergamon Press.

Rachman, S. (1980). *Contributions to Medical Psychology*, Vol. 2, Oxford: Pergamon Press.

Revans, R. W. (1964). *Standards for Morale*, London: Oxford University Press, for the Nuffield Provincial Hospitals Trust.

Roberts, A. W. and Visconti, J. A. (1972). 'The rational and irrational use of systematic anti-microbial drugs', *American Journal of Hospital Pharmacy*, **29**, 1054–1060.

Robinson, G. and Merav, A. (1976). 'Informed consent: recall by patients tested post-operatively', *Annals of thoracic surgery*, **22**, 209–212.

Roskies, E. (1979). 'Evaluating improvement in the coronary-prone (Type-A) behaviour pattern', in D. Oborne, M. M. Gruneberg, and J. R. Eiser (eds), *Research in Psychology and Medicine*, London: Academic Press.

Roskies, E. (1980). 'Considerations in developing a treatment program for coronary-prone (Type-A) behaviour pattern', in P. O. Davidson and S. M. Davidson (eds), *Behavioural Medicine Changing Lifestyle*, New York: Brunner-Mazel.

Roskies, E., Spevack, M., Surkis, A., Cohen, C., and Gilman, A. (1978). 'Changing the coronary-prone (Type-A) behaviour in a non-clinical population', *Journal of Behavioural Medicine*, **1**, 201–216.

Scheckler, W. E. and Bennett, J. V. (1970). 'Antibiotic usage in seven community hospitals', *Journal of the American Medical Association*, **213**, 264–267.

Schwartz, S. and Wiedel, T. C. (1979). 'Psychology of patient management: normative versus descriptive adequacy of decision-analytic approaches to neurological decision-making', in D. Oborne, M. M. Gruneberg, and J. R. Eiser (eds), *Research in Psychology and Medicine*, London: Academic Press.

Stevens, D. P., Stagg, R., and Mackay, I. R. (1977). 'What happens when hospitalized patients see their own records', *Annals of Internal Medicine*, **86** (4), 474–475.

Stimson, G. V. (1974). 'Obeying doctor's orders: a view from the other side', *Social Science and Medicine*, **8**, 97–104.

Stuart, R. B. (1973). 'Teaching facts about drugs: pushing or preventing?', *Journal of Educational Psychology*, **66**, 189–201.

Stunkard, A. J. (1979). 'Behavioural medicine and beyond: the example of obesity', in O. F. Pomerleau and J. P. Brady (eds), *Behavioural Medicine: Theory and Practice*, Baltimore: Williams and Wilkins.

Suinn, R. M. and Bloom, L. J. (1978). 'Anxiety management training for Pattern-A behaviour', *Journal of Behavioural Medicine*, **1**, 25–35.

Suinn, R., Brock, L., Edie, C. (1975). 'Behaviour therapy for type-A patients', *American Journal of Cardiology*, **36**, 269–272.

Suveges, L. (1977). 'The impact of counselling by the pharmacist on patient knowledge and compliance', *Proceedings of the McMaster Symposium on Compliance with Therapeutic Regimens*, Hamilton, Ontario: McMaster University.

Svarstad, B. L. (1974). *The doctor–patient encounter: an observational study.* Unpublished PhD. thesis, University of Wisconsin.

Triggs, T. J. and Bennett, M. J. (1979). 'An analysis of some characteristics of clinical judgement', in D. Oborne, M. M. Gruneberg, and J. R. Eiser (eds), *Research in Psychology and Medicine*, London: Academic Press.

Turner, R. and Ball, K. (1973). 'Prevention of coronary heart disease', *Lancet*, **2**, 1137–1140.

Ullman, L. P. and Krasner, L. (1975). *A Psychological Approach to Abnormal Behaviour*, Englewood Cliffs, NJ: Prentice-Hall.

Watkins, R. L. and Norwood, G. J. (1978). 'Pharmacist drug consultation behaviour', *Social Science and Medicine*, **12** (4A), 235–239.

Webb, B. (1976). 'The retail pharmacist and drug treatment', *Journal of the Royal College of General Practitioners*, **26**, Supplement 1, 81–88.

Weibert, R. T. (1977). 'Potential distribution problems', *Drug Information Journal*, **11**, Special Supplement, 45s–48s.

Wieland, G. F. and Leigh, H. (eds) (1971). *Changing Hospitals*, London: Tavistock Publications.

Weiner, I. W. (1969). 'The effectiveness of a suicide prevention program', *Mental Hygiene*, **53**, 357–363.

Wertheimer, A. I., Shefter, E., and Cooper, R. M. (1973). 'More on the pharmacist and drug consultant', *Drug Intelligence and Clinical Pharmacy*, **7**, 58–61.

Wright, P. (1977). 'Presenting technical information: a survey of research findings', *Instructional Science*, **6**, 93–134.

Psychology in Practice
Edited by S. Canter and D. Canter
© 1982, John Wiley & Sons, Ltd.

CHAPTER 4

PSYCHOLOGY AND MENTAL HANDICAP

Jeanne Males
Principal Clinical Psychologist
St Lawrence's Hospital, Caterham, Surrey

It is becoming increasingly evident that one of the major handicaps of that group of people in society whom we label 'retarded' (or more correctly in the UK 'mentally handicapped') is their public image. Confusion between mental illness and mental handicap still abounds (Office of Health Economics, 1978). Along with all the prejudices and misconceptions associated with the former there is a general mistrust and frequently an unwillingness for handicapped people to participate fully in the life of the community (Harris, 1978). Mentally handicapped people were for many years strictly separated from the rest of the community, and while treatment was at times quite humane, this reflected far more the moral climate of the period than a real understanding of the needs of the individuals involved. Segregation was encouraged on the assumption that the intelligence of the nation would be reduced if mentally handicapped people were allowed the same rights of reproduction as the rest of the population. During the 1960s and 1970s an increasingly liberal model of care was fostered which was based on a more accurately researched understanding of the problems which are associated with mental handicap. This model has been reflected in several Government publications (DHSS, 1971; 1979; National Development Group, 1977a, 1978), and in a host of papers based on research and on clinical practice (see Clarke and Clarke, 1974a).

Mental handicap is an area where there is a meeting of psychological expertise: in clinical and educational psychology. Indeed Williams (1979) suggests that it could potentially require a link between clinical, educational, developmental, and occupational psychology. At present the most frequent link is between clinical and educational psychology with mentally handicapped children up to school-leaving age. While clinical psychologists often specialize in mental handicap, many educational psychologists spend a large part of their working lives with 'normal' children. This latter model must allow for a healthy comparison. It is vital that the two disciplines work together with school-age children and particularly that they allow for a smooth transfer at school-leaving age: the importance of this period has been clearly described (National Development Group 1977,b,c). The worst result of a lack of communication between the two groups can be the repeated and unnecessary testing of a child, conflicting advice to parents, and at worst an inappropriate placement for adult life.

The links that must develop between educational and clinical psychologists as representatives of education and other services are clearly essential from personal experience but are potentially problematic. Locally, we have found that steps forward in this area can only be achieved by setting up good communication channels, and by meeting together in an attempt to understand areas of individual expertise as well as areas of common ground.

This chapter focuses its attention on the contribution of clinical psychologists. It seems appropriate therefore to consider the number of clinical psychologists at present working with mentally handicapped people. Such statistics are difficult to establish with any absolute accuracy, but indications may be obtained from a number of sources. One such indication, by the National Development Group for the Mentally Handicapped (1978) suggests that there were the equivalent of 114 whole-time psychologists in the hospital service working exclusively in mental handicap. This figure does not necessarily represent all those psychologists who work with mentally handicapped people during some part of their working week. A recent working party (Williams, 1979) attempted to identify the manpower needs for mental handicap and suggested either 0.5 whole-time employees per 100 hospital residents or 1:250,000 of the general population. Both these estimates were considered modest. On a pessimistic note Williams points to the statistic that there was an increase of only 6 whole-time employed psychologists between 1975 and 1976 in health service provisions. It is difficult to envisage either the financial resources or the interest amongst newly qualified clinical psychologists needed to allow for a doubling of the numbers available to work with mentally handicapped people.

Locally, it may be interesting to note the comparative numbers of clinical psychologists working in mental handicap and in other specialist fields. Robertson (1980) identified 102 psychologists working for the South West Thames Regional Health Authority: of these 32 were working in mental handicap (figures are approximate full-time equivalents). This represents 31 per cent of psychologists working in this speciality.

The changes in the philosophy of care for mentally handicapped people — which allow them increasing respect as individuals — have occurred at the same time that clinical psychology has been undergoing changes in orientation and approach. Indeed, the development of a variety of behavioural techniques for treatment which moved the psychologist's priorities away from assessment and towards practical intervention, has in many ways paralleled this philosophical reorientation. Recent developments in attitudes towards the expectations of mentally handicapped people could be assumed to be the results of the linking of the two developments: behavioural techniques which promote independence in turn foster a new attitude towards more competent handicapped people.

It has now become accepted on a general basis that mentally handicapped people should expect as of right a place in the community and that they have rights as individuals (Tymchuk, 1976). It is possible to examine in detail the various definitions and criteria for the description of mental handicap, but that has been discussed at length elsewhere (Clarke and Clarke, 1974b). It has become most useful to regard mentally handicapped people as individuals whose intellectual development falls at the bottom of the normal range, whose major handicap is in the ability to learn new skills, and whose major weakness is in the area of social competence. One writer has expressed this succinctly in an 'alternative' definition:

> Mental retardation refers to a level of functioning which requires from society significantly above average training procedures and superior assets in adaptive behaviour, manifested throughout life. (Gold, 1975)

This approach—which emphasizes the special needs of mentally handicapped people in terms of training—sets the scene for the changing role of the psychologist. This chapter attempts to discuss some of the issues involved in the changing interests of the psychologist away from the assessment towards training, so that the mentally handicapped person may have the choice to move away from institutional care towards a more independent life in the community.

In this context it must be emphasized that this is one area where the concept of 'illness' and subsequent 'recovery' cannot properly be applied: mentally handicapped people do not reach 'normality' but can be encouraged to live as normal a life as possible within their own limitations.

The aim of the work of a psychologist with people who are mentally handicapped is viewed in terms of the application of psychological knowledge in order to improve the quality of life of the individual. This usually involves reaching an understanding of the individual's level of functioning so that he may be helped to reach an improved level of independence. Such independence may involve improved self-care skills, improved literacy and numeracy, or merely the improved ability to express one's opinions more freely and forcefully. The level of independence at which one aims, very much depends on the possibilities for an individual's future—whether that be a move from hospital to hostel, from hostel to independent living, or merely a continuing dependence on others for the organization of many aspects of daily life.

In order to achieve these aims for the handicapped person I have found that it is vital to have a broad view of the scope of the work. It would be easy to work with one person—the so-called client—and assume that this would achieve all the necessary aims. This is not possible, however. Many people are involved in one individual's life in an influential way, and in order to achieve a structured approach in dealing with his behaviour their co-operation and understanding must be gained. Thus the psychologist works not only with his client, but with those around him. In order to facilitate progress for a handicapped person in a hospital ward, for example, it is important both to plan and to carry out specific procedures in conjunction with the ward staff who will have a close working knowledge of him. In this context therefore, it would be fair to regard the psychologist as having several different client groups with whom he must work in order to achieve his aims for the handicapped person who is the 'true client'. It is intended that these different groups will be discussed in turn so that at the end of the chapter a picture will emerge of the multifaceted role of the psychologist in this developing field. These groups are:

Handicapped people;
Their parents and relatives;
Direct-care staff;
Professionals in training;
The general public;
Management.

In many respects a psychologist's work with these groups involves elements of teaching: teaching new skills to handicapped people utilizing behavioural training techniques; teaching direct-care staff and parents how to train the people in their care and how to manage difficult behaviour; teaching the public the facts about mental handicap so that handicapped people may be better integrated into the community. Prior to any teaching, however, must come assessment in the broadest possible sense so that the problem can be properly understood before its solution is identified. It is usually expected that psychologists will counsel the parents and relatives of mentally handicapped people, and perhaps also direct-care staff; but a counselling relationship with a mentally handicapped person will often be therapeutic and thus warrants discussion. The breadth of the psychologist's role will be understood when the broadly managerial contribution is realized, as this may be far-reaching in its effects on wider aspects of the care of mentally handicapped people. In summary then, a psychologist in mental handicap will work with several client groups, and will use an approach based on teaching and training. Underlying this will be a thorough assessment of problem areas, and therapeutic intervention by counselling when appropriate. Involvement in management will be critical to all this, and may indeed be the factor which will facilitate progress in other areas. All these activities on occasion will demand a practical research-based approach in order to evaluate and develop the most useful situations to the problems presented.

WORK WITH MENTALLY HANDICAPPED PEOPLE

Psychologists have long been involved in work with mentally handicapped people. This originated in the one-to-one contact which was demanded of psychological assessment aimed at defining the level of intellectual functioning. It was in fact at the beginning of this century that the first formal intelligence test was devised by Binet, and this was with the specific intention of identifying the educational needs of subnormal children. Thus the now much criticized intelligence testing movement began with mental handicap! Since that time, much has been written about psychological testing in general (Anastasi, 1968) and about the particular applications of testing to mentally handicapped people (Mittler, 1970; Clark, 1974) and this will not therefore be reviewed here. From the practical viewpoint it has become evident that many tests are inappropriate for the assessment of severely mentally handicapped people especially if there is associated severe physical handicap or communication disorder. In these cases response mechanisms may be so limited that the choice of test for the psychologist is very narrow indeed. Few tests have been designed with these sorts of handicaps in mind. Even for the severely mentally handicapped adult with no physical problems the basal level of the test may be above his level of functioning, or the number of responses so small that any statistical calculations would be made on the basis of very few observations. On the commonly used Wechsler Adult Intelligence Scale (WAIS), for example, the basal level on the verbal scale is over 40 and on the performance scale is 35 or over (depending on age), and this renders it inappropriate for the individuals who function at below this level (Wechsler, 1975). Additionally the unsuitability of some tests for use with people with a restricted level of verbal functioning has long been demonstrated (see Berger, 1970). The psychologist therefore uses his skills in selecting the test according to the purposes of the assessment and the needs of the client; in maintaining optimum conditions for testing via good concentration and minimal distractions; and interpreting the test results accurately and openly in terms of their implications.

It seems, however, that despite the difficulties formal psychological testing will continue with mentally handicapped people even if the purposes of the assessment become somewhat different. This is because the identification of level of functioning is in many cases useful in deciding on the sort of occupation or employment that is suitable for an individual, and changes in such level may be important in reaching an understanding of why, for example, problems have suddenly arisen in a person's mode of behaviour. An understanding of a person's level of functioning can help to give some idea of his potential for learning and thus of the suitability of an educational programme. More than that, the psychological testing situation and all its rigorous demands gives the psychologist an opportunity to observe the mentally handicapped person responding to an unfamiliar situation which by definition involves a considerable degree of stress. These observations will be invaluable in predicting how an individual will respond in other relatively stressful situations.

It has already been intimated that the purposes of psychological assessment have changed over the years and this will now be examined. Historically, IQ was closely associated with the whole process of the labelling and often subsequent institutionalization of the mentally handicapped person. Terms like imbecile, idiot, and moron which have now passed into the English language as terms of abuse were all precisely associated with IQ ranges (Clarke and Clarke, 1974c). Thus the assessment of an individual's intellectual level became an administrative exercise and brief but systematic tests were carried out at the annual review when the person's Order was renewed by the Reviewing Body. Once conditions became more relaxed in hospitals after the 1959 Mental Health Act and mentally handicapped people became informal patients, there was less emphasis on this aspect. There was, however, a continuing wish for the psychologist to carry out a test 'to fill up a gap in the records'. Such a sterile and unthinking approach has now disappeared and a new philosophy has taken its place. This new approach demands that any psychological assessment will attempt to solve a particular problem in practical terms: thus an assessment might be carried out with a view to recommending suitable work opportunities. The aim is that the mentally handicapped person should demonstrably benefit from the assessment, as a result of the tests being carried out in the context of a problem-solving approach.

This changing attitude has led to an increase in the measurement of social competence. If any aspect of assessment has really practical implications, it must be this, for in the examination of assets and deficits in social competence, areas in need of training can be thoroughly examined and priorities identified. The champion of this sort of assessment in the UK has been Gunzburg, who has developed a range of assessment charts at different levels which must now span the complete range of abilities represented in mental handicap (Gunzburg, 1977). The amount of interest in this type of assessment from all professional workers has meant at least that the system is used, which of course adds to its practicality! The reporting of the results is essentially visual, thus moving away from the use of a definite score which might be open to abuse by misquotation. Other assessments of social competence, for example the American Adaptive Behaviour Scale (Nihara *et al.*, 1969), all perform the same function of identifying the gaps in a person's development in a way that can have practical implications for the practitioner—priorities are determined by the needs of the handicapped person and not by the needs of the system!

Having achieved an assessment which can be expressed in usable terms it is possible to work with handicapped people in a meaningful way in order to improve their level of independence via training. This involves working with both individuals and groups, and must always be preceded by an answer to the question 'what do they need to learn?' rather than 'what do we need them to learn?'

The incongruity of teaching mentally handicapped people in a social training unit to make 'Welsh Rarebit' demonstrates this point. A group about to be given an independent living situation was taught to grate cheese and mix it with other ingredients instead of being shown how to make 'Cheese on Toast' by placing sliced cheese on buttered toast. The latter approach, which could be described as 'Survival cookery' was more suitable to their needs.

Training programmes should aim at increasing independence, and in doing this they give the handicapped person something he would not otherwise have: an element of choice as to how to lead his life. It may well be that when given that choice some would definitely opt for community living even of the style that has been harshly but often deservedly criticized (e.g. Oswin, 1978), but until handicapped people are in a position where they can make that choice the issue cannot be truly resolved. Independence skills allow acceptance by the community, and permit real experiences of the alternatives to hospital or hostel care.

Training programmes for mentally handicapped people—and the work of the psychologist here is described as training and not treatment as the client is not ill—are based on an understanding of how people learn new skills, and utilize a behavioural technology. The concept of positive reinforcement is now well understood and its value should never be underestimated in the unrewarding life of a mentally handicapped person. The consequences of a piece of behaviour are powerful determinants of future actions in all situations, and the psychologist can use this knowledge to clarify situations so that these methods are used appropriately.

A case discussion on a profoundly handicapped person revealed that at times he became most distressed, screaming continually. This behaviour could start at any time but appeared to be particularly noteworthy at mealtimes. A member of staff had observed that he was often placated if given extra food. On the assumption that his food requirements were in excess of what he was being given, it was suggested that whenever he screamed he should be given extra food to decrease his hunger-related distress. Even if the initial assumptions were correct, this approach would result in a considerable increase in screaming. An alternative scheme was therefore devised whereby he would receive extra food at the defined meal-times in order to satisfy his extra requirements. In this situation the psychologist's task was to pin-point the potential consequences of making food contingent on screaming.

Less widely understood is the concept of task analysis in the teaching of new skills, both in methodological terms (Gold, 1976) and in the possible applications of such an approach by making each stage of a task so easy that it is unlikely that an individual will experience failure (Cullen, 1976). At a basic level systematic behavioural programmes aim at teaching self-care skills such as feeding, washing, dressing, and toileting (McDonald *et al.*, 1976): all these will improve life for the handicapped person and those around him, releasing time and energy for more interesting and challenging activities. The same sort of structured approach can be applied to the teaching of 'higher level' skills, such as cooking, using the telephone, crossing the road and so on. (See for example Jones and Phillips, 1979; Taylor and Robinson, 1979.)

Sometimes differing methodologies exist for teaching specific skills and when this happens it is often useful to utilize an experimental approach in training in order to identify the most useful method. This is essentially a practical research-based approach: the clients receive the necessary training and we as psychologists learn about the best techniques at the same time. A recent example has been in teaching coin recognition—an essential prerequisite to learning how to use money (Joyce and Thorpe, 1981).

The most important intervention for profoundly handicapped people and for people who have been institutionalized over a long period of time will take the form of general activities providing stimulation at an appropriate level. Many seriously handicapped people find themselves excluded from activities because of the serious nature of their problem, and may therefore be unoccupied for long periods of time. Cortazzi (1973) has described the problems of this type of individual and has documented the work of a psychologist in setting up such activities, beginning with music and art and extended into simple traditional educational games. Such activities may be sufficiently successful to allow the client to be eventually included in the more conventional units as provided for mentally handicapped people. Such a programme of stimulation may be vital in helping to combat the institutional effects not only of the hospital, but also of the hostel and training centre.

Increasing independence is inevitably challenging for the handicapped person himself, and it becomes necessary to deal with the individual's feelings about his new situation. These may be expressed verbally, or by implication in action, or overtly in manifestation of behaviour not usually seen in the individual. Taking account of this sort of response, and indeed of responses to many other situations (such as the death of a relative) is perhaps a new concern of professionals in mental handicap.

The difficulties in judging the depth of emotion experienced by a handicapped person have perhaps caused these very emotions to be disregarded through the ignorance of those around him. Reports of the serious discussions which have taken place at conferences for mentally handicapped people (Campaign for the Mentally Handicapped, 1972) and of the opinions of handicapped people in hospital (Cortazzi, 1975) have forcefully illustrated that the judgements and wishes of such people are worthy of serious recognition. Similarly the success of residents' councils in some hospitals and the range of discussion (from politics to the quality of hospital food) indicates that many mentally handicapped people are keen to express their own opinions. The psychologist uses his skills in counselling to listen to an individual's wishes and problems, and begins to guide that person towards a solution. It must be remembered, however, that even mentally handicapped people with a comparatively high verbal ability may have extremely limited powers of abstract thought, and this may hamper therapeutic progress if it is not taken into account in advance.

It is often the task of the psychologist to provide some means of intervention when a person is exhibiting awkward or bizarre behaviour patterns. These are very difficult to deal with as their causes are often obscure: they may be well-established habits, or a cry for attention resulting from long-term institutionalization. They may well be the result of unidentified epilepsy or over- or undermedication. They may be the outward sign of a psychiatric condition, or perhaps truly of 'no identifiable cause'. Sometimes the most positive long-term contribution can be via a research programme in advising on suitable assessment measures (see Matin and Rundle, 1980, for example).

Behavioural methods for dealing with problem behaviour have been well documented (Murphy, 1980; and at a less academic level Perkins *et al.*, 1976) but these present some difficulties for a psychologist in his daily work. It is often difficult to control all the factors that might be implicated in an individual's behaviour disturbance, and achieving consistency of response among differing numbers of staff will be problematic. It is clear that the most appropriate course of action is to deal with small aspects of a problem in the first instance so that the chances of success are maximized: and to emphasize methods of control that focus on the positive rather than the negative (for example, by providing a more positive set of activities which would exclude the opportunity for inappropriate response).

The whole concept of 'normalization' which emphasizes the necessity of the right to normal experience and development whilst allowing for a specific handicap (Nirje, 1970) demands that the views of a mentally handicapped person be taken into account. Beyond a philosophical or moral obligation there is the practicality that progress in other areas of an individual's life will otherwise be hampered. So far the implication has been that the expression of problems will mostly take the form of some sort of verbal communication, but it is well known that a significant proportion of mentally handicapped people have difficulties in expressing themselves in this way. It therefore becomes vital that the psychologist should recognize the expression of serious difficulty when it takes other forms. Overt behaviour problems, perhaps involving considerable violence, can sometimes be viewed in this way, although other problems such as epilepsy must be excluded. It is often possible to allow the individual other forms of non-verbal expression, via for example, art, music, or drama therapy. These developing areas of work are not always well-documented, but their contribution to the development of the handicapped person should not be underestimated (Males and Males, 1979), and the psychologist will work closely with other therapists in examining the nature of the communication within these contexts.

In areas of clinical work where there is little background information available psychologists use their skills in evaluation to examine the effectiveness of various methods. Art therapy is an area where little formal research has been carried out, particularly in mental handicap, and I have attempted to consider the background to this as well as to put a research project into operation. There are often problems in applying research methodology to progress in creative therapy, but various methods have been used (Males, 1980) and the issue of research is now increasingly considered to be important (Wadeson, 1978). This has meant applying different methods of evaluation at different times: beginning with a single case study, through a nationwide survey and now to a thorough research programme financed in part by the Department of Health & Social Security. We are now trying to identify the behavioural outcomes of two types of approach in art therapy with a control group. The problems of identifying the most useful measures and of realizing appropriate controls have been great at times, and other psychological skills have been brought into play in order to achieve consistency of management! We are at present attempting to look not only at behavioural outcome but also at the 'carry over' effect from the therapy situation to the living situation: observational data is being collected here. (Skellett, C., Hattersley, J., and Tennent, L., 1976). This sort of information is vital if we are to understand how to develop the therapeutic services for mentally handicapped people and how to provide the most appropriate remedial service in this area.

Sometimes the overriding need of the individual is in creativity for its own sake. It has been said mentally handicapped people are not creative (McDermott, 1954) but this cannot be borne out when the artistic and literary achievements of retarded people are considered (Deacon, 1974; Males, 1979a; Stanovich and Stanovich, 1979) and when the story of a handicapped individual's life is vividly told (Meyers, 1979).

Given the respect which as individuals they deserve, mentally handicapped people respond willingly and forcefully and provide a stimulating working situation for any professional.

WORK WITH THEIR PARENTS AND RELATIVES

In the Victorian era, which saw the building of many large institutions for mentally handicapped people, a primary aim was to separate them from their families, thus allowing those families to deny the existence of their handicapped relatives. It is not surprising that attitudes have changed within a hundred years, and an increasing openness about handicaps in general and the growing availability of help from the Social Services in the 1960s has led to a recognition of the importance of the family to a handicapped individual—this is perhaps merely a part of the recognition that he too has emotional ties. Indeed it is now general policy that any handicapped child should remain with his family of origin for as long as possible, provided that this is in his best interests (National Development Group, 1977a). It is surprising that the recognition of the contribution of parents in the professional care of their handicapped offspring has only just been made, and the importance of family links has recently been underlined in a report to the Government on hospital facilities for mentally handicapped people (National Development Group for the Mentally Handicapped, 1978). This recognition of the importance of family contacts—whether the handicapped person remains at home or not—has led to a considerable amount of reporting of the stresses and strains on such families both by the families themselves (Hannam, 1974) and by research workers.

There are several problems with which the psychologist deals in this field. First, the issue of how the parents are told that their child is handicapped. This most crucial time appears often to have been mishandled by those with the responsibility of telling the parents, perhaps because it is due to their own failure that the situation has arisen and perhaps because of their limited knowledge of the long-term development of people who are handicapped in this way. This results sometimes in reassurance being given that is unwise in reality, and sometimes in an unncessarily gloomy picture being painted. Wolfensburger (1967) has reported work which describes many of the unfortunately mishandled situations involving parents where they have been told of their child's handicap in an insensitive manner. Although there are individual differences amongst parents in how much they want to know and how soon, it is vital for the questions to be dealt with honestly and with an accurate examination with the parents of areas in which the professionals themselves are uncertain.

It is a matter of considerable concern to find parents of a child who is being considered for special education who are still unclear as to the severity of the handicap and of the long-term possibility of 'cure'. The psychologist who gives either educational or other practical advice at this stage must be clear about the extent of the parents' knowledge so that the issues can be dealt with in an honest but sensitive manner. This will inevitably involve close working relationships with paediatricians and community physicians. From the ethical point of view there may be a serious dilemma if parents wish to know facts that have not already been divulged. This has to be solved by the individual psychologist in conjunction with the team: whatever has been said or is to be said must be followed by an appropriate level of support to the family.

As the child begins to develop, family problems may be categorized into two distinct groups. First the emotional aspects of having a handicapped child—

this may involve feelings of guilt and inadequacy for the parents. Counselling in order to deal with some of these issues may take place individually or in groups and will include the feelings of the siblings, for continual focus on the handicapped person may otherwise cause considerable tension. Young people can easily find themselves socially isolated if they find it difficult to admit their brother's or sister's handicap to their friends.

A family's request for help may nonetheless easily be misinterpreted. It has been pointed out that many families feel insulted when they are offered psychotherapy while their real needs are practical (Carr, 1974). This second aspect of a family's difficulties has been increasingly recognized and psychologists have been in the forefront of finding solutions to these problems. The first approach has been in a reorientation of psychological services. At one time most psychologists who worked with mentally handicapped people were based in hospitals and spent almost all of their working time there. Nowadays there are few such psychologists who do not consider it to be an essential part of their job to undertake some work in the community, both with recently discharged 'patients' and with individuals for whom admission to hospital could be prevented if the family were given some practical assistance, for example in training procedures or in the management of behaviour problems. In addition, there is an increasing number of psychologists working from a community base and specializing in mental handicap. Psychologists now usually carry out their work not only in centres and workshops for handicapped people, but also in the home situation. In the context of the home, there has been considerable advance in the publication of material that can be used by the parents at home in training their offspring, and in learning to make objective observations. Such books may focus on one topic, for example the all-important area of toilet training (Azrin and Foxx, 1973), or on the general issues relating to practical management tasks (Carr, 1980), and enable them to work on relevant issues at their own pace. Practising psychologists need to be well-informed about the advice given in such publications so that day-to-day problems can easily be resolved. It is often humbling to discover just how much initiative has been taken by the parents themselves on these issues. Some parents require more structured advice, and here the Portage Home Teaching Programme has made a significant contribu-tion (Bluma et al., 1976). This provides both an assessment format and a series of structured activities based on the development of specific skills. It is a programme which requires considerable follow-through from professionals and 'home teachers', and can thus be very time-consuming. It has been shown however to be a productive programme where there are sufficient resources for its institution, both in its practicality and in its general behavioural approach to structured learning situations.

To continue discussion of methods of helping parents to help themselves, the concept of parents' workshops should not be excluded. It has long been recognized that families with similar problems may well derive a great deal of support from contact with each other, and the notion of parent workshops combines this with the possibility of practical advice from professionals (Cunningham and Jeffree, 1971). Most workshops consist of a regular series of meetings covering a programme of topic areas with a speaker and small group discussion, as well as the oft-needed social element. Some workshops have focused on specific behavioural teaching techniques while others (for parents of older children) have aired further important issues such as sexual development and the consequences of a death in the family. Some parent workshops in the United Kingdom were run by psychologists (Callias, 1976) but other ventures on the same model have often involved a wide variety of professionals (Attwood, 1977, 1978). Such workshops allow the parents to examine and try new ideas while they have the ongoing support not only of a group of professionals, but also of a group of parents with similar difficulties. It is clear that parents value such opportunities, and have requested workshops according to their individual needs. It is these needs that must be of prime importance when running a workshop; they must be considered even when administrative factors militate against them. In one area, the suggestion that a workshop should be run once a year because finance is available is only worthwhile if it is useful to the parents.

There are times when the needs of a parent do not even stretch to requiring special teaching or training programmes: one of the most grateful parents I have ever seen was one whose face became a picture when she was told of the free nappy service for older incontinent children! It would of course be presumptious to assume that every need is deeply psychological, and the professional will be aware of the very practical and valuable assistance which may be available from the Health or Social Services. The ever increasing number of booklets describing local resources usually available from Area Health Authorities, Social Service Departments or Parent Organizations is a reflection of the attempts to disseminate information of this nature (for example see 'Help for the Mentally Handicapped in Croydon', 1979).

Psychologists are at last becoming aware of the need to explain themselves and their methods to others. It is often the case that an assessment of perhaps a very formal nature has been carried out on a child or adult, and it is only natural that the relatives will want to be told the results of the tests. This is an understandably difficult issue, especially if there are statistical technicalities in the test results. It sometimes appears that the worst problems arise when a figure has been assigned as this is very specifically open to misinterpretation. However, the family of an individual should be involved in an assessment wherever possible as they are holders of valuable information (Jones, 1973), and parents will very often benefit from a written explanation of the practical implications of an assessment, so that they can take it away and assimilate it at their leisure (Jones, 1975). It has been observed that one of the most tense periods for the parents of young mentally handicapped children is when the child is about to be assessed with a view to the provision of special education. Parents tend to view the psychologist with suspicion, seem afraid to ask questions, and feel that they will not be believed if they point out that their child sometimes behaves in a different fashion. It has become the responsibility of the professionals themselves to explain the degree to which they rely on the test results and to have a full discussion on what has been achieved and the subsequent implications. It is easy to remove the mystery of psychological assessment by clarity of discussion and explanation: the psychologist's job will include such explanation. On these occasions the handicapped person's assets as well as deficits will be emphasized: it is always possible to build on one to help in the improvement of the other. The psychologist will make a positive attempt to identify such assets, even in the profoundly handicapped person, who is otherwise likely to be described in terms of his limitations.

Work with the families of handicapped people can at the same time be very taxing and extremely rewarding, but it is essential in maintaining the all-important links with the handicapped member, whatever his living situation.

WORK WITH DIRECT-CARE STAFF

The proliferation of different types of full-time care situations for mentally handicapped people has meant that more and more staff, both qualified and unqualified, become responsible for the well-being of the handicapped person. For the period of time that a handicapped man or woman is in a hospital, hostel, or other care situation, many of the tasks that would have been undertaken by parents and relatives will be undertaken by care staff with all sorts of different backgrounds. Thus the practical problems remain the same — how to cope with the demands of a situation where all basic care needs to be given to an adult, and how to encourage a person to become more independent through the learning of new skills. How can psychologists assist in this situation?

First, by giving factual help. A psychologist's knowledge can be invaluable in interpreting what is known about an individual's level of intellectual functioning. Some mentally handicapped people whose intelligence as tested may be in the subnormal range, may appear at first sight to be quite verbal and one might assume a relatively high level of comprehension. This is not necessarily the case, however, and the capacity for abstract thought may be very limited. If this is made known to direct-care staff they will be better prepared for difficulties in reasoning a situation through with the individual concerned.

A young mentally handicapped woman had a tested IQ of about 55, but presented herself well from the social point of view, and was able to converse quite fluently. In the institution she was rightly seen as being comparatively bright, and it was therefore thought that she understood the consequences of her actions, and even quite complex arguments. The staff consequently suffered considerable frustration when they found that she could not comprehend the logical nature of an argument and instead resorted to ideas which were almost 'magical' in quality ('. . . it won't happen to me . . . because it won't happen to me'). It was helpful when this aspect of her development was appreciated and discussions were able to proceed in more 'concrete' terms.

Likewise, the results of an assessment of social competence may be extremely helpful in determining how much should be expected of an individual in terms of self-care, the extent of training needs, and whether the client should be trusted with crossing the road, or handling his own financial affairs. The proper sharing of this type of information should make the care staff's task a great deal easier, and in turn improve the situation for the handicapped person, not least in preventing the development of overprotective relationships. This can only be achieved if there is a close working relationship with the care staff such that both sides can ask questions, and if the written reports from psychologists are careful in their explanation of technical terms and in the implications of the information obtained. An element of informal contact is also necessary so that well-established channels of free communication can be used for discussion. It should be mentioned at this point that the changing role of the psychologist in terms of contact with the family has meant that he will be able, along with the social worker, to provide some insight into the situation from that point of view. Factual help may also be of a much more practical nature based on a knowledge of the books and courses available which could be relevant to a person working in the direct-care situation.

Psychologists will also have a teaching role in this context. At the present time most Nurse Education Centres which prepare students for the RNMS examinations use psychologists to teach part of the course, as do other training courses that are relevant to mental handicap. Whatever happens in the future to nursing training in this field (DHSS, 1979) it is likely that psychologists will be involved in teaching in this context. More than this, there is a specialist teaching function. A good example of this would be in the teaching of behavioural techniques as this is closely related to the psychological theories of learning. Many methods of teaching these have been devised — from programmed texts (Gathercole and Rucker, 1972) to illustrated manuals (Perkins *et al.*, 1976) and workshop opportunities (for example the travelling workshops run by the British Institute for Mental Handicap). A common reaction to the teaching of behavioural methods is in the first instance that it is no different from what is already being done and that if it is, then it is too time-consuming. Part of the teaching time must therefore be given over to the differences in terms of consistency and of the pay-offs for all concerned if a handicapped individual can achieve a more independent style of life, as well as their right to be able to do just that. This sort of teaching need not of necessity be very formal although part of it may be very structured, but it is usually more successful if there is time allowed for the discussion of individual problems and in the difficulties of practical intervention.

Within the context of this type of teaching, a degree of compromise has to be reached in terms of the staffing levels that should be achieved in order to ensure consistency of approach and regular application of techniques. If staffing levels descend to a very low level it will be extremely difficult to carry out therapeutic programmes, although the work of Grant and Moores (1977), which reveals that staff–client ratios may have little effect on the application of specific procedures, must be taken seriously.

It would be unwise at this point to suggest that psychologists should 'go forth and teach' and expect everyone not only to listen, but to put what they have learned into practice. It is common, especially in institutional settings, for the care staff to hold psychologists in considerable suspicion and to feel that their own day-to-day experience of the handicapped people in their charge is sufficient to deal with all problems. This must be countered by a relationship of mutual trust over a long period of time, and through practical understanding of the problems experienced by direct-care staff. Raynes (1978) has pointed out that change can only really be effected if psychologists, along with other professionals, have a good understanding of day-to-day life on the ward. In this context psychologists in training and indeed new staff, in the Psychology Department at St Lawrence's Hospital, Caterham, undertake to work for at least one week as nursing assistants on one of the hospital wards. This experience not only gives them basic practical information about ward routine and the times at which the ward staff are most under stress, but it also fosters a relationship based on empathy with the ward staff as all the basic tasks of the nurse are shared. In addition, an improved understanding of the daily life of mentally handicapped people is reached (Males et al., 1979). In the last two years, ten psychology trainees have undertaken this task, and all have reported that the experience contributed to a deepening understanding of the life and problems of mentally handicapped people and those who work closely with them. Thus the teaching role of the psychologist in working with direct-care staff must be supported by the fostering of the sort of relationships that will allow for something to be taken from the teaching situation and put into practice — without this, clinical teaching would be but a sterile exercise.

Psychologists will also have a significant role in providing emotional support to the direct-care staff. It is true today that many care situations are chronically short of staff, and this leads to inevitable pressures. It would be hard to define a specific function here except to say that empathy developing out of a real understanding of another profession's role may facilitate help of both a practical and an emotional nature. The importance of informality and the sharing of ideas and the fostering of true community life within the care situation has an inevitable effect on the handicapped people in a beneficial way, and must be encouraged. Matthews

(1977, 1978) has emphasized this with particular reference to the mental handicap hospital which is perhaps particularly susceptible to rigidity of internal structure modelled on that utilized by general hospitals. Any action that helps to decrease the amount of stress experienced by the direct-care staff can only be beneficial to the true client—the mentally handicapped person.

It is usually the direct-care staff who have the most consistent contact with handicapped people, and they see them at important times of the day—meal times, getting up, and going to bed. They may therefore have very great scope in helping such people to reach the aims set them, such as increasing independence in a given area. It is of the utmost importance that professions which are perhaps a little more on the periphery of the care situation should help more indirectly by following up practical assistance with a service which attempts to give support in emotional terms to individuals who are working in an inevitably stressed situation.

WORK WITH PROFESSIONALS IN TRAINING

Anyone who works in one of the caring professions is likely to come into direct contact with people who are mentally handicapped and who thus have particular needs. This contact may not of course be readily identifiable, for some people who do not bear the perhaps overhandicapping label 'mental handicap' may still be functioning at a significantly low level and will have problems in learning new skills. It is interesting, for example, to see the reactions of a group of general nurses in training when they visit a mental handicap hospital: they would of course deny that their jobs have anything much to do with mental handicap, and yet they immediately see the relevance of some aspects of the situation to their own working life. Perhaps they become rather more able to deal with the low-ability patient, and realize the relevance of careful explanation of treatment in very simple terms. The situation just described inevitably involves all members of the caring professions with mental handicap of some degree at some time in their careers, even if this sort of contact is quite infrequent. However, the changing philosophy relating to the care of mentally handicapped people will significantly alter this in the future. The normalization principle (Nirje, 1970) suggests that mentally handicapped people deserve the same rights as any other citizen, and this philosophy has been carried over into expectations in terms of specialist care. The Peggy Jay Report (DHSS, 1979) has taken up this philosophical stand and put some of the ideas in a rather more practical framework: 'Mentally handicapped people should use normal services wherever possible . . . "Specialized" services or organizations for mentally handicapped people should be provided only to the extent that they demonstrably meet or are likely to meet additional needs that cannot be met by the general services' (p36). Thus mentally handicapped people from home, hostel, or mental handicap hospital should expect to be admitted to a general hospital ward when the need arises. Spencer (1979) has described some of the reactions of staff to such admissions, and has outlined some of the information that might be provided to the hospital staff in order to alleviate fears and make the handicapped person's stay more comfortable and thus in many instances the treatment more successful. If an element of mental handicap were to be included in staff training for other caring professions, this sort of paper would be unnecessary in so far as the facts suggested by Spencer would be given automatically on the request of the general staff. Failure in this area is observed when mentally handicapped people are discharged from general hospitals even before post-operative care is fully complete. Much could be done in a short course on mental handicap to outline the sort of self-care difficulties that such people might have as well as their communication problems which may well prevent them from understanding the reasons for their admission. A neglect of any of these factors could lead to the patients becoming unco-operative and less communicative about their condition, thus making them more difficult to treat successfully.

The situation which applies to treatment of physical conditions also applies to the facilities provided by the social services as well as to dental treatment, and so on. It is therefore necessary for such aspects of all courses to be expanded. This necessity is not, however, always rewarded with appropriate funding, and compromise may need to be reached by the provision of pamphlets or other written teaching material on mental handicap in order to fill the need within courses more economically.

At the present time psychologists may have contact with courses on an occasional basis, or in the context of covering behavioural science as a general topic. It is important to emphasize the psychological needs of mentally handicapped people both as a topic for a short course, and also in conjunction with an educational visit to some sort of facility that provides care for people who are mentally handicapped.

There has long been teaching on mental handicap in courses for psychologists in training although there are differences in emphasis and balance between the courses. It is easy, however, in psychology to remain 'academic' and make this element of the course emphasize the experimental psychological aspects of work with this particular client group—and indeed the work here is of a high standard and has been important in the understanding of some aspects of mental handicap. At this point, however, it becomes easy to cease to regard the subjects of the experiment as truly 'human', and subsequent clinical practice in this field may become a rather academic exercise completed for the sake of a qualification.

Two issues need to be discussed at this point in considering the importance of mental handicap in a psychologist's training. First, it is true that a minority of psychologists spend their working career in mental handicap. This is not due to lack of opportunities, as positions for psychologists in mental handicap remain unfilled, but it often seems to be the result of a general reluctance to work with this particular client group. Secondly, many psychologists who do not work primarily with mentally handicapped people will nonetheless have a very critical contact with them. A shining example of this sort of contact is the powers held by educational psychologists in determining placement in special schools for mentally handicapped children. For these two reasons, then, the psychological study of mental handicap will have to become more than an academic exercise, and in fact become a study of the behaviour of individuals who are as fascinating as those people whom we label 'normal'.

It is indeed humbling to see that if they are allowed to do so, handicapped people can become very 'real' indeed. Stanovich and Stanovich (1979) have emphasized the necessity of allowing mentally handicapped people to talk about themselves as this takes them away from the subordinate position which is usually dictated by society. The work of Joey Deacon reveals that both in autobiographical work (Deacon, 1974) and in fictional work (Deacon and Roberts, 1977) he has something unique to tell.

Practical experience of mentally handicapped people living their lives contains a lesson of even greater validity. It is in this way and not in the office or consulting room that we learn about them as individuals; the relevance of experience as a nursing assistant in this context has already been described. The inclusion of this experience and the experience of handicapped people in social situations (at parties, on holidays, etc.) can help to put the academic knowledge into perspective.

The educational needs of all caring professions in this particular field appear to be the same; to combine factual and academic knowledge with a practical experience and understanding of the needs of mentally handicapped people as individuals. The weight of psychological research in the area has made the teaching of mental handicap to trainee psychologists an area which is particularly susceptible to a sterile academic approach. As this situation is recognized, it is more easily rectified and mental handicap will develop into an area which holds sufficient interest for skills to be carried over from a course into a person's professional career. It is therefore part of the working duty of a psychologist in mental handicap to ensure that a balance is maintained wherever possible in training courses for the caring professions.

WORK WITH THE PUBLIC

The general public is becoming increasingly involved in the care of mentally handicapped people. The emphasis for the future will be that as few mentally handicapped people as possible will enter any sort of long-term care situation, and that those who do so will live in hostels and group homes which are located in the community itself. This is an exciting, challenging task for everyone working in the field, but it is not without its problems. While this community care stance has been taken up enthusiastically by some, and while successful models are being described (Campaign for the Mentally Handicapped,

1978), it is still possible to read descriptions of the very real problems some mentally handicapped people experience at the hands of the community at large (Harris, 1978). It often seems that such problems arise from ignorance and misunderstanding rather than from deliberate malice. It has already been suggested that a community cannot care if it does not understand those for whom it should be caring (Males, 1979b). Research has been carried out on the effects of prior knowledge on attitudes towards a new community home for mentally handicapped people and the paradoxical conclusion that prior knowledge resulted in negative attitudes was reached (Locker et al., 1979). This prior knowledge was, however, based on informal contacts which are misleading; and the need for accurate information for the community was identified.

Other studies of the attitudes of people towards general aspects of mental handicap have revealed that there is a considerable confusion about the subject — both in the United Kingdom and in the USA (Latimer, 1970; Pushkin, 1976, 1979). It would seem to be nonsensical to imagine that the community can really be expected to have a realistic attitude towards mentally handicapped people until some of the confusions about the cause, nature, and behaviour associated with mental handicap have been clarified. How can psychologists contribute to the clarification of such issues? First by research. We ask the question: 'To what extent are the confusions in the understanding of mental handicap spread right across the community?' It is only in this way that the extent of the work required will be ascertained. A recent survey has examined some of the issues in this context that are relevant to teenage schoolchildren (Males et al., 1980). This study showed how influential the media can be in moulding beliefs about, for example, the causes of mental handicap. This is a multidisciplinary piece of research and it is worth identifying the specific contribution expected from psychology in this type of approach. The four researchers are a nurse, a doctor, a psychologist and a therapist with a psychology background. The idea for the project originated from the nurse, but I was expected to provide some initial input on questionnaire design and a major part of the project is now under analysis by the therapist, who is undertaking an MA degree in psychology. The different professional backgrounds of the contributors provide useful additions to the project: psychology particularly in research design and analysis, but the other professions in an understanding of mental handicap from differing viewpoints. One major aim is to identify attitudes towards mental handicap and we all have particular interests here: the nurse in models of care, the doctor in the aetiology of mental handicap, and the therapist and psychologist in the confusion between mental handicap and mental illness and the effect of prior contact on attitudes towards handicapping conditions. We have worked together on this project in an attempt to answer some questions which will be important for the future care of mentally handicapped people, but in doing so, are providing a professional service in the here-and-now. This research based approach has a teaching component in its commitment to providing factual information (a series of short talks) on the same occasion that the paper-and-pencil questionnaire is completed. Once again, we undertake the teaching part of the project from our four different professional backgrounds: this often generates lively discussion from teenage schoolchildren. This illustrates two important aspects of work in a relatively new area—research aimed at clarifying the extent of a problem associated with its remediation via an educational approach—and it demonstrates how the skills a psychologist has in research methodology can become an integral part of everyday work.

In dealing with children it is easy both to find out their current attitudes and to remedy mistakes. Once one is dealing with the adult population it becomes more difficult. Attitudes and beliefs become more entrenched (this is why work with the younger group is so important) and people are perhaps a little less willing to engage in educational activities. Psychologists will apply both their knowledge of mental handicap and their understanding of teaching techniques in order to present the material appropriately. It is again always important to combine factual information with the capacity to emphasize the humanity of mentally handicapped people.

Attitudes and opinions that are commonly held by the general public are easily influenced by the mass media, and direct contact with the media will be an exciting and influential aspect of the work. A recent article in the 'popular press' of mental handicap was devoted to advice on dealings with the media (Shennan, 1980) as was a recent article published by the British Psychological Society (Harvey, 1979), thus demonstrating the importance attributed to this. It is of course true to say that it is sensational events that receive the most attention from the press, but it is equally true that good reporting can have a significant influence on community attitudes, and this should have a most beneficial effect on the lives of mentally handicapped people. It will be argued that in order to educate the general public, we must first educate the media, be they local or national.

It may be paradoxical, therefore, that in serving the best interests of a handicapped individual psychologists will find themselves working with those whose full-time career has little to do with mental handicap but who have significant national or international influence on attitudes towards this minority group.

WORKING AS A PART OF A MANAGEMENT STRUCTURE

It should be clear from what has already been said that psychologists can play a very wide-ranging role in mental handicap. It should be especially clear that unless channels of communication with other professions and with administrative departments are open, and unless the right facilities exist, their role will be narrowly restricted and the client will suffer. For example, a good toilet-training programme cannot be carried out if sufficient laundry to allow for frequent changes of clothing is not made available. Likewise, if psychologists do not contribute to the design of new units for mentally handicapped people, they cannot hope to achieve an environment ideally suited for the implementation of training programmes to the benefit of the clients. We must therefore participate fully in the management structure of our place of work.

Psychologists often regard themselves (and are sometimes regarded) as 'agents of change' within their places of work, and sometimes this is thought to mean that the system should be revolutionized. It seems to me that more appropriately things can only be helped to change if one works with the existing 'system'. One department has tried to abandon a hierarchical system of working within the department, but still finds itself represented at all levels within the hospital framework (Bexley Hospital Psychology Department, 1980). This function of a psychologist will often seem remote from the individual needs of a mentally handicapped person, but this very view must encompass an opinion that new services develop without any planning or effort, and that is clearly untrue. If psychology has anything to say about mental handicap, it must do so at the highest levels of planning as well as those of individual assessment, ward-based programmes, and social skills training groups. Indeed this is one of the strengths of a psychologist working in management, because the experience of working at so many levels (with individuals, their relatives, direct-care staff etc.) is an invaluable source of knowledge which can be applied to future planning. At the same time, an in-depth understanding of behavioural principles will often help not only to formulate plans and principles, but also in dealing with the committee structure.

What resources are available to us in this aspect of our work? First, people and second, documents. We need to understand and appreciate the roles of our professional colleagues and examine with them how to work together as well as where they stand on issues that are mutually important. This requires an investment of time prior to any truly co-operative work. It is always possible to back up local ideas with plans that have been made more centrally: it is possible to progress only with a knowledge of what has been written at many levels—this may produce agreement or disagreement. A recent "rough estimate" gave at least seventeen publications of national significance which need not be regarded as tedious documents to be read and discarded, but as documents which will aid our thinking, strengthen our case, and allow for the development of new and creative services. Discussions on 'Community Mental Handicap Terms' (National Development Team, 1978) for example, have not produced a set of identical services throughout the country, but a variety of approaches aimed at meeting local needs.

Having established the direction in which new services should move, psychologists will once again become involved in monitoring and evaluating their effectiveness as well as participating in the provision of the services. This is perhaps a role which is not always clearly understood as it is expected that we would normally spend a large amount of time in direct clinical work, but unless our research skills are used in evaluation we may never really consider how effective a service is, and this could result in the unnecessary perpetuation of a model that is less than effective.

CONCLUSIONS

This chapter has attempted to look at various aspects of the work of psychologists in the special field of mental handicap. It has been seen that the philosophy of care for mentally handicapped people has undergone radical changes in the last twenty years, and that the work of psychologists has had to change accordingly. Indeed, the role of psychologists in all fields has changed during this period and these changes themselves may have been influential in the developing philosophy of care. Psychologists have been able to break away from the rigid model of institutional care, and take on a wider role in caring for people in a variety of living situations. They have become involved in putting research into practice as well as furthering research, and have been able to examine the wider issues of helping mentally handicapped people to achieve that which they find most difficult — the learning of new skills. The implications of the work are such that psychologists will find themselves involved in work with various different groups of people in order to meet the needs of the handicapped person in the best possible way. While these other groups have at times been the focus of attention in the chapter, it is vital that the conclusion must rest with the needs of the mentally handicapped individual. In the final analysis, psychologists will be working with many other groups in order to fulfil one aim for the mentally handicapped person — that of the maximum possible independence so that he may have an element of choice in taking his place in the community amongst 'normal' people.

REFERENCES

Anastasi, A. (1968). *Psychological Testing*, 3rd edn, London: Macmillan.
Attwood, T. (1977). 'The priory parents workshop', *Child: Care Health and Development*, **3**, 81–91.
Attwood, T. (1978). 'The Croydon workshop for parents of pre-school mentally handicapped children', *Child: Care Health and Development*, **4**, 79–97.
Berger, M. (1970). 'The 3rd revision of the Stanford–Binet (Form L-M): Some methodological limitations and their practical implications, *Bulletin of the British Psychological Society*, **23**, 17–26.
Bexley Hospital Psychology Department (1980). 'The evolution of democracy in an NHS psychology department', *Division of Clinical Psychology Newsletter*, No 28, 24–30.
Bluma, S., Shearer, M., Frohman, A., and Hilliard, J. (1976). *Portage Guide to Early Education*. London: Coop Education Service Agency.
Callias, M. (1976). 'Parent group training', *Parents Voice*, **26** (1) 5–7.

Campaign for the Mentally Handicapped (1972). *Our Life*, London: CMH.

Campaign for the Mentally Handicapped (1978). *Encor—a Way Ahead*, CMH Enquiry Paper 6.

Carr, J. (1974). 'The effect of the severely subnormal on their families', in Clarke, A. M. and Clarke, A. D. B. (eds), *Mental Deficiency: The Changing Outlook*, London: Methuen, 807–839.

Carr, J. (1980). *Helping your Handicapped Child*, Harmondsworth, England: Penguin Books.

Clarke, A. M. and Clarke, A. D. B. (1974a). *Mental Deficiency: The Changing Outlook*, London: Methuen.

Clarke, A. M. and Clarke, A. D. B. (1974b). 'Criteria and classification of subnormality' in Clarke, A. M. and Clarke, A. D. B. (eds), *Mental Deficiency: The Changing Outlook*, London: Methuen, pp.13–30.

Clarke, A. D. B. and Clarke, A. M. (1974c). 'The changing outlook' in Clarke, A. M. and Clarke, A. D. B. (eds) *Mental Deficiency: The Changing Outlook*, London: Methuen, 3–12.

Clark, D. F. (1974). 'Psychological assessment in mental subnormality', in Clarke, A. M. and Clarke, A. D. B. (eds), *Mental Deficiency: The Changing Outlook*, London: Methuen, 387–481.

Cortazzi, D. (1973). 'The bottom of the barrel', in Gunzburg, H. C. (ed), *Advances in the Care of the Mentally Handicapped*. British Soc. Study of Mental Subnormality, distributed by Bailliere Tindall, London.

Cortazzi, D. (1975). 'The needs of mentally handicapped people as they themselves see it'. Unpublished paper presented at the 2nd Annual Congress of the Association of Professions for the Mentally Handicapped, 14–17 April.

Cullen, C. (1976). 'Errorless learning with the retarded', *Nursing Times*, 25 March, 45–47.

Cunningham, C. C. and Jeffree, D. M. (1971). *Working with Parents: Developing a Workshop Course for Parents of Young Mentally Handicapped Children*, NSMHC (North West Region).

Deacon, J. (1974). *Tongue Tied*, NSMHC.

Deacon, J. and Roberts, E. (1977). 'I will', *Special Children*, **3** (2) 44–68.

DHSS (1979). *Report of the Committee of Enquiry into Mental Handicap Nursing and Care*, Cmnd. 7468–1, London: HMSO.

DHSS and Welsh Office (1971). *Better Services for the Mentally Handicapped*, Cmnd. 4683, London: HMSO.

Development Team for the Mentally Handicapped (1978). *First Report: A76:77*, London: HMSO.

Foxx, R. and Azrin, N. (1973). *Toilet Training the Retarded*, Illinois: Research Press.

Gathercole, C. E. and Rucker, W. L. (1972). *Introduction to Behaviour Modification*, Rainhill Hospital, Psychology Department.

Gold, M. W. (1975). *An Alternative Definition of Mental Retardation*, (mimeo) Austen, Texas: Mark Gold and Associates.

Gold, M. W. (1976). 'Task analysis of a complex assembly task by the retarded blind', *Exceptional Children*, **43**, 78–84.

Grant, G. W. B. and Moores, B. (1977). 'Resident characteristics and staff behaviour in two hospitals for mentally retarded adults', *American Journal of Mental Deficiency*, **82**, (3) 259–265.

Gunzburg, H. C. (1977). *Progress Assessment Chart Manual*, Vols. I and II, 5th Edn, SEFA (Publications).

Hannam, C. (1974). *Parents and Mentally Handicapped Children*, Harmondsworth: Penguin Books.

Harris, G. (1978). 'Can the community offer this service?', *Parents Voice*, **28** (2) 4-6.

Harvey, P. (1979), 'Media matters', *Division of Clinical Psychology Newsletter*, No. 26, 18-21.

Help for the Mentally Handicapped in Croydon (1979).

Jones, A. (1975). 'Assessment: A means to an end', *New Psychiatry*, **2** (9) 10-11.

Jones, L. and Phillips, G. (1979). 'Further training for adults', *Apex, Journal of the British Institute for Mental Handicap*, **7** (1) 32-33.

Jones, N. (1973). 'Family-oriented psychological assessments', *Parents Voice*, **23** (4) 12-13.

Joyce, T. A. and Thorpe, J. G. (1981). 'Learning without errors', *Apex, Journal of the British Institute for Mental Handicap*, **9** (1), 25-26.

Latimer, R. (1970). 'Current attitudes towards mental retardation', *Mental Retardation*, **8**, 30-32.

Locker, D., Rao, B., and Weddell, J. M. (1979). 'Public acceptance of community care', *Apex, Journal of the British Institute for Mental Handicap*, **7** (2), 44-46.

McDermott, W. H. (1954). 'Art therapy for the severely handicapped', *American Journal of Mental Deficiency*, **59**, 231-234.

McDonald, G., McCabe, P., and Mackle, B. (1976). 'Self-help skills in the profoundly subnormal', *British Journal of Mental Subnormality*, **XXII** (2), 105-111.

Males, J. (1979a). 'The world of George Ellis', *Parents Voice*, **29** (1), 18.

Males, J. (1979b). 'The mentally handicapped child: a plan for action', *Royal Society of Health Journal*, **99** (2) 79-81.

Males, J. (1980). 'Art therapy: investigations and implications', *Inscipe*, **4** (2), 13-15.

Males, J. and Males, B. (1979). 'Art therapy: A creative approach to the care of mentally handicapped people', *Apex, Journal of the British Institute of Mental Handicap*, **6** (4), 16-17.

Males, J., Males, B., Parrish, A., and Harris, G. (1980). 'Schoolchildren today: caring community tomorrow'. Unpublished paper given at the Annual Congress of the Association of Professions for the Mentally Handicapped, University of Keele.

Males, J., Painter, L., Joyce, T., and McGill, J. (1979). 'Making positive change possible', letter to *Apex, Journal of the British Institute of Mental Handicap*, **6** (4), 30.

Matin, M. A. and Rundle, A. T. (1980). 'Physiological and psychiatric investigations into a group of mentally handicapped subjects with self-injurious behaviour', *Journal of Mental Deficiency Research*, **24**, 77-85.

Matthews, D. R. (1977). The therapeutic community for the mentally handicapped, *Apex, Journal of the British Institute for Mental Handicap*, **4** (4), 12.

Matthews, D. R. (1978). 'Towards a therapeutic community for the mentally handicapped', *Apex, Journal of the British Institute for Mental Handicap*, **5** (4), 8-9.

Meyers, R. (1979). *Like Normal People*, London: Souvenir Press (E & H).

Mittler, P. (1970). *The Psychological Assessment of Mental and Physical Handicaps*, London, Methuen, espec. Chs. 10 and 17.

Murphy, G. (1980). 'Decreasing undesirable behaviours', in Yule, W. and Carr, J. (eds), *Behaviour Modification for the Mentally Handicapped*, London: Croom Helm, 90-115.

National Development Group for the Mentally Handicapped (1977a). *Mentally Handicapped children: A Plan for Action*, DHSS.

National Development Group for the Mentally Handicapped (1977b). *Helping Mentally Handicapped School Leavers*, DHSS.

National Development Group for the Mentally Handicapped (1977c). *Day Services for Mentally Handicapped Adults*, DHSS.

National Development Group for the Mentally Handicapped (1978). *Helping Mentally Handicapped People in Hospital*, DHSS.

Nihara, D., Foster, R., Shellhaus, M., and Leland, H. (1969). *Adaptive Behaviour Scales*, Washington: American Association of Mental Deficiency.

Nirje, B. (1970). 'The normalization principle — implications and comments', *Journal of Mental Subnormality*, **XVI**, 62–70.

Office of Health Economics (1978). *Mental Handicap: Ways Forward*, Paper no. 61.

Oswin, M. (1978). *Children Living in Long-Stay Hospitals*, Spastics International Medical Publications, Lavenham Press Ltd.

Perkins, E. A., Taylor, P. D., and Capie, A. C. M. (1976). *Helping the Retarded: a Systematic Behavioural Approach*, British Institute for Mental Handicap.

Pushkin, R. (1976). 'Community confusion over abnormality needs a remedy', *Health and Social Service Journal*, 1856–1857.

Pushkin, R. (1979). 'Lay criteria for defining and recognising mental subnormality', *Journal of Practical Approaches to Developmental Handicap*, **3** (1), 3–8.

Raynes, N. V. (1978). 'Making positive changes possible', *Apex, Journal of the British Institute of Mental Handicap*, **6** (2), 4.

Robertson, J. (1980). *South West Thames Regional Health Authority: Clinical Psychologists*. Unpublished paper.

Shennan, V. (1980). 'Making friends with the media', *Parents Voice*, **30** (1), 4–5.

Skellett, C., Hattersley, J., and Tennant, L. (1976). 'Observation and recording of dayroom activity', *Apex, Journal of the British Institute of Mental Handicap*, **4** (2), 24–26.

Spencer, D. A. (1979). 'The mentally handicapped person in the general hospital ward' *Apex, Journal of the British Institute of Mental Handicap*, **6** (4), 22.

Stanovich, K. E. and Stanovich, P. J. (1979). 'Speaking for themselves: a bibliography of writings by mentally handicapped individuals; *Mental Retardation* (USA), **17** (2), 83–86.

Taylor, P. D. and Robinson, P. (1979). *Crossing the Road*, British Institute of Mental Handicap.

Tymchuk, A. J. (1976). 'A perspective on ethics in mental retardation', *Mental Retardation*, **14** (6), 44–47.

Wadeson, H. (1978). 'Some uses of art therapy data in research', *American Journal of Art Therapy*, **18** (1), 1–18.

Wechsler, D. (1955). *Manual for the Wechsler Adult Intelligence Scale*, The Psychological Corporation.

Williams, C. (1979). 'Clinical psychology manpower in mental handicap', *Division of Clinical Psychology Newsletter*, No. 25, 12–17.

Wolfensburger, W. (1967). 'Counselling parents of the retarded', in Baumeister, A. (ed.), *Mental Retardation*, London: University of London Press, Ch. 13, pp. 329–400.

Psychology in Practice
Edited by S. Canter and D. Canter
© 1982, John Wiley & Sons, Ltd.

CHAPTER 5

FORENSIC PSYCHOLOGY

Lionel R. C. Haward
Professor of Clinical Psychology
University of Surrey

PSYCHOLOGY AND LAW

Law and psychology are alike in that they are both concerned with human behaviour. Psychology attempts to understand and explain it, and applied psychologists try to influence it for individual or corporate purposes. Law, in contradistinction, has a more limited interest in human conduct, and is concerned solely with its social regulation. The law is a mature profession, counting its age in centuries and, except when suffering a frenzy of reform and legislation by impatient, short-sighted politicians, changes slowly and cautiously. Modern psychology, born of philosophy and sired by an assortment of paternity-denying biological Don Juans, is a lusty and demanding infant, anxious to get its fingers into everything.

Thus it is that psychology has initiated all the approaches to law, while lawyers themselves call upon psychiatry rather than psychology whenever they require help of a perceived 'mental' kind. However, while preferring this branch of a profession of vintage similar to their own, lawyers still regard mental science with suspicion tinged with scepticism. At a trial for murder not long ago, the country's most eminent forensic psychiatrist was introduced to the court as a man 'with a strange and esoteric science, which is not, to my knowledge, a recognised branch of science but rather a matter for the library shelf or discussion between medical gentlemen', (*Attorney General* v. *Norton*, 1966). If this is the law's view of psychiatry, then modern experimental psychology is clearly beyond the pale. The psychology dear to the heart of the lawyer is that fallacious commonsense and unacknowledged conglomerate of prejudices of the so-called reasonable man, a mythical character of legal fiction who spends his time riding on a Claphan omnibus. Today's jurist contemplates the behavioural scientist with all the emotions of a Victorian spinster facing the neighbourhood rapist, curious as to what might be revealed, but dreading the consequences.

89

What psychology *has* to offer law in full frontal behaviourism is enough to fill many a sister discipline with penis envy. Indeed, the sheer potential of it all is enough to give law an acute attack of vaginismus. Inevitably, on some occasions, this leads to denouement and anti-climax, when some particular application of psychology is found to possess the potency of a papal chorister.

Yet the bravura of psychology is neither premature nor unjustified. At one end of the psycholegal spectrum, psychologists have made a substantial contribution to criminology; at the other extreme, applied psychologists are playing an increasing part in law enforcement and the treatment of offenders. Between these two long-standing fields of endeavour, psychology makes a unique and distinctive contribution to the principles, procedures, and particular cases of substantive law itself. Some indication of these activities is given in Figure 1, which shows the main groups of psycholegal activities as they exist today.

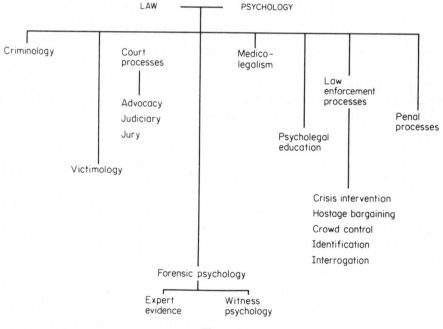

Figure 1.

Criminology is certainly the oldest, and probably the most developed, of our psycholegal activities (Clinard, 1956), while victimology is the youngest (Drapkin and Viano, 1975). The notion that victims may contribute to the crime is not new, but the *extent* to which the victim is a factor comes as a surprise to many (Myers, 1978). Many cases of assault, for example, start out as a simple alcohol-induced disagreement, and who becomes the victim and who the offender will often be decided on the basis of physical strength or a chance blow. To talk of the 'personality of the victim', or the 'personality of the criminal' in such a context is scientifically meaningless. Moreover some crimes are said to be 'victimogenic', because they are, wholly or in part, instigated by the victim; some sex offences fall into this category, as when so-called 'jail-bait'—girls below the age of consent—encourage sexual advances for their own needs or satisfaction, physical, psychological or financial, although the partner's compliant behaviour then becomes unlawful; sometimes the initiation or encouragement is not within the conscious aware-ness of the potential victim, whose coquetry may be the innocent and premature practice of atavistic feminine conduct. Some evidence suggests that crime reduction would become more effective if the emphasis were placed upon influencing the behaviour of the victim rather than the criminal; an inversion of ideas which confounds commonsense yet which has some scientific support (Viano, 1976). Psychologists are also interested in victims of crimes because in consequence they frequently suffer long-standing psychological distress. This is rarely notified to the police, so that the offender is not held responsible for the full consequences of his crime and the victim loses the compensation which goes to those with the more obvious physical sequelae. In 117 consecutive crimes against individuals (as distinct from crimes against companies and institutions), no less than 71 per cent were sufficiently distressed to require professional psychological help. Of these half were cases of burglary, theft, malicious damage, etc. where the victim had no contact with the criminal; it is not uncommon for severe psychiatric reactions to occur in such cases, sometimes to the extent of requiring hospitalization for long periods.

Medico-legalism (Nagle, 1970), a not altogether appropriate title coined north of the border but gaining currency among the sassenachs, is concerned with the legal consequences of professional activities. Of special importance to a profession of ever-widening interpersonal activities in an increasingly litigious society, this tends to be the haunt of those who view their own professional pathology with a morbid expectancy of legal repercussions. Although the UK scene has not yet reached the frenzy of litigation for which California has become infamous, where one in three medical practitioners have been sued, psychologists in this country have no cause for complacency, and there are enough complaints going through the channels to make professional indemnity insurance a *sine qua non*. The widespread use of behaviour therapy, where such techniques of flooding, aversion, and time-out procedures are potentially tortious, makes the clinical psychologist particularly vulnerable (Krasukopf and Krauskopf, 1965).

Psycho-legal education (Brown, 1966; Watson, 1963) concerns itself with educating lawyers in psychology (Smedley, 1963) and psychologists in law (McGillis and Mullen, 1977), a two-way communication in which the emphasis at present favours lawyers rather than psychologists. Post-graduate clinical psychology students at the University of Surrey receive two courses of legal content, one concerned with forensic psychology and law of evidence, the other with the law of tort, but this is somewhat exceptional in the UK, where few psychologists have received formal legal training in addition to their own professional qualifications.

Experimental psychologists, mainly but not exclusively drawn from social psychology, are actively researching a variety of court activities. These include such matters as the consistency of sentencing by magistrates (Green, 1961), the effects of the order in which advocates put their case (Howland, 1957), how jurors are selected (Diamond and Zeisel, 1974), how they evaluate psychiatric testimony (James, 1960), how they reach their verdict (Weld and Danzig, 1940), and how the foreman of the jury gets selected (Strodbeck and Hook, 1961). Caesar's plea to have about him men that were fat, has been echoed by many a plaintiff since psychologists discovered plump jurors award higher damages than the ectomorphs (McCart, 1964). Moreover, yon Cassius, with his lean and hungry look, would today be excluded at the jury challenge for reasons other than his somato type (Strodbeck et al., 1957). Many law enforcement processes owe their present efficacy to the experimental work of psychologists, who are presently engaged intensively in improving identification (Clifford and Bull, 1978) and interrogation procedures (Haward, 1974), and in training police officers how to cool and control crises, especially hostage situations (Danish and Brodsky, 1970). Prison psychologists continue their research into the effectiveness of various penal methods (Mannheim and Wilkins, 1955) while at the same time carrying out a variety of duties concerned with the selection (Argyle, 1961), training (Fineman, 1968), and rehabilitation of prisoners, (Andry, 1963). Last, but by no means least, is forensic psychology (Haward, 1973). Concerned exclusively with evidence (Haward, 1969), forensic psychologists either collect and tender their own expert testimony (Haward, 1972), or examine experimentally the evidence of others (Haward, 1963) in that special branch of the subject known as witness psychology (Trankell, 1965).

In all the other branches of psycho-legal endeavour, the psychologist has assumed one of three roles, namely, experimenter, teacher, or practitioner. In forensic psychology, four roles may be distinguished, that is experimental, clinical, actuarial, and advisory, and these may be assumed exclusively, sequentially or interactively, by the same psychologist in any one case. Of all roles, the experimental one is the most important, both in terms of the weight and the uniqueness of the evidence which the psychologist tenders to the court. In 1979 psychologists celebrated the centenary of Professor Wilhelm Wundt (1897), the father of experimental psychology, who founded the first psychological laboratory in Leipzig 100 years ago. It is rather fitting that the two earliest and still the most famous forensic psychologists in the world were pupils of Wundt who studied under him at Leipzig. One was Professor Karl

Marbe, who first introduced experimental psychology into the courtroom when he demonstrated the phenomenon of reaction time and so excluded from criminal responsibility the engine driver involved in a train crash. His contemporary was Professor Hugo Munsterberg (1907) who settled the case of the Flemish Weavers by bringing to court a knowledge of colour vision which he had acquired from Helmholtz himself.

THE EXPERIMENTAL ROLE

The modern forensic psychologist not only makes use of the wealth of experimental data accumulated during the past century, but conducts his own experiments. Many examples of forensic experimentation by the present writer have been published elsewhere (for example Harvard, 1961a, b, 1964, a, b, c, 1969, 1972, 1973, 1976). The experimental role utilizes what Allport (1937) called the 'nomothetic' approach, being a normative one based on the norms of an experimental sample selected to resemble the witness in the legal proceeding in terms of the relevant criteria. This raises problems of admissibility of expert evidence, since the experimental sample would need to give evidence *in toto* unless hearsay evidence is to be admitted on this principle. It also raises problems of scientific validity: the fact that 100 individuals with perfect eyesight failed to perceive a vehicle registration plate under the visual conditions identical to the original situation was held, by the magistrates in one particular case, to be irrelevant to the evidence of a policeman who claimed he had perceived and recorded the registration in question (Haward, 1973).

In the experimental role the psychologist provides previously non-existent data by experiment and this becomes evidence. In many cases brought under the obscene publication Acts, psychologists have been called to describe experiments in which the actual effects of pornography upon human behaviour have been measured, both in laboratory and field settings. As with all psychosocial experiments, such studies are fraught with methodological difficulties, and clearly demonstrate the research paradox that as the methodology is made more precise, the generalization of results becomes less valid. Attempting coitis when wired up to the multichannel recorder, surrounded by TV monitors and one-way viewing screens, and illuminated by spotlights, may not be conducive to trying out the latest variation illustrated in the current number of *Bizarre Capers*. On the other hand, showing blue films regularly over several months to married couples and monitoring their reports of sexual behaviour may give relevant, valid, and meaningful results which nevertheless lack objectivity and may be held inadmissible as evidence under the Rule of Hearsay.

However, sex, as Freud discovered, is a complicated business. In less emotional areas of the human psyche, experimentation can produce satisfactory evidence which is both relevant and admissible.

The manufacturer of a certain tinned food was preparing to sue the manufacturer of a similar commodity on the grounds of infringement of copyright, the labels from the two manufacturers having a certain resemblance. The question was whether the two labels were sufficiently alike to deceive the shopper into mistaking one brand for the other, and as is so often the case in law, this question was argued in the abstract by both sides, at great length and with absolutely no reference to empiricism. Finally it was suggested that this was a question of perception, in which subject psychologists professed expertise, and the author was called in to proffer advice. Facilities were provided by the manager of a supermarket, and quantities of both brands in question were placed in different sites, but at the same height and in racks of comparable convenience. The shelves were monitored from a special viewing position designed to detect shoplifting, and a film was made of customers selecting the tins used in the experiment. Each of these customers was then interviewed after leaving the cashpoint, the interviewer having recorded the particular brand concerned. Many of the customers were unaware of the precise brand they had purchased, being only concerned with the contents; all those who knew they had purchased the plaintiff's brand said this was the brand they wanted, but 19 per cent of those who purchased the defendant's brand said that they thought they were buying the brand of a third manufacturer. Many of these mistaken customers found it difficult to believe that they had not brought the brand of their choice, and insisted on emptying their shopping bags and trolleys to find the erring tins. While a simple *post facto* enquiry of this kind leaves much to be desired methodologically, the evidence was clear enough that *some* customers were confused by the similarity of labelling and that the plaintiff had a *prima facie* case, which was then expeditiously settled out of court.

Forensic experimentation is undertaken for criminal as well as civil offences. In a case for which a court martial was pending, an airman who had gone berserk pleaded being under the influence of a particularly obnoxious brew distilled from a mixture of petrol and rotting vegetation in a Displaced Persons Camp; the illicit still being constructed of copper tubing taken from the engines of abandoned Wehrmacht vehicles, and sealed with birdlime. The airman's drinking pattern on the night in question was obtained to the best of his, and his friends', recollection, and with his consent, and indeed his enthusiastic co-operation, he was plied with a repeat prescription of the equivalent volumes over the appropriate time-scale, using a sample which the service police had managed to procure from the same source. Despite the fact that the 'guinea pig' was being held on a serious charge at Police HQ and had shown exemplary behaviour since the time of his arrest, he gradually became more and more violent and maniacal in proportion to the volume of brew ingested, until the staff on duty were unable to restrain him and substantial damage to the experimental room was sustained. The detailed record of his behaviour by the author was accepted as evidence of the effects of the brew upon his behaviour; single case studies of this sort are often apposite in forensic psychology, and although such one-off experiments lack the methodological perfection of the ABAB and cross-over trials exhorted by the textbooks, they are often more convincing. In this case the author's suggestion of a repeat run met with vehement protest from a heavily bandaged and contused constabulary; not everyone is prepared to make the necessary sacrifices for science.

THE CLINICAL ROLE

In the clinical role, the psychologist is usually, though not necessarily, a clinician, and the area of his expertise concerns behavioural disability — arising from a road traffic accident for example — or mental state. In court he is presented as a 'medical witness' because the questions on which his expertise is required are medical ones. He will thus be giving evidence which inevitably overlaps, and sometimes contradicts, that from medical practitioners, and frequently finds himself on opposite sides to eminent neurologists and psychiatrists. Psychiatrists, of course, have their own problems in court, without these being complicated by evidence given by another profession. The so-called Battle of the Psychiatric Experts is an all too common phenomenon: sometimes, as in the Sofaer case where four psychiatrists gave four different interpretations of the facts, it becomes not so much a battle as a mêlée.

Nevertheless, the forensic psychologist, in the clinical role, generally simplifies rather than confuses the issue although this may not always be obvious to the jury. The fact is that psychological evidence *supplements* that of other medical experts: the psychologist comes to court as a behavioural scientist and presents his evidence primarily in quantitative terms. Because of this, forensic psychologists in the UK have rarely been in dispute. Naturally enough, differences of opinion exist in all professions, and psychologists do not always agree on the interpretation, but in forensic cases such disagreement is the exception rather than the rule. In many hundreds of appearances in court as expert witness, the author has only twice been confronted by contradictory evidence put forward by members of his own profession. One of these was a case involving pornography, where the author, in the clinical role, was describing his use of explicit sexual material in therapy. His views were contrasted with those of another psychologist, whose scientific standing has been seriously questioned by the Williams Committee looking into the working of the Obscenity Acts. During the era when psychologists were in great demand as expert witnesses in porn trials, the prosecution were unable to find one psychologist in the UK to bolster their case, and had to reach out to the Antipodes to find this particular witness for the prosecution.

The second case was one of fraud, and proved to be the longest running trial in English legal history, with a seven-figure estimated cost to the taxpayer. Here the evidence of three clinical psychologists that the accused was of borderline mental handicap was opposed by an academic psychologist who, while agreeing with the psychometric data, was of the opinion that the accused was faking bad. The three clinicians gave convincing evidence of the validity of their case, and prosecuting counsel, unable to fault their logic, could only undermine their case by ridiculing the psychological tests, a not too difficult task when the items are taken out of context, and the jury, confined to the jury box for seven weary months, were glad of a little light relief.

In this case mental subnormality, a legal defence against *mens rea*, or guilty mind, was at issue. Sometimes other mental states are the concern of the forensic psychologist in the clinical role. Was Nielson, the triple-murdering Black Panther (Valentine, 1976), really insane? To find out, the author spent many hours with him in the special cells at Winchester and Oxford, administering standardized tests and comparing his test performance and mentation with that of criterion groups. Did John Stonehouse MP (1976) really suffer fugue states when he believed himself to be someone else? Again the answer came from the precision of comprehensive long-term psychological testing which could be presented to the court in quantitative form. Other mental states which preclude *mens rea* and which the forensic psychologist in his clinical role investigates include automatism, such as sleepwalking, psychopathy, certain types of alcoholic states—as in the airman's case mentioned earlier—and amnesia. If the jury believes *mens rea* was absent at the time of the crime the accused may be acquitted. Sometimes the mental state of the accused suggests that he is incompetent to stand trial, since the British sense of justice decrees that a man must be able to follow the proceedings, instruct his solicitor, and understand the nature of his offence. A plea of amnesia is too easy an excuse for incompetency to be readily acceptable by the courts, especially as there is no easy way of proving it, and since Podola's (*R. v. Podola*, 1959) it has been considered a non-starter. For purposes of rebutting *mens rea*, however, the issue is still open, and some techniques in the hands of the experienced clinician enable objective quantitative data to be obtained on the memory processes of the accused. Of these Luria's Combined Motor Method (Luria, 1932) enables deliberate suppression of response to be detected, whilst the sensitive use of GSR technique reveals differential responses relating to facts which are unknown, those known but genuinely forgotten or repressed, and those known and deliberately suppressed (*R. v. Trotter*, 1957).

In one case of attempted murder, for example, an elderly widow living alone had been struck down unconscious and robbed of a copy of the *Sporting Times* (not all old ladies restrict their interests to pampered poodles or petit point). The chief suspect was an itinerant milestone inspector of the old school, found sleeping in a haystack and in possession of a blood-stained copy of the missing periodical, and who, after helping the police with their enquiries, was found to have fingerprints which matched those on a poker used in the assault. Well known to duty officers in casualty wards and mental hospitals up and down the country, he was a chronic epileptic prone to *grand mal* attacks and twilight states of automatism. He claimed complete amnesia for the assault, and said that he must have done it in an attack. Now although the medicolegal literature is replete with cases linking violence with epilepsy, of which the case of Jack Ruby, who killed President Kennedy's assassin Oswald, is the most notorious, the modern view is that epileptogenic violence is extremely rare and that in most of the classic cases, violence and epilepsy exist coincidently without any causal relation between them. In this case the author used the Luria technique and assured himself that the accused was not deliberately suppressing his responses, and then used the GSR in which it was hypothesized that the mean responses to three classes of facts, unknown, forgotten, and remembered would be different. The police had, of course, contaminated the issue by reminding him of certain facts relating to the crime, but there were some they had not mentioned, including the poker. If the alleged amnesia was genuine, the GSRs to this group of facts should lie between those for facts clearly known to the tramp, such as the *Sporting Times*, and those facts of the situation he was unlikely to know about at all. Although not reaching statistical significance, the means came out as hypothesized and helped to support the earlier finding. Finally, hypnosis was used to assist recall, when memory of the poker, *inter alia*, was regained by the accused, and provided sufficient corroboration for evidence to be given in his defence using a plea of insanity. Later, when the old rapscallion learned he would spend longer in Broadmoor than he would in prison on a grievous bodily harm conviction he quickly changed his plea to guilty and a short time later was seen convulsing his way through the Shires again.

Investigative hypnosis, the third tool of the forensic psychologist examining amnesia, has become a prominent technique in helping the police in the acquisition of new evidence and the discarding of false clues. Although not confined in its use to the clinical psychologist it nevertheless forms part of the clinical role because of the special human relationship formed between psychologist and client which is absent in other roles.

Hypnotic techniques, according to Bryan (1962), have four different applications in forensic psychology. One, the hypnotic screening of individual jurors prior to what is called jury challenge, has not been used in England, and is indeed more suited to the court procedure of the USA, where in-depth studies of the attitudes and prejudices of the jury are sometimes made. The second, whilst not unknown in this country, is still rare: this is the preparation by hypnosis of the nervous witness. The court draws its inferences about testimony from the demeanour and appearance of the witness as well as from the actual content of the testimony itself, and witnesses who become demoralized by an aggressive cross-examination can be frequently made to contradict themselves, suffer thought-blocking and dysmnesia for significant events as the stress in court becomes excessive. This can be prevented by desensitizing the witness under hypnosis, and giving post-hypnotic suggestions which enable the witness to deal competently with the cross-examining counsel. Most witnesses of this kind rely on anxiolytics from a sympathetic medical practitioner or resort to alcoholic self-help, either of which may calm the nerves but befuddle the intellect.

Studying the mind of the criminal is the third use of forensic hypnosis. This enables the psychologist to investigate motivation for the crime or to assess the mental state of the offender at the time of the offence. Hypnosis, according to Gulotta (1976) is the only method we have at present which can help us determine the true mental state of the offender. Suspects are unlikely to agree to be hypnotized unless they are innocent, but sometimes those guilty of the charge are prepared to co-operate in hypnosis in the hope of gaining access to information which would mitigate the offence. One persistent larcenist of phallic-shaped objects revealed under hypnosis intense childhood fears of ostracism from his peer group and the existence of three meati in his penis which made him urinate (and ejaculate) in three directions at once—an accomplishment of some status value to an adult but which had led to repression-engendering ridicule in his adolescence. A simple surgical operation immediately cured both his urinary extravagance and his recidivism. There is every reason to believe that but for this hypnotic revelation the unfortunate victim of such an anatomical joke would still be in and out of prison.

But it is the innocent suspect who has most to gain from forensic hypnosis, and at least two men facing the death penalty have been saved from capital punishment solely by information obtained from them under hypnosis.

The suspect or accused is not the only person for whom forensic hypnosis may be used with benefit. Victims are particularly good subjects for hypnosis, especially in sexual offences, where the emotional trauma is often intense enough to create strong repressive barriers to recall. Forgetting due to shock is, of course, the easiest form of dysmnesia to deal with, a fact well-known since Brown (1918) treated shell-shock amnesia in the First World War. While victims of assault, especially sexual assault, appear to be most prone to difficulties of recall after the offence, victims of non-sexual, non-assaultive crimes can also show the amnesia of psychological trauma. One victim seen by the author had returned home from a social visit to find her house ransacked and burgled; in consequence she went into a state of shock which necessitated hospitalization and long-term psychiatric care, and was unable to provide any information about the stolen items until placed under hypnosis.

Apart from victims and suspects, the forensic psychologist in the clinical role will also be concerned with independent witnesses. There is usually some emotional involvement on the part of the witness, if only from fear of being hurt, empathy with the victim, or even the sheer drama of the situation. This is rarely enough to evoke amnesia of the kind seen in victims, nevertheless, the recall of events may be impaired by distractions, and in the hypnotic state such recall may be improved. Some foreign constabularies, including the USA, now employ full-time forensic hypnotists, and in Israel, the leading exponents of this technique, some twenty arrests have been made on the basis of evidence derived from hypnotic interrogation. In the UK forensic hypnosis is less frequently used, although the enthusiasm of one police department is exemplified by the three-day marathon session in which the author was asked to hypnotize no less than seventeen witnesses. The validity of evidence obtained by hypnosis and its admissibility in court raise some interesting questions which have been discussed elsewhere (Haward and Ashworth, 1980; Reiser, 1980), but these authors argue that there are now sufficient grounds for the acceptance of hypnotic evidence within the usual safeguards of procedural law. Nevertheless, this particular field of forensic psychology does raise some ethical dilemmas. How far, for example, should the hypnotist be trusted by the court not to influence the testimony of the nervous witness he has been preparing for cross-examination? The witness will happily swear on oath to tell the truth, but what he or she believes to be the truth may be no more than a suggestion unconsciously (or experimentally) implanted by the hypnotist. Again, in treating amnesia encountered during hypnotic interrogation, the psychologist's clinical ethics may clash with wider social ethics. Should he remove a repression — a natural safety device to protect a vulnerable psyche from overpowering emotion — knowing it will cause the victim intense distress and serve no therapeutic purpose, in the interests of justice or the safety of the community? Does he owe a clinician's duty to his patient or a citizen's duty to his neighbour? This is often a real problem, and not just an academic exercise, especially when a rapist is at large. These are moral issues which have to be considered by the forensic psychologist and on which decisions have to be made at short notice. The psychologist has to live by his professional code of ethics, but he also has to live with his conscience, and nowhere are the conflicts and problems more acute than in forensic psychology.

THE ACTUARIAL ROLE

The clinical and experimental roles occupy the major portion of the forensic psychologist's activities. The third role is an actuarial role, where the psychologist is asked to predict the probability of an event or circumstance based on existing or specially obtained data. Probability calculations are making an increasing impact in law enforcement (Eggleston, 1978), and the psychologist's knowledge of the mathematics and statistics of probability theory enable him to use his numerate skills for this purpose. We cannot all match the expert who, after reviewing the scene of the crime, told the police:

'the man you want will be found wearing a double-breasted coat, with the top button done up' (he was!). But it is possible to narrow down the list of suspects, or to connect a suspect with a particular crime, by particular behaviour patterns. Forensic psychologists call this 'the finger printing of cognitive style' (Cunningham, 1964) and the method has been used successfully on war criminals in both the Second World War and Korea. Like the man who suddenly discovered he had been speaking prose all his life without knowing it, the police have used the concept of cognitive style in relation to criminal behavour for many years. With a classical touch which can only have come from the Hendon Police College, they call it *modus operandi*.

In one sense, of course, most convictions are based upon probability, albeit unquantified, because in most cases the evidence is circumstantial. The prosecution build up their cases by a cumulative display of evidence, each element of which increases the probability of the accused being guilty. The role of the jury, in this view is to assess the overall probability and compare it with the notional level of probability they conceive to be embodied in their concept of 'beyond reasonable doubt'.

The imagination boggles at the daunting task placed by society upon the 'twelve good men and true', some of whom may be illiterate, innumerate and/or mentally subnormal. Psychologists, free from such cognitive dissonance by the use of operationally defined levels of chance and happenstance, still argue over the real world significance of a 'twenty to one' probability: what chance has justice when each juror chooses his own levels and summates the evidence on his own innumerate system? It is precisely these basic psychological problems of law and justice which the forensic psychologist in the actuarial role examines for the individual case, using numerate data to replace the varying insights of the jury.

On one occasion, a pedestrian had her bag snatched by a young couple, consisting of a bearded negro and a white girl with blonde hair arranged in a pony-tail, who escaped in a yellow car. Sometime later, a couple answering to this description and driving a yellow car were picked up by the police in another part of the town, and brought to trial for larceny. Was this a collection of coincidences or were there two separate but similar couples involved? On such circumstantial evidence the jury often have to reach a decision. In this case, however, probability figures could be worked from the known population of negroes, white females, yellow cars, hairstyles, and so on, within the specific area. For example, the probability of finding a mixed-race couple in a car in that city was $p = 0.001$: multiplying this figure by the successive probabilities of the other noted and agreed characteristics gave the final odds of 12 million to 1. On such odds many a punter would happily put his shirt, and the trial court had no 'reasonable doubt' in reaching a guilty verdict (*People* v. *Collins*, 1976). Actuarial evidence was also given to the

House Assassinations Committee investigating President J. F. Kennedy's untimely demise on which occasion it was stated that in legal terms a probability of 95 per cent could be described as 'beyond reasonable doubt'.

THE ADVISORY ROLE

The final role of the forensic psychologist is the advisory one. In this role the psychologist does not present expert testimony under oath, but advises the court, or the legal representatives of one of the parties, from the basis of his specialized knowledge and experience, and using the great wealth of accumulated experimental data to support his opinions. In the advisory role, the psychologist not only finds himself in the civil and criminal courts, but in courts of enquiry, tribunals, and Royal Commissions.

CONCLUSIONS

Space does not permit one to do more than hint at the uses of psychology vis-à-vis law, nor to evaluate any of the many and varied contributions which the profession of psychology makes to legal process. Results in this respect must stand trial at the bar of scientific scrutiny; while they generally meet the standards and criteria insisted upon in laboratory work, their social relevance and political implications are less reassuring.

In the first place, it should be noted that psychology has made the most unique contribution in the least important area of law—that of the individual case. It is here that forensic psychology makes the headlines and can produce a complete reversal of the expected verdict. However important the consequent judicial decision is to the future of the person in the dock, the psychologists' contribution may have no influence upon the future of law whatsoever. Such contributions may well go unreported and therefore remain unknown to the legal world in general. Cases which have involved months of experimental work and bibliographic study and called upon the impassioned pleading and brilliant reasoning of some of our greatest thinkers, have left little or no mark in the legal archives nor engrams in the memory circuits of lawyers. Yet, in those areas where the problems are the most profound, and the social implications of prime importance, such as legal reform, psychologists have made, and continue to make, little effective contribution.

The fault perhaps lies less with psychologists than with lawyers, who fail to invite the former to investigate the socially important psycholegal problems, and who provide no guide as to what problems deserve investigating, nor suggestions as to the hierarchy of interprofessional activities which would be of most benefit to either or both professions or to society in general. Left to their own devices, psychologists choose the activities which best suit their own interests, inclinations, local facilities or ideas of what needs to be done. This results in a bewildering patchwork of psychological activities and unco-ordinated misapplied efforts. By generating their own contributions to law in ignorance of the problems and priorities seen by lawyers, a costly mismatch between need and effort ensues.

The abuses also stem mainly from the legal side, especially in the subordination of modern psychological knowledge to the psychology of the man in the street. Courts still reach verdicts by blind prejudice rather than scientific objectivity, as when a paternity suit was awarded on the basis of resemblance plus evidence of copulation despite the genetic evidence to the contrary (*Barry* v. *Chaplin*, 1946). The introduction of the breathalyser in place of a commonsense judgment of drunkenness was described by Bicknell (1961) as 'freakish and fallacious foolishness'. The law has assumed, and has entertained no doubts on the matter, that such things as a picture of Venus in a Municipal Art Gallery, a birth-control pamphlet, and one of the choices for the BBC's 'Book at Bedtime' have a tendency to deprave and corrupt. Offenders have been imprisoned on the basis of such assumptions yet the evidence available would suggest that these things were actually of substantial benefit to society socially, psychologically, and culturally. Much of our legislation contains ambiguities and false assumptions, which could be eradicated with a modicum of psychological sophistication. Until psychologists expend considerable efforts to produce good communication between the two professions, the present problems are likely to remain. The information flow must be improved before any significant advances can be made. The law, blissfully unaware of psychology or its potential contribution, cannot be expected to initiate or indeed even encourage an information flow. While not complacent about their own profession, lawyers have little knowledge of what psychology can do, and little belief in the relevance of psychology to law. Their attitude was adequately summed up by one well-known judge, who likened psychology to a doctor who was called in to treat a child. The mother explained that the boy suffered from nausea, cramps, and fever. 'But does he have fits?' asked the doctor. The mother said 'No, only nausea, cramp, and fever'. 'That's too bad', said the doctor, 'I'm terrific on fits.'

This may be an unfair image of psychology, and if we are seen to study fits, it is because the lawyers have not yet told us about the other symptoms. The time has come, however, when we must accept the onus of examining the whole corpus of law, and directing our efforts in the way the cognoscienti think best. But we cannot progress very far without acceptance and recognition by our legal colleagues. Psychologists are poor trumpet-blowers, and would have been a sore disappointment to Joshua at the Battle of Jericho. Yet only by publicizing our uses, rectifying the abuses, and integrating our activities more closely with lawyers, can our contribution to society match our capacity and so be both substantial and cost-effective.

REFERENCES

Allport, G. W. (1937). *Personality*, New York: Holt.

Andry, R. G. (1963). *The Short Term Prisoner*, London: Stevens.

Attorney General v. *Norton* (1966). Jersey, CI.

Argyle, M. A. (1961). *A New Approach to the Classification of Delinquents*, Sacramento: Board of Corrections.

Barry v. *Chaplin* (1946). 74 Co. App. 652, 169 Pac. 442.

Bicknell, J. (1961). *The Stethoscope*, January, p.4.

Brown, H. (1918). *Advanced Suggestion*, London: Bailliere, Tindall and Cox.

Brown, L. (1966), 'Experimental preventive law course', *Journal of Legal Education*, **18**, 212–220.

Bryan, W. J. (1962). *Legal Aspects of Hypnosis*, Springfield: Thomas.

Clifford, B. C. and Bull, R. (1978). *Psychology of Person Identification*, London: Routledge) Kegan Paul.

Clinard, M. B. (1956). Research frontiers in criminology', *British Journal of Delinquency*, **7**, 110–122.

Cunningham, C. (1964). 'Forensic psychology', *Bulletin of the British Psychological Society*, **54**, 7.

Danish, S. J. and Brodsky, S. C. (1970). 'Training policemen in emotional control and awareness', *American Psychologist*, **25**, 368–369.

Diamond, S. and Zeisel, H. (1974). *Courtroom Experiment on Juror Selection and Decision-making*, Proc. 82nd Ann. Conv. APA, New Orleans.

Drapkin, I. and Viano, E. C. (1975). *Victimology: A New Focus*, Lexington: Lexington Books.

Eggleston, R. E. (1978). *Evidence, Proof and Probability*, London: Weidenfeld & Nicolson.

Fineman, K. (1968). 'An operant conditioning program in a juvenile detention facility', *Psychological Reports*, **22**, 119–120.

Green, E. (1961). *Judicial Attitudes to Sentencing*, London: Macmillan.

Gulotta, G. (1976). *Psychoanalysis and Criminal Responsibility*, Milano: Giuffre.

Haward, L. R. C. (1961a). 'Forensic psychology', *Bulletin of the British Psychological Society*, **43**, 1–5.

Haward, L. R. C. (1961b). 'Psychological evidence', *Journal of Forensic Science Society*, **2**, 8–18.

Haward, L. R. C. (1963). 'Reliability of corroborated police evidence', *Journal of Forensic Science Society*, **3**, 71–78.

Haward, L. R. C. (1964a). 'Psychologists' contribution to legal procedures', *Modern Law Review*, **27**, 656–668.

Haward, L. R. C. (1964b). 'Psychological experiments and judicial doubt', *Bulletin of the British Psychological Society*, **17**, 23A (Abstract).

Haward, L. R. C. (1964c). 'Thematic appreciation analysis as a forensic technique', *Journal of Forensic Science Society*, **4**, 209–216.

Haward, L. R. C. (1969). 'Role of the psychologist in English criminal law', *International Journal of Forensic Psychology*, **1**, 11–22.

Haward, L. R. C. (1972). 'Role of the forensic psychologist', *Prison Medical Journal*, April, 53–57.

Haward, L. R. C. (1973). 'Forensic psychology', in Haward and McGann, *Psychiatry, Psychology, and the Law Courts*, Dublin: Institute of Psychology.

Haward, L. R. C. (1974). 'Investigation of torture allegations by the forensic psychologist', *Journal of Forensic Science Society*, **14**, 299–309.

Haward, L. R. C. (1976). 'Experimentation in forensic psychology', *Criminal Justice and Behaviour*, **3**, 301–314.

Haward, L. R. C. and Ashworth, A. (1980). 'Some problems of evidence obtained by hypnosis', *Criminal Law Review*, 469–485.

Howland, C. I. (1957). *Order of Presentation in Persuasion*, London: OUP.

James, Rita, M. (1960). *Jurors' Evaluation of Expert Psychiatric Testimony*, Ohio State L.J. 21 75.

Krauskopf, J. M. and Krauskopf, C. J. (1965). 'Torts and psychologists', *Journal of Counselling Psychology*, **12**, 227–237.

Luria, A. R. (1932). *Nature of Human Conflict*, New York: Liveright.

Mannheim, H. and Wilkins, L. T. (1955). *Prediction Methods in Relation to Borstal Training*, London: HMSO.

McCart, S. (1964). *Trial by Jury*, New York: Chilton.

McGillis, D. and Mullen, J. (1977). *Neighbourhood Justice Centers*, Washington DC: USA Government Printing Office.

Munsterberg, H. (1907). *On the Witness Stand*, New York: McClure.

Myers, D. (1978). *Responses to Victimisation*, Abingdon: Professional Books.

Nagel, R. (1970). 'Medico-legalism', *Medicine, Science and Law*, **10**, 158.

People v. *Collins* (1976). 438, p. 2d. 33.

R. v. *Podola* (1959). 3 W.L.R., 718.

R. v. *Trotter* (1957). Court Record, Durham Assize.

Reiser, M. (1980). *Handbook of Investigative Hypnosis*, Los Angeles: Lehi.

Smedley, R. (1963). 'A pervasive approach on a large scale', *Journal of Legal Education*, **15**, 435–443.

Stonehouse, J. (1976). *My Trial*, London: Wyndham.

Strodbeck, F., James, R., and Hawkins, C. (1957). 'Social status in jury deliberations', *American Sociological Review*, **22**, 713–718.

Strodbeck, F. and Hook, H. (1961). 'Social dimensions of a 12-man jury table', *Sociometry*, **24**, 397–414.

Trankell, A. (1965). *Witness Psychology* (Vittnes Psychologin), Stockholm: Liber.

Valentine, S. (1976). *The Black Panther Story*, London: New English Library.

Viano, E. C. (1976). *Victims and Society*, Washington DC: Visage Press.

Watson, A. J. (1963). 'Teaching mental health concepts in law school', *American Journal of Psychology*, **53**, 518–536.

Weld, H. and Danzig, E. (1940). 'A student of the way in which a verdict is reached by the Jury', *Amer. J. Psychol.*, **53**, 518–536.

Wundt, W. (1897). *Grundriss der Psychologie*, Leipzig: Engelmann.

Psychology in Practice
Edited by S. Canter and D. Canter
© 1982, John Wiley & Sons, Ltd.

CHAPTER 6

PSYCHOLOGISTS IN THE PRISON DEPARTMENT

Bernard Marcus
Principal Psychologist
HM Prison Grendon, Buckinghamshire

SETTING THE SCENE

Psychologists were first employed in the Prison Service in 1946 to assist Governors and Medical Officers in preparing reports to Court. In 1953 a Chief Psychologist was appointed at Headquarters to supervise their functions. (Since 1975 he has been designated Director of Psychological Services.) Over the years the numbers of psychologists have increased and the work changed according to service needs and individual expertise. Currently there are about eighty-five psychologists and thirty psychological assistants located in some thirty-six establishments in England and Wales. These include two research units at Headquarters; four regional offices and the Prison Service College at Wakefield, which is the Staff Training Centre.

Broadly, the job of psychologists is to help improve the efficiency and effectiveness of systems in the Prison Department. A review of Prison Psychological Services has recently been carried out and a report published (Home Office Prison Dept., 1980). This contains some discussion of the problems of managing a group of specialists who, unlike other specialists in prison, have no statutory duties, are not on the staff of every institution and who carry out a wide variety of work. The latter is seen as falling into four areas: clinical, organizational, staff training, and research. Heads of Psychology Units in institutions are accountable to the Governor of that institution and also to a psychologist in Headquarters. Over the years Prison Psychologists have learned that it is essential to forego whatever ivory tower inclinations they might ever have had, to work very closely with administrators and managers to maintain an understanding of *their* problems, and for *them* to understand the nature of the psychologists' potential contribution, and what facilities are needed to maximize it. Without such interchange hostile two-way stereotypes are easily established.

CURRENT WORK

This ranges very widely from basic psychophysiological research to involvement in evaluating the tougher regimes in detention centres, from assessing individual cases to running therapeutic community wings; from designing computerized management information systems to consultancy work on management structures. It includes both social skills training for prisoners and training courses for various grades of staff members. All kinds of theoretical orientation are found, behaviourist, dynamic, humanistic, social skills, etc. Before attempting to bring some order into this varied field, it might be helpful if I say a word about my own line of work, not because this is the most fascinating or important job of any prison psychologist, but to help clarify the perspective from which this chapter is written and perhaps to correct for bias. I am head of the Psychology Unit at HM Prison Grendon, a unique prison in that its primary task is treatment. That is to say the entire inmate population are there to receive psychotherapy. Because Grendon operates a treatment regime the Governor is a Medical Superintendent. The prison is divided into five wings, each under a therapist who may be a psychologist or psychiatrist. Each wing is a self-contained therapeutic community unit and it is to the therapeutic community ideology that Grendon bears the strongest affinity. It is, indeed, an attempt to operate a therapeutic community within the constraints of the penal system. I will simply make a point now, which will be developed later on not only in the context of Grendon, that being a 'therapist' is not simply or mainly a matter of clinical skills but rather a way of social interaction that creates a certain kind of culture.

The therapeutic community ideology on which Grendon is based insists that treatment is everybody's business, inmates and staff alike. It is not the sole prerogative of those with certain specialist qualifications. Many consequences follow from this, all of which have been observed by several authors (Jones, 1968; Clark, 1965; Rapoport, 1960), for example permissiveness, role blurring, lessening of social distances, openness of communication, suspension of status prerogative. This means a certain kind of culture, different from and quite antithetical to the culture which is a normal expectation of anyone in prison. This is something quite different from the one-to-one confidential relationship popularly associated with psychotherapy. All treatment occurs in multiperson situations, in small groups or large community meetings. There is a great deal of pressure for openness and self-revelation. This itself is strongly opposed to the prison habit of secrecy. I hope that from this brief statement you will be getting the message that being a psychologist involved with treatment in the prison service means something very much more than being a clinician. Already I am touching on such fields as culture creation, which inevitably means management involvement, a theme to which I shall be continually returning.

Taking an overall view, prison psychologists' work can be divided into four main areas (my wording is not quite the same as that of the review referred to above).

(1) *Organizational:* that is, aids to management. I will always use this term broadly, including not simply the official business of management but also the interpersonal dynamics that creep into management deliberations.

(2) *Treatment:* both individual and group. Here the concern is with changing people's behaviour rather than conducting medical-type operations. (Prison Service psychologists ceased to be part of the Prison Medical Services in 1963.)

(3) *Staff training.*

(4) *Research.*

The above should not be seen as a list of disparate areas but rather as a matrix of intercorrelating variables. In other words these areas are bafflingly inter-linked, such that it is hardly possible to be engaged in one area without also being engaged in one or more of the others. If this were to be factor-analysed, by whatever technique, my guess is that we would emerge with a general component of which area (1), Organizational, has the highest loading. It might be a bit oversimplistic to say that all other problems stem from management problems. It would not be an exaggeration to say that issues which are ultimately management issues seem to permeate every aspect of what prison psychologists do, and I give you notice that this topic will be a King Charles' head entering into discussion of all other areas. Still, convenience always demands that we discuss each topic under separate headings.

Organizational

It is well established (though even this needs a certain amount of qualification) that psychologists in the prison service are nowadays heavily involved in the management problems of their institutions; for example at Feltham Borstal the psychology unit is involved in management from the top down. At each layer of decision-making, from house management up to institutional policy, a psychologist is involved. At Grendon, as stated above, apart from involvement at institution level, psychologists in charge of wings are in fact managers of those wings. At the large women's prison at Holloway psychologists are involved in the most crucial of management problems in any kind of institution. It is interesting to note that in this institution, when management was confronted with a problem such as analysing communication, it was automatically accepted that the psychologists were the people in the institution to ask. Examples could be multiplied but it would be more profitable to point out the rationale for why I consider psychologists to be an appropriate group of people to consult in problems of penal management.

Because they *are* psychologists, and I mean by this psychologists in the popular sense, they know what makes people tick. (Mind you I have known lots of psychologists who do not and many non-psychologists who do but you will get my general drift.) Let us be a little more technical about this. It is no great revelation these days to say that whatever the official task of an organization management might be, the interpersonal dynamics of the institution can hamper the carrying out of that task. Often the carrying out of a primary task is held back by unspoken assumptions, unverbalized tensions, the hidden agenda and so on. Prisons, after all, are only one form of organization and in any organization you do not really know what goes on unless you understand the clash of various interest groups. Certainly, you do not have a hope of resolving them until you see that they are there. At Grendon, for example, the primary task of the institution is treatment but like every other prison, Grendon has to cope with problems of security and discipline. There is no logical reason why the security and discipline systems should clash with the institution's treatment task but it is easy to see how they might and certainly the treatment task cannot efficiently be carried out unless the clash is resolved, or rather unless the clash is transformed into something more like a harnessing arrangement.

A simple example: the training committee has the task of carving up the time available for training prison officers. How much time should be allocated to training in conducting small groups, which is a very important, indeed a key element, in Grendon treatment and how much on the more conventional prison officer duties, which are related to the more general issue of advancing the prison officer's career? Apparently a simple administrative problem, but it is clear what interests are involved and what the scope might be for rivalries and hostilities. Naturally, as a psychologist and therapist, I am anxious to advance the cause of training for treatment, but it would in fact be extremely bad psychology to ride roughshod over the other very legitimate and worthy interest.

At Holloway, it is reported that the job is mainly an exercise in public relations which means that before ever they can exercise their technical skills (the field of staff training here also provides a good example) psychologists need to be aware of pre-conceived ideas and suspicions about their own role. If these interpersonal tensions are not resolved then resistances remain, but it has increasingly become an expectation that psychological skills, whether these be intuitive, scientific, or combinations of both, are relevant in conceptualizing these situations and helping management get over them. For many years the small groups situation has, amongst other things, been seen as a microcosm whereby human interactions in a larger organizational setting might be revealed. Psychologists have played a large part in training in small groups for all grades of staff.

Whatever controversy there might be about whether psychologists can really judge people and interpersonal situations better than intelligent and sensitive non-psychologists, I hope there will be rather less doubt about the fact that psychologists do know rather more than the average about methodology and quantification. This is the other entrée a prison psychologist has into the field of helping with institutional management. Management needs information. To be meaningful information must ultimately be about quantity and statistics. Here we see a close interplay between management and the area of research mentioned above. If management is to be based on real information and not on stereotypes it needs research. At both simple and sophisticated levels it is increasingly common for psychologists in prison to help in precisely this direction. 'Monitoring' has become a very OK word with prison psychologists. Basically it means putting a figure on such questions as: 'what's going on?' 'what kind of people are we getting?' 'what kind of people do so and so?', etc. Typical examples are population monitoring and studies of absconding at Feltham Borstal.

The intelligent lay person is able to make perhaps quite penetrating global statements about social atmosphere. The psychologist is, or should be, able to make much more specific statements which can provide numerical indications of what is going on. For example, psychologists conducting an encounter group at the Girls' Borstal at Bullwood may or may not have made overall statements such as 'The groups seem to do these girls good'. What was more typical of the psychologist, in the scientific sense, is that they looked at a specific and easily countable indication of institutional atmosphere, such as the number of offences committed within the borstal, and ascertained that this had dropped for the treated group. This is typical of the way in which prison psychologists try to make objective and quantitative statements, rather than relying on impression and anecdote.

The quantitative-minded psychologist can test myths. For example, all social organizations seem to need a golden age myth, a myth that things were much better at some point in the distant past. Grendon is no exception. A frequent verbalized myth is that in the past (Grendon has existed for nineteen years) we had a much better type of inmate fed to us from the general prison system. It is easy to see the social usefulness of this myth. When things are not going too well, it is convenient to be able to say that we are not doing so well now because we have much worse material to work on than in the past. In point of fact psychologists at Grendon have continuously monitored the intake. All the objective quantifiable information available on Grendon inmates shows that the intake has been remarkably constant over the years. This has been frequently reiterated by psychologists but the myth persists. I am sure this is not the only example of a myth persisting despite evidence to the contrary. To understand why also needs psychological skills, but of a kind different from the statistical.

An interesting and more sophisticated piece of management-orientated research is the use of the simulation model at Grendon. This is based on the work of Poole and Szymankiewicz (1977). This in effect introduces a kind of board game model to institution management. An aspect of the real world is presented visually in simplified or stylized form so that the effects of a change anywhere in the system become readily visible. It is particularly relevant in a queuing situation, where a number of outside sources are seeking a smaller number of places. What for example would be the effect of the adoption of a particular rejection and/or acceptance policy? The simulation model gives a visual and quantitative answer. It is easy to see the potential value of this as an aid to management in policy-making.

Two recent projects carried out for local management at Birmingham illustrate the national relevance of some matters of local concern. Losses and destruction of prisoners' kit such as shirts and underwear were running at an alarmingly high rate in early 1979. The picture appeared to be the same in other local prisons which have a high turnover of prisoners and suffer from overcrowding and staff shortages. The project, in which the Psychology Unit collaborated with other departments within the prison, involved pinpointing through data analyses and interviews where kit losses and damage were likely to be occurring and then making recommendations aimed at rectifying the situation. A small working group, which included a member of the Psychology Unit, was responsible for looking into this issue. The group was aware that the complexity of the situation meant that it should be striving for improvements rather than a total solution. The required action, it seemed, would need to stem from an identification of the most straightforward changes of procedure which would generate the greatest improvements. Certain staff changes, the effects of which would be monitored, appeared to be the key.

The second project of national interest stemmed from concern expressed by the Governor about the level of overcrowding within the prison. The Psychology Unit was commissioned to analyse the prison's population with a view to identifying groups of prisoners for whom non-custodial sentences might have been more appropriate than imprisonment. The purpose of this was twofold. The Governor could be provided with information with which he could address magistrates, the judiciary, and the media to argue the case for non-custodial sentencing. Secondly, criteria for selecting prisoners potentially suitable for non-custodial dispersals could be developed and validated so that these criteria might be used as and when reductions in levels of overcrowding become feasible. This project has focused on an issue at the interface of a number of departments within the Home Office and consequently interest has been expressed by departments other than the Prison Department. The preliminary data have also been reported in the media as part of the general theme of concern to improve conditions within the penal system.

A very fundamental task of management is to see that the organization is properly staffed. Public concern about prisons results in the service taking long and critical looks at itself. An evolving service needs to be very aware of its recruitment of key management figures, in this case Assistant Governors, who are of course the Governors of the future. An elaborate and rigorous selection procedure has been devised for selection of Assistant Governors, and it has long been recognized that psychologists are part of the team that undertakes this selection.

To sum up this section, it is a reasonable statement that psychologists who work in penal institutions, at some point or other, have to involve themselves with the question: 'How should this place be run?', and they might have to fact this question on the level of overall institutional management or subsectional management or both. Indeed, as I have implied, whatever other work they will be doing they will have to face this question, and may well have to face the same question precisely arising out of other kinds of work which you might think of as more typically psychological. Furthermore they are likely to have to face this question at what might be called the experiential, relational, intuitive level, as well as at the methodological, quantitative level.

It is worth referring you to a recent publication, *Unlocking the Facts* (Home Office Prison Dept., 1979). This is a review of psychologists' research which has a bearing on managerial decisions.

Treatment

I use the word 'treatment' here rather than the more generic term 'clinical' to underline what I see to be a very important theme in the expansion of psychologists' functions within the Prison Department. It is very different now from those early days when psychologists were part of the medical services, and when it was assumed that the word treatment automatically meant medical-type activities. Certainly medical treatment remains medical treatment, the health of prison inmates must remain a prime responsibility of the Department and this is the job of doctors. I refer however to treatment which does not involve physical intervention, which in one way or another amounts to behaviour change or, if you prefer it, changes in attitudes and social perceptions. This is a psychological rather than a medical activity. Historically this has come to be increasingly accepted by psychologists themselves and the Department as a whole. To take a personal perspective—in the early 1960s I would have been seen as a somewhat exceptional figure amongst prison psychologists in doing a treatment task at Grendon, nowadays I am simply one amongst several psychologists fulfilling this kind of role. Behaviour therapy, behaviour modification, social skills training, group work, are clearly good examples of psychologically orientated treatment (whether the word 'treatment', with its medical implications, should continue to be used in this context is questionable, but it is hard to change people's verbal habits, so I shall continue to use it in this chapter).

Being very topical, the concept of 'Life and Social Skills Training' (LSST) currently exercises the interest of a good many prison psychologists and this is of course a commonsense expectation as lack of social skills is a very common characteristic of people who find their way to prison. Two recent examples of such training programmes undertaken by prison psychologists are the social skills training group for young male offenders at Feltham Borstal, and a problem drinkers' course for borstal trainees at HMYOC Glen Parva. It is worth pointing out that in these quoted examples psychologists in charge of the treatment also undertook some kind of quantitative evaluation of results albeit that the results are not always startling. Also deserving of mention in this context is pre-release training at Ashwell and Ranby, again with a built-in scheme for quantitative assessment.

Over the past few decades those of us who work in the penal field have become used to a long dreary series of negative findings in which it has been shown that various forms of treatment have no effect on reconviction rates and maybe it was not even reasonable to suppose that they would do. The trend in the direction of developing social skills and pre-release training places emphasis much more on what the person will actually be doing when she or he is released from penal confinement. Frankly I do not know as yet whether the new lines of approach will have any effect on reconviction rates but it does seem imperative that this is an area which should be looked at.

This outward going, beyond the prison gate, emphasis in treatment is well illustrated in Birmingham prison where the Psychology Unit has developed formal links with the Midland centre for forensic psychiatry, probation, and after-care service, the West Midlands police department, and the administration of a psychiatric hospital. Thus a large proportion of the treatment cases seen by the psychology unit are dealt with entirely in the community, recognizing the fact that treatment begun in a prison setting is more likely to be effective when carried out in the offender's natural environment.

Involvement in management is certainly important in the area of treatment. Often indeed psychologists are undertaking a particular form of treatment or training precisely because this has been asked for by management. Treatment is very often rather more than the situation of one therapist seeing one referral, although of course this does happen. In the penal setting, treatment in the sense of behaviour change very often means running a particular kind of regime no matter what the theoretical orientation of the regime organizer may be. Running regimes is self-evidently a management-type task and very often it may happen that no matter how great your therapeutic or clinical skills may be you will come unstuck if you do not acknowledge and deal with management-type problems. Here I will quote my own experience. I run a therapeutic community of about thirty young prisoners, many of them with very violent histories. Treatment in the sense of changing attitudes and behaviour operates through large and small group pressures. The point I want to make is that, in so far as I run the wing successfully the key skill is not the depth of clinical institutions into group dynamics. Rather it lies in the ability to run a particular kind of social organism. The situation is a society composed partly of young offenders, partly of prison officers, and my problem is how to keep the show going. I started by asking what was the nuclear situation from which all else, not only on my wing, at Grendon prison derives? I see this not in the plethora of professional, that is psychological and psychiatric skills which exist at Grendon, but in the officer/inmate relationship which perhaps distinguishes Grendon from all other penal institutions in this country. This relationship is, in a word, relaxed, natural, with a minimum of social distance, so that running a regime at Grendon means the kind of social engineering which will preserve this kind of relationship intact.

Since there is a good deal in conventional prison culture which maintains and reinforces the idea of distance between inmates and custodial staff it follows that being a Grendon therapist means establishing a certain kind of culture among people whose experience and/or training orientates them to a completely opposite culture. I mentioned the crucial importance of reduction of social distances; this must mean that hierarchical assumptions are strongly questioned or even declared irrelevant. Everybody is in a state of permanent accountability irrespective of their official position or rank, status is no defence against public criticism. The very mechanics of the system require that everyone in it must accept the role of therapeutic agent, this means both uniformed staff who might conventionally see themselves as fulfilling a custodial role, and even more importantly, inmates who might well imagine that they are there to act in the purely passive role. Even from this brief description it is easy to see how anxieties and hostilities might be aroused all along the line. For the therapist, whether psychologist or psychiatrist, there is nothing for it but to acknowledge that there is no division between management and therapy skills. Both roles involve listening, encouraging the airing of feelings, picking up unspoken messages by using observation skills. The therapist must in fact let the culture do his work for him, since getting people to trust each other more, breaking down barriers and so on, can rarely if ever be achieved by direction or exhortation. Obviously clinical skills are important but in practice it is far more important that the therapist acquires skill in a management style of democratic team work. Without this the most penetrating clinical and therapeutic skills would be not much more than white elephants. For a fuller discussion see Marcus (1978).

We cannot discuss the question of treating incarcerated offenders without acknowledging that ethical issues are involved. Psychologists cannot claim any monopoly of wisdom or indeed any special expertise in resolving ethical issues but the obligation is on them as on everybody else to be sensitive to such issues. Where, as is for example the case at Birmingham prison, much of the treatment activity is carried out within a broadly behavioural framework, psychologists so engaged have had to develop a sensitivity to the kinds of objection which are often voiced about behavioural techniques. As against the argument that nobody is forced to have such treatment without his own consent, it has been urged that no imprisoned offender can give truly free consent to any procedure of intervention such as behaviour modification. As you will probably know, it has also been said that because behaviourism provides particularly powerful techniques for changing behaviour it can be used to manipulate prisoners against their will. There is no ethically watertight answer to this, since neither psychologists nor anybody else can get away from the basic fact that people are by and large in prison against their own will, but care is always taken to ensure the informed consent of clients undergoing such treatment, and their freedom to opt out of therapy is fundamental and unconditional. Incidentally, substantially the same issues arise when, as at Grendon, inmates are offered the therapeutic community model of treatment. Grendon is generally seen as a very relaxed and permissive prison but in point of fact peer group pressures can be very intense and arouse the same kind of ethical issues as are encountered with behaviour therapy. Here again the most we can do, ethically speaking, is to set out the options honestly at the beginning, defining boundaries clearly and giving people the absolute freedom to terminate the treatment if they so wish.

Prison psychologists engaged in treatment are pretty certain to come up against interprofessional issues. I have said above, somewhat cavalierly, that treatment which does not involve physical intervention is a psychological and not a medical activity. I feel fairly sure about this but it would be sanguine to expect doctors to accept the same view. Basically doctors and psychologists, by virtue of their different training, would tend to have different views of disordered behaviour. Doctors often see this sort of behaviour in terms of an 'illness' model. It is easy to see how this comes about — certain behaviour is highly deviant, causes much suffering to the individual concerned and to other people, and thus is easily assimilated to the sickness model. One must respect this point of view, but the fact remains that psychologists often look for an understanding of disordered behaviour to factors within the individual's previous history and present circumstances, so that the concept of illness becomes redundant.

The skills needed to detect and remove abnormal behaviour are not analogous to those used by a doctor when diagnosing and treating illness. For a more extended discussion on the inappropriateness of sickness language in conceptualizing abnormal behaviour see Ullman and Krasner (1975). Such differences in modes of conceptualization do not in practice have to lead to conflict but it is very necessary to be aware of them and develop some kind of *modus vivendi*, if only agreeing to differ where psychologists and doctors work together in some kind of treatment programme. Ethical considerations alone demand that the interests of treatment come uppermost. Even setting aside the ethical paramouncy of the client's interest (it is deliberate that I use the work client or inmate rather than patient), it is notorious that interpersonal tensions, such as rivalry between professional groups, can wholly disrupt the primary task of an organization. On the whole doctors and psychologists work amicably, but frictions do arise, and it is hoped that these will be minimized when a planned joint consultation machinery is set up. On the whole both sides manage to live with the fact that the other side uses a different kind of language.

In summary, prison psychologists engaged in treatment cover a wide spectrum. On the one hand there is behaviour therapy with individuals, on the other hand (of course no value judgement is implied) there is experiential-type treatment with groups. It may be dangerous to try and impose a unity on such diversity but I would guess there is a common element in that we tend to set out as target criteria some kind of change in behaviour or social interaction, and I think this is as true for those of us engaged in group work as for those engaged in behaviour therapy. This kind of approach is in contrast to the kind of therapy that aims at insight or deep self-awareness. Long and sad experience has taught us that there is little to be gained from converting criminals into criminals who understand why they did it! Taking a historical look, I think it true to say that over the years, or even decades, this has represented a real shift in the interests of prison psychologists, from insight-orientated to behaviour-shaping types of therapy, but this is a bit of an armchair speculation and I cannot pretend to speak for eighty or so colleagues.

Staff training

First let me make the bald statement that prison psychologists are heavily involved in the training of prison staff at both local and national levels.

The psychologists' involvement in staff training is only a subheading of the more general topic of psychologists' involvement in management. I will enter the topic via my own preoccupation, that is, the issue of staff identification. Organizations, including penal establishments, cannot fulfil their primary tasks unless the staff are attuned to the values of management. Adequate training is a necessary pre-condition for such identification (which does not alter the fact that there are other equally compelling reasons for training staff). Management, whether it be administrative or technical, may have excellent ideas about types of regime, treatment programmes, etc., but there is a good deal of chastening experience that there is effectively no chance of such ideas getting off the ground if there is a wide divergence of values between management and front-line staff. Staff training in its broadest sense is essential if such divergences are to be avoided. I have mentioned above the crucial importance of the prison officer in implementing the therapeutic regime in Grendon and I have no doubt that similar statements could be made about other penal institutions. If prison officers feel themselves to be inadequately trained to carry out the task of their institution their reaction not unreasonably is that management is indifferent to their needs, is in effect too remote. From here it is not a very long step to arguing 'if management doesn't care about us why should we care about management?' Here we have the beginnings of a situation in which basic staff feel no identification with management goals. There is no need to labour the disastrous results of this: there are many ways of sabotaging management objectives, apart from downright insubordination. It is of course universally recognized that the provision of staff training programmes is a *sine qua non* for carrying out organizational tasks, and the Prison Department is only one of innumerable organizations which have recognized this. The physical and visible manifestation of this is the presence of the Prison Service College at Wakefield. The sheer growth in its physical size over the years is only the tangible aspect of the growth in the complexity of its programme. What is relevant from our point of view is that as the Prison Service College (it has had different names during the course of its history) has expanded so has the psychological presence within it. In the early 1950s a solitary psychologist (myself) who belonged primarily to Wakefield Prison had, so to speak, one foot in the Imperial Training School as it was then called. Nowadays a whole psychology unit is stationed within the college, psychologists collaborate with tutorial staff on formulating objectives for staff training and on the design of evaluative procedures that are related to course objectives and which enable students to carry out some self-evaluation of their learning. On the topic of evaluation we shall have more to say when we talk about research. In the meantime it is worth labouring the point that at the very centre of prison service staff training it has been found essential to put a Psychology Unit and this is as it should be. However psychologists differ in their own theoretical orientations it can scarcely be denied that the psychological field of expertise includes the learning process and motivation factors associated with it.

Talking about learning leads fairly naturally on to a discussion of the work of psychologists in regard to social skills or, to fill out the topic somewhat, life and social skills (LSST) with the closely allied topic of pre-release training. Raising this topic will be useful in showing the close relationship betwen staff training, treatment, and institutional management issues. LSST is attractive to psychologists because its basic premises involve comparatively simple statements which satisfy our need for scientific parsimony. Instead of 'high-falutin' global statements about human personality we start off with the basic statement that in order to live it is necessary to acquire skills to do with people, and skills to do with objects. Hence life skills may be divided into social and practical skills, or perhaps rather we should think of a continuum. This simple statement has its attractions because it fairly easily leads into a programme of treatment or training. If coping with life needs certain kinds of skills then in devising a treatment programme we are helped by the literature on the acquisition of skills. Work on learning indicates that a skill can be taught, it can be improved with practice and suitable feedback, it can be generalized to a variety of situations. It involves the smooth sequence of actions which are directed towards a goal. Coaching, modelling, rehearsing, and feedback then become crucial. All (but it is of course a big all) that needs to be done is to devise the paradigm real-life situations which are to be learnt. Managerially speaking, what is of interest is that at a high level, that is that branch of Head Office organization which is concerned with regime development, there is an interest in LSST and, perhaps most significantly, a realization that psychologists are the appropriate experts to call in to advise on the implications of its implementation. This is a systematic rather than an *ad hoc* use of psychologists.

It is worth, at this stage, talking about social skills and pre-release training in relation to what I call the deprofessionalization of treatment. (I shall shortly also be talking on this theme in the different context of Grendon treatment.) The psychologist's viewpoint, which is clearly one with which the department agrees, is quite simply that prison officers are the most appropriate staff to run such courses. It is felt that this extension of the role of prison officers is intrinsically highly desirable, quite irrespective of any follow-up effect (that is, on reconviction rate) which such training might have. It is intrinsically desirable because of a rise in staff morale, a better feeling throughout the institution, a lowering of social distances and a feeling of identification with management goals. This is really not much more than the commonsense expectation. Numerically the greatest number of face-to-face contacts within the prison are those between the prison officer and the inmate. Anything which improves these lessens the overall amount of institutional tension, which is a good and worthwhile goal in itself. When I talk about the deprofessionalization of treatment this is in no sense a denigration of the prison officer's role. It is meant simply as a denial of the long-held superstition that treatment can only be carried out by people with the right kind of letters after their name. However, neither prison officers nor any other group can be expected to undertake courses of treatment or training without themselves receiving training and it is pleasing to report that within this field psychologists have really come into their own in the sense of being perceived as the appropriate training agents. For example, in the well-established pre-release courses at Ranby and Ashwell conducted by officers, psychologists have undertaken a training needs analysis, listing the needs of instructors and a series of objectives, in effect devising a miniteachers' training course for officers undertaking this task, and carrying out both basic courses and developmental courses for already experienced officers. I see this as a very significant example illustrating significant trends in the prison department's way of thinking. An important piece of inmate training is being carried out by a section of staff who in days gone by would have been seen as fulfilling almost a purely custodial role, and psychologists are seen as the most appropriate professional group for providing the training support.

One can perhaps best illustrate a unity of theme by switching to a completely different setting and still seeing the same kind of mechanism at work. At Grendon the treatment set-up looks much more conventionally professional in so far as there are a lot more professionals around, both psychologists and medical. Here the goals are the more vague and global goals generally assumed in psychotherapy rather than the much more specific areas which are worked at in social skills, life skills, and pre-release programmes. Nevertheless, it is still very much a case of the essence of the treatment being carried out by officers. The nuclear treatment situation is not a dyadic doctor/patient interview but the small group conducted by an officer, and perhaps equally important are the innumerable informal officer/inmate contacts. At this stage it is not necessary to stress how vital the officer role is in maintaining the therapeutic ethos at Grendon but again it cannot be done without adequate training and support and again psychologists play a crucial role in trying to devise the most appropriate training programme and offering the most appropriate form of training, both experiential and didactic. Here is a field in which there is scope for fruitful co-operation between doctors and psychologists. But examples could easily be multiplied of psychologists as training persons. Feltham Borstal, for example, is another place where psychologists run their own courses in training officers to be social skills operators, and on interviewing skills. Difficulties here are those faced by teachers everywhere — explaining the complex and being proficient in teaching skills. Interestingly enough, the psychology unit here reports that management has a kind of natural expectation that psychologists possess these skills.

In summary it can be said that staff training, apart from its intrinsic desirability, has been invaluable as a means of facilitating dialogue between psychologists and management at both institutional and national level. In the earlier days there was a good deal of puzzlement as to what psychologists could do in prisons and whether in fact they could do anything and such puzzlement easily shaded off into hostility. No-one can doubt, however, that effective management needs adequate staff training and it is almost equally self-evident that psychologists have the most relevant expertise in this field.

Research

It will be helpful to begin this section with a straight quote from the review of the Prison Psychological Services referred to above. Under the heading 'Research and Evaluation' this document writes:

Psychologists undertake a number of research and evaluative studies in order that their contributions to the understanding of operational problems and institutional processes are founded on a sound empirical basis. These can range from straightforward fact finding enquiries to professional research tasks which may appear to have no immediate practical application but which, as in the case of catastrophe theory, can be seen to be of considerable potential relevance.

This quotation makes two useful points, firstly that prison psychologists' research goes through the whole spectrum of straightforward fact-finding to complex interactive designs, and secondly, that research is closely bound up with management needs. Almost every psychology unit in the penal system has at one time or another carried out operational research of varying degrees of complexity. The word 'operational' is important here since increasingly psychologists have seen their research function closely bound up with their function as an aid to management (in earlier days there was a much stronger tendency for psychologists to do research simply because this was interesting to psychologists). The idea of research being a means of providing information and advice to management is neatly illustrated in the example of the women's prison at Holloway where psychologists have provided information from surveys on such matters as the care provisions made for the children of mothers in prison, the levels of disturbance in borstal girls, the criminal history of prostitutes, and the occurrence of fire-raising incidents in the prison.

A very long list could be made of researches carried out by psychology units in the prison service, but I want rather to show how the psychologist's inclination towards research ties in with the needs of institutional management, and indeed *above* institutional level, via the Adult Offender and the Young Offender Psychology Units, and in service-wide tasks called for by relevant headquarters divisions.

It is a link which has become stronger by an evolutionary process over the years. In earlier days where the role of psychologists was much less certain (I would not pretend that it is all that certain now) there was much more of an atmosphere, at least amongst the more scientifically minded of prison psychologists, of a need to do research for its own sake, in the interest of scientific enquiry. I am not saying that such 'pure' research does not go on now, and certainly would not belittle its value (at Grendon for example quite a lot of work is done on the internal structure and multivariate analysis of psychometric tests, which is probably of not much interest to anyone but psychologists) but it is a fact that the development of activity has shifted towards operationally directed research and this has quite clearly been a parallel development with the perception of psychologists as a management resource.

Increasingly there is a general realization that many questions in the realm of management eventually boil down to number questions. If you want to know the answer to such questions as: 'What is the atmosphere like in this institution?' 'Did such and such a course of treatment for inmates do any good?' 'Was this staff training course of any use?' then eventually your question comes down to the question—'how much?' Or 'what kind of a figure can you put on it?' Psychologists do at least think in terms of number at all levels from simple head-counting up to complicated mathematical models such as linear regression techniques. They tend to push their colleagues into asking the sort of questions which can be eventually answered in terms of number. Certainly management is concerned to evaluate what it is doing, and since psychologists are scientifically and numerically conscious, there is here an obvious confluence of interest.

It is hoped that psychologists are an important source of help in the question 'What shall we evaluate?'. It is a formidable question because in the complex interplay of a social organism it is not always easy to find things that are both quantifiable and of general interest (it is easy to find simple pieces of numerical information which nobody thinks very exciting, it is also easy to ask profound questions which nobody can quantify). For a long time, and to some extent this is still the case, it was held that the key piece of evaluation was reconviction rate. The only 'real' way of assessing the value of the regime or system of treatment was to demand that it reduced the reconviction rate of those going through it. Typical experimental design would be the comparison of the reconviction rate say, after a two-year follow-up, of a treatment group as against a matched controlled group that had had no treatment. This was certainly worth investigating and still is, but the sad truth is that the criminological literature is full of examples of negative treatment results. Even quoting the examples mentioned in this paper there is no reason to believe that the group-orientated regime at Grendon reduces reconviction, and the same thing almost certainly has to be said about the life-skills training mentioned above. Surveying the literature as a whole on reconviction the melancholy truth seems to be emerging that the number of positive studies is very small and, perhaps more ominously, the better controlled the experimental design the less likelihood there is of a significant difference to arise. (I should make it clear here that I am not referring only to the British penal system.)

Maybe the search for something that will reduce reconviction is entirely chimerical, and it is not reasonable to expect that anything done for a man while he is in prison will be carried over when he goes into the quite different situation outside, which might well have been criminogenic in the first place. For an argument that reconviction is not a suitable measure of success of a treatment regime see Gunn et al. (1978). However, many people feel a need to continue regimes or modes of treatment despite proof that it does not reduce reconviction, and this is not necessarily an unscientific stance provided other means of evaluation are suggested. (I am far from saying that scientific stances are the only valid stances, and would be quite prepared to justify, for example, the continuance of the Grendon regime with extra-scientific arguments.) It might be argued that a regime is worth continuing because it makes for a better atmosphere in the prison, with more normal staff/inmate relationships; it in some way improves the personality of inmates even if it does not reduce their likelihood of reconviction; it improves staff morale, and so on. These are perfectly valid arguments but people making such claims still need to evaluate them quantitatively.

We may be challenged—what is the point of the treatment prison at Grendon? If we judge by the criterion of reconviction, we have to admit that on the whole (there are qualifications) Grendon does not reduce reconviction. It can be argued that Grendon is a civilized and humane prison and that this is quite sufficient justification in itself. Personally I think this is a valid argument, but it is not a scientific argument, and we are at present concerned with the topic of research, and even the claim that Grendon is civilized and humane needs to be scientifically evaluated. Here we come to the question of criterion consciousness, the identification of the criterion by which effects are measured. Psychologists at Grendon have concerned themselves with finding quantitative backing for the moralistic opinion that Grendon is a good prison. We find for example that although Grendon has a more than averagely trouble-prone population (I mean trouble in the sense of committing prison offences), the number of disciplinary offences is in fact comparatively small compared with other prisons and with the behaviour of the same men in their previous institutions. Again, it has been possible to show that over the years the level of drug administration has dropped dramatically, which is very relevant quantitative information in a regime which purports to be a therapeutic community, and where the pressure is on people to take responsibility for their own actions and work on their own self-change without passively trying to let drugs do it for them. A number of other quantitative indices point in the same direction. The point we have stressed is that even value judgements need criteria to point them up. We have had to sell the point of view that little bits of numerical data, and the relationship between them, can in fact point up a very complex and dynamic social reality.

Another example of using disciplinary reports as a piece of operational research is their use as a criteria in assessing the value of an encounter group at the girls' borstal at Bullwood Hall. Here is a simple piece of quantitative information—the eight weeks prior to the group the weekly average number of reports per girl was 0.73, in the eight weeks after the group the corresponding figure was 0.19. Obviously this simple but telling piece of information is not the same thing as describing the rich and tempestuous occurrences that usually characterize encounter groups, but operationally speaking the important thing is that it shows the group was probably doing something to its members or, more accurately, as a result of the group they had decided to do something about themselves. Looked at in terms of the relationship between treatment, research, and management the implications are that something has been found that it is hoped could lead eventually to a reduction in what is said to be the prison department's highest rate of borstal offending.

Examples could be multiplied of the psychologist's way of using measurement to tell management what is going on, for example psychometric tests, tailormade questionnaires for particular projects, official records, consumers' responses to the effects of staff training courses and so on. A very neat statement of the psychologist's research job in relation to management has been made by the senior psychologist at Feltham Borstal. This is so universally true of prison psychologists that it is worth quoting his words:

> management research is almost exclusively institution bound: population monitoring, studies of absconding, security procedures, style of inmate training . . . . Whilst it is obviously necessary to attempt to comply with the rigours of theoretical research, this must be balanced against the practical dictates of applied research . . . . The final report must be tailored to suit the reader; which may mean rendering simple the psychologically or statistically complex.

This could not be bettered as the statement of prison psychologists' research activity and its relation to institution management.

CONCLUSION

The above summary is of course not an exhaustive statement of what prison psychologists do. I am aware, for example, of having said nothing about individual inmate assessment. This is not to deny that it goes on or to belittle its importance, but rather to reflect the feelings of the review team whose report is referred to above. They considered that although individual-centred tasks would always remain important, psychologists' main functions should be organization and system-centred.

You may feel that this summary of psychologists' work in the prison service could be repeated, *mutatis mutandis*, for psychologists working elsewhere, and there obviously is no need to make any apologies if this is the case. One final historical comment — over the years prison psychologists have talked and agonized endlessly on the topic of 'what is the role of the psychologist?', inevitably, perhaps, since as was said above they are a group with no statutory duties, so that the topic of their role is bound to be unstructured. Such discussions have at times tended to verge on the metaphysical, but the gist of this paper has been to try and show you that, though the question is by no means fully answered, the answer is moving towards the empirical and the pragmatic. That is to say the role of the prison psychologist is that area where what psychologists can do most nearly resembles what management wants done.

ACKNOWLEDGEMENTS

I am indebted to a good many of my colleagues in the composition of this chapter, but special acknowledgement is due to the following whose opinions and findings I have quoted liberally:

Peter Shapland, Director of Prison Psychological Services
Eric Cullen, Senior Psychologist, HM Borstal, Bullwood Hall
Phillipa Low, Principal Psychologist, HM Prison Holloway
Howard Sleap and Smish Dinnage, Senior Psychologists, HM Prison Grendon
Clive Hollins, Senior Psychologist, HM Borstal Feltham
Derek Perkins, Principal Psychologist, HM Prison Birmingham
Mary McMurran, Psychologist, HMYOC Glen Parva
Keith Baxter, Principal Psychologist, Prison Service College
Barry Conlin, Senior Psychologist, HM Prison Gartree

This Chapter is published with the permission of the Prison Department Home Office, but the views expressed are the author's own.

REFERENCES

Clark, D. (1965). *Administrative Therapy*, London: Tavistock.
Gunn, J., Robertson, G., Dell, S., and Way, C. (1978). *Psychiatric Aspects of Imprisonment*, London: Academic Press.
Home Office Prison Department (1980). *Review of the Prison Psychological Service*, Home Office.
Home Office Prison Department (1979). *Unlocking the Facts*, Directorate of Psychological Services, Home Office.
Jones, M. (1968). *Social Psychiatry in Practice*, Harmondsworth: Pelican.
Marcus, B. (1978). 'Small group work in psychiatric prisons', in *Training in Small Groups*, Babington-Smith, B. and Farrell, B. A. (eds), Oxford: Pergamon.
Poole, T. and Symankiewicz, J. (1977). *Using Simulation to Solve Problems*, Maidenhead: McGraw-Hill.
Rapaport, R. N. (1960). *Community as Doctor*, London: Tavistock.
Ullmann, L. D. and Krasner, L. (1975). *A Psychological Approach to Abnormal Behaviour*, Englewood Cliffs, New Jersey: Prentice-Hall.

Psychology in Practice
Edited by S. Canter and D. Canter
© 1982, John Wiley & Sons, Ltd.

CHAPTER 7

PSYCHOLOGY AT WORK IN EDUCATION

Keith J. Topping
Educational Psychologist
Calderdale Psychological Service, Halifax

When on the first day of my appointment I duly appeared, top hat and striped trousers in the doorway of the Education Officer's private room, asking, very humbly asking, for my terms of reference, I was greeted in his Aberdonian accent with a curt 'Young man, ye've all London at your feet . . . go away and draw 'em up yerself'.

This was the first workaday experience of the first applied educational psychologist, Cyril Burt, who was appointed on a part-time basis by the London County Council in 1913. His sphere of operation was to be the whole of London, and in due course his role became largely that of researcher and adviser to the education department, resulting in classic studies such as *The Young Delinquent* (1925).

The fifty years that followed saw an initially slow but accelerating growth in the numbers of educational psychologists, whose functioning became enmeshed in the accompanying spread of special schools for 'defective' children and of Child Guidance Clinics. The long-established medical model of internal causation, and the equally long-established bureaucratic model of heirarchical categorization, came to dominate, and psychologists resorted increasingly to the application of that small part of psychology which is psychometrics. Educational psychologists became ancillary technicians, used by doctors for routine preliminary 'diagnostic' tests, and by administrators for the routine labelling and disposal of children.

However, as the profession began to establish itself, it became evident that practice along these lines was quite inadequate to cope with changing social reality. From an established base, educational psychology was able to become more assertive and more self-critical and from the 1960s onwards, acceleration in the rate of change in the profession became the order of the day (Topping, 1977).

Currently there are about a thousand educational psychologists working for local education authorities in England and Wales. (The structure is rather different in Scotland.) Ways of working often vary greatly from one Psychological Service to the next, with particular differences apparent between County Services, often spread over large and mainly rural geographical areas, and urban Services, which are often operating in much more compact areas with more obvious and tangible, if frequently less soluble, problems.

The national (and indeed international) trend is certainly towards diversification in role and function. In the pages that follow, descriptions will be given of psychology at work in education in five different forms, namely: (i) individual casework; (ii) in-service training; (iii) consultation on organizational issues; (iv) research and evaluation; and (v) policy formulation. It is, however, worth emphasizing that the five subdivisions used here are in no way rigid. On the contrary, the boundaries between ways of working are often blurred.

INDIVIDUAL CASEWORK

Most educational psychologists spend between 40 per cent and 80 per cent of their working time dealing in some way with the problems of individual children, although this varies considerably between different psychologists and different services. Individual casework is the largest single component of the educational psychologist's job, and is likely to remain so for some years yet.

The label covers a multitude of different approaches, however. In recent years, the term has lost a good part of its quasi-medical connotation pertaining to the 'assessment and treatment' of the child by the psychologist himself. Data-gathering by observation in the situation where the problem presents itself is increasing, and the old practice of testing and interviewing the child in an office is declining. Information-collecting and negotiation with the adults responsible for the day-to-day care of the child is now likely to take up far more time than actual contact with the child; indeed, in a number of cases, the psychologist might never see the child at all.

The 'problem' presented is rarely seen by the psychologist to be totally 'within' the child, and the average educational psychologist has a much more social, interactionist, and organizational perspective than hitherto. In almost all casework, therefore, the first step is to establish a clear definition of the problem, and its 'ownership'. What is the child said to *do*, which is creating stress, anxiety, disturbance, etc., and to whom is this behaviour a problem? (The child himself may not regard it as at all bothersome.)

Secondly, corroboration of the existence of this behaviour is required. A more precise definition and systematic recording of the 'problem' may well radically alter the perceptions of the complainants as to its nature and seriousness.

Thirdly, the psychologist will consider what changes are necessary. These will include changes in the behaviour of the adults surrounding the child as well as in the behaviour of the child, and probably also changes in the development of physical resources. The educational psychologist might set 'objectives' for change, which he would hope to see achieved within a stipulated time-span. Intervention and negotiation of the implementation of changes are then attempted. Very often only a portion of the desired changes are realistically accomplished, as will be seen in the example below.

Subsequently the psychologist will follow up the case, partly to ensure there are no undesirable side-effects which require dealing with, and partly to evaluate the effectiveness of the intervention.

While the elaboration of these five stages may strike the reader as largely self-evident and more than a little redundant, nevertheless they will be worth considering in the light of the examples that follow. It will be apparent that when the educational psychologist adopts a problem-solving rather than a 'clinical' role, the question of 'who is the client?' often becomes unanswerable, if not completely meaningless. Working in this way is not without its insecurities, one of which is the need to make far more sweeping value judgements than hitherto. Thus it is perhaps worth emphasizing that there are three stages which should occur in casework *before* the psychologist attempts to intervene directly. While this may not result in psychologists' acquiring great reputations for reacting instantly to crises, it does mean that some glimmer of their social science training becomes discernible in their routine practice.

The case of Michael

Michael is 10-years-old, lives in the centre of the most socio-economically deprived area of town, and attends the neighbourhood Junior School. The head of the school is full of energy, dramatic in all that he does, and a fine teacher. He is also tense and overactive, and the multiple pressures over the years have worn him down. Now he suffers from heart trouble, and plans to take early retirement. His reactions have been a little erratic of late.

The Psychological Service has had a lot of involvement in the school in the past, and a few of the staff have been on the Service's in-service training courses. So in Michael's case, the psychologist's first surprise comes when it is learnt that the head has referred the boy, not to the Psychological Service, but to the local psychiatrist, of whom it is known that the head has a poor opinion. The head's lengthy and histrionic letter of referral complains of bizarre and aggressive behaviour, impulsiveness, and Michael's total unawareness of the consequences of his actions, all of which is said to have been going on for the last two and a half years. Why, then, has no-one heard about it before?

The psychiatrist sees Michael, says that his main problem is being bullied by other children at school, that psychiatric treatment would not accomplish anything, and that the boy should be sent to a residential school for maladjusted children. (The authority has no day schools or units for disruptive children of this age.) The psychologist has some difficulty following the thread of this argument. Fortunately the Education Department administrative officers have learnt to ignore educational recommendations which emanate from non-educationalists, and their reaction is automatically to refer Michael to the psychologist.

Meanwhile the headteacher, under great pressure and in despair, has suspended Michael from school. It is completely unclear whether Michael is a behaviour problem at home or not. The headteacher says the parents say he is, but other educational officials the parents have seen say that the parents say he is not. There is also a feeling that antagonism and mutual recrimination are building up between the school and the parents.

So who is the client? And where do you start? The initial objective set by the psychologist is to get Michael back into school. Even in this fraught situation, the problem-specification and data-collection stages are not to be omitted — indeed, they become even more important.

But this first task is complicated by two factors. One is that the psychiatrist has told the headteacher of the 'medical' recommendation for residential special school, a straw which the head grasps eagerly, although if he wanted to stop to think, the head would realize how little weight that carried with the decision-makers in the Education Department. While the head dreams of keeping Michael on permanent suspension until the boy gets 'sent away', no-one knows what the parents think about the boy going to residential special school — neither the psychiatrist nor anyone else appears to have thought to ask them.

The other complicating factor is that the local authority have no agreed policy on the suspension of pupils. Draft policies have been produced, but were never put to the Education Committee because the officers decided they preferred the flexibility of dealing with each suspension on an *ad hoc* basis, by relying on 'goodwill' and personal relationships. So there are no rules in the suspension game, and the psychologist is left in a managerial vacuum.

Step one in achieving the initial objective is clearly to soothe and reassure the head, listen for a long time, and make him feel the psychologist is going to be supportive to the school. If heavy-handed action by the administration precipitates another heart-attack in the man, all the children in the school would suffer.

A little more is learnt about the boy. His mechanical reading skills are good but comprehension is weaker, his fine motor skills are poor, and his concentration is dreadful. There are some suspicions that his father batters the boy. Two main ploys are used by the psychologist, both loosely based on a combination of learning theory and organizational considerations. One of these is gently to work into the discussion reminders to the head that if a child has special educational needs, this has to be formally stated by an educational psychologist before any effective recommendations can be made. As the psychologist is professionally bound to assess the problem behaviour *in situ* before any conclusions can be made, it follows that the child will need to be readmitted to school. (Or, to put it more crudely, if the head is to have any hope of getting rid of Michael, he will have to accept him back into school first.)

The other tack is to point out to the head that the boy's behaviour at home is not definitely known to be highly disruptive, and parental reaction is decidedly ambiguous, so even if Michael is found to have special educational needs, for the £8000 per annum cost of a place in a residential special school the lad could practically have his own personal teacher locally. There are many children with behavioural difficulties in the area, and the setting up of a small unit for such children in a mobile classroom attached to the school would be far more economically viable, would give employment to local teachers, and would enhance the size and status of the school. In fact, although the psychologist does not say this, the chances of establishing such a unit in the near future are negligible. Nevertheless, this serves to divert a debilitated teacher from the immediate crises on to more futuristic notions of positive planning, and encourages him to regard Michael's behaviour as a golden opportunity rather than a source of stress.

At the start of the following week, Michael is readmitted to school. Having achieved the initial objective, the psychologist now starts problem specification and data collection. But there is a need to ensure that the psychologist does not alienate the parents, and come to be perceived by them as yet another authoritarian bureaucrat. A gentle letter is sent to the parents, suggesting that the psychologist is sure they would not object if he saw Michael in school, and fixing a date to see them subsequently to discuss Michael's educational needs and see what help can be offered by the authority. The psychologist also checks the boy's school medical records. There is no history of birth trauma or developmental abnormality, and Michael seems, so far as is recorded, to be a perfect physical specimen.

Observation of Michael in school is undertaken. The psychologist fully expects to find that the boy presents very few problems in objective terms, and that the whole episode is one of teacher overreaction under stress, confounded by inappropriate initial referral and subsequent mishandling by another agency.

During two visits to school, the psychologist observes the child in class. There is often an initial Hawthorne effect in such situations, but school-children quickly get used to being scrutinized by arbitrary intruders into their classroom, and soon come to ignore them. Michael is also observed, unknown to him, in the assembly hall and in the playground. There are also long discussions with the classteacher, who has already been keeping highly detailed records of Michael's behaviour, as well as notes of the various strategies that have been tried to improve it. Such strategies had included seating Michael in isolation from other children, seating him next to other children who presented good models of acceptable behaviour, providing carefully selected work tasks of great interest and exactly the right level of difficulty, repeatedly reminding him of a few simple personal rules of good conduct, using a simple reward system with house points (which Michael likes) as reinforcers, and so on. All of these have proved ineffective. The classteacher himself is impressive; a big, burly man, with a firm but very caring manner, who runs an orderly and well-organized but lively and stimulating classroom. The psychologist realizes that the Michael episode is rather more than a flash in the pan.

A consistent stream of disruptive behaviour from Michael is observed to occur in a wide range of situations. The boy is extremely overactive; constantly out-of-seat and attention-seeking. He is continually tense and fidgeting. All his perpetual movements are quick, jerky, and impulsive. Sometimes he seems completely unaware of his surroundings, at other times he overreacts violently to the slightest stimulation. He shows little sign of empathy with, or responsiveness to, other human beings. In and amongst he pokes a pencil in a girl's face, kicks another two children, and digs his elbow in the ribs of a fourth—and all this in full view of the teacher. Instructions from the teacher are either ignored or forgotten in a span of seconds. In summary (but be careful with those labels) Michael presents as hyperactive, inconsequential, impulsive, egocentric, distractible, and aggressive. Some of his behaviour seems deliberately manipulative, but most of it appears to be entirely beyond his control.

Subsequently the psychologist takes Michael out of the classroom to see how the boy will function in a one-to-one situation. Michael functions pretty much the same. His egocentricity is emphasized by his grossly immature tirade against all his persecutors in school. An attempt is made to discover if any specific learning difficulties exist which might be relevant to his behaviour. Michael sprints unrestrainably through a series of tests and tasks. Nevertheless, he performs at a level at least average for a child of his age on tests of receptive language and abstract visual motor skills. He does a little less well on reading and fine motor skills, but at the end of the day the psychologist finds nothing which might impede the boy's learning, other than his grossly inefficient general learning behaviour.

Somewhat sobered, and armed with the data from the school, the psychologist visits Michael's home in the evening, to enable him to see both parents and all the children in that situation. On arrival, it transpires that the father is not going to be there after all, and his absence is unexplained. The house is fairly squalid: broken windows covered with cardboard, lumps missing from the doors, very little furniture, all rather greasy, with a big colour TV and half a set of encyclopaedias on the mantlepiece. The mother is surrounded by an innumerable brood of grubby, manipulative, tempestuous children. She looks young, probably in her early twenties, and responds in a very immediate, erratic way to the children's demands. With a carefully non-threatening approach from the psychologist, the mother is pleasant and co-operative, and by no means lacking in flashes of insight. What the psychologist says sinks in fairly slowly, but this is hardly surprising when she has already been confused so thoroughly by other 'helping' agencies.

Is Michael a problem at home? Well, says his mother, he's a bit more of a problem than the others, but then he's the eldest. He plays me up a bit, but his dad can 'make him do'. Our conversation is punctuated by the odd altercation while Michael, his siblings, and various of the neighbourhood children squabble and fight outside. However, the psychologist observes nothing to contradict the mother's view—Michael does seem just like the others. The household is obviously disorganized and inconsistent in patterns of management, but so are many others in the area. In relation to the local cultural norm, there are no signs of any great 'pathology' in the family.

By now the psychologist is fairly convinced that a residential special school would not be appropriate for Michael, since the problem is mainly in the school context rather than the domestic one. However, Michael is not satisfactorily educable in an ordinary classroom, that is certain. The ordinary school would need additional physical and human resources to manage Michael and protect other children, and however cost-effective this might be, there is no realistic chance of the LEA making these available in the near future. The psychologist explains all this frankly to Michael's mother, and goes on to describe the residential schools for 'maladjusted' children used by the authority, and their advantages and disadvantages. The mother is made aware that there is virtually no research evidence to suggest that children do any better in such schools than if they stayed in the ordinary school. Finally, the psychologist says to the mother that the short-term options are residential school or staying in the existing ordinary school. The possibility of more appropriate special help locally in a year's time is irrelevant, since by then Michael will be on the verge of transfer to secondary school. If his mother wanted Michael to go to a 'boarding school', the psychologist would not stand in the way of such a course, although he could not recommend it whole-heartedly.

The mother does not really know what to think or say. While she is left to do all the communication with the various agencies, at the end of the day she is totally subservient to the father's decisions, even though he sees little of the children. She does not know what her husband would think: 'he doesn't discuss things, but he got real mad when Michael was suspended—he reckons it's the teachers up there'.

Michael comes in, and with Mum's agreement the psychologist explains the situation again in simple terms. (This is useful for Mum, too.) Michael seems interested and excited, but does not say anything. His mother agrees to have a talk with Michael on his own, discuss the issues with her husband as best she can, and ring up to let the psychologist know what they think. A few minutes later, the psychologist is in his car, driving to the wealthy middle-class part of town where he lives, thinking: 'Why should I deny the kid the opportunity to get away from all that for a year or two?'

The next day the mail contains a further long report from Michael's head-teacher, listing numerous further acts of aggression. Shortly after that, Michael's mother telephones. All the family, including Michael, were unanimous that a residential school would be the best for the lad, and they wanted to thank the psychologist for the trouble he had taken.

Of course, this is not the end of the psychologist's work, only the beginning. A series of official forms have to be filled in, and reports written. Then there is the question of finding a suitable school. The psychologists have collected detailed information on what different schools offer, and an attempt can be made to match the most appropriate school to the child's needs.

A list of schools to try in Michael's case, in order of suitability, is produced. The administration will be lucky to find a vacancy in any of them at short notice, and Michael and the ordinary school may still have to face a six-month waiting period. The psychologist rings the Principal of the school that heads Michael's list, to attempt a little gentle persuasion. Miraculously, owing to a freak circumstance, a place is available immediately. Well, it's about time something started going smoothly in this case. Provided Michael and his parents go for interview, and both they and the school are happy about admitting the boy, he will be given the place.

All the psychologist has to do now is review Michael's progress, both at school and when at home in the holidays, as frequently as necessary and at least once a year. Care has to be taken that the residential school does not hang on to him too long, and that he is reintegrated to ordinary school at the earliest reasonable opportunity. Then there will be protracted negotiations to effect his reintegration, and continued support for the family and the ordinary school that receives him. Through all this, the psychologist has been juggling with a couple of hundred other active cases at the same time, as well as carrying out a wide range of other duties. The psychiatrist says: 'it took you a long time to agree with me'.

What is to be learnt? It is left to the reader to pick his or her own holes in how the psychologist proceeded, and the value judgements that were made along the way. Some particular questions that may arise: 'was Michael brain-damaged—and if he was so hyperactive why did not the psychiatrist spot it and do something?' For the psychologist, any possible physical or genetic causation of Michael's behaviour was irrelevant, since only environmental factors were under the psychologist's control—and precious few of those. Just as the doctor's educational recommendation was disregarded, so it was not in the psychologist's purview to comment on possible physical factors. In any case, Michael was considerably less hyperactive at home than he was at school — or was it just that this aspect of behaviour was less noticeable in the home environment? But if Michael dies of a brain tumour in nine months time, how will we apportion the blame?

As has been said, for many psychologists individual casework is the largest single component of their work, although it should be emphasized that very few 'individual case' involvements end with the child, like Michael, placed in a special school. It is certainly the casework function which is most demanded of them, although there is some evidence to suggest that the very people who demand it are often those who are not satisfied with the results (Hibbert, 1971; Topping, 1978), yet they continue to ask for it. Perhaps part of the dissatisfaction results from psychologists' frequent failure to solve the problem totally in the terms in which the referring agent initially perceived it. But if the educational psychologist's primary professional responsibility is to children, surely the referring agent must expect the psychologist's main aim to be to solve the problem in favour of the child, rather than be preoccupied with reducing stress and anxiety in the referring agent? Unfortunately this is not always the case, and while there is nothing to stop a psychologist choosing the reduction of stress or anxiety in the adults surrounding a child as the main aim of an intervention, a great deal of clear thinking is necessary to ensure that, by so doing, the psychologist does not sell the child down the river.

The Shepherd, Oppenheim, and Mitchell study (1971) was the first in the United Kingdom to case doubts on the effectiveness of individual casework. There has subsequently been further research, in both the United Kingdom and the United States of America, which has tried to evaluate this area of a psychologist's work (see Topping, 1977a; Topping, 1978; and Wright and Payne, 1979). There is still no conclusive evidence that individual casework activity by educational psychologists results in improvements greater than those which would occur anyway by spontaneous remission. Readers will appreciate from the foregoing example that casework is extremely difficult to evaluate. With a clear theoretical model and a structured approach, it is usually possible to see whether ongoing 'process' objectives have been met (Denton, 1976), but it is less frequently possible to evaluate casework in terms of the meeting or otherwise of any ultimate or 'outcome' objectives, especially not in comparison to what would have happened had the psychologist never been involved. It is small wonder that educational psychologists are increasingly turning to other activities, the effectiveness of which is often considerably easier to evaluate. One of these is the in-service training of other professional and lay groups.

IN-SERVICE TRAINING

A survey by Wolfendale (1980) shows that educational psychologists make a far greater contribution to in-service training than is generally realized. Of the

Psychological Services providing data, 76 per cent ran their own courses for teachers. The vast majority of these provided courses based in schools as well as in central meeting places. A larger proportion, 95 per cent, provided input for courses run by other LEA officers (usually advisers).

On the courses which were run and controlled completely by psychologists, a wide range of topics was covered. Listed in order of frequency of occurrence (starting with the most offered topic), these were: Behaviour Problems and their Management, Learning Problems, Methods of Assessment, Special Education, Language, Child Development, Remedial Education, Pastoral Care, Pre-school Education, Reading, Perceptuo-motor Development, Curriculum Development, and Careers Guidance.

In response to the question: 'Should the setting up of INSET courses be central to the educational psychologist's role?', 52 per cent of the Services said 'Yes'. Interesting data also emerged on the issue of evaluation. Of those Services who ran their own in-service training courses, 77 per cent also carried out some form of evaluation of their success. But of other LEA courses not involving psychologists, only 41 per cent were ever evaluated.

At the moment, psychologists are spending between zero and 25 per cent of their working time on in-service courses, depending on the Service in which they work and on individual predilection. There seems to be no doubt that this proportion of time will increase in the future, a trend which has been adumbrated by authoritative central sources (Warnock, 1978; Cranmer, 1979). To accommodate this development, a reduction in individual casework will be necessary, and of course the hope is that effective in-service training will reduce both need and demand for individual casework. There are already signs from some Services that this is beginning to happen.

To put some flesh on these bones, a review of the INSET activities of one particular Psychological Service may be useful. This Service makes numerous one-off inputs into courses run by other agencies (for example the local College of Further Education, LEA Advisers, the local branch of the National Association for Remedial Education, the local Association for Parents, and so on), where the target audience may be nursery nurses, play-group leaders, residential child care officers, etc., as well as parents and teachers of all sorts. However, the psychologists tend to be fairly dubious about the effectiveness of these gap-in-the-programme filling exercises, and regard the utility of this kind of involvement as mainly in terms of fostering good public relations. (Good public relations having become of greater significance since the onset of cuts in education budgets.)

The real thrust of the Service's INSET work lies in its own courses and workshops, almost always completely controlled and 'tutored' by psychologists from the Service, with aims, objectives, course inputs, and structure clearly specified well in advance. The idea is to have the whole set-up well enough organized for any one of the team of psychologists to be able to switch tasks at a moment's notice. Far from resulting in an excessively rigid structure, this gives the flexibility needed to cope with organizational hiccups which are beyond the psychologists' control (like staff illness, floods, power failures, and the sundry other acts of God which always beset any attempt to organize anything). The courses are equally spread between the centrally-based (for students from a large geographical area) and the school-based (for the whole, or a large part of, the staff in a school). The latter are finding increasing favour among the psychologists, since they allow the continuing social dynamic within the school to be more easily manipulated, thus increasing the likelihood of long-term behaviour change in the school staff by a process of on-going mutual reinforcement.

The courses are closely tailored to local needs, but most of the longer courses have some common features. Each session is likely to have some information input from a psychologist, using written hand-outs, overhead projector displays, or video. Also, each will have a period for discussion in small groups ($n = 6$ to 8), with each group led by a psychologist, where the information input is chewed over and practical problems resolved. In addition, and more importantly, in the groups the students feed back information to each other and the psychologist about their success or otherwise with the task (framed as a behavioural objective) which was set them at the preceding session. Thirdly, the small-group sessions are used for discussion and rehearsal of the next task, set during the information input, the completion of which will be reported on at the next meeting of the course.

Subject areas covered in courses for teachers include: the assessment of learning difficulties, motivation and learning style, enthusiastic teaching and classroom control, behaviour modification in the classroom, resources for children with learning difficulties, remedial education in secondary schools, language development, stress management and coping skills, precision teaching, curriculum structure, physical handicap, mental handicap, and 'maladjustment'. Courses for other groups have included: toy librarianship (for volunteer assistant librarians from the community), foster-parenting (for foster parents!), behavioural techniques in casework (for probation officers), 'dyslexia' (for parents and teachers), children under 5 (for parents), introduction to psychology (for any adults).

Many of these have already been repeated several times. Future plans include courses in behavioural techniques for social workers, in the management of 'school phobia' for education welfare officers, in the effectiveness of alternative educational systems for managing disruptive pupils with senior secondary school staff, and so on.

How, then, have these courses been evaluated? It is clear that where short-term behaviour changes in the students are specified as part of the course structure, in terms of set tasks which are the subject of later self-report, it is fairly easy to tell whether such behavioural objectives have been met.

But although the evaluation of INSET is easier than the evaluation of case-work, since in the former the setting of objectives is a much more open exercise which is considerably less muddied by organizational confusion and interpersonal tensions, it nevertheless proves to be not terribly easy to do it well (Topping and Brindle, 1979). Two major problem areas are evident.

The first is the question of the duration of behaviour changes in the students. No evaluation is complete without a long-term follow-up, at twelve months or two years. A further problem is distinguishing between lack of long-term behaviour change in the student which is due to inadequacies in the course, and that which is due to circumstances beyond either the student's or the psychologist's control (for example, in the case of teachers, restrictions from an antagonistic headteacher, precipitate redeployment to another school as part of cuts in the education budget, changes in the catchment area of the school which make the course content irrelevant to the new population, and so on).

The second major problem area is the question of the relationship between post-course behaviour changes in the student and resultant changes in the behaviour of the children with whom the student interacts and for whom he or she is primarily responsible. To gather reliable data on long-term behavioural change in the student is difficult enough, and while it may be possible to gather long-term data about changes in the behaviour of the children by observation, test results, or verbal feedback, it is difficult to ensure that the latter are a *result* of the former when control or comparative samples are not easily establishable.

Many INSET course students are emphatically practitioners rather than theorists, and regard their own *modus operandi* as reflective of art rather than science. They may find the 'scientific' approach wearisome as well as more than a little threatening. It is rarely easy to convince anyone of the necessity of evaluation in practice. However, educational psychologists are progressing in this area, albeit slowly, and new models and methods of evaluation are evolving. This movement will certainly gather speed and force during the next decade, as happened in the United States some fifteen years ago. It is clear that, particularly in the current economic climate, any move by psychologists to change their way of working will need to be justified via evaluative data.

CONSULTATION ON ORGANIZATIONAL ISSUES

In local government, there are many people whose job has some kind of managerial function. Very few, however, have any training in management or organizational method, and this is particularly true of headteachers. While many psychologists are equally innocent in this respect, they at least should have a practised objectivity, a preoccupation with data rather than speculation, and a sequential approach to problem-solving. It occasionally happens that the most inane and tautological comment on managerial matters by a psychologist is perceived as a blinding revelation by someone who is so embedded in the minutiae of day-to-day practice that they cannot see the wood for the trees.

However, lacking management training as they do, psychologists need to take some care that, intoxicated by this extension of their role and/or personality, they do not completely leave behind the body of knowledge and skills with which they are officially equipped. A psychologist making sweeping statements which are not founded on any theoretical or empirical base is unlikely to be any better than a street sweeper doing the same, and may well be worse. Where psychologists might be of genuine and professionally valid assistance is in the area of clarifying the nature of the organizational problem. Indeed, the model of problem-solving we applied to individual casework problems is likely to be of equal relevance to organizational issues. The model is merely a simple way of expressing that which is 'scientific method'; in organizational consultation the psychologist is only 'aiming at larger targets', as Stratford (1979) expresses it.

With the current emphasis on tighter curricular structure in schools, and greater accountability to both central government and the local ratepayers, a psychologist's familiarity with evaluation methodology may be seized upon by headteachers, and utilized by them as an early warning system, and possibly also as a weapon which can be deployed in an aggressive or retaliatory manner. Management is about power, especially in the traditionally hierarchal structure, and as educational psychologists become involved in managerial problems they inevitably become embroiled in political problems (with a small or large 'p').

The proportion of time spent by educational psychologists on this kind of consultative work is very variable, but it is most unusual for more than 20 per cent of working time to be so allocated. Often the more senior or experienced psychologists in a Service will be the most involved in this area of work, which requires confidence balanced with great sensitivity. We will consider an example which illustrates the potential complexity of the genre.

The Central High School

Secondary schools are large and organizationally complex, and by virtue of this almost always much more difficult for educational psychologists to work in effectively. This school is a secondary modern school in one of the 20 per cent of towns in England which still have 'selective' education at secondary level.

Until two years previously, the Central High School had been a 'semi-selective' school—a very strange animal indeed. Once the grammar-school children had been 'creamed off' via the 11-plus results, a second layer of the apparently more able children were taken off for the High School, with the watery milk remaining being despatched to the ordinary 'secondary moderns'. This anomalous structure had been eventually dispensed with, and the High School became an ordinary secondary modern. This resulted in a lot of teachers who were primarily adapted (through long and, in some cases, highly repetitive experience) to pursuing academic achievement in their own pet subject areas suddenly being confronted with a mixed intake of children, many of whom had very weak communication and literacy skills. (A similar phenomenon occurs when grammar schools go comprehensive.)

Before long a spate of referrals of individual children at the High School came to the psychologist, with the implicit complaint that the school could not cater for their learning needs. To have removed these children to other ordinary secondary schools or special schools might have been better for the children, but the psychologist's feeling was in line with the LEA's policy, that the school had to learn and change to provide for the needs of such children.

Data-gathering had its complications. For the past four years, the first-year intake had been 'screened' with reading, English, and mathematics tests. However, the raw scores from these had never been referred to standardization tables or compiled to give an overall picture, they had merely been used to list the children in rank order to facilitate dividing them into 'sets' of more or less homogeneous ability for the various subjects. The data were scattered round the school on odd scraps of paper. Eventually the psychologist retrieved them all, standardized all the scores, and performed a very crude analysis of the data. The analysis vividly demonstrated how radically the skills of the intake had changed since the reorganization two years before. By using highly arbitrary cut-off points in the test results, the psychologist was able to give some indication of the numbers of children needing a full-time remedial class of a specified (small) size, those needing some small-group withdrawal help, and those needing specially devised resource materials in other subject lessons.

The head convened a staff meeting where the psychologist elaborated, and indeed laboured, the impact of these results, and emphasized the need for the internal reorganization of resources to meet the needs of these children. To underline the point, research evidence on the link between learning frustration and behaviour difficulties was cited, and the teachers were told that if they neglected the needs of the academically weak children, it would be at their own peril.

The reaction of the teachers left a great deal to be desired. Some had not even come to the meeting. Some came and merely launched into a tirade of complaint about how they could not possibly 'do their job' with these children in their class. Some expressed concern but did not see what they could do. One teacher offered to try to help. The psychologist, a handy scapegoat, was showered with a mixture of apathy and ill-feeling.

Further follow-up, advice, and help was offered to the head. The offer was never taken up. The head, although concerned, was caught in too many conflicts. He was under enormous pressure to maintain the high academic standards the school had traditionally upheld. There was little opportunity to draft in more sympathetic teachers, since the state of the teacher labour market was such that everyone was hanging on to their old jobs, however much they disliked them. Cuts in resources funding meant there was little opportunity to purchase new materials for the slow learners. It was not surprising that the head had difficulty grappling with the problem in its entirety, and did not really think a psychologist could help him further.

What the psychologist could and did do, in the months that followed, was support the teacher who took over some responsibility for remedial work, by advising about resources and materials and on programming for the very worst children, by involving the teacher in various support groups and in-service training activities, and by continuing to suggest and pressurize for a better 'remedial' structure. The head still occasionally made an individual referral of a child, but since he came to realize that by doing so he merely exposed himself to further pressure from the psychologist about the organization of the school, referrals tailed off.

What went wrong with this involvement? The crucial missing link was the absence of a strong relationship between the head and the psychologist, which had never had much chance to develop. The time and place were all wrong, and all that was left to do was scurry round on the periphery sweeping up as well as the psychologist was able.

In time, changes occurred anyway. The LEA made an extra half-time teacher available to the school, who was deployed in full-time remedial work in small groups. At this point, the psychologist became able to step up his input, for there was another point of focus for supportive intervention. However, no long-term objectives could be set, since the extra teacher was likely to be removed as suddenly and arbitrarily as she had been appointed. In addition, the local council finally approved plans for the High School to go fully comprehensive in a further two years' time. It was more than a little difficult for the psychologist to act as organizational consultant when the rules of the game were constantly changing. Perhaps the best that could be hoped for was that, by the time the High School did go comprehensive, the psychologist would be sufficiently well known to the head and some of the other key staff to be involved more closely in the consultative role when the next wave of chaos broke.

Secondly, another example, also one where the name of the game changed as the psychologist went along, but one where increasing control was exerted over outcomes, and all ended happily ever after.

The politics of language handicap

Over the years, the psychologists and the speech therapists had become increasingly aware of the needs of a small but significant number of children with specific and complex impairment of language functioning. The psychologists felt it worthwhile to bring together the parents of such children, and a parents' group for children with severe specific language impairment was formed. The group meetings proved emotionally and socially supportive for the parents, and the psychologist, speech therapist, and various visiting 'experts' advised the parents about ways they could help their children when they were at home.

As time went on the parents began to question the desirability of sending very young children away to the residential schools specializing in the education of such children. The psychologists considered the issue, and decided it would be perfectly feasible, and of equal benefit to the children, to set up a unit locally to cater for them. The psychologists could train the teachers for such a unit, and advise about its organization and methods. In a time of financial cutbacks in education, the economic argument for the establishment of such a unit was substantial.

The psychologists prepared a document on this issue for the Chief Education Officer. This sank without trace in a bureaucratic quagmire, and no action resulted. A second more detailed document was prepared, citing relevant research evidence and laying out policy options in great and lucid detail. This went the same way as the first.

Then the parents' group got hold of the issue. Some of the more vocal middle-class parents joined AFASIC (The Association for all Speech-Impaired Children), a national advisory and pressure group, and armed themselves with relevant literature. They began to lobby their local councillors, write to the local paper, and telephone the Education Officers at inconvenient times of the day. Before long the issue was on the agenda for the next Education Committee meeting, and the Education Officers were feverishly trying to find their copies of the documents the psychologists had prepared months previously.

The councillors on the Education Committee were divided on the issue— while many were in favour of saving money, they were not too keen on having to accommodate to any change in the status quo. The establishment of a unit involved short-term increases in expenditure, albeit in order to effect economies in the long term. They were also irritated that the Education Officers had not briefed them much earlier on this issue, which alarmed the officers, who reacted by kicking the nearest available scapegoat, namely the psychologists. The psychologists were accused of stirring up mass agitation, politicking, and grossly overstepping the boundaries of their job definition.

Eventually the Committee agreed to the establishment of the unit. The officers' annoyance subsided, and the psychologists were involved in the choosing of site and staffing for the unit. They later committed a substantial in-service training input to the unit, and as it became established and the teachers' skills developed, children were phased back into it from the residential schools. The psychologists had a large degree of control over admissions to the unit, and were able to set up a satisfactory procedure for the monitoring of children's progress and the evaluation of the work of the unit. Reports could subsequently be prepared for the Education Committee detailing not only the unit's effectiveness, but also its cost-effectiveness in comparison to previous alternatives.

The main moral of this story is: never underestimate parents. Consultation on organizational issues is a developing area of the role of the educational psychologist, and it is certain to be an area where psychologists will learn by their mistakes. There is some interesting literature in the field, such as the article by Goldberg (1968), who reports that the major factor affecting the efficiency of such involvements is the quality of the interpersonal atmosphere in the institutions and agencies where such projects take place. Work of this kind calls for a keen awareness on the part of the psychologist of the political structure and power struggles around him. As psychologists tend to have a preoccupation with data as a basis for meaningful decisions, it is sometimes difficult for them to remember that for the people with whom they are working, self-preservation is often the first, if unspoken, rule, and the objectives these people state may well not be their real or primary objectives. Also, it is difficult for psychologists to adapt to working in a situation where the entrenched cultural values are radically different from their own. In such cases, not only is there a lack of common language or shared meanings, but the psychologist has to devote substantial time to understanding the subgroup norms—the rules of the game—before being able to proceed at all, and this experience in itself could engender considerable stress and frustration in the psychologist.

So far as the United Kingdom is concerned, educational psychologists will continue to need to approach this area of their work cautiously, remembering that they have no monopoly of wisdom.

The latter reminder is less applicable to the fourth area of an educational psychologist's work to be considered, the area of research, since psychologists will frequently find themselves to be the only profession in a local government setting which can claim training in research methodology.

RESEARCH

Ever since educational psychologists were first invented, they have been saying they ought to do more research. By and large, however, they have proved to be singularly unwilling to take their own advice. It will by now be evident that the traditional experimental paradigm of research is virtually useless to a practising educational psychologist. However, there are many alternative paradigms, such as those lucidly outlined by Campbell (1969). Also, there is the strong trend for evaluation 'research' to be built in to a great deal of the routine work of educational psychologists, following the methodology of behaviourist psychology and the urgings of such writers as Deniston *et al.* (1969) and Burgoyne and Cooper (1975). In addition to routine internal evaluation of their own work, educational psychologists also sometimes act as research 'consultants' on particular projects. However, it is unusual for this part of their work to take up more than 10 per cent of their professional time. Two examples of research 'projects', with different political and administrative ramifications, will be considered here.

The effectiveness of remedial teaching

The Psychological Service had a teaching unit attached to it, which had functioned for some years as a remedial centre, with children attending full-time for two to four years for intensive small-group teaching to boost basic literacy and numeracy skills. The teachers in the unit were happy enough with their results, but the psychologists were more dubious, being aware of the mass of research evidence which suggested that the long-term effectiveness of such teaching was minimal in comparative terms.

Before any change in the functioning of the unit was considered it was agreed that the long-term effects of the work so far should be looked into. Of the 130 children admitted to the unit over a seven-year period, only 33 proved to be subsequently traceable and still at school. For these 33, records of their tested reading ages before entry to the unit, at various stages during their stay in the unit, and at various time intervals after their discharge from the unit were available.

The records showed that most children had improved while attending the unit, by an average of 0.87 years of reading age for each year they had spent there. However, a few had made no progress at all, and some had gone backwards. After leaving the unit, the mean yearly gain in reading age fell by a half. A substantial number of children made no further progress, and 25 per cent went backwards. The possibility remained that, had the children not been admitted to the unit, instead of a relative spurt in the unit and a marked deceleration on discharge, they would have made steady gains to arrive at the same point. This is a situation which many studies of the effectiveness of remedial education have shown to exist (Chazan, 1967; Carroll, 1972), but this hypothesis for the unit children was not testable on the available data.

Other fascinating information emerged. The unit had always worked on the policy of admitting children as young as possible, on the assumption that this would maximize long-term effectiveness. In fact, the data showed that the unit was more effective with the children who were admitted at a later age. Likewise, the unit had always favoured the admittal of 'bright' children with 'specific learning difficulties', rather than the 'generally dull slow learners', on the basis of a similar assumption. The data showed that the unit had been more effective with the so-called 'slow learners', who had learned faster than the 'bright' children! The children's IQs bore no relationship at all to their reading progress. (This is also a fairly common finding.)

The results of the project were written up and published (Topping, 1977b), but the main uses were in terms of influence on local action. The demonstrated effectiveness of the unit was regarded as less than satisfactory by all concerned, and its functioning was radically changed. The unit became a part-time, short-stay placement for the assessment of children by experimental teaching, and moved much more towards the provision of a 'remedial resources' library and an advisory and in-service training function.

The project highlighted the fact that retrospective research is at best difficult and at worst downright impossible, and that evaluation methods have to be built in when planning a new development, if any reasonable standards of reliability and validity of outcome measurement are to be attained.

The effect of socio-economic variables on school achievement

A councillor who was a member of the Education Committee, from a ward in a depressed and deprived part of town, expressed great concern to the Committee about the very small number of children in the schools in his ward who managed to pass the 11-plus and go to grammar school. (It could have been argued that the fact that he was shortly to stand for re-election, and that none of his children had passed the 11-plus, might have had something to do with this.) Was this not an indication, he stated, that the standard of education provided by the local schools was sadly lacking? And what did the Chief Education Officer propose to do about this dreadful state of affairs? (One of the things the Chief was trying to do was turn the whole authority compre-hensive, but that did not meet with universal approval.)

The issue rapidly hit the local press, with the result that parents started removing their children from the schools in question, and the school rolls shrank, and some of the teachers were redeployed elsewhere. Staff morale was at rock-bottom, and the whole affair became a fine example of a self-fulfilling prophecy.

The CEO was in a cleft stick, since there was no way the councillor concerned could publicly accept the likely truth of the matter, which was that the domestic language and cultural deprivation which characterized the area was the major relevant factor in the children's failure to 'achieve'. The Chief advised the Committee that he was asking the LEA Advisers to 'inspect' the schools concerned. The members cried 'Whitewash, whitewash', and morale in the schools sank even lower.

Then somebody had the bright idea of asking the psychologists if they could help. Yes, they could, and with a speedy reanalysis of data from various screening exercises carried out over the years, together with the mounting of one or two other rapid testing and data-gathering exercises, a formidable body of factual and incontrovertible evidence was compiled into a report for the Committee. Sensing what was in the wind, the councillor concerned now resorted to delaying tactics. He delayed just long enough and was re-elected with a greatly increased majority. When the report was eventually presented to the Committee, interest in it was curiously lacking, and the whole affair died a quick death. At least it did so far as the councillors were concerned. Back in the schools, the teachers were still just as depressed, and their motivation levels were to remain low for many months thereafter.

These examples demonstrate the essential feature characteristic of almost all research done by applied educational psychologists in the field—that of relevance to action. 'Academic' research is largely out of the question for the practising educational psychologist. While the examples described lack a great deal in design finesse, they represent the application of research skills to messy, intractable and very real problems. If psychologists do not provide some data base for decision-making, there may be no-one else around who will. The roles of the psychologist in research and in policy formulation are inextricably linked.

POLICY FORMULATION

The ability of psychologists to generate useful theoretical models of action, retrieve relevant research evidence, and mount research to answer new or idiosyncratic questions, is often locally unique. Under the circumstances, it is perhaps unfortunate that educational psychologists do not make a bigger input into policy formulation, within their own Service, within the Authority which employs them, and at a national level.

Contributing to policy formulation at local authority level should be an important feature of psychologists' work, since one policy decision can affect the lives and welfare of thousands of children for many years. Time spent sitting on a deliberating working party is rarely as immediately rewarding for the psychologist as individual casework, but the potential pay-offs are vastly more substantial. Whether or not psychologists become involved in policy formulation at authority level depends partly on their own level of confidence and willingness to do so, and partly on interdepartmental politics within the LEA. The relationship between the Service and key administrators is likely to be critical, and these relationships are by no means uniformly placid, since educational psychologists not uncommonly find themselves advocating for children and criticizing 'The System'. However justified such criticism may be in rational and empirical terms, it nevertheless does little to make friends and influence people within the system. Administrators are unlikely to be too happy about admitting psychologists who are known not to be tame or bureaucracy-oriented to any kind of policy formulation exercise.

Nevertheless, it does happen sometimes, and psychologists have been involved in a wide variety of areas, including:

(i) the reorganization of special schools;
(ii) the restructuring of procedure for multidisciplinary liaison;
(iii) the issue of confidentiality in record-keeping and data-processing systems;
(iv) procedures for dealing with the suspension of pupils from school;
(v) the establishment of authority-wide 'screening' (both to monitor overall standards of achievement in an authority's schools, and to pick out those children needing special programming or additional help);
(vi) methods of recording the continuing educational progress of all children in schools;
(vii) the review of an authority's policies on educational provision for the under-fives;
(viii) curriculum development on 'education for parenthood' in secondary schools;
(ix) multicultural education and patterns of provision for those children for whom English is a second language;
(x) provision for special groups of children (e.g. the 'autistic' and 'language-impaired');
(xi) tertiary education for handicapped pupils;
(xii) job creation and 'youth opportunities' projects.

In these policy formulation exercises, psychologists usually try to restrict themselves to offering conceptual clarification and information about relevant research evidence, and try to resist the temptation to allow their own value judgements or personal prejudices to intrude into their contributions. This latter is not always done, however, particularly since psychologists may have greater skills in manipulating group dynamics than many other members of such working parties or committees.

At a national level, practising educational psychologists have made very little contribution to policy formulation, although more recently two psychologists were members of the Warnock Committee (Warnock, 1978). The British Psychological Society has various Divisions, Boards and Committees which submit evidence on a host of issues, but the end result is often akin to a very small voice in a storm of representations from other vested interests.

A number of psychologists have expressed dissatisfaction at this state of affairs (e.g. Tizard, 1976; Raven, 1977), and it may be that as the small but significant profession of applied educational psychology extends its boundaries and refines its methods, a more coherent approach to input to central policy formulation will evolve. However, it is by no means impossible that the profession will develop unevenly, and even greater fragmentation and lack of political voice will result. One encouraging recent development is that educational psychologists are publishing more about their activities. This increased flow of information can only serve to assist greater homogeneity in the development of Psychological Services.

MORAL JUDGEMENTS

The examples of educational psychologists' practice that have been discussed in the previous pages were riddled with examples of moral judgements in operation. This is particularly obvious in individual casework, where the impact of the psychologist's work may be more immediate and the relationships with the people involved are more direct than in the other areas of work.

Every individual case accepted involves making value judgements. If the psychologist contracts to modify the behaviour of a child, is that in the child's best interests, or only those of the surrounding adults? Whose welfare is the psychologist trying to promote, and whose perceptions of 'welfare' are we talking about? How should the psychologist balance long- and short-term considerations, or, to put it more crudely, is there such a thing as 'being cruel to be kind'?

It could be argued that it is safer to err on the side of advocacy for the parents and the child, rather than act as agent for the big battalions buttressed by institutional power, thereby acting as a sort of compensatory political counterweight. But this is far too simplistic an assertion.

The moral issues inherent in other aspects of an educational psychologist's work tend to be less obvious. Although they might be hidden, they still loom large under the surface, particularly in the area of policy formulation. For example, a psychologist may pressurize for the establishment of an attainment screening programme in an authority, to help identify inefficient schools which are failing their children. The LEA may agree to this, carry out the exercise, then respond by deploying additional teachers blanket-fashion in the weakest schools, thereby rendering them even less cost-effective, and depriving other children of resources. The net result is that the children in the authority are worse off than they were before.

However, if psychologists in the field stopped too long to consider the moral aspects of their every action, they would never do anything. Life, alas, is not like that. There are many questions, and it can only be left to individual practitioners to grope towards their own answers. It may be of little comfort to psychologists to feel that they are, through their training, more keenly aware of the moral issues than some other local government employees, but at least this signifies that the profession is now secure and confident enough to be self-critical.

FUTURE DEVELOPMENTS

Over the next ten years, the major growth area for educational psychologists is likely to be in-service training. The other three non-casework areas are likely to show some, but slower, growth. In terms of particular topics within the field, the effect of local and central governmental changes on the patterns of activity is interesting. Right-wing government tends to produce an emphasis on the 'gifted', 'dyslexia', the monitoring of educational standards and 'disruptive' children, with a strong undercurrent of cost-cutting, while a left-wing government is likely to result in an emphasis on education for the under-5s, the social benefits of education, and special programmes of help for the disadvantaged.

So far as the longer term development of educational psychologists' work is concerned, there is a distinct trend away from total preoccupation with schools, towards a much broader involvement with many other sections of the community, and this movement is likely to gather momentum over the next decade (see Lehmann, 1971; Bender, 1976, 1979; Tully et al., 1978; Murphy, 1979). Whether a separate discipline of 'community psychology' will ever be viable, or useful, is another matter.

One important implication of these developments is that directors of first-degree courses will need to consider ever more carefully the weight of their emphasis on the social, interactionist perspective in psychology. As data retrieval systems become more sophisticated, the acquisition of knowledge per se will decrease in importance. Correspondingly, a psychologist's ability clearly to conceptualize the scientific method of his discipline, and assess the significance and utility of new information, should receive increasing emphasis. If psychologists are to survive in practice outside the universities, they will need training in applied skills as well as being pumped with information, and as the rate of change in society accelerates, psychologists will above all need to be trained for flexibility.

TRAINING AS AN EDUCATIONAL PSYCHOLOGIST

Educational psychologists in England and Wales are almost always required to have a first degree in psychology, a post-graduate certificate in education to qualify them as teachers, at least two years' teaching experience, and a post-graduate degree in educational psychology, i.e. a minimum of seven years training.

These requirements have become more rigid in recent years, despite the fact that there is little evidence to suggest that the teacher training and experience components are particularly useful (for example Carroll, 1975), and despite the trend for psychologists to extend their work beyond the narrow confines of schools. Educational psychologists used to have a habit of regarding themselves as 'super-teachers', but a majority now regard themselves as primarily psychologists, and consider their post-graduate degree in educational psychology as the most important section of the total training experience.

Encouragingly, the post-graduate training courses for educational psychologists are showing increasing rigour in analysis of the skills required to be taught, and are beginning to structure real experiences for students which have a chance of enabling the right kind of learning to occur. Attempts are being made to train for flexibility, with appropriate emphasis on consultation skills and 'systems change'. Efforts are even being made to evaluate the courses (Thompson, 1980), although they vary enormously in nature and orientation.

As we have seen, for educational psychologists the process of expansion and development is coloured by two opposing trends, one towards fragmentation and one towards a new cohesion. Which of these trends will eventually predominate is an empirical question.

Note: The author's views do not necessarily represent those of the local authority which employs him, and the events described do not necessarily bear any relation to any actual event.

REFERENCES

Bender, M. P. (1976). *Community Psychology*, London: Methuen.
Bender, M. P. (1979). 'Community psychology: when?', *Bulletin of the British Psychological Society*, **32**, 6–9.
Burgoyne, J. C. and Cooper, C. L. (1975). 'Evaluation methodology', *Journal of Occupational Psychology*, **48**, 1, 53–62.
Burt, C. (1925). *The Young Delinquent*, London: University of London Press.
Campbell, D. T. (1969). 'Reforms as experiments', *American Psychologist*, **24**, 409–429.
Carroll, H. C. M. (1972). 'The remedial teaching of reading: an evaluation', *Remedial Education*, **7**, 1, 10–15.
Carroll, H. C. M. (1975). 'Teacher training and teaching experience: their contribution to the expertise of a group of educational psychologists', *Bulletin of the British Psychological Society*, **28**, 277–279.
Chazan, M. (1967). 'The effects of remedial teaching in reading: a review of research', *Remedial Education*, **2**, 1, 4–12.
Cranmer, G. (1979). 'The contribution of the educational psychologist', *Trends*, **3**, 13–16.
Deniston, O. L., Rosenstock, I. M., and Getting, V. A. (1969). 'Evaluation of program effectiveness', in *Program Evaluation in the Health Fields*, H. Schulberg *et al.* (eds), New York: Behavioural Publications.
Denton, L. R. (1976). ' "Noc Noc" — What's there?', *Canada's Mental Health*, **24**, 2, 19–23.
Goldberg, H. (1968). 'The psychologist in head start: new aspects of the role', *American Psychologist*, **23**, 10, 773–774.

Hibbert, K. A. (1971). 'Teachers' attitudes towards psychologists' *Journal of the Association of Educational Psychologists*, **4**, 3, 4-9.

Lehmann, S. (1971). 'Community and psychology and community psychology', *American Psychologist*, **26**, 554-560.

Murphy, A. (1979). 'Some pressures of working in a community psychological service', *Bulletin of the British Psychological Society*, **32**, 278-280.

Raven, J. (1977). 'Government policy and social psychologists' *Bulletin of the British Psychological Society*, **30**, 33-39.

Shepherd, M., Oppenheim, B., and Mitchell, S. (1971). *Childhood Behaviour and Mental Health*, London: University of London Press.

Stratford, R. J. and Cameron, R. J. (1979). 'Aiming at larger targets', *Occasional Papers of the Division of Educational and Child Psychology, British Psychological Society*, **3**, 2, 47-62.

Thompson, D. (1980). 'Evaluation of E.P. training', *Journal of the Association of Educational Psychologists*, **5**, 3, 53-55.

Tizard, J. (1976). 'Psychology and social policy', *Bulletin of the British Psychological Society*, **29**, 225-234.

Topping, K. J. (1977a). 'Evaluation of Psychological Services: a bibliography (Research Paper No 12)', Halifax: Calderdale Psychological Service.

Topping, K. J. (1977b). 'An evaluation of the long-term effects of remedial teaching', *Remedial Education*, **12**, 2, 84-86.

Topping, K. J. (1977c). 'The role and function of the educational psychologist', *Journal of the Association of Educational Psychologists*, **4**, 5, 20-29.

Topping, K. J. (1978). 'Consumer confusion and professional conflict in educational psychology', *Bulletin of the British Psychological Society*, **31**, 265-267.

Topping, K. J. and Brindle, P. (1979). 'The evaluation of in-service training', *British Journal of In-Service Education*, **5**, 2, 49-51.

Tully, B., Doyle, M., Cahill, D., Bayles, T., and Graham, D. (1978). 'Psychology and community work in mental health', *Bulletin of the British Psychological Society*, **31**, 115-119.

Warnock, H. M. (chairman) (1978). Report of the Committee of Enquiry into the Education of Handicapped Children and Young People, London: HMSO.

Wolfendale, S. (1980). 'The educational psychologist's contribution to in-service education of teachers: A survey of trends', *Journal of the Association of Educational Psychologists*, **5**, 3, 45-53.

Wright, H. J. and Payne, T. A. N. (1979). *An Evaluation of a School Psychological Service*, Winchester: Hampshire County Council.

Psychology in Practice
Edited by S. Canter and D. Canter
© 1982, John Wiley and Sons, Ltd.

CHAPTER 8

PSYCHOLOGY AND ADULT EDUCATION

Athalinda McIntosh
Lecturer in Educational Studies
University of Surrey

INTRODUCTION

A substantial number of psychologists have dabbled in teaching adult education classes, yet few have taken up full-time employment in the field. Nonetheless psychologists constitute approximately 5 per cent of full-time staff in British University Adult Education departments and there are thirty-two British universities that offer psychology as a subject in adult education programmes. However, as far as I am aware I am the only full-time qualified clinical psychologist in this area.

University adult education has many faces but for the purpose of this paper I would like to make the distinction between two major areas, that of extra-mural education and other adult education programmes. The latter type of adult education, largely post-graduate or professional training courses, is self-financed or financed by the usual university sources. Extra-mural courses are grant-aided by the Department of Education and Science (DES) which is the Government department with legal responsibility for them. This means that all extra-mural courses are vetted by government appointed inspectors (HMIs). It is this area of adult education that I am principally concerned with here.

Extra-mural courses, or as they are now referred to, Responsible Body (RB) courses, are organized on the basis of a partnership between the universities, voluntary bodies, predominantly the Workers' Educational Association (WEA), the local education authorities (LEAs) and the DES. In the 1979–80 session university adult education courses catered for 236,500 students in 10,569 extra-mural classes (UCAE, 1980) throughout Britain. Of these 412 courses were in psychology, representing 4 per cent of the total.

AIMS OF ADULT EDUCATION

Whereas previously adult education has been considered either in the remedial sense for people who need to compensate for earlier shortcomings, or alternatively as some sort of leisure activity, it is now seen as having a much wider function (Janne, 1976). That is, it is viewed as a continuing process guided by the overriding goal of improving the quality of life (Carelli, 1976). The individual is always at the hub of this process. Thus, adult education is conceived as serving to facilitate personal development, to include becoming psychologically equipped to cope with personal tensions resulting from rapid economic, vocational, social, and cultural changes (Cropley, 1977), which are characteristic of almost all spheres of modern life. It is an expanding field and one in which psychologists along with others have an increasingly important role to play.

ROLES OF THE PSYCHOLOGIST

The work of the psychologist in adult education is, of course, similar to that of any other lecturer in adult education, in so far as he or she will be responsible for the organization and administration of programmes and the teaching of specific courses. However, as a psychologist there is a particular responsibility for the education of the public in the theory and practice of psychology, and a unique role to play in the development of teaching methods appropriate to adults, as well as the generation of information through research that will contribute to useful policy decisions in the field.

As yet the potential contribution of psychologists to adult education has not been even partially realized. Most psychologists, myself included, have concentrated on establishing themselves within extra-mural adult education by concentrating on the teaching of psychology and by becoming involved in National Adult Education Groups such as the Standing Conference for University Teaching and Research in the Education of Adults (SCUTREA) in which we are attempting to promote psychology in adult education. We are only in the initial stages of planning for a more systematic research contribution to the area.

Organization and administration of RB courses in psychology

Each year courses in psychology have to be planned for the county of Surrey for which our Department is the Responsible Body. It is part of my job to ensure that a balanced programme is provided that meets the needs of the community, is practical in terms of availability of tutors and is acceptable to the DES. In order to achieve this I am involved with three major groups.

(1) The local authorities and adult educationalists, usually principals and

staff of institutes of adult education and local WEA committee members with whom I consult and advise on courses.

(2) Prospective tutors of courses with whom I draw up syllabi for specific courses.

(3) The DES who receive the syllabi and with whom I justify the courses if necessary.

This work presents a number of challenges other than administrative ones, in particular the 'selling' of the subject of psychology to others in adult education and the selection and guidance of psychology tutors.

'Selling' the subject

Although DES guidelines state that RB subject areas can include, at the least, those which would be offered at first or second year undergraduate level (Stock, 1978), in practice there are certain unwritten norms about what is included under the RB rubric. As these courses are for the general public and receive wide publicity they seem to need to be seen to conform to public expectation of morality, at least as seen by adult educationalists and some course tutors. There are a number of attitudes, prejudices, and fears that have to be contended with in order to shape and provide the programme that the public will respond to. Other professionals still have misconceptions of what psychology is about and there is also reluctance amongst some psychologists to present anything other than a traditional academic course to the public. Most of the effort has to go into persuading others to accept psychology and to promote their understanding of it. I have to make courses attractive, interesting, and morally acceptable to those responsible for accepting them in their programmes.

When I first took up the post, few centres offered courses in psychology and those that did offered either introductory courses or those in the field of adolescence and child-rearing. I have managed to increase the number of courses offered and expanded the range of subject areas covered. The current programme does to a large degree reflect my own interest and concerns and many of the courses are within the area of applied psychology, particularly as they relate to general application of theories and practices of psychology to the everyday life of the students attending.

The present provision has been achieved by my circularizing all providers, asking them to consider including psychology in their programme if they did not already. I meet those interested and discuss the possible courses with them. Usually I suggest a short introductory course in psychology as an initial course. I have to convince them of the viability of such a course since their income depends on students attending it. Where classes have been established for two or more sessions I ask tutors to check with the students what they wish to study next. Once a demand for psychology has been established in this way, it is easier to introduce new courses of a more applied or specific nature. These courses have in fact proved so successful in terms of attracting students, that requests from adult education providers will often now be in terms of 'something in the way of applied psychology'.

None the less some of the courses acceptable to local educational providers continue to be challenged by the DES inspectors and even by potential tutors. For instance, a DES inspector queried a course on 'Hypnotherapy', despite the fact that it had been conducted by a very experienced clinician and senior academic. Psychology tutors have questioned the provision of courses such as those on 'interpersonal communication' as they feel that people might want to use them to air their personal difficulties. It seems to be the view that if people find out more about themselves, they will immediately embark on a sort of do-it-yourself psychotherapy, to some detriment of their own health and that of those around them. This is a central issue in my approach as a clinical psychologist to adult education and one which I shall address in the next section.

I have been subject to much well-meaning advice against running a class on 'Clinical Psychology'. Time and again there is the question about whether or not it is 'dangerous' for people to find out about the theory and practice of psychology. This fear is expressed even more strongly with regard to clinical psychology which is often equated with medicine. Potential organizers find it difficult to imagine a surgeon or a general medical practitioner telling prospective clients about what they actually do in their work.

Apart from convincing the providers of the suitability of courses for their programmes it is, of course, necessary to attract the public to them. In my second year of RB teaching I drew posters and delivered them personally to all the local shops, libraries, and police stations to advertise a new course on which I was teaching in a new area. I have also written articles for local newspapers, as well as having an article written about me and my work, to encourage adult students to attend university adult education courses.

Rogers and Groombridge (1976) drew attention to the need for adult education to have constant promotion and visibility. They mention a study by Keele University which found that eight out of ten of the local population in two nearby villages were unaware that the university provided classes for adults.

Tutor support

RB tutors I recruit in various ways, including sending invitations to meet to discuss possible courses to psychologists working in hospitals, colleges, industry, etc. Whenever I am involved in a teaching programme with psychologists, I include an invitation to anyone interested to discuss with me the possibility of becoming a tutor. I usually discuss with potential tutors their attitudes toward teaching psychology to the general public and how they envisage themselves in this role. Usually I recommend that they begin by offering a short course in some aspect of psychology in which they are most interested. When a course is agreed I discuss with them, at length, issues such as dealing with mixed ability groups, student expectations, class organization, and the construction of a syllabus and booklist. In our department we run RB tutor-training programmes and I run workshops for all RB psychology tutors and anyone interested in being one.

Contact with tutors continues throughout the course and I act as a counsellor in the university for any tutor running a course. This may involve giving advice in the practical aspects of their teaching and administrative role. I may also visit the classes in an advisory capacity to discuss the course with tutors and students. So far I have had no serious complaints about psychology tutors from RB providers or students. If there were I would have the responsibility to intervene, at least in the first instance.

TEACHING ADULTS

A large proportion of my teaching activities involves teaching adults who have a whole range of background interests, ages, and activities. Whereas some of these students are selected for post-graduate and professional courses, the adult RB education classes are comprehensive in that they have open entry. Newman (1979) describes RB adult education as 'a cruel test of a tutor's skill'. As he succinctly points out 'if a tutor does not have what it takes, people stop coming'. In order for the courses to be successful they have to be relevant in content and taught by methods that are appropriate to the particular group.

Considering that adult education is a growth area whilst school populations are falling there is still very little work and information on adult learning and methods of teaching. Derrick (1980) found that in a review of journals of educational psychology 25 per cent of the articles were concerned with adults but out of these only 2 per cent were concerned with adults other than undergraduates and teachers. As Knowles (1979), Apps (1979) and others have pointed out, the assumption has been that adults learn in precisely the same way as children. Allman (1981) points out that scientific theories of learning have been largely derived from studies of learning in animals and children, and calls them 'childomorphic'.

More recently there have been various proponents of a theory of adult learning which has come to be known as andragogy (Knowles and Klevins, 1978; Knowles, 1979). There are at least four assumptions in andragogy that are different from those of pedagogy. These are relevant to the whole issue of adult education and the role of psychology in it. They are briefly:

(1) The point at which an individual achieves a self-concept of essential self-direction is when adulthood is achieved.

(2) Because of a person's reservoir of experience he or she is already a rich resource for learning. At the same time, that experience can act as a base on which to relate new learning.

(3) An individual's readiness to learn . . . is the 'product of the developmental tasks required for the performance of evolving social roles'.

(4) An adult enters into education with a problem-centred orientation to learning, so the time perspective is one of immediacy of application to what is happening in the learning situation.

Miller (1965) describes an adult as 'an experienced veteran who approaches each sighting with a complicated set of expectations and a great deal of experience against which to check what he sees; every field identification for him is structured by these experiences'.

A tutor as an adult must, by definition, be included in this identification. In other words he or she also brings his or her own expectations, previous experience, etc. to a class. Problems arise when expectations and needs of tutors and students are not congruent, particularly in regard to what is relevant to whom.

Psychology and real life

In 1970 an Association for the Teaching of Psychology (ATP) was formed with the aim of supporting and raising the standard of teaching of psychology at all levels and to aid teachers of psychology in their professional work. In the first Bulletin of the Association (*Psychology Teaching*, 1973) there is a report on a conference entitled 'Psychology is People' which was convened by a Birmingham University undergraduate student with the aim of 'unifying critical students to provide constructive alternatives to their courses'. Among the ideas for reform were that there should be a larger experiential dimension to courses, and a demand that greater emphasis be placed on people-as-they-live aspects of psychology (Britter *et al.*, 1973).

In the same Bulletin, Hearnshaw (1973) in his article on 'The teaching of psychology in Great Britain' says that 'students . . . are increasingly turning to psychology as a source of illumination on the meaning of life'.

In 1981, my experience in adult education is that these sentiments are ones which are expressed by students of all types. These include many students in professional training who have been disillusioned by earlier exposure to psychology teaching.

Consistently teachers, doctors, nurses and other groups say that what they have been taught is not relevant to their everyday work, or 'real life'. Others in professional courses have had similar experiences (see for example the collection of papers by McWhirter, 1974; the Division of Clinical Psychology, 1974; and Nicolson, 1981). Academic psychologists, according to these findings, are not meeting the needs of these students, particularly in the question of 'relevance' to 'real life' situations.

There is no work that I am aware of that has investigated RB students' views on the relevance of psychology classes to themselves. I have found from my own classes when asking students to declare their expectations of a course in writing, at the outset and from informal talks to tutors, that students expect 'to understand people, including themselves, better' as a result of attending psychology classes. Hetherington's (1981) experience supports this finding. However, studies on why students leave are few (Rogers, 1971, 1978) and responses are not consistent over a range of classes. It could be surmised that when students leave psychology classes it could be that they are not finding the courses relevant to their hoped-for understanding of people. Howarth (1974), Britter et al. (1973), Hearnshaw (1973), and Stone (1980) draw attention to the fact that psychologists who work in the professionally accepted sense of applied psychology have to do some form of post-graduate training. Not enough attention is paid in undergraduate courses to the relevance of psychology as an applied discipline. Stone (1980) says that at present many graduates leave university in a state of being 'half-baked' for the want of some professional training as part of their degree. If tutors have met only this academic as opposed to applied emphasis, before themselves going into teaching, then clearly that is what and how they will expect to teach adult students without psychology degrees.

Education and therapy

Public professional expectations of any psychologist are that they are there to solve people's problems. Hetherington (1981) stated that in his experience of seven years at the Headquarters of the British Psychological Society, every day letters and telephone calls from people in trouble were received, specifically asking for the services of a psychologist. Yet, as I have mentioned previously, tutors often fear that students will use classes to air personal problems and feel that they could not cope if they did.

Obviously, being trained in, and practising clinical work, influences my own way of thinking in this matter. Moreover it seems to me (and others, for example Nelson Jones, 1981) that the teaching of psychology in an applied context is one in which the expectation should be that problems will be raised and solutions sought. If in adult education we are aiming for self-management for students then their problems cannot be ignored.

Central to this viewpoint, it is recognized that there is a thin line between education and therapy. Nearly every book in adult education refers to the link between education and psychotherapy (in its broadest sense) and it is from the work of clinical psychotherapy practitioners, particularly Carl Rogers, that the process of adult education has been seen to be synonymous with other forms of psychological intervention. Kovel (1977) talks about adult education as a model for therapy. In contrasting therapy and education, he argues that therapy has to take into account emotional and subjective need and assumes an inbalance which has to be righted, whilst education works by teaching new rules of conduct. I believe that such a division is an artificial one, but agree with Kovel when he says that therapy, like education, can be of use to everyone who needs it. Where I would differ is that the 'need' has also to have emotional and subjective dimensions in education, otherwise adult education continues to be perpetuated as school-based information, giving, as opposed to facilitating, self-development.

My own approaches to teaching are governed by:

(i) my gut reaction against being a student at the end of pedagogical teaching at school;
(ii) an introduction to the theory and practice of humanistic psychology as an undergraduate, and the idea of free choice;
(iii) my experience as a clinical psychologist, which has influenced some of the teaching techniques that I use;
(iv) the writings of Carl Rogers in clinical work and education;
(v) the theory of andragogy;
(vi) my belief in the relevance of psychology as the study of human behaviour and experience to the lives of any student and tutor.

I approach my teaching therefore with the needs of adults in mind and adopt my methods of teaching accordingly. I am concerned with teaching in terms of both cognitive input and skills transmission.

Curriculum planning

In planning a curriculum or course of study, whether there is a set syllabus (as on a professional course), or not, the aims of any course needs to be embraced under the general aim of adult education. With RB classes there is tremendous scope for experimentation. I use a thematic approach to the planning of my syllabus. That is, I identify a theme of study and areas of study within that theme. Students are invited to develop their own curriculum within those themes. For example, my themes could include: 'clinical psychology', 'the psychology of communication', 'the psychology of interpersonal relationships'.

Before we shape the syllabus I ask the members of a class to identify their aims, which is a great help in identifying students' perceptions of a proposed course.

Increasingly I use behavioural contracts such as are suggested by Knowles

(1979: 198–203) in which students are invited to diagnose their own learning needs and objectives, the resources and strategies they hope to use to accomplish their directives, and what they might use to show as evidence of what they accomplish. For example, if 'understanding' is an objective then how will they utilize knowledge gained in solving problems?

With professional groups with specific syllabi where I am only making a 'one-off' input, I always go to great lengths to check with course organizers the context in which a psychology input is being made. Then I endeavour to incorporate material that is being/has been used in other parts of the course, to establish the link or relevance of the psychological input to the course. An example of this is with a course with District Nurses. I link behavioural theory with practice to their sessions on establishing a nursing contract.

To involve students in planning the curriculum is often not easy as they may have been used to didactic styles of teaching in other contexts. They may hold the viewpoint that a teacher with his or her background of knowledge, expertise, and skill is in the best position, not only to interpret the needs of students, but to meet those needs by offering his or her knowledge, expertise, and skill to the students. To suggest that a student can ever be self-directing is in direct contradiction to this notion. How can a student be self-directing when it is the teacher who has all the knowledge and skills? Students may feel confused and cheated, however, by a student-centred approach. This problem has been identified by others (for example, Elsdon, 1975; Legge, 1974).

To cope with this, during a university class I always do what Feltwell (1981) suggests for RB tutors. That is, I include a brief explanation of the student-centred approach, inviting students to be involved in their own learning. This always leads to a debate on the role of a teacher so I discuss with them where I see my role in relation to them. The guidelines I use for this are those suggested by Rogers (1969: 164–166).

Class organization and approaches to teaching

In order to promote active involvement of students in the class I am concerned to create a social context which is conducive to this. This would involve ensuring a proper arrangement of furniture, promoting social interaction and always including some student-centred activity where possible in dyads or small groups.

The guidelines I use for myself when making a contribution is to allow students to be silent for no more than about ten minutes. If that has occurred I immediately stop and 'check-off' their understanding with students. That is asking them to think of examples in their own lives to illustrate the theory. If this does not have a quick reaction, I automatically then carry out with the students some sort of exercise and/or small-group work related to what we are doing.

Approaches to teaching in adult education are infinite. I use as many as I can with the exception of a 'straight lecture' which was total anathema to me as a student, and I therefore feel justified in not imposing it on other students. The following approaches are just a few that I have used in clinical and adult education work. In discussing Freudian concepts I will use projective techniques, getting students to participate by using their own responses to such material as ambiguous stimuli, free association to stimulus words, etc.

In teaching a behavioural approach I increasingly use behavioural contracts (see Knowles, 1979: 198–203) with students; systematic desensitization as described in Korchin (1976) in which students construct their own behavioural hierarchies; modelling, such as described by Lange and Jakubowski (1977); and social skills exercises such as described by Priestley *et al.* (1978).

Sculpting (Satir, 1967) is one technique which I use when the family is the theme of a class. Others I use, such as listening skills and emphathy exercises, are taken from client-centred psychotherapy, especially in courses related to communication.

For problem-solving exercises I sometimes present situations and ask groups or pairs of students to work out what they would do if they were faced with such a problem. This is useful with professional training groups who may have previously identified problem areas for consideration.

I integrate the teaching of research methods in discussions of various areas of psychology. For example, after students for one group had responded to a questionnaire, I invited small groups of them to do frequency distributions of the responses, and graph and analyse them.

In a class on the media and its presentation, one-half of the students did a content analysis of 'womens' magazines such as *Woman's Own* while another group did one of *Men Only*. Considering the first was predominantly advice to women on self-catering holidays that week, and the latter was predominantly aids to improve sexual performance, there was plenty of data for future debate.

Often I ask students to do 'homework'. This can range from looking up definitions, to some sort of experimental work, or book reviews and seminar presentations. This 'homework' will usually come from something which has occurred in class. Whatever work a student does outside class I use, or have the class use in some way. When students have the confidence they sometimes take some or all of a class themselves, using me as a resource. If a student has a particular skill this is very helpful in utilizing it.

The main objective in using these techniques is to involve students and enable them to draw on their own experience and knowledge to illustrate the content of what is being taught.

Evaluation

The function of evaluation is to find to what extent the aims and objectives of a tutor and student have been achieved. It needs to be done continuously throughout as well as at the end of a course (see Stephens and Roderick, 1974). Since the students will have identified their own objectives they, at least, will have some criteria for evaluation at the end of the course. In conjunction with an evaluation of achievement of stated objectives there is often a 'ripple-effect' which is worth investigating. For example, skills that have been learned in the classroom situation may be tried and tested in other contexts. One recent student from a class related how her relationship with her father-in-law had improved as a result of some practice we had had in class on interpersonal communication. This had led to an improved relationship with her husband and mother-in-law.

There is little work on the efficacy of different teaching methods. The Society for Research into Higher Education (SRHE) have done some work in this area (see Ross *et al.*, 1977 for example), but their work is based in Colleges of Education. As Karl Mackie (1981) writes, the application of effective learning in effective teaching is 'fairly well concealed'.

In professional training courses and higher degrees the usual criteria, such as examinations, are used to evaluate courses. This will be an issue of debate if part-time degree courses are incorporated into the RB system as the University of London has already done. I am ambivalent towards any examination system in that the skills of passing examinations are rarely built into a curriculum, nonetheless they probably do have a part to play in the assessment of certain skills.

RESEARCH

Psychologists are especially skilled in carrying out research, and since psychology has a significant if not a primary part to play in the study of adult education, it is surprising that more is not being done. Part of the reason for this must be that the distinction between pedagogy and andragogy is still not widely accepted by many research psychologists. Yet even from a simple practical viewpoint, the large number of willing and capable people, throughout the country, who make up adult education classes do have great potential as an easily reached subject pool. But as I have emphasized, they cannot be treated as passive subjects like undergraduates or schoolchildren usually are. Any co-operation requested of them for research will need to be explained and its relevance to their own experiences made clear.

Such co-operation need not be difficult to achieve. The central questions for research are essentially questions about the contribution which adult education makes to the lives of those who attend classes (although as I have indicated, the 'spin-off' effects on the lives of others may also be worth exploring).

At the simplest level we need to know why some people come and others do not. Why some continue to come for years and others 'drop-out' after a few weeks (Rogers, 1978). The answers to these questions, in their turn, raise questions about differences between people in what adult education does for them and differences between adult education teachers in what they encourage or provide. Do the formulations of Carelli (1976) in his insistence that the quality of life is improved by adult education fit the expectations of all those who attend classes? Does the approach I have advocated here, from the viewpoint of a clinical psychologist, really lead to people perceiving a benefit in their personal lives?

When considering differences between adult students, stages in development may be still worthy of attention. The writings of stage theorists such as Neugarten, Sheehy, and Erikson may be tested against experiences of adult classes. How does attendance relate to life crises which writers such as Caplan suggest are inevitable? Can adult education play any part in an intervention process?

The answers to questions such as these, about the purposes of adult education, can therefore help to answer those other more practical questions about the most appropriate skills for tutors of adults and the most appropriate teaching methods. They could also give us a basis for dealing with the public awareness of classes and other matters related to publicity identified by Rogers and Groombridge (1976). They would certainly tell us whether there is any basis at all to the view that psychology can be dangerous and give us firm evidence for questioning those fears.

One current standard textbook on psychological research and applications in adult education is Howe's (1977) book *Adult Learning*. It is in three parts, covering 'Human Learning in Adult Life', 'The Acquisition of Knowledge', and 'Learning and Modern Society'. The book shows that there is no part of psychology that is not involved with the development of teaching and learning and vice versa. For although, as Shea (1979) puts it in his review of Howe's book, 'psychologists are in no position to instruct educationalists how to do their job', they are in a better position than most to think about their own approaches as adult educationalists. Now is the time for them to take advantage of that position.

CONCLUSION

In the future, with the increasing interest in educational opportunities for mature students in universities, it could be that adult education will be seen as the 'norm' for universities, not only for full-time but for part-time courses as well.

The Universities Council for Adult Education (1970), in its first statement on behalf of the Council to the Committee on Adult Education, stated that 'extra-mural' classes should not be thought of as outside the main stream of university work, but 'rather in terms of opportunities for university education occurring at intervals throughout life'. Also 'if adult students wish to build some of these courses into study for a degree or other qualification, they should be helped to do so'.

Psychologists, therefore, will not only have to regard adult classes as leisure activities for students and a source of extra income for themselves but as an integral part either of their university or practical work. As adult education has it the explicit philosophy of equal educational opportunity for all, psychologists as adult educationalists will want to work to that end. This will mean university staff going into community and other settings rather than always expecting people to come to them.

Because of the nature of the organization of adult education, different subject specialists currently work together. Lifelong education has its basis in many disciplines. Thus psychologists will find themselves working as part of a multidisciplinary group. Indeed, as I hope has been shown, psychologists have an essential role to play in the development of the education of adults.

REFERENCES

Allman, P. (1981). 'Adult development: an overview of recent research', in Allman, P. and Mackie, K. J. (eds), *Adults: Psychological and Educational Perspectives*, University of Nottingham, Department of Adult Education.

Apps, J. W. (1979). *Problems in Continuing Education*, London: McGraw-Hill.

Britter, L., Hawley, C., and Monck, T. (1973). 'Psycho 73, psychology and revolution', *Psychology Teaching*, 1, no. 1.

Carelli, Dino, M. (1976). Foreword to Dave, R. H. (ed), *Foundations of Lifelong Education*, Oxford: Pergamon.

Cropley, A. J. (1977). *Lifelong Education: A Psychological Analysis*, Oxford: Pergamon.

Derrick, T. (1980). 'Some recent trends in British educational research', *Bulletin of the British Psychological Society*, 33, 341–343.

Division of Clinical Psychology (1974). 'Teaching psychology to nurses', *Bulletin of the British Psychological Society*, 27, 272–283.

Elsdon, K. T. (1975). *Training for Adult Education*, Department of Adult Education, University of Nottingham, in association with The National Institute of Adult Education, Leicester.

Feltwell, J. (1981). 'It will be all right on the night', *The Tutors' Bulletin for Adult Education*, 4, no. I, Spring.

Hearnshaw, L. S. (1973). 'The teaching of psychology in Great Britain: historical background and general problems', *Psychology Teaching*, 1, no. 1.

Hetherington, R. (1981). 'The changing role of the clinical psychologist', *Bulletin of the British Psychological Society*, 34, 12–14.

Howarth, C. I. (1974). 'Teaching psychology at Nottingham', *Psychology Teaching*, 2, no. 2, 145–152.

Howe, M. J. A. (ed). (1977). *Adult Learning: Psychological Research and Application*, London: Wiley.

Janne, H. (1976). 'Theoretical foundations of lifelong education—a sociological perspective', in Dave, R. H. (ed), *Foundations of Lifelong Education*, Oxford: Pergamon.

Knowles, M. (1979). *The Adult Learner: A Neglected Species*, 2nd ed, Houston, Texas: Gulf Publishing.

Knowles, M. S. and Klevins, C. (1978). 'History and philosophy of continuing education', *Materials and Methods in Continuing Education*, Los Angeles: Klevens Publications.

Korchin, Sheldon, J. (1976). *Modern Clinical Psychology*, London: Harper and Row.

Kovel, J. (1977). *A Complete guide to Therapy*, Hassocks, Sussex: Harvester Press.

Lange, A. J. and Jakubowski, P. (1977). *Responsible Assertive Behaviour*, Illinois: Research Press.

Legge, D. (1974). 'Discussion methods' in Stephens, M. D. and Roderick, G. W. (eds), *Teaching Techniques in Adult Education*, Newton Abbot: David and Charles.

McWhirter, E. (1974). 'Teaching psychology in interpersonal professional courses: a collection of papers', *Psychology Teaching* **2**, no. 2.

Mackie, K. J. (1981). 'The application of learning theory to adult teaching', in Allman, P. and Mackie, K. J. (eds), *Adults: Psychological and Educational Perspectives*, University of Nottingham.

Miller, Harry, L. (1965). *Teaching and Learning in Adult Education*, London: Collier-Macmillan.

Nelson-Jones, R. (1981). 'Counselling psychology and the society: the report of the PAB working party on counselling', *Bulletin of the British Psychological Society*, **34**, 314–316.

Newman, M. (1979). *The Poor Cousin: A Study of Adult Education*, London: Allen and Unwin.

Nicolson, P. (1981). 'Psychology teaching for social work students', *Bulletin of the British Psychological Society*, **32**, 6–7.

Rogers, C. R. (1969). *Freedom to Learn*, Columbus, Ohio: Charles E. Merrill.

Rogers, J. (1971). *Adults Learning*, Harmondsworth: Penguin Books.

Rogers, J. (1978). *Adults Learning*, 2nd ed, Harmondsworth: Penguin Books.

Rogers, J. and Groombridge, B. (1976). *Right to Learn: A Case for Adult Equality*, London: Arrow Books.

Ross, A., McNamara, D., and Whittaker, J. (1977). *An Experiment in Teacher Education*, Society for Research into Higher Education Limited, University of Surrey, Guildford.

Satir, V. (1967). *Conjoint Family Therapy: A Guide to Theory and Technique*, Science and Behaviour, Palo Alto, California.

Shea, P. (1979). Review of Howe, Michael (ed.), *Adult Learning: Psychological Research and Application in Adult Education*, **50**, no. 4, 264–265.

Stephens, M. D. and Roderick, G. W. (eds) (1974) *Teaching Techniques in Adult Education*, Newton Abbot: David and Charles.

Stock, A. (1974). 'Role-playing and simulation techniques', in Stephen, M. D. and Roderick, G. W. (eds), *Teaching Techniques in Adult Education*, Newton Abbot: David and Charles.

Stock, A. (1978). *Adult Education in Great Britain*, National Institute of Adult Education, Leicester.

Stone, V. (1980). 'University Reform', *Bulletin of the British Psychological Society*, **33**, 15–16.

Universities Council for Adult Education (1970). *First statement submitted on behalf of the Council to the Committee on Adult Education*, University of Birmingham: UCAE.

Universities Council for Adult Education (1980). *Annual Report of the Universities Council for Adult Education 1979/80*, UCAE.

Psychology in Practice
Edited by S. Canter and D. Canter
© 1982, John Wiley & Sons, Ltd.

CHAPTER 9

PSYCHOLOGY AND WORK: THE GROWTH OF A DISCIPLINE

Pat Shipley
Lecturer, Department of Occupational Psychology
Birkbeck College, London

That field of psychology most directly concerned with people in the context of work and industry is usually referred to as 'occupational psychology'. This label covers a broad range of diverse activities. In subsequent chapters the work carried out by practitioners in each of the identifiable areas of the field is described. The purpose of the present chapter is to provide an overview of the growth and development of the field of occupational psychology as a whole. Occupational psychologists are interested in individuals and their jobs, occupations and careers; they study behaviour at work and the variables thought to influence it; they attempt to describe and perhaps change the nature of organizations that employ those people. How far individual occupational psychologists are prepared to lend their services to help to change individual workers, groups of workers, work places, or employing organizations, will depend on their own value orientations and who is paying them. Psychologists based in institutions of higher education also may do consultancy and applied research in order to augment either their salaries, their fieldwork experience, or both.

Occupational psychology is not much younger than its parent discipline of psychology, if we were to trace the empirical origins of the latter to Galton's work in eugenics and individual differences in inherited characteristics and their statistical treatment, towards the end of the last century, and to Wundt's experimental laboratory in Leipzig at the turn of the century. An often-used construction of the history of industrial psychology is typified in the article by Cronbach (1957) in which he refers to two disciplines or traditions of scientific psychology: the individual differences tradition, and a tradition associated with the experimental investigation of behaviour. The first represents the basis of personnel psychology with its psychometrics and methods of assessment and allocation, and the second presages applied experimental psychology and the study of the effects on behaviour of changes to the physical and social dimensions of the working environment.

The earliest recognized textbook of the field was written by a Professor of Psychology at Harvard in America (Munsterberg, 1913). The book was about how to promote industrial efficiency and major tactics recommended by him were: (i) selecting the best people for the work; (ii) giving them the best possible conditions of work; and (iii) influencing potential buyers and consumers of their products through advertising and salesmanship. The first two have become well-established as legitimate areas of concern for occupational psychologists. The respectability of consumer psychology has waxed and waned and is discussed in Chapter 13 of the present book.

The classification of topics in occupational psychology into individual differences, personnel selection and appraisal, on the one hand; and the organizational context of work, including the job and its physical situation, on the other, invokes the person–environment dichotomy which is implicit in the most well-known and influential definition of the field, which has been attributed to Alec Rodger, who held the first University Chair in Occupational Psychology in Britain, at Birkbeck College in 1961. Building on a simple model which had been in circulation for some time, 'the person–environment fit' model (or 'job-fit' model) Rodger and Cavanagh (1967) maintained that occupational psychologists were trained to diagnose and deal with work problems of the FMJ-FJM (FMJ—fitting the man to the job, FJM—fitting the job to the man) kind. 'FMJ' was to be brought about by means of vocational guidance, personnel selection, and training, as appropriate, whereas FJM would be achieved by the design and development of work methods and equipment, and the suitable arrangement of working conditions (social and physical) and the provision of suitable rewards.

This way of viewing the phenomena of interest has a medical ring to it: the diagnosis and treatment of problems by qualified experts and consultants. The 'FMJ-FJM' formulation still holds sway in many places of professional practice. Notice that the perspective is from that of the person and that the level or unit of analysis, that of the individual, is a characteristically psychological one. *Individuals* are adapted to meet the needs of the organization, or the organization is modified in some way to meet the interests and abilities of the *individual*. The discipline's development has to some extent been held up by a thought block at the level of the individual.

Further, there has been a mutual relationship between occupational psychology and the managers of organizations, public and private, with the result that the occupational psychologist has attracted the reputation of acting mainly in the role of management technologist. In principle, however, there is no reason why the services of these professionals should not be engaged by other influential 'clients', such as organized groups like Trades Unions (cf.

special issue of *International Review of Applied Psychology*, April 1981), and other registered societies, although such liaisons have so far been a minority interest.

MAIN COMPONENTS OF THE DISCIPLINE
AND THEIR HISTORICAL ORIGINS

At this point it may help us to return to the historical threads of the discipline specifically in the two countries of Britain and America, where the subject has taken deepest root. This historical perspective points to the influences on the development of the field from larger forces in society, such as industrialization; the pressing needs of the war effort and the defence systems of the two countries; the impact of major technological changes; and strong trends in societal values.

The historical view offered here identifies three main threads, traditions, or components to the discipline; that of engineering psychology or 'human factors' as the Americans call it and which is referred to as 'ergonomics' in Britain (and illustrated in the present book in Chapter 12); the component of personnel psychology (cf. Chapter 10); and the area of industrial social and organizational psychology (Chapter 11). This tripartite view is reminiscent of the Rodgerian framework mentioned above. The personnel psychologist is more concerned with 'FMJ' questions and is particularly interested in how people differ, whereas the 'FJM'-oriented ergonomist is more interested in group data which can be aggregated and more easily accommodated in standard and fixed solutions used by designers for the physical and spatial problems of buildings, equipment, and furnishings. The socio-organizational frame of reference is also 'FJM'. General principles of organizational structure and function may be sought, along with collective views and opinions, by those more interested in the social aspects of industry and in organizational change and development.

At the time Munsterberg's book was published, an American engineer published his treatise on a doctrine or philosophy of work entitled 'scientific management' (Taylor, 1911). Taylor's ideas and motivations were clearly a product of his time and place occurring during the main phase and thrust of industrialization in a young and dynamic country imbued with the Protestant ethic of industriousness, self-discipline, thrift, and materialism. The assiduous fervour with which he carried through his ideas in the Bethlehem Steel works in Pennsylvania is a reflection of a strong and obsessive personality. The ideas of scientific management have had a lasting effect on western industry including British working life. Some of these ideas were also a foundation for the early industrial psychology and continue to serve as meat for the academically-based critics of industry.

The idea behind 'scientific management' is to seek to improve the firm's productivity through increased efficiency and the rational and systematic analysis of work processes. The main method of securing efficiency was thought to be through designing efficient methods of work and through controlling the work pace and effort put into their work by production operatives. The advent of mechanized production and the assembly line in industry developed from the original concept of Henry Ford, made this ideal attainable in practice. Attempts to standardize the methods of work of so-called 'indirect workers' (for example maintenance workers such as fitters and machine setters, storemen and porters) have been less successful, because of the irregular nature of such work and the necessary degree of discretion available to such workers. (Mentally-complex tasks have always eluded the time-study man's grasp.)

The main human concession made by time-study experts is in the form of fatigue allowances. By national agreement every job has its share of tea and toilet breaks, but those jobs judged by the experts to be more physically tiring are given extra time. No concessions, however, are made to the more psychological, higher-order needs, for variety, a meaningful set of tasks, the application of skill, etc. The job enlargement/job enrichment movement of the 1950s and 1960s was intended to replace scientific management, but the latter is still widespread in industry. In its extreme form the philosophy promotes an image of production workers as mindless machines, and/or as individuals motivated solely by economic considerations. Workers are as necessary a part of the production process as machines, but less attractive than the machines because they are rather unreliable and variable, having 'off days' and inclined to sickness, fatigue, and slowing down, and sometimes going on strike.

The stock-in trade tool in the time-study expert's kitbag is the split-second stopwatch. Typically, the expert can be seen standing white-coated over the production line operative, meticulously recording on a study sheet the minutiae of movements performed by the worker whilst simultaneously operating the decimal-minute stopwatch. The 'expert' is referred to by a variety of names, such as time-study engineer, work-study observer, industrial or production engineer. The latter have wider functions than basic work measurement whereas the time-study man's job is more restricted to standardizing methods and times, and periodically doing spot checks or audits to determine if standards have slipped in any way.

The industrial or production engineers, on the other hand, tackle all manner of production assignments; involved at the start in the design of all methods of work once the company's marketing and production policy is decided. It is possible to take a degree in production engineering here and in the States. Increasingly this category of professional is paying attention to the social as well as technical aspects of production, and occupational psychology and ergonomics are beginning to occupy a substantial part of the degree syllabus. There are some 13,000 or so qualified professional production engineers in Britain and over 20,000 work-study practitioners, compared with less than 1000 ergonomists and about 400 professionally qualified occupational psychologists. The work-study equivalent in the office-working environment is called 'Organization and Methods' and these specialists have amalgamated with work-study practitioners to form the Institute of Management Services. Occupational psychologists are therefore heavily outnumbered by those other claimants to work-design expertise.

Human factors

Industrial psychology in Britain probably had its clearest beginnings in the government-initiated investigations into accidents in our munitions factories in the First World War. These were conducted under the auspices of the Health of Munitions Workers' Committee in the period of 1915 to 1917. They were continued by the Industrial Fatigue Research Board in 1918 which was later to be renamed the Industrial Health Research Board. This tradition has been carried on by the Medical Research Council's Applied Psychology Research Unit based at Cambridge. A classic study from this early era of scientific intervention into industrial behaviour is the statistical work reported by Greenwood and Woods (1919) on the minor accidents sustained by women munitions workers. This report later served as the stimulus for attempts by early industrial psychologists to establish the phenomenon of 'accident proneness' (Farmer *et al.*, 1933), a quest which continues to attract considerable attention.

Farmer and his associates were employed by the National Institute of Industrial Psychology (NIIP) which was founded in 1921 by a remarkable man called Charles Myers, who was also founder of the Cambridge Psychological Laboratory, as well as becoming first president of the BPS around that time. (The BPS was soon to get an industrial psychology section to it and Alec Rodger changed its name to 'Occupational Psychology' when he occupied the office of Secretary.) The NIIP was funded partly from Myers' own pocket and partly out of funds from consultancy work. (The drying up of the latter after Myers' death contributed to its eventual downfall.) The researchers at the NIIP worked on many human factors problems, bringing as far as possible an orthodox scientific approach to bear upon their work (Rose, 1975) in true British empiricist fashion. Many of their projects about the physical conditions of work, methods of work, fatigue, accidents, rest pauses, and hours of work, can be found published in the pages of the NIIP's journal, which was later to be named *The Human Factor* in 1932, and subsequently in 1938 the *Journal of Occupational Psychology*.

The Ergonomics Research Society was founded in 1949 as a scientific forum for applied researchers working in interdisciplinary teams of engineers, psychologists, and physiologists, formed as part of the Second World War effort to help build men and machines into efficient fighting systems. Ergonomics was then applied to industrial as well as military problems, later broadening to include the needs of domestic consumers. The emphasis has been on the design of equipment and physical conditions of work to accommodate the psychological and physiological capacities and limitations of workers. Alec Rodger's view was that in addition to skills ergonomics should take account also of workers' interests, attitudes, and motivations to be fully successful. The Society was eventually renamed to exclude the work 'Research' in the title in recognition of the strong practical and applied orientation of many ergonomists.

Personnel psychology

Munsterberg's book was produced during the First World War in Europe. The American army made wide use of mental tests developed from developmental and educational psychology, for classifying and assigning soldiers, from which the first major test data bank was compiled. The British also used psychological tests with lower-rank military personnel and variants of these were later incorporated in officer-selection schemes conducted by the War Office. These schemes were developed during the Second World War and included various forms of individual assessment other than psychological testing, and the ideas were borrowed later by the Civil Service Selection Board in the processing of applicants for the administrative class of the Service.

The NIIP 'Myersians' (see Rose, 1975) also had an interest in individual assessment and played their part in the development of this major branch of the discipline. Alec Rodger was for a time an employee of the NIIP specializing in vocational guidance and personnel selection, as was the psychometrician, Cyril Burt. This branch of the field is referred to as 'personnel psychology' in America, and in this country there is the wide misconception that this *is* occupational psychology. Further discussion of this area is given in Chapter 10 of this book.

Industrial social psychology and organizational psychology

A third branch of occupational psychology derived from the studies of the Harvard group in the 1920s and 1930s in America, of which the best known are the studies of the effects of the experimental manipulation of human factors variables such as lighting and rest pauses on the performance of assembly workers at the Western Electric Company at Hawthorne, a suburb of Chicago. Although it seems that 'social man' was known earlier to anthropologists and sociologists, it is often stated that the insight did not come to industrial psychologists before the Hawthorne studies were done! It is claimed that the Hawthorne researchers discovered more or less by accident the power social factors such as supervisory style and work group norms have to influence output levels and productivity.

The birth of the 'human relations' movement is dated about this time. It is not surprising, therefore, to see the dominant emphases in the discipline on human factors and personnel selection being shifted somewhat in the 1940s and 1950s to studies of social and group factors at work. In the Second World War, for example, the morale of soldiers was investigated using attitude-survey techniques. The American textbook on industrial psychology by Tiffin and McCormick (1960), first published in 1942, contains sections on measuring attitudes and morale, job satisfaction, and motivation. A research centre for Group Dynamics was established in the late 1940s at Michigan University. A spate of investigations followed emphasizing the human relations aspect of industry, focusing on leadership style and supervision, group dynamics, social communications processes, attitudes, and morale, primarily in relation to questions of efficiency.

Another related movement, the Humanistic Psychology movement, was also gathering momentum at this time, based primarily on the Utopian ideas about personal growth and self-development of Abraham Maslow (Maslow, 1943), the American psychologist, ideas which have had a lasting effect. Maslow saw human motivation in the shape of a hierarchy of basic physiological needs, intermediate social needs, and ultimate 'self-actualization' towards which everybody is supposed to be driving, given the right circumstances and opportunities. Self-actualization is meant to include feelings of achievement and self-esteem and reaching one's maximum potential as an individual. Interest in human welfare as distinct from human efficiency was beginning to take firm root in the discipline.

The modern variant of occupational psychology referred to as 'organizational psychology' owes some of its origins to the humanistic movement. Douglas McGregor (McGregor, 1960) is perhaps the best known example of an organizational theorist who has built his ideas of organizations on this movement. He proposed that working organizations could take one of two forms. An organization was typically 'theory X' or autocratic, run by a management which believed that workers could only be motivated by coercion. On the other hand, McGregor argued, a more desirable and enlightened way of running a firm was according to a democratic 'theory Y' model based on trust and individual development.

Out of these kinds of ideas have grown industrial experiments on job design. Job enlargement and enrichment have given workers more variety and responsibility in their work. Decentralization of power and partici-pative leadership are also recognized characteristics of democratically-run organizations. The 'theory Y' proponents would also argue that authoritarian organizations cause psychological distress, and actual ill-health as well as inefficiency.

The job-design principles advocated by the Tavistock School here in Britain in the 1950s and 1960s are partly based on humanistic principles and partly on the earlier human relations movement ideas about group work. The most well-known job-redesign or -restructuring notion promoted by the Tavistock workers is the 'autonomous working group'. The 'AWG' is an answer to the Tayloristic approach to work design and its supposed undesirable side-effects of absenteeism, fatigue, and high labour turnover. The group comprises a team working together, often on the whole product, sharing duties by agreement and with enlarged responsibility delegated to the group. It is also the norm for the group to appoint its own leader, thus displacing the conventional supervisor or foreman. Modern examples of work-design experiments enshrining such ideas and principles are the work-design experiments of Volvo and Saab in Sweden and Philips in Holland (discussed in Chapter 11). The modern 'Quality of Working Life' movement could also be traced to such origins.

It is possible to identify another important strand in the evolution of occupational psychology. The study of organizations has been enriched by the insights of sociologists and social anthropologists focusing on structures and functions, and the norms and values of groups and cultures. Relevant structural theorists include Michigan's Rensis Likert (Likert, 1961) and his concept of organizations comprising overlapping groups. His idea was refuted, however, by Burns and Stalker (1961) who argued that structures of viable organizations are related to the demands and characteristics of the organization's environment, and that Likert's structure is only efficient in a rapidly-changing outside world.

The Tavistock Institute of Human Relations was founded in 1947 for psychologists of interdisciplinary orientation and the 'socio-technical systems' model was proposed by these workers to take account of both the technological and social realities of modern organizations. Technical and human activities are seen to be the interrelated contents of a dynamic socio-technical system whose aim or goal is to hit on the optimum mixture of all components for maximum efficiency and satisfaction. A viable system, according to this model, is also an open one which encourages a flow of information and intelligence across its boundaries which are kept open to the outside world. This means that the system is ready to change, is adaptive, when the environment demands such a change. The environment is defined in commercial terms (for example labour market and product market needs) and in cultural terms (for example societal norms and values about how organizations should operate, and the statutory influence of employment law, etc.).

CHANGES IN THE DISCIPLINE OF
OCCUPATIONAL PSYCHOLOGY

These last few years have seen some quite remarkable changes in the definition and practice of the discipline of occupational psychology. After the relatively short-lived toying with the 'systems' concept, an organizational frame of reference has become widespread within a wider social context. Although the subject has not lost sight of its parent discipline, and primary unit of analysis (the person), insights and revelations from other disciplines, such as industrial sociology, are being allowed to bear upon the subject matter. A problem-oriented approach forces us to confront the complexity of those problems and to respond in a more 'eclectic' interdisciplinary way than a unidisciplinary solutions-oriented response would allow. The failure of many project reporters to get their recommendations implemented is because what is offered is not seen to be relevant by the client. Experts have too often gone in search of problems to apply their solutions to.

Although our primary focus is the individual worker, various units and levels of analysis from the starting point of the individual, through small groups to the larger organization, groups of organizations, and even societies at large, may need to be explored in a particular problem-solving effort. Multinational organizations, for example, have considerable influence on people's lives, transcending the narrow boundaries of single nation states. The individual can be viewed as a figure, and the organization and the society in which it is embedded are the background against which the figure is seen. This kind of holistic thinking is evident in particular sub-areas of the discipline.

Many occupational psychologists, for example, spend most or all of their time working with a single independent client in a careers-counselling relationship. Until quite recently a narrow conventional approach was brought to this role, with services offered mainly to young people looking for a career path, or a first job, and a standard assessment procedure was used, comprising a personal record form, a set of aptitude tests and an interview. The modern counselling approach, however, is more holistic and considers the client's complete life-space including social and domestic sectors of that life-space, taking a more forward-looking view and helping the client to develop his or her own life-planning skill. Mature clients are also welcomed for counselling, especially those who have been made redundant in mid-career.

The modern view is careful to place the individual in context and to understand how far individual attitudes and behaviour are a product of social relationships. A worker's responses may differ as a function of the sex of the other person being related to and/or their position in the organizational hierarchy. A situation in which such factors may become salient is the appraisal interview. These contextual and holistic approaches also require acknowledgement of the potential relevance of the personal history that individuals bring to the workplace, and of a future which potentially extends beyond the confines of a single place of employment.

I have become convinced over the years that the successful applied psychologist uses a high degree of interpersonal and social skill whatever the assignment, and that such skill may often be insufficient but is certainly necessary for the job. It is debatable how far such skills can be taught in the classroom and laboratory. My belief is that something (but not everything) can and should be done by teachers to protect the aspirant from committing professional errors prior to actual practice. In my own case most of my solid learning has come from making mistakes on the job, finding out for myself. 'Many colleagues have shown how well they swam when thrown into deep water', said Dick Buzzard when he worked for the NIIP (Buzzard, 1970).

A good training, in my view, not only includes a grounding in psychology, but a borrowing of useful knowledge and insights from other disciplines. As far as skills are concerned I would want emphasis to be given to higher-order conceptual skills of analysis and synthesis, at least equal to the emphasis given to specific skills to do with the application of closely defined techniques such as psychological testing or noise measurement. Interpersonal and social skills important for dealing with clients and for working in teams, often multi-disciplinary teams, will also be paramount.

A further fundamental consideration which has nothing directly to do with skill is that of general awareness. Embraced by this notion is the values dimension, not only your own value orientation and the personal motivation behind taking on a particular project, but the motives, values, and interests of those in the 'client system' you will be dealing with. Ours is not a value-free science in the sense that values have no bearing upon what we do and what we find. Even when we take a neutral and independent stance we risk jeopardizing the whole project if we deny the existence and operation (often covert) of values and interests of all those involved in the project.

A major principle in organizational change exercises is that of involving fully all those likely to be affected. Full participation means that people's interests are bound to surface and be recognized.

The values question also has an ethical component. Ours is no more an ethics-free science than it is a values-free science, although ethical questions can be very salient in one project and may not constitute an issue in another. The practitioner has to be constantly alert to the possibilities. Often the true position does not surface until well into the project and a choice of continuing with or curtailing your involvement has to be made.

Given the values aspect of the discipline and the particular idiosyncrasies and local characteristics of particular organizations, it is questionable how far generalizations and principles can be applied, or even derived from such studies. Furthermore, whose values and interests are we primarily concerned with? Our own or our client's? If we exclude our own needs and interests, we are still often confronted with the challenge of identifying who is the client in a complex system. The reality is that organizations are rarely smoothly functioning and harmonious wholes; more likely considerable tension and potential for conflict is being contained and managed within their boundaries. To complicate the picture even further, if you pin down 'the client' the latter's values and interests are still open to change, perhaps as a result of influence from yourself as an agent of change!

This general awareness of the change agent's role should include an understanding of why you have been taken on in the first place, and what the motives of your sponsor really are. These may not be what they seem. For instance, you may be used occasionally as a façade to make it look as if management really cares about its workforce by employing a psychologist to listen to their problems. Trouble may arise in due course, however, if no changes to benefit that workforce ensue from the psychologist's involvement. You may inadvertently get involved in the organization's power game. When things go wrong, when management fails in its attempt to introduce a change in a covert fashion without workforce consultation for example, the psychologist may get scape-goated and blamed for it.

The blaming may be more easily executed if the psychologist is employed as an outside consultant. On the other hand, internal agents on the pay roll of the firm may be neutralized effectively by their economic dependency on their employer which may lead to their own job dissatisfaction at failing to get valued changes made, or sheer indifference about change so long as the monthly salary cheque gets paid into the bank account. There are many difficulties associated with both relationships, internal or external. Unfortunately, we are not usually willing as outside consultants, or allowed to stay in the system long enough, to work with the client for the level of independence to be established which enables clients to solve their own problems.

Psychology is often seen as an added luxury rather than as an essential ingredient in a society where values and practices are based on 'hard' technology and economics. When funds become tight we may be dispensed with as something the organization cannot afford.

But the near future may see some important changes and opportunities which we should not be too slow to grasp. Increasing problem complexity may force upon us the breaking down of boundaries between subjects. External pressures of all kinds seem to move us in this direction. Increasing leisure and joblessness, for example, may lead to all kinds of flexible job arrangements and demands for help by the long-term unemployed. Sticking rigidly to old definitions of subjects and disciplines (in knowledge, skills, and goals) will result in us failing to adapt to change ourselves and missing these opportunities. Remaining locked in traditional concepts and methods of science will also hold us up. Our discipline has a different kind of understanding to offer from that of the exact sciences, because our subject matter is people and their attitudes and values. We are observers, if we are not agents, it is true, but observers holding potentially a compassionate view of our subject matter.

REFERENCES

Burns, T. and Stalker, G. M. (1961). *The Management of Innovation*, London: Tavistock.

Buzzard, R. B. (1970). 'Field training in occupational psychology', *Occupational Psychology*, Jubilee volume, **44**, 89–94.

Cronbach, L. J. (1957). 'The two disciplines of scientific psychology', *American Psychologist*, **12**, 671–684.

Farmer, E., Chambers, E. G., and Kirk, F. G. (1933). 'Tests for accident proneness', *Industrial Health Research Board Report No. 68*, London: HMSO.

Greenwood, M. and Woods, H. M. (1919). 'The incidence of industrial accidents upon individuals with special reference to multiple accidents', *Industrial Health Research Board Report No. 4*, London: HMSO.

Likert, R. (1961). *New Patterns of Management*, New York: McGraw-Hill.

Maslow, A. H. (1943). 'A theory of human motivation', *Psychological Review*, **50**, 370–396.

McGregor, D. (1960). *The Human Side of Enterprise*, New York: McGraw-Hill.

Munsterberg, H. (1913). *The Psychology of Industrial Efficiency*, Boston: Houghton Mifflin.

Rodger, A. and Cavanagh, P. (1967). 'Personnel selection and vocational guidance', in *Society: Problems and Methods of Study*, Welford, A. T. *et al.* (eds), London: Routledge & Kegan Paul.

Rose, M. (1975). *Industrial Behaviour: Theoretical Development since Taylor*, London: Allen Lane, Penguin Books.

Taylor, F. W. (1911). *The Principles of Scientific Management*, New York: Harper.

Tiffin, J. and McCormick, E. J. (1960). *Industrial Psychology*, London: Allen and Unwin.

Psychology in Practice
Edited by S. Canter and D. Canter
© 1982, John Wiley & Sons, Ltd.

CHAPTER 10

THE OCCUPATIONAL PSYCHOLOGIST

Andrew M. Stewart
Consultant Industrial Psychologist, Surrey

The purpose of this chapter is to try to convey what an occupational psychologist does, and how it fits into a more general scheme of employment. A map is offered on which can be traced most of the openings for a useful contribution from an occupational psychologist. A few examples have been selected for a more detailed discussion. No serious attempt has been made to present the work as tightly organized and researched to high academic standards. Instead, a narrative account is offered of what actually happened in a number of situations.

There is continual discussion about what an occupational psychologist *is*. The argument might be easier to resolve if we were to concentrate instead on what the occupational psychologist *does*. Those who are concerned with definitions can then infer what such a person is from the hard evidence resulting from what has been done. Dunnette (1976) devotes nearly 200 pages to a thorough exploration. It is with some hesitation, therefore, that I offer a definition, based on a review of what I and my colleagues seem to have been doing. Our job seems to have been *to help individuals and organizations to make informed judgements about how to use the potential talent available to them.*

A number of points are contained within this suggested definition which warrant further investigation. First, we can only *help* individuals and organizations. We cannot make up their minds for them, nor should we. To assist where we can is commendable; to take over and actually make their decisions for them adds nothing to their competence. In contrast to the clinical psychologist, we are dealing for the most part with normal, healthy, sane individuals who have work-related problems. So far as an organization is concerned, we can only recommend. Implementation lies in the control of the managers for whom we are working. This is not to say that, on occasion, we do not find ourselves asked to implement our recommendations and to carry responsibility for the consequences. In these cases, we are no longer working as occupational psychologists, but have become managers. I believe that this barrier is highly permeable and that the profession would benefit from a more frequent osmosis. This view is perhaps reflected in the increasing number of requests from industry for facilitation of the managers' own efforts in preference to the superimposition of an outsider's solution to a problem. A facilitator can only function when he or she understands enough about the client's world and its problems to know when to speak and when to remain silent.

Second, we are concerned with both *individuals and organizations.* The occupational psychologist may have an individual as a client, for career guidance or redundancy counselling purposes for example; an organization can equally well be the client. Given that organizations are in many ways no more than the sum of the individuals within them, the dichotomy should not be preserved too rigorously, but it can be helpful for the purposes of exposition. Problems that are often defined as organizational might include selection, training, counselling, or initial definition of the type of employee needed to fill a given post.

Third, we wish the individual or organization to make *informed judgements.* By this we mean that there should be some initial collection of facts, using the tightest methodology available and acceptable, upon which the decision-maker can rest his or her judgement. It is here that the occupational psychologist's research expertise is most fruitful, provided he has an acute awareness that neither the time nor the conditions of the laboratory are likely to be available. Experiments at work tend to be less than watertight in their design and execution. That is no reason for not doing them, but it is a good reason for being as careful as one can and for exercising one's ingenuity to the full. It is the function of the occupational psychologist to provide the decision-makers with the best information that is available, so that they stand the best chance of making accurate guesses about what to do next. If they receive bad information they will make bad decisions, and eventually both the organization and the individuals in it will suffer.

Fourth, we are concerned with *how to use the potential talent available to them.* There is another decision concealed within that statement. People may also wish to decide *whether* to use the talent available to them. A frequent assumption is that whatever talent exists should be used to the full all the time. My personal preference may be for that course, but that does not attract everyone, and I have no right to force my value-system upon them. All an occupational psychologist can do, it seems to me, is to point out what the individual or the organization has at its disposal. It is then up to that individual or organization to decide whether or not that talent should be used. No such decision is possible, of course, until the nature and extent of the talent has been uncovered, hence the use of the word *potential*. We are trying to answer the questions: 'Who have we here? What can they do? What do they want to do? What does the organization want them to do? How can we make a match? If no match is possible, what do we do instead?' Overlaid on the answers to those questions is the right of the individual to agree that, while his talent may well lie in the direction of becoming a management trainee, what he actually wants to do is to work as a wood-turner in a rural crafts workshop. Provided that he has the talent for that as well, there is no reason why he should not do so, always provided that he does not expect the pay and conditions which go with the first course of action. The role of the counsellor can also involve reminding people that they have to sell whatever it is that they want to do, and that people will only pay what they think a particular product or service is worth in a free market. Desire and talent are not enough if there is no call for what the individual wants to do.

If the foregoing view of the job of the occupational psychologist is approximately acceptable, it then follows that it is desirable that some specific kinds of competence and experience be found in occupational psychologists. Experience in the market-place suggests that the following are necessary:

(1) Numeracy.
(2) Good foundation in general and theoretical psychology with special emphasis on experimental design and analysis, learning theory and cognitive psychology, and on physiological psychology. If a strong applied psychology option is available, this is an obvious bonus.
(3) Direct experience of earning a living in industry or commerce, preferably both as an employee and as a manager.
(4) Sufficient clinical psychology to be able to handle all forms of psychological test with facility, and to be able to undertake personal counselling without undue fear of raising issues beyond his or her competence to handle.

Such people do exist, although the level of numeracy is still too low. This has been a long-standing problem for psychologists generally. The fact that many managers are still virtually number-blind does not excuse the occupational psychologist from being able to substantiate what he is saying. This implies that both the statistics of psychological experimentation and the analytical tools of business and commercial life should be readily available to the practitioner.

Finally, the occupational psychologist has to be able to sell his or her wares. Like any other profession, the job is not complete until the client has understood what is being offered, has accepted and implemented it, and has evaluated the result. Nothing will happen if the solution, however elegant, is rejected because it is inelegantly communicated. The fact that the solution offered by the occupational psychologist may be the correct one is possibly self-evident to that psychologist, but it will not sell itself. We are not dealing with rationality, but with irrational, emotional people. They have likes and dislikes founded on all kinds of strange notions. One of those notions may be that no good ever came out of psychologists of any kind, implying that your first selling job is not your solution but yourself. The techniques for doing this are also capable of rational analysis (Rackham, 1980), which may render the task slightly less distasteful.

Having given some preliminary indication of what an occupational psychologist does, and about the circumstances under which it is done, it would now seem timely to offer some specific examples of occupational psychology in action.

In order to understand where each contribution fits in to the overall pattern of employing people, a map of the territory is needed. Table 1 offers a simple flow-chart of what happens in employment, from the point of view of both the individual and the organization. It will be possible to locate each example on this flow-chart. It should be added that a flow-chart of this simplicity, purporting to portray something as complicated as employment, must leave out a great deal for the sake of clarity. It should also be noted that we have by no means identified all the places where an occupational psychologist may have a contribution to make. To some extent this is because we are still discovering what we can do. Occupational psychology, in anything other than the applied commonsense variety, is a comparative newcomer. Part of the reward for the practitioner lies in knowing that much of what one is attempting has not been done that way before.

Some brief explanation should be offered concerning Table 1. This flow-chart is not prescriptive. It represents merely a record of what we have observed to be the case in many industrial settings. Since employment occurs of necessity over time, it follows that there is a logical sequence to be followed in the ideal case. An occupational psychologist may find useful employment at any or all stages of the sequence offered. Each stage in the sequence is now outlined, beginning with the left-hand branch, then moving to the right-hand branch, then following the common stem down until the two feedback paths are encountered and the final entry—retirement.

A. Organizational preparation

Before entering the flow-chart proper a box should possibly rest containing the organization's business plan. This will provide an organizational context within which all else happens.

(1) *Diagnosis*—a systematic approach to determining what jobs need to be done and what characteristics should be sought in those selected to do the jobs.

Table 1

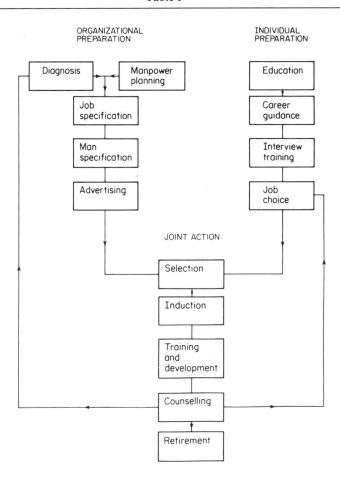

(2) *Manpower Planning*—an analysis of the stocks and flows of people in the organization, related to both internal and external change, in so far as such change is predictable. Morris (1972) gives an excellent introduction to the subject while Bartholomew and Forbes (1978) offer a more mathematical treatment. Both the human (psychological) and numerical (commercial) components of an organization's needs merit investigation. Either without the other will offer an unbalanced picture.

(3) *Job Specification*—the production of a carefully defined statement of the job to be done, quite independently of the person who may be asked to do it.

(4) *Man Specification*—the production of carefully defined statement of a variety of ways in which the job might be done, each requiring a different kind of person, but all leading to effective performance. Our first example illustrates a diagnosis leading to such a man specification.

(5) *Advertising*—the means of making attractive both the position available (to the labour market) and the product (to the potential customer).

B. Individual preparation

The right-hand branch of the flow-chart attempts to show what the individual can do to prepare himself for making the best choice of job.

(6) *Education*—the process of becoming equipped for a variety of roles which others in a society may be prepared to buy, thereby permitting the individual to earn a living. While the educational process itself has been subject to a great deal of research to render it more effective there seems to have been far less research into bridging the gap between education and a productive adult life.

(7) *Career Guidance*—assisting an individual to make an informed choice about the range of appropriate career opportunities available. This is one of the longer established areas to which the occupational psychologist contributes. It requires both a wide knowledge of the different careers available and facility with many different investigative instruments. Our second example is drawn from this area.

(8) *Interview Training*—in the same way as it is possible and desirable for an employer to be trained to interview, so is it possible to be trained to be interviewed. A poor performance at interview can unreasonably block an otherwise good choice of career.

(9) *Job Choice*—assisting an individual to make a decision about a specific job, rather than a more general identification of areas of work. This might be thought of as a more tightly focused form of career guidance.

C. Joint action

In the remaining stages of the employment sequence, both employer and employee are jointly involved. Both have to work to make a success of employment.

(10) *Selection*—both parties having now thoroughly prepared themselves it is possible to come to an informed judgement about the suitability of an individual for a particular position. The occupational psychologist has been heavily engaged in this area, and our third example is concerned with selection.

(11) *Induction*—helping the individual to settle down quickly in a new post or new organization. The knowledge of the psychologist about the management of stress and the special problems of adult learning could have a major application here, but are at present underutilized (cf. Chapter 8 of the present volume).

(12) *Training and Development*—equipping individuals to perform new or more complicated tasks in the organization. This may range from learning to operate a microcomputer-controlled machine tool to acquiring an understanding of the implications of the international money market for domestic strategy. Not only are techniques of training applicable here, but also an understanding of motivation. The occupational psychologist should have an input into both the technology of training and development and its direction. Adults who see no sense in what they are being asked to do often do it badly. Our fourth example is drawn from the area of training and development.

(13) *Counselling*—involving both counselling of individuals and training others to give work-related counselling. This may range from quite small items concerned with the performance of the immediate task to much larger items concerned with career change. Redundancy-counselling figures unhappily large at the time of writing.

The feedback loops which occur in the flow-chart at this point represent the possibility that counselling may lead to a new job choice for the individual, or that the cumulative record of such counselling discussions may lead to new diagnosis of the organization's needs. Redundancy counselling may be thought to suggest a further loop back to career guidance if below the age of 55, and possibly to pre-retirement counselling if over 55.

(14) *Retirement*—preparation for retirement and post-retirement counselling are both offered by a number of organizations. The incidence of early death after retirement is high. Assistance with the transition from a guided and circumscribed life to one of relative freedom in time coupled with reduced financial security is greatly needed.

It is now proposed to consider four examples of the application of the special skills of the occupational psychologist.

EXAMPLE ONE: DIAGNOSIS

The problems with which clients most often approach us tend to fall in the areas of selection or training. These problems are usually presented in the form of a request for a psychological test of some kind—sometimes specifically named—or for some other technique which has attracted the client's

Table 2

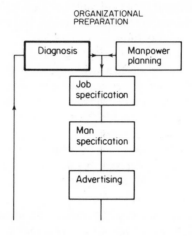

attention. We call this the 'flavour-of-the-month' syndrome. There is a serious tendency, particularly at the more commercial end of the market, for clients to be presented with solutions in search of problems to which to apply them. This is dangerous for two reasons. First, the solution may be wholly inappropriate to the particular problem that the client has. Secondly, a perfectly good technique may be rejected because it did not work in a situation for which it was never designed. We can therefore find ourselves in the paradoxical position of responding to a client's request for help with a firm 'No'. We then have to give reasons and suggest what we think he should do instead.

For example, a client approached us some time ago with the following problem. He was recruiting salesmen for the insurance-broking industry. The job of these salesmen is to identify their customers' insurance needs and then to find that insurance company, or combination of companies, whose policies will best meet those needs. Note that their first task is to identify their customers' needs. However, the logic of this approach did not transfer itself to their recruitment procedures. After discovering that they were losing something over half their recruits within six months of appointment, and that hardly any of them stayed long enough to grow into more senior posts, the managing director decided that he needed to tighten up his recruitment methods by testing the intelligence of his prospective salesmen. It was never explained satisfactorily why he thought this would help.

They acquired three of the old National Institute of Industrial Psychology tests. The NIIP no longer exists and the need for something like it—a source of excellence for *practitioners* in occupational psychology—is great. The company elected to use a test of general intelligence, a test of verbal ability, and a test of numerical ability. Norms used were those from the general population. No appreciable difference could be detected in the number of new recruits leaving after six months, so they concluded that they needed different tests.

We began by looking carefully at the records that were available, noting any relationships that might exist between length of stay and test score. There was no correlation at all. All that one could say was that on both general intelligence and verbal ability the recruits tended to be somewhat above general population means, with surprisingly little spread. On the numerical ability test, all recruits fell in the 95th percentile of the general population! This was clearly unusual. One question about the background of the recruits solved the problem. They had all worked for a number of years as an actuary, or in some allied post. One wonders what need there was to test their numerical skills further. A more searching inspection of the data yielded the information that the reason for the tight distribution of all three sets of scores was that such selection criteria as there were had defined cut-offs below which no applicant would be considered. No data had been kept on the unsuccessful applicants. It was therefore not possible to say anything about the characteristics of the population from which applicants had been drawn. On the basis of our highly critical review of their current practice we were given permission to suggest ways in which we felt the job could be tackled more effectively.

Our first question surprised them. 'How much does it cost you every time you lose one of these recruits?' We then added, 'And how much does it cost you to replace him?' They did not feel that this was at all the kind of question that they had expected a psychologist to ask. We told them that, until we knew how much the problem was costing them we could not help them to decide how much it was worth spending on the solution! The notion that any kind of psychologist could be concerned about profit was new to them. Once they had realized that we were in business in part to help them to stay in business and to perform their chosen function more cost-effectively, much of the opposition to being interfered with by 'one of those damned trick-cyclists' vanished.

The answers to our questions, incidentally, at 1973 prices, were that it cost £6000 to advertise for, select, and train a salesman to a position from which he could be sent to a customer unaccompanied. Each time they lost a salesman they had effectively wasted £6000 because he had not yet had time to pay back his costs in revenue. They then incurred a further £6000 in advertising, selection, and training costs for his replacement. This, of course, is repeated as often as there are mistakes in salesman selection. Since our intervention was going to cost no more than one-third of the price of one mistake we encountered little further opposition on the grounds of expense. It is not normally difficult to show that the cost of a consultant under these circumstances is very quickly recovered with a relatively modest improvement in performance, but it still needs to be demonstrated to the satisfaction of the client.

We then attempted to discover what an effective salesman *did*. Note that we were not looking for personal characteristics but statements of what was done that led to the completion of a sale. We achieved this in two stages. After familiarizing ourselves with the nature of the business, so that we had a common language and could understand what we were being told, we interviewed a sample of existing salesman—half defined by the company as successful, half as less successful. We had no foreknowledge of which was which. The interview technique used was a variant of Repertory Grid. A fuller account of the technique is given later in the Career Guidance example. For this example it may suffice to say that we became involved only to the extent of construct elicitation. A complete account of the procedure we used will be found in Stewart, V. and Stewart, A. (1981). Interestingly, from the theoretical point of view, we were able to distinguish between effective and less effective existing salesmen, almost without error. The successful ones produced a large number of constructs, of considerable variety, with comparative ease. The less effective ones were far more restricted both in the number and the range of constructs produced.

Next, we designed a questionnaire, on the basis of the construct list, and administered it to all existing salesmen. They were asked to describe an effective person by means of their responses to the questionnaires, bad points as well as good ones. Nobody is perfect, and it might just be the case that an apparent fault turns out to be a good predictor! About three weeks after those questionnaires had been returned, a second set was issued. This time respondents were asked to think of an ineffective person, and then to complete the questionnaire in exactly the same way as before. Three kinds of information were extracted in this case. First, there was a list of those items which discriminated between perceived effective and perceived ineffective performers; second, there was a list of those behaviours associated solely with being effective; third, there was a list of those behaviours associated solely with being ineffective. Those last two lists did not match because we were dealing with real people who shared many characteristics, regardless of whether they were effective as salesmen or not. Further, one item might produce a nice tight distribution of responses on the first, or 'effective' administration, but yield a sufficiently wide spread on the second, or 'ineffective', administration that no coherent picture could be drawn.

The origins of this technique will be found in Warr *et al.* (1970), but we believe we have evidence that it has been improved considerably since. For instance, as originally used, about 15 per cent of the questionnaire items yielded a statistically significant difference between the effective and the less effective picture. By prefacing the construction of the questionnaire by the construct elicitation interview that percentage rose to 60 per cent or better.

In earlier applications, items were generated by brain-storming amongst personnel specialists and the consultants; now we seek out the people actually doing the job, and their superiors, and obtain the information directly in behavioural terms that are closely related to the job to be done.

After the statistical analysis, presented in detail in Stewart, A. and Stewart, V. (1981), the items have to be grouped in some way and presented in a form that management will find accessible. What emerges at the end of this analysis and presentation is a series of paragraphs describing, under a variety of headings, what it is that effective performers, salesmen in this case, are thought to do — and what the ineffective ones do that is different. But this is at best only a reflection of the collective wisdom of those presently doing, or responsible for, the job. What if the needs are going to be different in the future? Or, worse, what if the collective wisdom is simply wrong?

To have collected all that information and to have presented it back to the decision-makers is, in fact, usually quite a step forward. It is, after all, an account of the basis — the perceptions — upon which decisions about appointing people have so far been made. But it is not enough. It is now necessary for senior managers, acting upon the best information that the technicians have been able to provide, to make policy decisions about what they are going to do in the future. After the data have been thoroughly questioned and revised by line managers, then and only then can informed decisions be made about what to do in selection, or training, or whatever the eventual purpose of the exercise is. In this case we were concerned with selection.

The outcome was the removal of the existing tests. A more recent test of intelligence was substituted, and a new and highly disciplined interview schedule was instituted. Every area to be explored was defined in terms of the questionnaire results and the exact questions and their sequence standardized. The interview record form was also standardized. Further, a group exercise was designed in the course of which applicants were asked to work on a problem which would reveal whether or not they could produce some of the behaviours which the interview was unlikely to be able to uncover. After some opposition to the change in the interview procedure — people do not like having to conduct disciplined interviews, which is why the interview is generally unreliable as a selection instrument — the managers settled down to the new routine. Nine months later we had a look at the number of new recruits who were leaving. The company was now losing less than half as many as had been the case before. This change has been shown to be enduring until the time of writing, deteriorating only when a manager departs from the imposed discipline. It is also the case that smaller follow-up studies have been conducted to keep the diagnosis up to date.

We have concentrated in this example upon one application only, and on two techniques used in tandem. There are many other applications for a systematic diagnosis. Team-building and management development within the organization come readily to mind. The diagnosis helps to determine where you are going. It also gives you the basis for measuring progress after you have carried out whatever selection, training, or development has been agreed. It becomes possible to check back to the original specification and to see how much change has occurred.

As there are many applications, so there are many techniques for conducting such a diagnosis. Stewart and Stewart (1978) list critical incident, self-report questionnaire, structured interview, diary method, content analysis of documents, behaviour analysis and others in addition to the two explored in detail above. Stewart (1976) provides an exhaustive account of the diary method which is probably a model of its kind.

We have spent a long time on this example because it can be thought to illustrate a fundamental principle. It seems most unwise to rush into recommendations for a client before gathering a thorough understanding of the problem. It would seem equally unwise for the client to rush into buying a solution until the problem that is to be solved has been adequately defined. To the extent that no proper preliminary investigation takes place, the advice offered by the occupational psychologist is likely to be misguided or actually wrong. The three remaining examples assume that such a diagnosis suitably modified to meet the particular case, has been carried out.

EXAMPLE TWO: CAREER GUIDANCE

Table 3

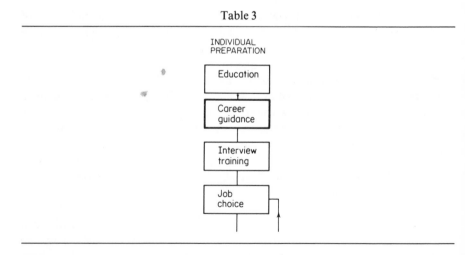

Part of the preparation for initial employment, or for a job change, which an individual may wish to undertake may involve some form of career guidance. We now offer a case of career guidance for a schoolgirl who seemed not to know what she wanted. After an initial discussion we concluded that, while she was aware of a number of aspects of employment which she found desirable, she was very short of words to describe working. We therefore used a fuller version of Repertory Grid than the one mentioned in the previous example. Our objectives were to find out what she thought about various kinds of job, and to extend both her awareness of new jobs which she might consider and her ability to choose between them.

This application of Grid is much closer to the mainstream of work with this technique and its associated body of theoretical knowledge. Indeed, the technique sprang from the theory. For a full understanding of the theory underlying Grid one can do no better than go to the source. Personal Construct Theory was propounded by Kelly (1955). An accessible account of the theory, usually abbreviated to PCT, will be found in Bannister and Fransella (1971). Shaw (1980) presents a useful collection of interactive computer programs for the analysis of full Grid data, using a cluster analysis approach. Stewart, V. and Stewart, A. (1981) offer a number of different applications of Grid in industry, including a self-administered version.

The essence of Kelly's position was that man can be considered as a personal scientist. By this he meant that we form hypotheses about that part of the world which presently concerns us, test those hypotheses, modify the hypotheses as a result of the test—or form new ones, test again, and so on. Those who detect a Hegelian note of thesis–antithesis–synthesis/new thesis, are probably right. Kelly identified a need for precision in defining that part of an individual's total life space with which one is concerned, followed by precision in exploring the ways in which the individual distinguishes between details in that part of the life space. All this was to be achieved while keeping the influence of the interviewer (one of the major sources of error in any interview) to a minimum. It follows that the purpose of any Grid interview must be exactly stated—in our example, to explore the feelings and knowledge of a young girl about possible jobs. That statement of purpose will determine the nature of the elements to be used. In the previous example, names of salesmen were used; here, the names of possible jobs that she might wish to consider formed the elements. Next, using the same triadic comparisons questioning technique as before ('Tell me some ways in which two of these jobs seem to you like each other and different from the third in terms of your feelings about them'), we elicited some constructs. Thus, comparing Journalist, Typist, and Cleaner, she decided that Journalist would be exciting, but the other two would be dull.

Our recording method, however, was different from that shown in the previous example. There, we simply listed the constructs for later conversion into questionnaire items. In this case the results were going to have to stand on their own. We needed more detail. We therefore asked her to create a five-point scale, from 1 = Exciting to 5 = Dull, and to place all the jobs she was

Table 4   Schoolgirl's first career construct

1	Journalist	Typist	Social worker	Air hostess	Cleaner	Secretary	Policewoman	Shop assistant	5
Exciting	1	5	3	1	5	3	2	4	Dull

considering somewhere on that scale. The result is shown in Table 4. It will be seen that she rated Journalist as 1 (exciting); Typist and Cleaner were rated as 5 (dull); Social Worker was rated as 3 (neither specially exciting nor specially dull); Air Hostess was rated 1 (exciting); Secretary was rated 3; Policewoman was rated as 2 (fairly exciting); Shop Assistant was rated as 4 (fairly dull).

Table 5

		Journalist	Typist	Social worker	Air hostess	Cleaner	Secretary	Policewoman	Shop assistant	
1.	Exciting	1	5	3	1	5	3	2	4	Dull
2.	Well paid	2	4	5	2	5	3	3	4	Badly paid
3.	Wear uniform	5	5	4	1	1	5	1	3	Wear own clothes
4.	Work odd hours	3	5	2	1	5	5	2	5	Work regular hours
5.	On your feet	5	4	3	2	1	4	1	1	Sitting down
6.	Romantic	1	5	3	1	5	4	4	5	Dull

Successive triadic comparisons of those and other career elements finally produced the grid shown in Table 5. This seemed a little sparse. That indeed reflected the basic problem quite accurately. She had too few ways of thinking about jobs. We therefore continued to the next stage, and looked for similarities in the ways in which she thought about certain jobs. We were able to show her that she seemed to think of Typist and Secretary as being rather similar. This process is called focusing, and was achieved by reading down the columns headed Typist and Secretary respectively and looking at the rating she had given the pairs of constructs: 5–3, 4–3, 5–5, 5–5, 4–4, 5–4. Could she think of any new constructs on which Typist and Secretary would score differently? She could, and produced two new constructs: high status–low status; work for one person–part of a crowd. For her, a Secretary was a high-status person who worked for one person, whereas a Typist was a low-status person who worked as part of a crowd. Whether she was correct or not is irrelevant at this stage. We were collecting information about how *she* saw the world of work, because that, in the absence of anything else, was going to be the basis for her judgements. We needed to know her view, unconfused by any of our notions. When we and she both had her views plainly in front of us, then we could start to negotiate on an informed basis. Similarly, Cleaner and Shop Assistant seemed much the same to her: 5–4, 5–4, 1–3, 5–5, 1–1, 5–5. Could she think of any new construct that would differentiate between Cleaner and Shop Assistant? She produced: clearing up mess–making things. For her, Cleaners cleared up mess and Shop Assistants made things. The beginnings of the extended Grid are shown on Table 6. By the time we had finished, she had

Table 6

1.	Typist	Secretary	Cleaner	Shop assistant	Journalist	Social worker	Air hostess	Policewoman	5.
1. Exciting	5	3	5	4	1	3	1	2	Dull
2. Well paid	4	3	5	4	2	5	2	3	Badly paid
3. Wear a uniform	5	5	1	3	5	4	1	1	Wear own clothes
4. Work odd hours	5	5	5	5	3	2	1	2	Work regular hours
5. On your feet	4	4	1	1	5	3	2	1	Sitting down
6. Romantic	5	4	5	5	1	3	1	4	Dull
7. High status[a]									Low status[a]
8. Work for one person[a]									Part of a crowd[a]
9. Clearing up mess[b]									Making things[b]

a Grid which had expanded from eight to fourteen elements and from six to twenty-three constructs. Having found out what was interesting and rewarding for her, we were now able to go ahead and give useful careers advice, based on our knowledge of her previous academic record and local job opportunities. She has been working happily as a policewoman ever since.

EXAMPLE THREE: SELECTION

Our third example concerns the selection of salesmen once again, but of a very different kind from those involved in the first example. From time to time one sees books with titles such as *The Profile of the Super Salesman*, or *How to Sell*, or *How to Find the Men to Make Your Profits Soar*. Those books, and many sales-training courses that we have met, seem to be founded upon the idea that all good salesmen everywhere are the same. From our emphasis on diagnosis it will come as no surprise to learn that there is no such thing as the ideal salesman in just the same way as there is no such thing as the ideal manager. Anyone who doubts the truth of this so far as managers are concerned should look at Minzberg (1973) to see the vast range of activities and styles that managers have to be able to produce in different situations. The same holds true for salesmen.

Table 7

There are perhaps three main sources of variation in what makes an effective salesman. The first is the product; the second is the personality of the individual; the third is the culture and style of the organization. The product may vary from a service (such as the brokering activity in Example One) to small, cheap items (like confectionery), small, expensive items (like jewellery), medium-sized and cost items (desk-top computers), to very large and high-priced items (cars, houses, ships, companies). The personality of the individual may range widely, from the stereotype extrovert to the frequently more successful sensing introvert. A salesman who does not listen is probably a liability. Two contrasting personalities can sell the same product for the same company equally well. The culture and style of the organization can vary along a number of dimensions. For example, it may be highly participative and consultative, or it may be very authoritarian. Both can work. The style will also be dictated by the market in which the organization finds itself, not just by the personality of the most powerful individual in it. Retail businesses have a quite different task from wholesalers. Direct sales are different from either of the previous two. The book trade is totally different in its requirements for salesmen from the chemical industry.

In this example, the company wanted to improve the way in which it selected salesmen for the heavy capital-goods sector—computers and office machinery. Selection at the outset was by a series of individual interviews. The first was given by a local line manager to assess general suitability for the post. The second was given by a personnel officer, also to assess general suitability, but also to go rather deeper into the skills and background of the applicant. These two interviews might occur in the reverse order. The third interview was with the Branch Manager, and was the one at which the decision to employ or not was finally taken. Clearly the first two interviews acted as a filter, so that the Branch Manager was only seeing those who were thought to be a fairly certain choice. Our intervention was triggered by one explosive occasion on which a Branch Manager was asked to spend the bulk of one week interviewing no less than thirty-six likely candidates. Not one proved acceptable to him!

In the course of our diagnosis we established that the interviews were unco-ordinated, relatively unsystematic, and that the recording system was only more standardized than a blank sheet of paper. Having established the range of behaviours that were thought likely to be effective for salesmen in that organization we were then able to construct a procedure different both in content and in administration from that which had gone before.

Administratively, all applications were now processed by Personnel at Head Office as a first stage. The practice of local initiatives was stopped. Any local potential recruit was given a standard application form and asked to send it to Head Office. Based on the diagnosis, a simple content analysis was performed on each application to sort out those who were clearly excluded for any reason —usually inappropriate experience. Those who remained after this paper-sort were interviewed at Head Office by a Personnel Officer, using a tightly constructed interview schedule based on the diagnosis. Those applicants who passed this stage of the process were then invited to a group selection day, based at the provincial office most geographically central to the manpower need. The group day was run initially by us, but this function was handed over to a Personnel Officer as soon as practicable. This is a largely procedural role, concerned with seeing that the exercises and interviews run smoothly and that those who are making the judgements are reliable and systematic in what they do. The judgements were made by the concerned Branch Managers and more junior local managers, who had previously been trained to observe behaviour likely to be generated by the procedures being used. In this way, up to sixteen applicants could be seen in one day by several managers, and decisions could be reached by the end of the day on all applicants.

The group exercises involved the applicants working in groups of no more than eight on problems quite like some of those which they might encounter if employed. This may sound unduly tough on those who had not worked in this kind of market before. It was intended to be. There was quite clear evidence that it was virtually impossible to sell this kind of equipment unless one had some first-hand experience of the kinds of business problems which the equipment was designed to solve. A high degree of numeracy was required, together with an ability to communicate the results of technical analysis in a form acceptable to those without that kind of knowledge. While the procedure as described here did improve the success ratio (number interviewed vs. number performing effectively eighteen months after employment), it was later found necessary to add a personality questionnaire to assess one critical factor which the group selection process was no better able to assess than was the interview: the ability to tolerate a high level of ambiguity. In operational terms, this means that a salesman in this field will often not know for eighteen months to three years after the initial contact whether or not he is going to make a sale. Traditionally, salesmen are thought of as preferring very low levels of ambiguity—they like to know at the end of each day how many sales they have made and, therefore, how much money they have earnt. Computers cannot be sold that way. There are too many variables to consider for any one installation to permit very rapid feedback on results. The salesman who can operate at this distance from his reward is quite rare, and we found that Form C or D of Cattell's 16 PF gave us the information readily, and could be fitted conveniently into the existing selection programme.

One other feature of this project may merit mentioning. We succeeded in training the line managers to take a highly disciplined approach to observing, recording, and analysing the behaviour generated during the group day. We had expected to meet opposition to this as it was in very marked contrast to the previous way of doing things, but we were quite wrong. Not only did the managers take to the new methods quickly, but they added new disciplines of their own. We ended by learning from them, and tend to take the view that this marks a successful assignment—we emerge able to do something we could not do when we started! For example, a discipline which they asked us to help them set up was a charting system, such that all observations could be seen on one large display and any differences explored and resolved. This is a standard part of our training of observers in some other circumstances, but we were pleased to see the need being generated from within a group of hard-bitten managers. We were particularly pleased to see the ready way in which evaluations that could not be backed up by specific behavioural observations were challenged and, if necessary, rejected regardless of the seniority of the individual concerned. In this way, the managers had effectively invented their own system of reliability checks—for inter-rater, observer, or conspect reliability. We do not always meet such ready acceptance of either the need for this or the associated discipline among senior managers, particularly in the more conservative of our employers.

EXAMPLE FOUR: TRAINING AND DEVELOPMENT

This field is so vast that it is difficult to decide which example to use. Whatever one chooses there is the frustration of knowing that much of value will remain unacknowledged. However, there is a recent example in which we have managed to combine a regard for theory with some very practical consequences. The application is in the public service, and the theory comes largely from the work of Revons (1976, 1980).

Table 8

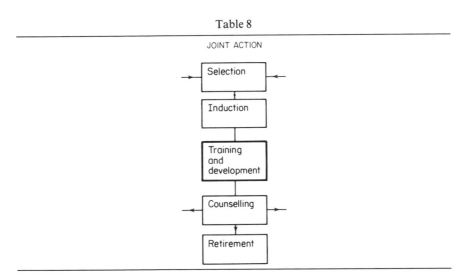

It is fashionable at the time of writing to be concerned with the problems generated by stress at work. We first began to address this issue in a rather detached fashion, running a series of one-day and two-day seminars during which we talked about the problem and some possible solutions with a number of people. We recorded our thinking (Stewart and Stewart, 1975), and among the places where this record was noticed was the Northern Ireland Public Service Training Council. This body has responsibility in Northern Ireland for introducing new programmes to senior people employed in the public service which their training staff can then pick up and develop. Public service includes the Northern Ireland Civil Service, Fire Service, Health Boards,

Education and Library Boards, nationalized industries, police—and usually a visitor or two from private industry as well. As a result of reading our paper a programme was built which involved many disciplines in addition to psychology, and which involved the participants far more actively rather than relying on passive listening.

The theoretical background is centred around some basic notions about adult learning which Revons has teased out of a mass of more or less disorganized business school practice and tested in the real world. Seven principles emerge, which are listed below. It should be said that we found out that this is what we had been doing *after* we had been running the programmes in Northern Ireland. It is often the way in practice that you only discover later that you have carefully reinvented the wheel!

The Basic Principles of Adult Learning

(1) Men and women only learn when they want to learn.
(2) An important reason for wanting to learn is a knowledge of one's inability to do something properly—or to earn a living.
(3) Learning is a social process.
(4) It is barren to argue without testing one's conclusions in specific action. 'Case studies, devoid of responsible outcome, are an academic imposture and business games, without risk of real loss, an arithmetical fraud.'
(5) Even deliberate action is a waste of time unless its specific consequences are assessed against a set of declared expectations.
(6) Successful ideas, even if generated in specific action, should be generalized as far as possible.
(7) Learning is not so much the acquisition of new knowledge as 'the reorganization of what is already scribbled upon the cortical slate'.

He goes on to imply that behaviour change in adults cannot be taught, it can only be individually learnt. The reader must now judge the extent to which our Northern Ireland programme meets the demands implicit in the principles listed above.

The objective of the three-and-a-half day event was to give the participants an understanding of what stress was and how it related to them at work, in order that they might change their own behaviour. The outcome of such a change would be a more suitable level of stress for themselves as individuals and, more importantly perhaps, the adoption of measures designed to achieve the optimum level of stress at work for their subordinates. It will be noted that we do not aim to remove stress. We were concerned to help individuals find and understand the right level of stress for them and their situation.

The team included a consultant cardiologist, an organization-development specialist, a senior manager from the public service so that we were constantly anchored in their reality, a dietician, a physical-fitness expert, two relaxation experts, and myself as the psychologist. Before each programme all fourteen or so participants were given a thorough medical check to establish their fitness for the physical component of the course and to set their individual baseline from which they could plan to improve. In addition, they were each asked to complete Cattell's 16PF, mainly to establish their scores in the second-stratum Anxiety scale, but also to see more generally what kind of people we had and who might be at risk. We detected eighteen individuals out of ninety-two, using 16PF, who were considered to have a dangerously high anxiety level. The cardiologist, working quite independently and using his own measures, identified the same eighteen individuals.

It might be questioned why, given our previously expressed enthusiasm, we did not elect to use Repertory Grid for the pre-examination. A number of reasons may be offered: we were unable to be physically present during the pre-testing, so whatever technique we used had to be amenable to simple administration by someone with limited training; we were interested in establishing Northern Ireland norms, in case they were different from English norms; we needed a standardized instrument so that internal comparisons could be made within groups and between groups. Grid would not offer the most fruitful path to these objectives. It should be added that, while administration of 16PF was given to someone else, scoring and interpretation remained firmly in our hands. Individual results remain confidential to the person who generated them and are retained for research purposes only with his or her specific permission. Among the curious results which have emerged from this exercise we find a Northern Ireland mean score of 2.2 on the Group Dependency/Self-sufficiency trait (Q2) as against a UK norm of 8.1. The reasons for this difference are not clear at present. We have possibly a skewed sample, largely self-selected. We do not know whether a similarly deviant result would be obtained from another self-selected group of roughly the same range of occupations and seniority, from a similarly small and well-defined community. It would be most interesting to pursue this in, say, Tyneside, South Wales, or the North-East of Scotland to try to discover whether this is a uniquely Ulster phenomenon or whether some other factor is at work.

The programme began with a restatement of objectives and a general overview of what we planned to do together. The physician then took over and talked for the rest of the morning about the medical aspects of stress at work. After lunch (all food, which was generally pronounced excellent, was planned to meet the requirements of healthy eating), the physician fed back to the group their medical pre-examination results. Clearly, individual results were not discussed in open forum, but the opportunity was extended for anyone who wished to do so to have a private session with him. Virtually everyone availed themselves of this offer at some point during the programme. One of the purposes of putting this feedback into the after-lunch session was to keep people alert (because the results were of personal interest) during what can be an extremely difficult time for both tutor and participants. People can go to sleep after lunch, to the extent that many lecturers refer to this time as 'the graveyard shift'.

At this point in the programme the participants met the physical dimension for the first time. They were sent orienteering (running, walking, or jogging between various check points on a planned route in hilly and wooded country). This exercise requires the expenditure of a small amount of energy and the ability to read a map and plan a workable route. Importantly, the tutors all go too. At the end of that exercise we were all welded together by mutual suffering and there was no shadow left of a division between tutors and participants. Once again, we did not realize at the outset how valuable this shared experience would be for the development of the team dynamic of the course. This experience was backed up during the evening by a film on the value of moderate amounts of physical exercise as part of a different lifestyle. The emphasis was on moderation. It is unwise for someone who has spent perhaps thirty years learning to avoid exercise suddenly to leap into strenuous action.

The next morning concerned the psychological aspects of stress—what it is, how you recognize it in yourself and others, and how to set your own optimum level. In the afternoon, in exactly the same way as with the physician, we discussed their 16PF results. Again, this was done on a group basis, with the opportunity for individual counselling should it be desired. It nearly always was.

In the late afternoon we went to a Sports Centre, where participants could take part in a wide variety of activities, ranging from squash and swimming through archery and softball to trampolining. In the evening, a dietician talked about sensible eating and revealed that all this splendid food they had been enjoying was part of a strictly controlled regime of healthy eating. She disliked the word diet, saying that people assumed that diet = pain. Sensible eating could be highly pleasurable—as they had by now discussed.

The next day, the physician and I combined forces to talk about what can be done about stress. Up till now we had concentrated on definition, diagnosis, and understanding. We now moved into corrective action, including the teaching of some very simple relaxation and control techniques suitable for use in the office. This session continued into the early afternoon. All then went back to the Sports Centre for a further session with whatever physical activity they wished. They returned from this session to find that all the tables in the conference room had been removed, leaving a large empty space, a soft, pleasantly coloured carpet—and two ladies who started to teach them relaxation techniques in earnest.

This session was, in fact, based firmly on Yoga. In Northern Ireland particularly, religious difficulties can arise if the label Yoga is used too freely, so the session was called 'relaxation'. Similar problems are often encountered in England. The assumption is made that Yoga means retreating into yourself, contracting out of the real world, and putting your left foot in your right ear. The ladies quickly dispelled any such idea by basic breath control exercises, followed by a session which can lead to the early stages of meditation for some people. For those for whom this part works, real personal insight can be achieved. Perhaps the most extraordinary example of what can happen was that of a very hard-bitten policeman who came out of the meditation session saying that he was astonished. When asked why, he said that he had started out by just going along so as not to spoil it for others who might be taking it seriously. For himself, he had expected, if anything, to feel drowsy and out-of-touch. Instead of that he said that he had never felt so alert and 'with it' in his life. That man's alcohol problem ceased at that point. In the evening a film was run which summarized all that had gone before and prepared people for the final day.

During the early morning of the final day, participants learned about the influence of management style on one's own behaviour and feelings, and on those of one's subordinates. Participants then moved into interest or occupational groups and planned two types of objective: first, something they were going to do for their own lifestyle to cope with their own problems; second, something they were going to do as managers to change the way in which they operated with their subordinates. Emphasis now began to move from cure to prevention. The final session involved all participants in declaring publicly their personal and organizational objectives (unless there was some pressing reason why they should keep their personal objectives private). A typical evaluative comment from a private-industry visitor was: 'I did not feel I was under stress before I came, and I still don't, but I now realize what I have been doing to those poor devils under me!'

Six months after each session, the participants received a further medical check and a parallel form of 16PF to ascertain what changes of an enduring kind had taken place. We now have data on over ninety participants and can claim that, both on medical and psychological criteria, considerable personal gains have been made: including weight loss; reduced alcohol intake; cigarette-smoking has ceased in all except one participant (from eleven); reduced skinfold thickness; increased muscle tone; and a highly significant reduction in the Anxiety scores. In four out of the ninety-two a reduction in excess of six scale points on a ten-point scale has been achieved and maintained. Twenty-three participants have achieved a better than three-point reduction. Forty-eight participants have reduced anxiety scores by two or more points. Five Anxiety scores have increased, only one by more than one point, and that individual has changed his job to one which is both demanding and dangerous.

The organizational results were disappointing. While considerable individual gains had been made, there was little evidence of real organizational change in the direction of prevention or management of stress. After a review meeting, involving sixty-eight of the participants, we concluded that one possible explanation might be that they had been drawn from too diverse a range of organizations. The latest course has therefore involved only three organizations, and all the participants were actively involved in setting up an organization to promote preventive health care. It is too early to be able to say how successful this attempt has been. A monograph on the entire experience is to be published in 1982 by the Public Service Training Council of Northern Ireland.

CONCLUSION

It has been my intention in these examples to illustrate some of the areas into which an occupational psychologist may penetrate. Not all of them are purely psychological. All of them are intended to be illustrative of helping people to help themselves and to make informed choices about what they can do and what they want to do.

In conclusion it should be noted that we are working in the real world, not the laboratory, where mistakes can cost money and can cause distress to individuals and organizations. This responsibility cannot be taken lightly. A conflict can occasionally arise between this sense of professional responsibility and a manager's need to get things done. This conflict can cause difficulties if it is not anticipated and managed. It is sometimes said that one difference between a manager and a professional is 'that a professional wants it good— a manager wants it Tuesday'. I hope to have shown that it is at least possible to try to get it good on Tuesday.

The rewards of being an occupational psychologist, for me at least, include being part of a growing body of knowledge to which one can occasionally contribute something; seeing that knowledge taken through to applications that make an appreciable difference to the way an organization behaves or to the competence and well-being of an individual; and the continual challenge of meeting new people and new problems that never quite fit into the previous mould and require some degree of original thought. The only major penalty that I can think of is the nagging fear that, one day, one may do something which damages someone whom one is trying to help, possibly through trying to do too much too quickly. Coping with pressure is a basic skill for an occupational psychologist, but it is also possible to have a great deal of fun.

REFERENCES

Bannister, D. and Fransella, F. (1971). *Inquiry Man: The Theory of Personal Constructs*, Harmondsworth: Penguin Books.
Bartholomew, D. and Forbes, A. F. (1978). *Statistical Techniques for Manpower Planning*, Chichester: Wiley.

Dunnette, M. D. (ed.) (1976). *Handbook of Industrial and Organisational Psychology*, Chicago: Rand McNally.

Kelly, G. A. (1955). *The Psychology of Personal Constructs*, 2 vols, New York: Norton.

Minzberg, H. (1973). *The Nature of Managerial Work*, New York: Harper & Row.

Morris, B. (1972). *Recruitment promotion and career management—the use of quantitative models*, University of Sussex: Institute of Manpower Studies, GN45.

Rackham, N. (1980). 'Selling to the low reactors', *Marketing*, 30 April, 58–59.

Revons, R. W. (1976). 'Management education: time for a re-think', *Personnel Management*, July, 20–24.

Revons, R. W. (1980). *Action Learning: New Techniques for Management*, London: Blond & Briggs.

Shaw, M. L. C. (1980). *On Becoming a Personal Scientist: Interactive Computer Elicitation of Personal Models of the World*, London: Academic Press.

Stewart, A. and Stewart, V. (1975). *Industrial stress: causes, costs and consequences*. University of Sussex: Institute of Manpower Studies, GN80.

Stewart, A. and Stewart, V. (1981). *Tomorrow's managers today*, London: Institute of Personnel Management.

Stewart, R. (1976). *Contrasts in Management*, New York: McGraw-Hill.

Stewart, V. and Stewart, A. (1978). *Managing the Manager's Growth*, Farnborough, Hants: Gower Press.

Stewart, V. and Stewart, A. (1981). *Business Applications of Repertory Grid*, New York: McGraw-Hill.

Warr, P. B., Bird, M., and Rackham, N. (1970). *The Evaluation of Management Training*, Epping, Essex: Gower Press.

Psychology in Practice
Edited by S. Canter and D. Canter
© 1982, John Wiley & Sons, Ltd.

CHAPTER 11

ORGANIZATIONAL PSYCHOLOGY

Frank H. M. Blackler
Lecturer, Department of Behaviour in Organizations,
University of Lancaster

INTRODUCTION

Only in recent years has the psychology of behaviour in organizational settings been acknowledged as an area of special importance. Nonetheless it is a particularly important subject. Not only industrial production but also heating, lighting, water supply, waste disposal, transport, health care, education, entertainment, and so on, all depend on the efficient functioning of organizations or, more correctly, on the effectiveness of the decisions and behaviour of people within them. Indeed it is not only by their outputs that organizations affect the quality of our lives. Most people can be said to spend most of their lives in organizations of one type or another, from the hospitals in which we are born, through the institutions in which we are educated and the organizations where we work, to the institutions that care for us in old age and in which we die. As members in schools and universities, at work, in unions, in clubs, as clients, patients, customers or citizens, organizations are a dominant feature of life. People may associate together sensibly and in a humanitarian fashion or their ways of organizing may be exasperating and degrading both for those whom they serve and for those who live and work alongside them.

The subject 'organizational psychology' can legitimately be understood to include all aspects of behaviour in organizations that may be studied from a psychological point of view. By common usage, however, the term is normally used to refer to applied social psychological studies of organization. Important areas of practical and theoretical concern have included motivation, attitudes and job satisfaction, job and organization design, interpersonal and group behaviour, leadership studies, approaches to participation and industrial democracy, conflict, decision-making, and the planning of change. The subject is problem-centred, however, and accordingly the boundaries that designate the topics that fall within the province of organizational psychology are in constant flux. As a research area organizational psychology is growing with, for example, topics of emerging concern including the psychological consequences of changes resulting from new technologies based on microelectronics and the consequences of the threat and reality of unemployment. Later in this chapter the history of the subject is reviewed and it is argued that prevailing social problems have been a major influence on the evolution of the subject area.

There is, however, a further reason why a certain vagueness exists concerning the exact position of the boundaries designating organizational psychology. Psychologists have not been the only social scientists interested in organizational behaviour. Sociologists, economists, industrial relations theorists, and systems theorists are amongst others who have made contributions. Areas of interest to people working in these sister disciplines have often overlapped with those of psychologists. (Sociologists, for example, have studied bureaucracies and the effects of routinizing tasks and the ways different technologies may affect organizational methods.) In consequence, to understand behaviour in organizations it is helpful not only to draw on concepts developed within psychology but also to utilize concepts from other social sciences. Problems in social life rarely fall within the exclusive province of one academic discipline. Whilst retaining the benefits of their particular training organizational psychologists in practice find it helpful to cultivate an interdisciplinary approach to their subject matter. In these circumstances the question of quite where a psychological approach ends and, for example, a sociological one begins seems largely to be an irrelevance.

Rather than seeking to draw strict lines of demarcation between topics that might be labelled 'psychological' or 'sociological', or whatever, it is more helpful to consider what it is that distinguishes a psychological approach to behaviour in organizations. Basically, psychologists working in this area focus upon the study and explanation of behaviour in particular contexts. In this they differ from occupational psychologists, who may not consider the immediate social environment of an individual, and from organizational sociologists, who may consider organizational and social structures separately from the actions of individuals within them.

Given that the distinguishing feature of the subject area is the study of behaviour in certain contexts, a number of possible roles for organizational psychologists present themselves. The first is a critical role, when psychological theories and concepts are used as the basis for an evaluation of common organizational practices. An example is the critique that has been offered of the ways in which jobs are conventionally designed. Jobs in modern organizations are typically designed by management to provide the minimum opportunity for workers to make choices and to exercise discretion (see, for example, the review by Davis *et al.*, 1955). This approach to organization centralizes control of the production process in management's hands. The psychological consequences for workers, though, are severe. Unable to identify with very routine tasks people become dependent, apathetic, withdrawn, or hostile. Organizational psychologists have predicted and studied such consequences and, more generally, have exposed some of the human consequences of decisions taken for technical or commercial reasons.

In addition to performing a critical function organizational psychologists can, from the insights of their discipline, develop a series of statements of what alternatives to the conventional are possible and desirable. In the case of job design the dimensions of motivating jobs have been explored (see, for example, Cooper's 1974 review) and a number of guidelines for sound job-design practice are now available. The presence of variety in a job, opportunity to exercise choices in planning and executing tasks, the nature, significance and difficulty of the job objectives are all factors that, typically, are associated with people's reactions to and feelings about their work. And, more generally, psychologists can take a broad look at the criteria that generally govern organization. Alternative scenarios of a fundamentally new nature can be proposed. A well-known example of this is Fromm's (1955) discussion of how the unchecked quest for productivity and material gain that is so characteristic of modern society is no guarantee at all of psychological well-being. His proposal was that psychologists working in industry should seek to study not 'the human problems of industry' but 'the industrial problems of humans'. On this view a respect for personal experience should take precedence over respect for organizational efficiency.

In addition to the roles of social critic and adviser on social policies there are two further roles organizational psychologists can fulfil. The first of these is to consider ways in which the alternatives that psychological theories and concepts have indicated to be desirable may be implemented. The subject of how changes may be introduced is an important aspect of organizational psychology. Managers, for example, often feel frustrated at the extent to which the proposals for changes that they make are, despite their apparent good sense and desirability, resisted by people affected by them. Junior members of organizations also, often feel frustrated at the failure of those above them in the hierarchy to take note of, or even to consider, their views. But it is not always evident to employees that the plans of senior management are justified nor, by the same token, to management that the wishes of workers are acceptable. As studies of people's reactions to changes have shown (e.g. Marris, 1974) the manner in which changes are contemplated, planned, and proposed is crucial in understanding people's reactions to them and psychologists can make important contributions to the development of techniques for intervening into organizations (see, for example, French and Bell, 1973).

Finally, psychologists working in organizations have a key role not only in introducing change as such but also in assisting in the efficient management of organizations as they are presently constituted. Given the importance of organizations in society today it is evident that the serious study of the effective use of society's resources is an important task for psychologists. Achievements have been recorded in several areas, not only at the level of the efficient routine functioning of organizations but also with regard to their effectiveness in non-routine circumstances. A dramatic example of the latter is Janis' (1972) analysis of decision-making procedures adopted by various American governments, in which he showed how pressures towards group conformity can, if unchecked, contribute significantly to such catastrophes as Kennedy's invasion of Cuba and Johnson's escalation of the Vietnam war.

In this chapter aspects of the work of organizational psychologists will be reviewed in a brief history of the subject area followed by a discussion of some recent developments and case examples. The objectives of the chapter are twofold. First, to illustrate the kinds of work organizational psychologists may do and the kinds of issues they become involved in. Second, to illustrate how important lessons can be drawn from this area that are of general relevance both to theoretical developments in social psychology and to the professional practice of organizational psychology. It will be evident from these introductory paragraphs that organizational psychology is concerned directly with social policies and the experiences of everyday life. In many respects because of this, it is rather an unusual branch of the discipline. Certainly some psychologists working in other areas have hoped that their work would assume an increasing importance in the formulation of social policies but in most spheres the years since the Second World War have not recorded psychologists as making much impact in this respect. In 1976, reviewing the impact of psychology on social affairs, the then President of the British Psychological Society took as the theme of his address to the Society the fact that academic psychology had only rarely taken the problems of everyday life as a main focus for theoretical enquiry and that even when significant social issues of the day had demanded their attention psychologists could record few substantial successes (Tizard, 1976). Yet, against the trend that Tizard noted there are, within the area of organizational psychology, a number of achievements and learning points that can be pointed to concerning psychology's relevance to policy matters. Typical such points will be introduced in the discussion that follows of some of the hopes, successes, and failures of people working in the field. It will be concluded that there are a number of shifts which have taken place, some of which are rather unexpected, in the approach organizational psychologists have taken to their work. These are:

(1) The realization that organizational psychologists must revise any view that they are strictly impartial 'value-free' scientists. It is necessary to

accommodate the fact that practical work in organizations is likely to serve some of the interest groups associated with organizations (possible groups include individual employees, trade unions, management, employers, customers, society in general) more than others. The question 'who is the client?' is a central one for organizational psychologists.

(2) There have been key changes in the professional roles organizational psychologists have sought to adopt. The role of expert adviser has, in general, given way to the role of specialized helper.

(3) There have been changes in the approaches psychologists have taken to encourage new behaviours. Attempts to introduce widespread and far-reaching changes quickly have been replaced by an incremental approach. Further, the importance of securing structural supports for changes at the interpersonal level in organizations has become more widely recognized.

(4) There is a growing recognition by organizational psychologists that the claims to knowledge and understanding that they can make must, of necessity, be less grandiose than many non-experts expect to be the case. Surprising as it may at first seem *certain* knowledge is not a feasible goal for organizational psychologists (or, for that matter, any psychologists interested in human actions) to work for. Despite the fact that many people who employ organizational psychologists would like them to offer definitive predictions about human behaviour and to formulate sure-fire prescriptions about what should be done, these are unrealistic expectations. Organizational psychologists tend to de-emphasize the quest for the formulation of 'laws' of behaviour and universal prescriptions of what should be done. Instead they point to the general relevance of psychological concepts, models, and theories to organizational problems and to the advantages of localized enquiry to determine their applicability in any particular case.

However, before turning to discuss these points further it is appropriate briefly to review the emergence of organizational psychology as an identifiable and recognized subject area. The potential of the field has only recently become fully clear as organizational psychology has become sanctioned as a legitimate area for specialized study.

THE EMERGENCE OF ORGANIZATIONAL PSYCHOLOGY AS A FIELD OF STUDY

Reviews of principal contributions to the developments of a particular branch of the social sciences tend, naturally enough, to focus more on the ideas characteristic of mainstream thought and less on the particular circumstances of their development. For example, Hall and Lindzey's (1957) classic review of theories of personality included short biographies of the principal theorists whose work was discussed but assembled and evaluated their work according to the type of theory each helped develop. The principal objective of such overviews is to introduce students to the nature of the theories themselves; an account of the history of thought in the area is very much a secondary concern. But although there may be debate about quite how exactly contemporary social events do influence the emergence of particular ideas few would deny the importance of prevailing social concerns to the shape of particular social scientific theories. For example, prevailing attitudes to sex undoubtedly influenced Freud's approach to personality theory; Carl Rogers' non-directive approach to counselling was, on his own admission (Rogers, 1974) strongly influenced by an ideology of the positive and hopeful side of human nature; and at least one theorist (Skinner, 1976) has set out to present a detailed autobiography simply to record the influences of contemporary events on his work. Although it is tempting to try and describe a field of scientific study as if it were made up only of studies and theories each adding a little more to what was known before, this would be to misrepresent what does, in fact, take place.

Within organizational psychology one review of the area which concentrates on the development of ideas without discussion of their social background has been provided by Pugh (1969). Having discussed various contributions, Pugh's argument was that psychologists interested in organizational behaviour should focus on theoretical concerns of their own devising and should not give priority to practical matters. However, this approach was soundly criticized by Cherns (1979) who argued that while the disciplinary origins of organizational psychology and the so-called 'pure' scientific concerns that might be generated in the area were of interest, in themselves they provided an inadequate understanding of relevant developments within and future prospects for the area. Cherns argued that developments in the field had depended (and would continue so to do) not only on the state of theory and method at any particular time but also on current social problems and on prevailing ideologies and values.

In explaining these points Cherns pointed to the major influences on the development of organizational psychology. These had included, for example, the work of F. W. Taylor before the First World War (who argued for the advantages of deskilling workers' jobs and motivating them to perform their routinized jobs by financial incentives); the emphasis on working conditions and selection tests of the First World War years (as the productivity of munitions workers was crucial, and as large numbers of service recruits needed to be deployed to various tasks in a reasonable way); the lessons of the Hawthorne experiments (Roethlisberger and Dixon, 1939) in the between-war years (where workers' greater respect for each others' views over any unbridled financial ambition or regard for management's exhortations for extra effort were convincingly demonstrated); the needs in the Second World War to design advanced fighting machines so that they might reasonably be operated, and to select satisfactory candidates for the rank of officer (which led to the emergence of 'ergonomics' as a special science and to social psychological work on small groups and leadership); and in the years after the war the needs for organizations to adjust to changing worker expectations and attitudes to authority, to accommodate new technologies, and to function effectively despite increasing size and complexity, problems that led to an inflow of personnel and resources to the area. Tangible signs of the growing legitimacy of the field in the post-war years include the appearance of specialized journals (in the UK, *Human Relations*), a prestigious consultancy centre (the Tavistock Institute of Human Relations in London), the funding of a major research centre (the Social and Applied Psychology Unit at Sheffield), and the introduction of a taught post-graduate course in organizational psychology (at Lancaster University).

The emergence of this area has thus been the result of a complex interplay of social problems and ideological climate, as well as of scientific advancement. Taylor's approach appealed to his contemporaries as it was in accord with the prevailing view that the righteous would prosper through hard work. Careful organization of work and fair administration of financial rewards seemed an appropriate and just approach. Later, the discovery at the Hawthorne works that employees value the respect of their colleagues inspired many who wanted workers to be happy as well as good. The emergencies of two world wars and the extraordinary problems of organization they presented greatly influenced the kinds of work psychologists in the area undertook. The orientation towards testing in the first war was reinforced by values of individualism. The concern with leadership issues of the second war allowed psychologists to work on an important issue of the day, namely whether democratic leadership forms were as efficient as authoritarian or fascistic ones appeared to be. After the war the changing problems of a growing peacetime economy and the emerging values of the western industrialized world combined with the theoretical concerns of psychologists interested in studying organizations to determine the shape of organizational psychology today. The trend in the area away from a concern with individual workers, their selection and motivation, towards an understanding of the importance of the context of behavioural events for an explanation of the behaviour itself did not result only from theoretical developments in the area.

However, it is specifically to the development of recent theory and practice in the area that we now turn. In recent years the author has been involved in a Social Science Research Council (SSRC) funded project reviewing aspects of the work of organizational psychologists. In the following cases and discussion some results of this research are introduced in a review of the increasing sophistication in approach that has been characteristic of this area.

SHELL'S NEW PHILOSOPHY OF MANAGEMENT

The first case is a landmark project undertaken in the mid-1960s. Its interest is mainly due to the fact that, certainly in terms of the declared aims of the people principally involved, it was something of a failure. It took place at a time when organizational psychologists were beginning to think that they had a science to apply. In many ways indeed, the way this project was run reflects popular expectations about how expert social scientists should operate yet, as we shall see, these expectations proved unrealistic.

The technological changes, changing expectations of youth, and increasing prosperity characteristic of the mid-1960s suggested to many contemporary observers that a totally new kind of society was beginning to emerge. So fast were changes occurring that it was also felt by some that their speed was outstripping people's abilities to adjust. Two such theorists were working at the Tavistock Institute of Human Relations in London. They had become convinced that prevailing assumptions about how best to organize were mistaken. They suggested that psychological and sociological concerns had been overlooked by managers with managerial and technological priorities for production processes having sole priority. Based on empirical studies by members of the Institute of the introduction of semi-automated methods of mining into coal mines (Trist *et al.*, 1963) Fred Emery and Eric Trist proposed that important organizational problems could be overcome if both psychological and technological concerns could be 'jointly optimized' in new approaches to organization designs. 'Socio-technical theory' was the name they gave to this approach.

The psychological ideas they sought to emphasize bore close resemblance to the ideas contained in an influential theory of personality of the time. Abraham Maslow, extrapolating from his experience in clinical work in the USA, had proposed (Maslow, 1963) that people's motives for behaviour could be arranged in a hierarchy of importance. Maslow thought that until satiated, basic physiological needs (hunger, thirst, sex) would dominate behaviour. Next, the need to secure an environment free from threat would predominate. Social needs would then assume importance, then a person's need for self-respect, finally the need for self-expression or 'self-actualization' guiding behaviour. This style of theorizing captured the imagination of people concerned with organizational problems and one managerial writer, Douglas McGregor (1961) popularized the idea that contemporary managerial practice recognized only employees' lower needs, with people's need for self-respect and fulfilment being largely denied by the authoritarian or bureaucratic organizations that were then very obviously the norm. This analysis was very close to that of Emery and Trist, who believed that, in addition to providing a living wage and reasonable working conditions, jobs should be demanding, should allow feedback on performance, scope for personal learning and decision-making, and should be valued by workers.

At just the time that Emery and Trist were developing these ideas the Tavistock Institute was approached by personnel from Shell UK Refining. Having read McGregor's book these people had come to believe that a new approach to management, based on a new set of principles, would improve industrial relations in the company. It was their hope that social scientists from the Tavistock Institute would write such a philosophy for them and would help to introduce it into Shell UK. Emery and Trist accepted the project and, equipped with their ideas of the need to develop 'socio-technical systems' proceeded to formulate a philosophy statement that they thought would be suitable for the company.

Over the two to three years the Tavistock Institute was closely associated with the Shell project four phases of their involvement can be identified. First, they drafted the philosophy statement. Next, after presenting the document to senior managers in Shell they helped organize a series of weekend conferences held over a two-year period to enable other managers in the company to discuss it. Third, they helped people work out strategies by which the philosophy could be implemented. Discussions with managers played a part here, especially counselling them on how to be more participative in their dealings with their subordinates, but the most visible aspect of work under this heading was undertaken in a handful of demonstration job-redesign projects. In these projects social scientists spent some weeks or months observing the techniques of oil-refining before submitting proposals on how rearranged jobs might better serve workers' psychological needs. Finally, the social scientists working in Shell carried out a survey of what changes had taken place in the company that might be attributed to the project.

It is interesting to note that the architects of Shell's philosophy had not, short of believing in the need to ensure wide acceptance of their ideas, any clear ideas about what particular developments their philosophy would encourage. In the event four 'main channels' for the implementation of the philosophy emerged. These were the demonstration job-redesign projects; the need for managers to act more participatively (they were referred to in reports of the project as 'change agents'); the productivity deals to be planned in the refineries by participative joint working parties of union-management representatives and not by management alone; and the 'socio-technical systems theory' being used to influence the design of a new refinery then under construction at Teesport. These channels of implementation were originally discussed by the Shell manager responsible for starting the project in an account (Hill, 1971) published some six years after the start of the exercise. Another six years after this the present author and a colleague undertook an independent retrospective study of events (Blackler and Brown, 1980a). In Table 1 our findings (which led us to the conclusion that few lasting benefits could be attributed to the philosophy programme) are summarized and compared to Hill's earlier, and rather optimistic report.

Table 1

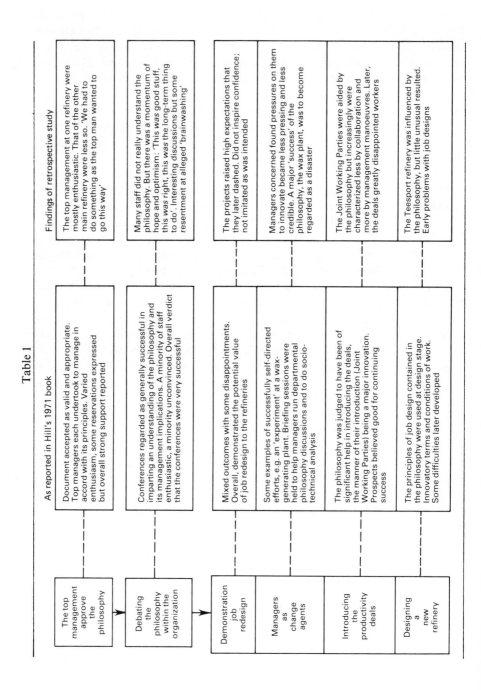

	As reported in Hill's 1971 book	Findings of retrospective study
The top management approve the philosophy	Document accepted as valid and appropriate. Top managers each undertook to manage in accord with its principles. Varied enthusiasm, some reservations expressed but overall strong support reported	The top management at one refinery were mostly enthusiastic. That of the other main refinery were less so. 'We had to do something as the top man wanted to go this way'
Debating the philosophy within the organization	Conferences regarded as generally successful in imparting an understanding of the philosophy and its management implications. A minority of staff enthusiastic, a minority unconvinced. Overall verdict that the conferences were very successful	Many staff did not really understand the philosophy. But there was a momentum of hope and optimism: 'This was good stuff, this was right, this was the long-term thing to do'. Interesting discussions but some resentment at alleged 'brainwashing'
Demonstration job redesign	Mixed outcomes with some disappointments. Overall, demonstrated the potential value of job redesign to the refineries	The projects raised high expectations that they later dashed. Did not inspire confidence; not imitated as was intended
Managers as change agents	Some examples of successfully self-directed efforts, e.g. an 'experiment' at a wax-generating plant. Briefing sessions were held to help managers run departmental philosophy discussions and to do socio-technical analysis	Managers concerned found pressures on them to innovate became less pressing and less credible. A major 'success' of the philosophy, the wax plant, was to become regarded as a disaster
Introducing the productivity deals	The philosophy was judged to have been of significant help in introducing the deals, the manner of their introduction (Joint Working Parties) being a major innovation. Prospects believed good for continuing success	The Joint Working Parties were aided by the philosophy but increasingly were characterized less by collaboration and more by management manoeuvres. Later, the deals greatly disappointed workers
Designing a new refinery	The principles of job design contained in the philosophy were used at design stage. Innovatory terms and conditions of work. Some difficulties later developed	The Teesport refinery was influenced by the philosophy, but little unusual resulted. Early problems with job designs

From the interviews we conducted with managers and employees, as well as with consultants involved in the project, and from the information that emerged from company reports of the time it became evident that early hopes for the success of the project were to be disappointed. In fact people who had attended the philosophy conferences had often resented being told their assumptions about human nature were misplaced. Many were downright suspicious of the exercise. One interviewee, for example, told us:

> A little bit must stick whatever you feel at the time. I don't remember what I thought was good but I was not very impressed. The general reaction of people was 'it's a bit of a giggle'. The only enthusiastic people there were the lecturers. Possibly other people were enthusiastic but I didn't meet any. We were being indoctrinated . . . Some of the ideas were good but whether they are ever followed up when you get back from these courses is questionable. I was suspicious because the 1964 'Golden Handshake' [a redundancy programme to reduce manning levels] had been preceded by consultants doing something, and other company exercises were followed by reductions.

And another recalled

> Most of us found it very convincing. We felt it was good, it could be a very good thing . . . And there were some good ideas coming out of it, like no clocking on, and the idea we are all professional people. Remember Shell used to be paternalistic, anti-union. In those days the 'boss man' counted. But at the conference they said 'You call me Eddie, I'll call you Jack'. We thought, what the bloody hell is going on here? But it made you feel good. Then we all got drunk!

Given the lukewarm reception that many people seem to have given the philosophy, later developments obviously faced difficulties. As it was, the demonstration redesign projects were disappointing, changes in managerial style did not come easily to many managers, the joint working parties produced a highly controversial productivity deal, and even at the new refinery problems soon developed. While the philosophy project was a fine endeavour, good intentions are not in themselves enough and the Tavistock workers failed rather spectacularly to achieve tangible results in the company.

There are, no doubt, a great number of reasons why the early and hopeful impressions of progress that Hill reported had not proved well-founded. For one thing, it is simply very difficult to achieve major changes in the ways large organizations are run. People within them become accustomed to the way things are arranged. Assumptions about what is possible and desirable pass unquestioned. Vested interests in the status quo run deep. The way factories are built, the technologies used within them, the tasks to be done, the social skills people possess, all these and much more contribute to what one writer (Schon, 1971) has described as a 'dynamic conservatism' in organizational life. No wonder then that the enthusiasm that inspired Emery, Trist, Hill and others associated with the venture proved insufficient to transform Shell.

More than these points, however, the Shell story above all else indicates that social scientists working in organizations are likely to serve one interest group more than others. The client in this case was senior management, yet the Tavistock theorists at the conference they ran to introduce their philosophy to employees at lower levels in the hierarchy presented their package as if it were of equal attractiveness to all. This (witness the quotes presented above) failed to convince employees who were themselves personally affected by the industrial relations situation in Shell at that time. Certainly life would be more congenial in a participative environment, with responsible jobs, etc., but employees introduced to the philosophy were well aware that, while social science consultants could afford to emphasize the potential for self-development in work, the company's interest in the effects of the philosophy was rather more pragmatic. Human problems in organizations cannot sensibly be treated like technical problems. Conflicts of interest play a major part in organizational life and any approach that promises benefits to all, while undoubtedly well-meaning, will almost certainly invite suspicion.

THE DEVELOPMENT OF ORGANIZATIONAL DEVELOPMENT

Since the years of the Shell project much has been learned about the theory and practice of organizational change. In particular many important lessons were learned from the appearance of an approach to planned change known as 'organizational development'. In this section we briefly review this phenomenon before considering further examples of recent experience.

The phrase 'an organization development approach to change' is somewhat misleading as it appears to imply a fairly coherent body of knowledge and practice. However, as This (1971) pointed out at the height of popular usage of the term as Kahn (1974) later repeated, organizational development (OD) is not a scientific term but a convenient label for a variety of activities. Despite attempts by some writers (e.g. French and Bell, 1973) to present writings in the area as if they amounted to a body of well-tried theory, OD is little more than a loose amalgam of ideas and practices. Yet even though a very wide range of activities has been lumped together under the term, there is some, albeit ill-defined, theme that does distinguish OD approaches from others.

An article by Chin and Benne (1969) identified what this might be. Chin and Benne set out to provide a typology of strategies for deliberate changing. Three types emerged. 'Power-coercive' approaches are one type. These include the activities of pressure groups, violent and non-violent protests, strikes, sit-ins and the like. An alternative type was 'rational-empirical' approaches. Research activities designed to identify the facts so that policies might better be formulated, rational argument, operations research, and attempts to restructure organizations and select more suitable personnel for key jobs are examples of rational-empirical strategies. Both these and power-coercive approaches are easily recognized of course and well-discussed. Both have their problems. Power-coercive approaches are likely to create resentment and to breed counter-reaction. Rational-empirical approaches exasperatingly often fail as research reports are ignored or as rational solutions fail to convince. It is correct to say that the third class of Chin and Benne's change types emerged from attempts to avoid such problems. Chin and Benne called it the 'normative-re-educative' approach. In this, attempts are made to utilize what is known about man's emotional nature in addition to what is known about his capacity for rationality and his response to moral, legal, or political imperatives. It builds on insights developed by psycho-therapists, counsellors, and social skills trainers. Normative-re-educative approaches encourage people to 'own' problems for themselves and, with their own resources, to explore new ways of coping rather than be directed by outside experts or pressure groups.

OD is best understood as one such approach to change. Writers in this tradition urged change agents not to impose solutions on their clients but to help their clients develop the skills and organization to employ their own resources for dealing with issues. (There is, evidently, a very considerable difference here to the one adopted in the Shell project.) The importance of group influences on individuals is very relevant to this approach. One psychologist who was interested in normative-re-educative approaches to change was to study the techniques of brainwashing used by the Chinese in the Korean war (Schein, 1956) and to conclude that groups served many important psychological functions (such as helping a person to define reality, confirming his self-esteem, providing an outlet for his affiliation needs and providing him with a security base). Accordingly Schein thought the importance of groups in our lives should not be underestimated and attempts to change behaviour should take note of prevailing group norms. Later he presented a model for changing group norms to managers (Schein, 1964) and wrote an account of how consultants might utilize group psychology in organizational development work (Schein, 1969). The essence of Schein's approach is to encourage open discussion about group norms to avoid interpersonal manoeuvrings and to encourage a supportive and innovatory group climate.

Foremost amongst consultants applying such approaches was Chris Argyris, whose model for OD consulting, at first sight paradoxically, argued that change should not be the change agent's first priority. Argyris (1970) recommended that a number of 'key tasks' should comprise the OD consultant's role. These were that the consultant should seek to help his clients to receive valid and useful information, to make free and informed choices, and to have internal commitment to the choices they do make. In itemizing these factors Argyris identified what the essential aspects of many professional interventions by organization psychologists amount to. The consultant/researcher acts as a catalyst, enabling his client group to review assumptions about events for itself, and to take better informed decisions with more conviction than would otherwise be likely. The 'doctor-patient' model (as adopted, for example, in the Shell project where the Tavistock workers, convinced of the diagnosis, wrote out a prescription) is self-consciously avoided.

Argyris felt that a crucial area where 'valid and useful' information was not, characteristically, put to use in organizational life was that of interpersonal behaviour. Given the bureaucratic structure of most organizations decision-making tends to be controlled at the top by unilateral management action, junior employees are expected to be conformist, their job tasks being rigidly defined and with the administration of information, rewards, and punishment being controlled by senior personnel. Argyris pointed out that psychological withdrawal, dependence, hostility, and mistrust are characteristic responses to such circumstances. Feelings are not discussed, rationality is falsely emphasized with the consequence that the motivation and inventiveness of an organization's members are stifled. In a very similar way to McGregor, Argyris pointed out that conventional assumptions about appropriate ways of organizing left much to be desired.

It was in the resulting plethora of techniques put forward by other writers as examples of ways in which people might be encouraged to explore group and interpersonal behaviour that the confusion about the nature of OD arose. Sensitivity-training groups, encounter groups, team-building activities, semi-autonomous work groups, leadership-style training, intergroup confrontation meetings, survey feedback procedures, these techniques and others reviewed by French and Bell (1973) were presented to managers as simple prescriptions to overcome deep-rooted organizational problems. There was much talk of moving from 'unhealthy' to 'healthy' organizations, where employees all collaborated 'In such a way that the goals and purposes of the organisation are attained at the same time that human values within organisations are furthered' (French and Bell, p.xiii). Indeed it must have been comforting to be reassured, as was Skibbins (1974), that radical change was possible and any reasonably intelligent and able manager *could* attain it in his organization.

The enthusiasm characteristic of such writings is very reminiscent of the Shell project. Like the Shell project too, early hopes were to be let down as the buoyant optimism of some of those inspired by OD began to flounder. Central in this process was the discovery that while increased openness was desirable in modern organizations within the reality of organizational life it would not necessarily guarantee much change. Organizations, people came to realize, are not coherent bodies with unitary goals but are made up of individuals, groups, and coalitions of groups that are engaged in both co-operative and competitive activities. The alleged aims or goals of an organization reflect the aims and ideologies of the present dominant group. Power, influence, and politics are important characteristics of organization life. The routines and structures of bureaucracy reflect not only, as McGregor and Argyris suggested, conventional views of the nature of man but also reflect interests vested in the maintenance of current arrangements. The lessons of the Shell project in emphasizing the significance of contextual arrangements for an understanding of localized behavioural events are evident here also.

Recognizing points such as these two recent trends in the literature on organization change may be identified. An article by Pettigrew (1976) represents one important development. Pettigrew analysed the OD consultant's role in terms of the various power bases he might be using in his attempts to influence other people. Part of the 'valid and useful information' Pettigrew believed people might make use of relates to the politics of organizational life, and how a consultant's activities are inevitably a part of them. Expertise in a certain field, control over information, access to powerfully placed individuals and the strength and number of links with them, the consultant's reputation and the opportunity he has to rely upon supporting resources, are the power bases Pettigrew suggested consultants had to depend on in their change attempts. Such a line of thought was developed also by Mangham (1981) who pointed out that, given the competitive aspect of organizational life, consultants should consider playing their political roles more self-consciously. Advocacy, confrontation, even covert and devious actions might, he suggests, become part of a change armory. However distasteful this might appear to psychologists like Argyris, this is probably realistic advice for change agents who decide to work for weaker groups in organizations, who will often find that more direct approaches to achieve change tend to fail. It does, however, clearly raise a number of important ethical and professional issues and the present author feels uneasy about the suggestion that deviousness is an acceptable way forward.

A second and related trend is the increased awareness amongst change agents of the importance of structural support for changes at the interpersonal level. This outlook suggests, for example, that within an organization if jobs stifle individual initiatives then new designs should be found, and if bureaucracies prevent involvement in decision-making then alternatives to hierarchies should be tried. Extended somewhat, the same point of view suggests that changes at the organizational level may need the encouragement and support of outside institutions, including government and legislation. This may offer a way forward which recognizes the power shifts that new approaches to organization may imply, but avoids the need suggested by Mangham for change agents operating at the organizational level to act covertly. Such issues are amongst those that are discussed in the following two case histories.

Job design in its organizational context

The first of these is concerned with developments in Volvo's truck division. Volvo itself has enjoyed, indeed has cultivated, a reputation for an enlightened approach to the utilization of social scientific theories. The motor industry generally has had a very bad press amongst social scientists and Volvo's achievements here are somewhat unusual.

The psychology of job design has been a topic of recurring interest to organizational psychologists in the last twenty years. As we have already noted, much of what is presently practised can be traced to the original ideas of F. W. Taylor, an engineer working in the first decade of this century. Management, he pointed out (Taylor, 1911), faced a problem in controlling workers when, as was often the case with skilled men, the workers knew more about what was required than did their managers. He suggested that brain work should be removed from the shop floor, work planning should become a job for managers, and suitable workers should be selected and trained by management, then motivated by appropriate financial rewards. It was only much later that the psychological consequences of Taylor's recommendations for deskilling work were systematically studied by psychologists. But in the mean time Taylor's prescription had taken a firm hold on industrial practice.

Nowadays the assembly-line characteristic of the motor industry is the prime success story of Taylor's self-styled 'scientific management principles'. A modern vehicle assembly plant is composed of a fast-flowing line transporting the vehicles through different assembly points where workers supplied with appropriate parts by a computer-managed system each complete tasks of a few seconds' or minutes' duration. As might be anticipated, a general trend nowadays is to automate as many of these assembly jobs as possible. Yet against this background social scientists (for example Dowling, 1973; Tichy, 1976; Walton, 1977) have rated Volvo's actions highly. In 1974 the company opened a new and expensive car assembly plant at Kalmar which attempted, by the introduction of some group working, the provision of buffer stocks and the creation of pleasant working conditions, to overcome the excesses of conventional vehicle assembly technology. There are some reasons to doubt that the design of the plant is as radical as was originally thought (for example, the pace at which vehicles pass through the plant is, as in more conventional plants, controlled by computer). But as a symbolic gesture to the effect that Volvo would no longer continue mindlessly to routinize and trivialize assembly workers' jobs the Kalmar plant was extremely successful. The company's image as an employer in Sweden rose dramatically.

Following an earlier study by Colin Brown (1973) in the company's truck division, in 1976 and again in 1979 Brown and the present author (see Blackler and Brown 1978, 1980b) were provided with an opportunity to study the course of a profoundly innovative method of assembling trucks in Volvo. The method devised was in marked contrast to approaches inspired by Taylor that insisted that vehicles being assembled be moved down an assembly line. In the case we studied it had been found that a team of men could build a truck working round a *static* chassis in less time than on the line, given certain technical innovations and a skilled, motivated, and co-operative work group. Put at its most simple the reason for this was that production engineers in designing the very impoverished tasks for operators working on the line are unable (quite sensibly) to assume anything other than an uninterested operator. Static assembly, on the other hand, offers workers far more interesting jobs (with a work cycle of perhaps five or six hours). Assuming the correct components may be stored accessibly because the work is not paced by moving conveyor or by computer terminal, the system allows workers to work at whatever pace they choose. As demonstrated mathematically by Rosengren (1979) and empirically on the experimental static assembly unit, savings of up to 30 per cent man-hours assembly time may be achieved over what is possible on a paced line. The psychological benefits of this method of organization to workers are considerable.

Our SSRC-funded study of the new method centred around the decision-making processes that firstly encouraged experimentation with it, later permitted it to continue, then put an end to plans for wider adoption of the method. To do this we interviewed all those who had played a significant part in the experiment. Industrial engineers, senior and middle managers, union officials, personnel specialists, and social scientists on Volvo's payroll were amongst those we interviewed first in 1976, then again (with some additions) in 1979.

One of our findings concerned the role of social scientists in Volvo. We found that the success that the company had enjoyed in adopting new ideas was partly due to the fact that social science ideas were known not only to a few expert advisers, but had been widely disseminated throughout the company. This, combined with the fact that responsibility for experimentation was decentralized in Volvo to an unusual degree meant that, while specialist advice could be and was sometimes sought there was no dependence on experts to produce solutions. Expertise had been developed in the company at divisional level and Volvo's managers were very knowledgeable about recent psychological theories of work organization.

Given this environment our studies in Volvo of the truck division showed that the static assembly method had been developed when a boom in customer demand had created a situation where Volvo's normal assembly factories found they were unable to cope. Rather than lose trade, warehouse space was found, and the necessary truck parts were provided for a small team to begin assembling the vehicles with none of the hardware normally associated with line assembly. Inevitably this meant a static-build method had to be used. A number of technical problems arose but a project group worked on these and monitored the progress of the experiment. It was soon found that the performance of the static-assembly unit was outstanding. Later, when the upsurge in demand for trucks died away the experimental site was not abandoned. In the belief that the company would need soon to invest in a new truck plant the possible design implications of the new method justified its continuation.

This was the situation at the time of our 1976 study. Of course not everyone in the company was happy about the experimental plant. Critics argued that the results of one small study would not generalize, that technical drawbacks could become acute, that the assumption that workers were trustworthy and could cope with long work-cycle times was mistaken. But we concluded that the experimental environmental created in the company by the Kalmar plant, the skills of the project team running the static-assembly experiment and the presence of co-operative unions all gave the project hope for success. We were optimistic that Volvo would build its new truck plant along truly innovative principles.

At the time of our return in 1979 plans were far advanced for the new truck factory. Although the excesses of the normal production line were avoided, to our disappointment, and to the disappointment of people in the company who had been impressed by the earlier experiments, plans for the assembly method involved work-cycle times of only forty-five minutes for assembly workers compared to the times of five or six hours we had observed previously in the experimental warehouse. The new factory was being designed to allow team working on parts, but not on all, of the total assembly. By such a design management could retain control of the speed of assembly to an extent that would not have been possible if the full static-assembly method had been used. Brown and I were to conclude that, paradoxically, by retaining such control management would, in all likelihood, lose the essential motivational advantages that the original static-assembly method had provided. Much of the attraction to workers of the experimental static-assembly unit had been the opportunity it gave *them* to exercise discretion. However it was clear that the tension managers had begun to feel between the possible commercial advantages of the static system and the loss of control it required of their role had been resolved by forsaking the possible financial gains.

At the time of our 1979 study it had become clear that the views of the sceptics we had originally heard had become the dominant view of the original experiment. Senior managers told us they believed that production savings could be achieved by static assembly but in their view the method was less reliable than other methods. A robust method, they argued, which did not, to the same extent, rely on the good will of, in their view, a possibly unreliable workforce was preferable. They also expressed hostility towards the static-assembly method for, allowing as it did the assembly workers to vary their work output, during some parts of the day the work team often decided to take extended rest breaks. Despite the fact the teams were nonetheless achieving their work quotas management felt such practices were unacceptable and encouraged an improper attitude towards work.

In this case therefore we have the interesting instance of a socio-technical invention that is both beneficial to workers and also commercially advantageous. Yet it was not adopted as it required a shift in responsibility downwards from management on an issue important to management's very existence. There is nothing very remarkable in management's suspicion of the static-assembly method. From their point of view there are limits to how far they can 'sensibly' go in introducing new ideas of job design. The unions in the company, while fully aware of what was happening, were not particularly concerned either. At a time of developing unemployment they were not too interested in a method of work organization less labour-intensive than it otherwise might be. Thus the politics of organizational life in the company meant that a work system, innovatory as it was on the psychological level, potentially challenged important interests and customary modes of thought. Accordingly, even in an organization as enlightened in the area of job design as Volvo the new work system was not to be adopted as thoroughly as psychologists would have liked.

Local initiatives and the role of legislation

In the cases and discussion so far presented a number of themes have been highlighted. Optimism for change inspired by new assumptions about how people can behave in organizations may be misplaced. Change in organizations is difficult to engineer. While social psychological variables are highly relevant so too are factors more usually considered to fall within the province of sociologists. There is a need for organizational psychologists who wish their particular social science to lead to social reforms to recognize the importance of supportive structures.

Points such as these may lead one to conclude that legislation to help ensure that private companies and public sector organizations put organizational psychology to use should be sought. The examples discussed in this chapter do not go against the idea that the changes in outlook stimulated by Shell's new philosophy were valuable despite the failure of the programme to achieve widespread change. Nor would it be correct to say that OD approaches have been a waste of time or that the job-design changes to be incorporated in Volvo's new plant, even though quite marginal compared to what might have been achieved, are pointless. Some improvement is better than none. Yet it is evident that organizational psychology has a potential for more than just minor improvements. Why not legislate for these?

This question has been discussed by Gustavsen (1980). Reviewing legislative efforts to improve health and safety at work, he concludes that laws of this type are normally used to create a set of rules about unacceptable practice that can fairly easily be applied by factory inspectors. The more concrete the rules the better for factory inspectors, for then they can be sure that a particular set of conditions in a given factory is either acceptable or not. Further, the more specific the rules about any necessary remedial action the less open to criticism inspectors might be about the changes that they do decide to enforce. Also, given that health and safety inspectors cannot normally spend long in any given factory it is in their interests to have safety rules phrased in such a way that problem cases are easily identifiable. The net result of such considerations is, as Gustavsen pointed out, that regulations and codes of practice following from health and safety legislation tend to specify minimum standards of acceptability. Not only do such standards help the work of factory inspectors, but managers also find them useful, for given that a government watchdog is going to scrutinize their practices it is better for managers that his decisions are governed by general rules and are not dependent primarily on his own personal views. To facilitate investment and planning managers evidently need to know with some degree of certainty what is and is not acceptable.

The 1974 Health and Safety Act in the UK is not untypical of the way such laws work. The Act empowers The Secretary of State through his Health and Safety Commission to draw up detailed regulations to improve conditions at work. Regulations and codes of practice for different industrial conditions have followed over the years. Working parties have sat and in preparing statements of the rules have sought to discover what factors are potentially harmful in work situations, how much exposure to potentially dangerous substances can be tolerated, and how such levels may conveniently be assessed.

As Gustavsen points out, social research can often help administrators identify what factors are relevant to poor environments. For example at a very general level statistics can be collected to show how certain workers are more at risk to early death than others. Or by more detailed work it may be shown how psycho-social factors like boring jobs or authoritarian bureaucracies can lead to unhappiness, alienation, stress, and ill-health. But Gustavsen is concerned also to point out that when the next question is posed — how *much* repetition in a job is bad or, how *much* bureaucracy is tolerable? — the social psychologist is stuck for something to say. Although much effort has been expended in attempts to define minimum levels, and some ingenuity employed to produce workable models, such questions remain unanswered. They are, as we shall see, unanswerable.

The question of the relevance of organizational psychology to the law raises the question of the nature of claims to knowledge in this discipline. The dominant approach in psychology has been to assume that in the study of behaviour 'external' rather than 'internal' causes should be sought. Experimental psychologists have tended to record small and detailed variations in stimuli that animals or people are exposed to, tending to discount attempts to explain behaviour by reference to 'goals' or 'intentions', unobservable as such phenomena necessarily are. After sufficient behavioural observations have been made, through abstraction more general statements (laws of behaviour) can be made. 'Positivism' assumes (see Hollis, 1977) that both the natural and the social sciences use the same methods in seeking to understand the world, that relationships in the social world can be identified as laws, that science is the search for such regularities. If such an approach proved to be feasible in social psychology then, clearly, laws of psychology could relatively easily be translated into legal requirements.

Recent years have, however, seen a shift in approaches in social psychology. Psychologists today are tending not to assume that their business is the identification and systemization of 'facts'. Berger and Luckmann (1966), Harre and Secord (1972), Armistead (1974), Shotter (1975), Brenner et al. (1978), and Ginsberg (1979) are examples of the many writings nowadays 'reminding' social psychologists of the importance of taking into account the point of view of the people whose behaviour they are studying. Having its roots in phenomenology and Gestalt psychology, this approach states that an active intellect is central for the explanation of social behaviour. The processes by which we construct and order reality, discover relationships in it, and learn to value different things are considered central in explaining what we do.

What this tells us of course is that human social behaviour cannot be treated 'as nature'. The present author takes the view that psychology should help provide generalized insights into the nature of human reactions and that psychologists should do more than simply record 'commonsense' explanations of events. But local understandings of different cultures or subcultures are crucial for social policies. In a real sense people help create their own worlds. The appreciations they develop may not be obvious, nor need they be fixed and unchanging. Indeed a characteristic of human behaviour is that once conventional modes of response are recognized people are often quite capable of choosing to behave differently.

A dilemma therefore exists for organizational psychologists interested in policy issues. Their research alerts us to issues of fundamental social importance. For example it seems that people who have influence in their work situation will feel responsible and motivated to perform well. Those given menial work, with little opportunity to exercise discretion, are likely to become alienated. But the facts are that wide individual and cultural variations mean that circumstances in which people feel involved will vary. Values and expectations are not uniform. It is impossible therefore to state threshold conditions below which some jobs can be said to be unacceptably routine, some organizations unacceptably bureaucratic, some individuals unacceptably authoritarian. Certainly, general guidelines can be drawn up but these do not provide a suitable basis for a conventional legislative programme.

At least four examples of ways through this problem can be cited, all of which involve the provision of structural supports for local initiatives. In Sweden changes in the law regarding the ownership of firms are under consideration (Meidner, 1976). Such laws would require that ownership of large companies be passed from existing shareholders to trust funds administered in the interests of employees. If such proposals ever do become law they might facilitate some decentralization of large companies as conventional management prerogatives would tend to diminish. Under such circumstances methods of work (like the Volvo truck static build, which requires only a warehouse, a good workforce, parts, and some machinery) which are consistent with decentralized plants might become more feasible (see Blackler and Brown, 1978). However, such corollaries to the new legislative proposals do require political will and/or grass-roots support. Frankly the chances of these developing seem slim.

The second approach that has been suggested is to introduce new methods of social auditing, charging to companies the cost of alienated employees that otherwise falls more generally on society (through sickness, or vandalism perhaps). This, it has been hoped, would encourage experimentation in new forms of organization. Optimistically discussed by Rhode and Lawler (1973), as Hopwood (1979) points out, even if feasible, such methods do not face the contradiction that arises when changes inspired by humanitarian ideals are costed against conventional economic criteria. Even if they are not 'economic' in a cost-effective sense, new forms of work design might nonetheless be highly desirable.

A third method is presently being tried in West Germany. Here local work-reform projects have been partly supported by government grants. This may help with long-term shifts in values. Production engineers in Germany have become more interested than ever before in exploring ways in which human considerations might be built into job designs (Klein, 1977). But in all likelihood the barriers to wide-reaching changes that were illustrated in the Volvo case remain unchallenged by this particular strategy.

Finally a new form of work environment legislation that has been tried in Norway should be mentioned. Norway is unusual in that it has maintained a consistent interest in job design since the mid-1960s when Emery (whose ideas so inspired the Shell project) helped formulate a national strategy for industrial democratization in the country. As might be expected from the Shell project Emery recommended autonomous work groups as a more significant way forward to democracy than legislation for board representation for employees. Later he and Einar Thorsrud set up demonstration job-redesign experiments and, much as in Shell, they then awaited for other companies to copy their efforts.

As with Shell it did not happen. In Table 2 events are summarized. In reality government, unions, employers, and social scientists had differing expectations of the project. While the social scientists were bitterly disappointed that the autonomous work groups did not widely catch on in Norway with people seeking increased opportunities to exercise choice and influence, the employers' organization was sorry for productivity reasons. Unions were less bothered, and pushed ahead with plans for worker directors. For a few years the social scientists involved in the project developed their approaches and skills but now

Table 2

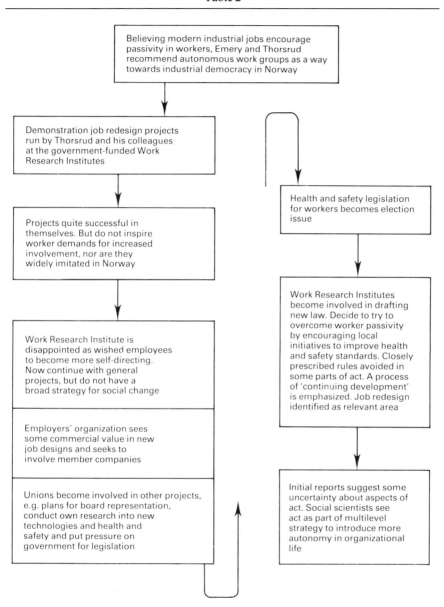

without a coherent strategy for introducing widespread reform. Then, given the emergence of health and safety for workers as a political issue, an opportunity arose for them to develop a new general approach. Under the direction at this stage of Bjorn Gustavsen, whose analysis of a mismatch between social science knowledge and legalistic rules was referred to earlier, the Work Research Institute sought to have certain unusual clauses included in the new health laws. Essentially these emphasized the role of local knowledge of certain problems, insisting that worker/management initiatives to improve (continually) present conditions was a priority. The direct instruction from a factory inspector to improve matters was not now to be the only widely recognized reforming force. The burden of proof shifted in the act towards employers having to prove the acceptability of present arrangements in certain areas, rather than the unacceptability of them having to be demonstrated as a pre-condition for reform. And in the area of job design the 1977 act stated:

> . . . conditions shall be arranged so that employees are afforded reasonable opportunity for professional and personal development through their work.
>
> The individual employee's opportunity for self-determination and professional responsibility shall be taken into consideration when planning and arranging the work.
>
> Efforts shall be made to avoid undiversified, repetitive work and work that is governed by machine or conveyor belt in such a manner that the employees themselves are prevented from varying the speed of work. Otherwise efforts shall be made to arrange the work so as to provide possibilities for variation and for contact with others in connection with individual job assignments, and for employees to keep themselves informed about production requirements and results.

As part of the SSRC-funded research project mentioned earlier the present author was able to interview representatives of the Norwegian government, unions, and employers, as well as the social scientists involved, to begin to assess the effects of this law. It would appear (Blackler and Brown, 1981) that despite the novelty of the law, or perhaps because of it, there are a number of problems associated with it. For example, while the open-ended nature of the legislation and its encouragement of locally specified improvements is impressive from a social-psychological perspective, from an administrative point of view there are difficulties. The pressures, mentioned earlier, for work-reform laws to specify minimally acceptable standards still remain. Further, the labour inspectorate is not sure that unshackled local initiatives for continuous improvements are a good thing. They could, for example, prove very expensive. At a time of economic stringency (even in oil-rich Norway) this would be unacceptable. Indeed the inspectorate probably does still hold the initiative as local safety committees do not yet feel especially competent to act in some areas. The job-design paragraph, quoted above, is not understood by many managers or workers. And it is probably true to say that neither is it widely and fully understood in the labour inspectorate itself. Yet despite the fact that, for reasons such as these, pressures may grow for the law to be reformed to specify precisely what is or is not allowable, the law as it now stands is of considerable interest. Above all it suggests that if legislators can find ways to emphasize less precisely what is required, and rather more to state why it is that changes need to be made, and also to indicate the ways in which progress should be made to make them, then the insights from organizational psychology can be used to provide the basis for a law-supported strategy for organizational reform.

OVERVIEW—THE WORK OF ORGANIZATIONAL PSYCHOLOGISTS

From the examples discussed in this chapter it can be seen that organizational psychologists cover a wide range of activities in their work. Their work can serve a number of purposes, to establish a critique of common practice and points towards alternatives, to explore approaches to the introduction of changes, or to study ways of managing institutions more effectively than they are presently arranged. Their work is both practical and theoretical in orientation. Further, the scope of activities in which they are engaged is extensive, requiring as it does knowledge of a wide range of social science theories, a sound grasp of various social scientific methodologies, and an ability to adopt high standards of ethical and professional practice.

Organizational psychologists are employed in various capacities. As academic researchers they can study particular issues in depth and contribute towards theory development. Employed as specialist psychologists in large organizations they can introduce new ideas to managers and workers. This is true also of organizational psychologists who work as freelance consultants. Consultants themselves can differ considerably in the kind of approach they take, choosing to specialize in particular areas (for example job design, or organization development), or choosing to work with a particular type of client (for example public or private organizations). While the detail of the activities of people engaged in these different types of work will obviously vary, a number of key tasks are common for all. Each has to decide who is to be their client, to determine in whose interests they are prepared to work. Each has to negotiate a method of working, which often involves exploring the expectations the client has of the psychologist as expert adviser or as specialized helper. Each has to help define the problem he works with, by undertaking special study of the local issues and relating these to relevant theory. Each has to work with his client in a consideration of possible options for any remedial actions and, later, in an evaluation of any progress made.

In this chapter it has been argued that the approaches organizational psychologists have taken to the issues raised by these key tasks have changed in recent years. In Table 3 the points that have been made are summarized. It is evident that an emerging professionalism is characteristic of the area. Easy solutions to the complex issues organizational psychologists deal with are no

Table 3 Key professional issues and emerging approaches within organizational psychology

Key issues	Old approach	New approach	Examples discussed
In whose interests is the psychologist working?	The psychologist as value-free expert	A recognition of the importance of the values of the psychologist	Shell's new philosophy
	Human problems treated like technical problems	A recognition of the differing interests within organizations	
What is the role of the organizational psychologist?	An expert analyst	A facilitator of localized activity	Organization Development
	To search for the 'best' ways of organizing	To encourage eclecticism	
How may changes best be introduced?	Consideration of particular problems only	A recognition of the interlocking nature of organizational problems	
	An attempt at once and for all change with respect to them	Incrementalism	Volvo's truck division
Nature of knowledge claims by psychologists	A search for 'laws' of behaviour	An emphasis on concepts, models, and theories	
	Prescription for what should be done	The need for local enquiry to determine the relevance of theory in any particular case	The development of the Norwegian Work Environment Act

longer expected and the complicated nature of organizational problems is now acknowledged. Psychologists are generally more concerned to help people solve their own organizational difficulties rather than to tell them what they should do. Ethical issues raised by work in the area are better recognized. The enthusiasm and confidence characteristic of earlier work in the area has become tempered with a certain cautiousness (a caution which one might say is highly appropriate for a professional group trained in the scientific method). While it is certainly true that organizational psychologists no longer expect to be able to introduce radical changes quickly the increasing sophistication of practice in the area suggests that, over time, their contributions will be considerable.

REFERENCES

Argyris, C. (1970). *Intervention Theory and Method*, Reading, Mass: Addison Wesley.
Armistead, N. (1974). *Reconstructing Social Psychology*, Harmondsworth: Allen Lane, Penguin Books.
Berger, L. and Luckman, T. (1966). *The Social Reconstruction of Reality*, Harmondsworth: Allen Lane, Penguin Books.
Blackler, F. H. M. and Brown, C. A. (1978). *Job Redesign and Management Control*, Farnborough: Saxon House.
Blackler, F. H. M. and Brown, C. A. (1980a). *Whatever Happened to Shell's New Philosophy and Management?*, Farnborough: Gower.
Blackler, F. H. M. and Brown, C. A. (1980b). 'Job redesign and social change: the case of Volvo', in K. D. Duncan, M. M. Gruneberg, and D. Wallis (eds), *Changes in Working Life*, Chichester: Wiley.
Blackler, F. H. M. and Brown, C. A. (1981). *The Law and Job Design: Comments on Recent Norwegian Legislation*. Paper presented at British Psychological Society, Occupational Psychology Section Conference, January.
Brenner, M., Marsh, P., and Brenner, M. (eds) (1978). *The Social Contexts of Methods*, London: Croom Helm.
Brown, C. A. (1973). *Job Design Change*. Unpublished research project report to SSRC.
Cherns, A. (1979). *Using the Social Sciences*, London: Routledge & Kegan Paul.
Chin, R. and Benne, K. D. (1969). 'General strategies for effecting changes in human systems', in W. Bennis, K. K. Benne, and R. Chin (eds), *The Planning of Change*, New York: Holt, Rinehart & Winston.
Cooper, R. (1974). *Job Motivation and Job Design*, London: Institute of Personnel Management.
Davis, L. E., Canter, R. R., and Hoffman, J. (1955). 'Current job design criteria', *Journal of Industrial Engineering*, **6**, 5–11.
Dowling, W. F. (1973). 'Job design on the assembly lines: farewell to blue collar blues?', *Organisational Dynamics*, **II**, 51–67.
French, W. L. and Bell, C. H. (1973). *Organisational Development*, Englewood Cliffs, NJ: Prentice-Hall.
Fromm, E. (1955). *The Sane Society*, New York: Harper.
Ginsburg, G. P. (ed.) (1979). *Emerging Strategies in Social Psychological Research*, Chichester: Wiley.

Gustavsen, J. (1980). 'Legal-administrative reforms and the role of social research', *Acta sociologica*, **23**, 1, 3-20.
Hall, C. S. and Lindzey, G. (1957). *Theories of Personality*, New York: Wiley.
Harre, R. and Secord, P. F. (1972). *The Explanation of Social Behaviour*, Oxford: Blackwell.
Herzberg, F., Mausner, B., and Snyderman, B. (1959). *The Motivation to Work*, New York: Wiley.
Hill, P. (1971). *Towards a New Philosophy of Management*, Farnborough: Gower.
Hollis, M. (1977). *Models of Man*, London: Cambridge University Press.
Hopwood, A. G. (1979). 'Towards the economic assessment of new forms of work organisation', in C. Cooper and E. Mumford (eds), *The Quality of Working Life in Western and Eastern Europe*, London: Associated Business Press.
Janis, I. L. (1972). *Victims of Group Think*, New York: Houghton Mifflin.
Kahn, R. L. (1974). 'Organisational development, some problems and proposals', *Journal of Applied Behavioural Science*, **10**, 485-502.
Klein, L. (1977). 'Designing jobs fit for the people who do them', *The Times*, 20 June.
Mangham, I. L. (1981). 'The limits of planned organisational change', in K. Trebesch (ed), *Organisational Development in Europe*, Berne: Paul Haupt.
Marris, P. (1974). *Loss and Change*, London: Routledge & Kegan Paul.
Maslow, A. H. (1963). 'A theory of human motivation', *Psychological Review*, **50**, 370-96.
Meidner, R. (1976). *Employee Investment Funds: An Approach to Collective Capital Formation*, London: Allen & Unwin.
McGregor, D. (1961). *The Human Side of Enterprise*, London: McGraw-Hill.
Pettigrew, A. M. (1976). 'Towards a political theory of organisational intervention', *Human Relations*, **29**, 453-469.
Pugh, D. S. (1969). 'Organisational behaviour: an approach from psychology', *Human Relations*, **22**, 345-354.
Rhode, J. G. and Lawler, E. E. (1973). 'Auditing change: human resource accounting', in M. D. Dunnette (ed), *Work and Non Work in the Year 2001*, California: Brooks & Cole.
Roethlisberger, F. J. and Dixon, W. J. (1939). *Management and the Worker*, Cambridge Mass: Harvard University.
Rogers, C. (1974). 'In retrospect, forty six years', *American Psychologist*, **29**, 115-123.
Rosengren, L. G. (1979). *The Potential Performance of Dock Versus Line Assembly*. Paper presented at 5th Annual Conference on Production Research, Amsterdam, Netherlands, August.
Sanford, N. (1970). 'Whatever happened to action research?', *Journal of Social Issues*, **26**, 46-54.
Schein, E. H. (1956). 'The Chinese indoctrination programme for prisoners of war', *Psychiatry*, **19**, 149-172.
Schein, E. H. (1964). 'The mechanics of change', in W. Bennis, K. K. Benne, and R. Chin (eds), *The Planning Change*, New York: Holt, Rinehart & Winston.
Schein, E. H. (1969). *Process Consultation*, Reading: Addison Wesley.
Schon, D. A. (1971). *Beyond the Stable State*, Harmondsworth: Penguin Books.
Shotter, J. (1975). *Images of Man in Psychological Research*, London: Methuen.
Skibbins, G. J. (1974). *Organisational Evolution: A Program for Managing Radical Change*, New York: Amacom.
Skinner, B. F. (1976). *Particulars of My Life*, London: Cape.
Taylor, F. W. (1911). *The Principles of Scientific Management*, New York: Harper.

This, L. E. (1971). 'Organisational development: fantasy or reality', *in* G. L. Lippett, L. E. This, and R. Bidwell (eds), *Optimising Human Resources*, Reading, Mass: Addison Wesley.

Tichy, N. (1976). 'When does job restructuring work?', *Organisational Dynamics*, **5**, 63–80.

Tizard, J. (1976). 'Psychology and social policy', *Bulletin of the British Psychological Society*, **29**, 225–234.

Trist, E. L., Higgin, G., Murray, H., and Pollock, A. B. (1963). *Organisational Choice*, London: Tavistock.

Walton, R. (1977). 'Successful strategies for diffusing work innovations', *Journal of Contemporary Business*, Spring, 1–22.

Psychology in Practice
Edited by S. Canter and D. Canter
© 1982, John Wiley & Sons, Ltd.

CHAPTER 12

PSYCHOLOGY AND AVIATION

V. David Hopkin
Senior Principal Psychologist
RAF Institute of Aviation Medicine, Farnborough

INTRODUCTION

In my work, I apply my psychological knowledge, and the findings from my own experiments and those of others, to the detection and solution of practical aviation problems. I need a very broad and up-to-date knowledge of psychology. I must assess the potential relevance of new psychological theories, constructs, and findings to the problems which I have to solve.

The standards of safety and reliability in aviation are most rigorous. I cannot afford blunders. Any mistakes of mine will not find a haven of oblivion in the pages of an obscure journal, but will become all too apparent wherever my recommendations are implemented. I must therefore ensure that my conclusions are correct and can be supported. I do not review existing psychological knowledge uncritically, but need to know the strength of the evidence on which it depends and the conditions under which it was obtained, in order to judge its generality and applicability, and the probable limits on its validity.

In the United States, there are hundreds of aviation psychologists: they work for government agencies, for the United States Air Force, for airlines or aircraft manufacturers, for universities or research organizations associated with them, for firms in avionics, or for human factors consultancies. Most of the countries in Europe with either their own air force or own national airline employ a few aviation psychologists. In the United Kingdom, aviation psychologists work in government research establishments or departments, for airlines, for aircraft or avionics manufacturers, in industry or in universities, but there are probably no more than fifty altogether. Generally they have an honours degree in psychology, and may have a post-graduate qualification, for example an MSc in ergonomics or a PhD on a topic of some relevance. Practical experience is often more highly prized than academic qualifications beyond a good honours degree. Some knowledge of engineering or physiology, and practical training or experience in aviation, such as a private pilot's licence, may also be helpful.

The main links between psychology and aviation date from during and soon after the Second World War. Then as now, psychological knowledge was used to define jobs, to select and train people to do them, and to measure efficiency and lapses in performance. Human capabilities and limitations had to be reconciled with each advance in technology so that its potential benefits could be realized. The ways in which man could be considered as a system component became clear. The importance of human characteristics with no technological counterpart, such as pride in work and the development of professional norms and standards, took longer to become apparent. The effects on performance of various physical environmental factors, such as heat, noise, and vibration, singly and in combination, were explored. Principles for the design of workspaces evolved. It was noted that the length of time during which efficient performance could be sustained without a break depended on the individual, on the nature of his tasks, and on the design of the system. The importance of human needs, for the development and use of skills, for job satisfaction, for status and responsibility, came to be acknowledged.

Aircraft are becoming more complex; operational requirements change; technological innovations proliferate; new forms of computer assistance are devised: these all imply new roles for the pilot in the air and for the air traffic controller on the ground. I am therefore faced continually with new problems or with old problems in new guise (Hopkin, 1981).

How can new technological developments be reconciled with human abilities and limitations to enhance safety and efficiency in aviation? An exciting technological innovation may not have any obvious practical use. It may entail new selection and training methods, introduce novel kinds of error, or be boring to use. I have to predict whether such problems will arise. It is far too late to discover only after an innovation has been installed that people cannot understand what it does or learn how to use it properly.

Aviation is international. Similar psychological problems therefore tend to arise in different countries at about the same time, and solutions on an international basis have to be found. There is therefore much international collaboration and exchange of information. Aviation is also interdisciplinary. Psychology is one of several disciplines contributing towards the solution of any given problem, and each discipline has its own unique contribution to make. The status of the individual psychologist depends considerably on his mastery of his own subject, on his ability to explain it to others, on his competence to make an effective practical contribution, and on his ability to work productively as a member of an interdisciplinary team.

The interdisciplinary and international aspects of aviation influence the publication of psychological findings, which generally appear in international rather than national journals. Papers are published in the psychological and human factors literature, but also in the professional journals of many other disciplines, such as air safety, aerospace medicine, air traffic control, cartography, navigation, and man-machine systems. Many papers are written for conferences or meetings convened to examine a single theme from an inter-disciplinary point of view, and are published as part of the proceedings.

EXAMPLES OF PROJECTS

Something of the nature of my work as a psychologist in aviation can be gauged from the following examples. However, one overriding consideration should be emphasized from the outset. Textbooks of academic and applied psychology alike partition the subject matter by headings under which literature, theories, constructs, and findings are reviewed and discussed. These headings may deal in academic psychology with such topics as memory, perception, social psychology, and individual differences, and in applied psychology with such topics as information displays, controls, communications, and workspace design. If the whole of psychology were not divided up and structured in this fashion, it would appear amorphous, disorganized, and diffuse. Nevertheless, this partitioning does not arise naturally in applied psychology but has to be imposed. It can therefore be misleading. Real-life problems do not occur in neatly partitioned form. Rarely is a problem concerned solely with workspace design, or displays, or controls. Decisions about any of these normally affect all the others. The whole of psychological knowledge is potentially relevant to aviation but the integrated synthesis of that knowledge, which is needed for practical applications, requires its appraisal and interpretation, and is not achieved merely by adding all the bits of it together.

Altimeter design

The first example concerns the design of an altimeter, an instrument in the cockpit of an aircraft which shows its height. It is important that the altimeter can be read easily and quickly and not misread, that there should be only one correct interpretation of each reading and no ambiguities, and that the altimeter cannot be mistaken for any other aircraft instrument, showing speed or heading for example (Dhenin, 1978). Some years ago, aircraft were fitted with three-pointer altimeters derived from sensors of atmospheric pressure. Occasionally accidents occurred, usually because the altimeter had apparently been misread by 10,000 ft. Figure 1 shows two altimeters on which the readings differ by 10,000 ft. It will be seen that such errors might be made even by an experienced pilot, particularly if overburdened, distracted, dealing with an emergency, concerned about adverse weather conditions, disorientated,

Figure 1   A difference of 10,000 ft in readings on a three-pointer altimeter

Figure 2   A simple counter-pointer altimeter display

or influenced by false expectancies about the altitude of his aircraft. At first, efforts were made to improve the conspicuity and discriminability of the pointers themselves, but the benefits of such changes were at best marginal. The root of the problem was the fact that there were three pointers. The integration of the information which they contained was potentially confusing, and the most vital information was given by the smallest pointer, which could be obscured by the others. Basically similar problems would recur as long as there were three pointers, no matter how they were modified.

Any alternative altimeter design must be engineered: this limited the solutions which were possible. Technological advances meant that a digital readout of height information could be provided. But given the variety of operational roles and usages of height information, would a digital readout meet all needs or would further information be essential? Are there characteristic errors, even in reading a row of digits? Note that I have to define the questions that have to be resolved, and that I need verifiable facts, and not common-sense or speculations, to answer them.

The first step was to consult many pilots of different kinds of aircraft, to discover what they needed and what they would like to have. As a separate exercise, from an analysis of operational requirements the height information which would be essential to meet them was deduced. Then various possible altimeter displays were derived and drawn, all of which would meet users' needs and operational requirements, would be technically feasible, and would be compatible with existing knowledge about human information processing and sources of error. These designs were canvassed among a large variety of pilots, to narrow the options and generate hypotheses for later testing, regarding possible benefits, ambiguities, and sources of error in alternative designs. Then simple dynamic instruments, portraying height in various alternative ways, were constructed, and used to obtain preliminary sample readings and measures of performance. Initially each instrument was tested in isolation, and then the more promising ones were put into flight simulators and evaluated more thoroughly and realistically in their workspace setting. Progressively more elaborate simulations refined the designs and reduced the options. It was found that a single row of digits could not provide adequate information about rate of climb or descent. The counter-pointer instrument (Figure 2) was required, in which the counters gave a direct reading of height in digits, and the pointer revolved once per 1000 feet to give information on rate of change of height.

Even this instrument, a great improvement in many ways, had at least one characteristic source of error. A pilot, instructed to descend to 14,000 ft for example, tended at first to watch the thousands digits and to level out at about 14,900 ft, and then correct his error. This only occurred initially and was soon overcome with practice. However, it is the kind of error which might recur under stress because the pilot has to learn not to make it. Nevertheless this is acceptable because the aircraft would be higher, and not lower, than intended, and therefore there would be no danger that the pilot would inadvertently fly into the ground.

The simulation trials suggested that this altimeter design would be safe and efficient, but the evaluation of it was still not complete; the proposed instrument was next installed in aircraft for extensive flight trials of thousands of hours to verify the simulation findings. Only then could the recommendation be given with confidence that three-pointer altimeters should be replaced by counter-pointer altimeters which would be efficient and safe and make a positive contribution to accident prevention. Most commercial aircraft today are fitted with counter-pointer altimeters.

The same problem of the depiction of height information in the cockpit is now recurring in a new form. In the relatively near future, hardware cockpit instruments will be replaced by cathode ray tube displays. How should the height of the aircraft be portrayed on a cathode ray tube display? Should a counter-pointer display be retained or could something even better be devised, now that advances in technology, in the form of the generation of displays by software, offer almost limitless display options?

A simple workspace

Much of my work looks to the future. Once systems have been designed and become operational, it can be highly expensive and perhaps technically impossible to modify them if for any reason they do not satisfy operational requirements. Care must be taken to try and ensure that the envisaged standards of performance will be reached.

One of the simplest applications of existing knowledge to future systems occurs in the design of workspaces. I would normally participate in working parties to agree on the principles for the design of a workspace to meet future operational needs. For example, future air traffic control systems will have pairs of controllers acting as teams: this is new. The broad principle of their tasks and the information they will need can be deduced from operational requirements. I work in consultation with system planners, those who define requirements, those concerned with equipment, the occupational health specialist, and representatives of numerous other disciplines to agree the design of the furniture at which the controllers will work and the location of items of equipment within it. I need to know the basic anthropometric data about body sizes, in this case for both men and women since either may occupy the workspace. All must be able to reach and see the facilities provided and be able to work in reasonable comfort, in sitting positions which do not induce any postural or visual occupational health problems. The basic knowledge of reach distances, of the design of suitable seating, of the layout of equipment, and of display legibility is applied. In this case some facilities are for one

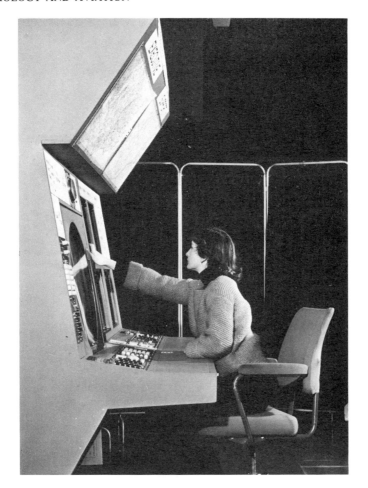

Figure 3   Posed photograph in prototype workspace — small body size

controller only, and some are designed to be shared. The workspace layout must reflect this.

Once a broad agreement has been reached, a mock-up can be built. Initially this shows the location of equipment; a suitable technique is to take posed photographs of extreme body sizes showing the postures which will be adopted at work (Figures 3, 4, and 5). These may provide firm evidence of any problems, in a form which is convincing to others with no relevant specialist knowledge. This kind of evidence is normally gathered before dynamic simulations are conducted to devise methods of training for the tasks and to evaluate performance of them. This kind of work does not entail research but the application of existing knowledge and principles. It should ensure that

Figure 4   Posed photograph in prototype workspace — large body size

there are no major psychological mistakes in the design of the physical workspace.

The evaluation of maps

A topographical map is one of the most complex displays of information designed for human use. It contains a great deal of information and elaborate information coding. Few psychological studies have ever been done using maps as experimental material, because maps are far too complex to permit a systematic control of the kind of variables which the psychologist is usually interested in when testing hypotheses about the laws of human behaviour

Figure 5   Posed photograph in prototype workspace — team members in position

and experience. The ergonomist dealing with the efficient portrayal of information for human use has also tended to avoid maps, with the result that it is not known if the findings obtained from studies with much simpler material, about colour, shape, alphanumerics, discriminable differences, and other visual coding dimensions, may be applied validly to maps, although there are strong indications that they may not be.

Maps are used extensively in aircraft cockpits. Many advances in computer technology are also being applied to cartography for the first time. Methods of map production are being revolutionized, and in the cockpit many new methods of presenting maps are in being or can be foreseen. For example, it is possible to reduce an existing map on to film strips projected on to a screen in the cockpit, and to link this device to the aircraft's navigation system so that the terrain over which the aircraft is flying is always shown on the map projected in the cockpit. Existing maps must be redesigned to remain legible after this photographic processing and projection. Conventional topographical maps in the cockpit environment may have to be viewed under red lighting and vibration. Developments in navigation provide continuously generated cockpit displays, based on radar or infrared sensors, of the terrain over which the aircraft is flying, and there may be a requirement to match these displays with maps, either side by side or by superimposition.

I therefore have to try and reconcile technological innovations in aviation cartography and in display technology, new operational needs for map reading and map comparisons, known human capabilities and limitations in information processing and in visual discrimination, and the confined workspace and unusual physical environment which the aircraft cockpit typically presents.

What I did first was look at the existing information about principles for the coding and display of visual information and draw up a specification for an experimental topographical map on the assumption that these display principles were valid. A series of experiments was then done to evaluate the experimental map and to compare it with other maps to establish which display principles appeared to remain valid and which did not. A means had to be devised to prove that the findings were not specific to the particular geographical region portrayed in the experimental map but could be generalized to maps of other regions and preferably to maps at other scales. Here it proved helpful to use information theory to express the information on the map as bits of information, which provided a means for describing maps and variations within them.

Many coding recommendations in the literature are suspect when applied to maps. The standard recommendations about the legibility of various type faces and typographical variables are wrong in the context of a topographical map, where each character is viewed against backgrounds varying greatly in contrast and where the face, case, size, and colour of type are themselves coding dimensions within the map. Similarly, with regard to colour coding, the normal recommendations about the number of permissible colours within a single display are inapplicable to maps which almost invariably contain far more discriminable colours than would be recommended for other information contexts. The map also relies, for example in the portrayal of hypsometric layer tints, on gradations of colour in subjectively equivalent visual intervals. The cartographer has traditionally used many effects which are far more subtle than those which the applied psychologist commonly encounters but which I must take account of. The cartographer's concept of visual balance has no obvious counterpart in psychological parlance.

The study of aviation maps poses a further problem. If it is desired to study aircraft cockpits or an air traffic control system, a great deal of reliable and valid psychological evidence can be gathered by constructing a simulation of the cockpit or of the air traffic control system, and by using this simulation to conduct experiments in which variables are controlled and manipulated within a fixed experimental design according to orthodox psychological practice. With maps the evidence is overwhelming that attempts to simulate maps for evaluation and research are futile. Drawings of maps cannot embody the subtlety or complexity of real maps. Findings from drawings of maps are not valid for real maps. Therefore, simulation is not a feasible technique in the study of maps. It is necessary to produce real maps for experiments: this means that the map must be compiled and drawn by professional cartographers and printed on their presses with their paper and their inks. Much of the experimentation on maps hitherto has been wasted because it has ignored this well-documented limitation.

I therefore have to enlist the active collaboration of professional cartographers for my work on maps. Here as elsewhere, as an aviation psychologist I rely on interdisciplinary collaboration in order to achieve results which are scientifically valid. Given this, much progress has been made during the last decade. A culmination of my work on maps has been a textbook on human factors in aviation cartography, in which I defined the subject matter, and which is the first systematic application of psychological knowledge to cartography (Hopkin and Taylor, 1979).

In dealing with maps I became aware of the gulf between the producers and users of aviation maps. The aviation cartographer generally knows little about how maps are actually employed in the cockpit or in preparation for flight. The pilot and the navigator generally know even less about the constraints which have influenced the specification and production of the map. A role of the aviation psychologist is to bridge this gulf. I cannot fulfil my own functions without some knowledge both of the uses to which maps are put within aviation and of the methods of producing them. I am also concerned with the skills in map production and usage. I therefore apply my knowledge to suggest how cartographers might be selected and trained, and to indicate how map reading might be improved by suitable training of the users. Very little is known about the ways in which children learn to understand maps and of how their understanding could be aided. The usage of aviation maps might be enhanced greatly by effective user training and an increased acknowledgement, in the principles of portrayal of cartographic information, of limitations in human information processing.

The measurement of mental workload

I have an eclectic approach to measurement: I cannot afford to discard on principle any source of information which could be useful. It is important to gather and evaluate as much relevant information as possible before decisions are taken. I have to decide what kinds of evidence are likely to be productive, and compare the effort and resources entailed in employing each measure with the amount of useful information it can yield. There are far too many measures to use them all. I must therefore be selective, being well aware that the reliability and validity of the findings may depend more on the correct choice of measures than on what each in fact reveals. I need a good knowledge of how various measures have fared in previous attempts to employ them.

Suppose that I want to measure the mental workload of an air traffic controller handling on a very busy day the air traffic in a region with which he is familiar (Hopkin, 1980). There are many ways of measuring mental workload, including system measures, performance measures, subjective assessments, physiological and biochemical indices, control theory, mathematical modelling, etc. (Moray, 1979). The concept of mental workload is sometimes used to refer to the demands imposed by tasks, but usually it refers to the impact of those demands on the individual: the implication is that the same task can result in different mental workload—often grossly different —for people who differ in knowledge, skill, and experience.

In the academic literature, these various measures of mental workload all have one common characteristic: they have been used to seek to explain the nature of mental workload and to devise a means of assessing it and they have normally been based on studies of high workload. The applied psychologist is not concerned with high workload as such. The judgement he has to make is not whether workload is high but whether it is too high (and often whether it is too low). Workload that is too high may result in a breakdown in performance, in impairments to safety, in an increase in errors, in the need to make an excessive effort, or in an inability to maintain performance throughout a normal work period.

One kind of measurement concerns the inputs and outputs to the air traffic control system. These can be expressed in terms of the number of aircraft which the controller handles in a given time, the peak aircraft traffic flow, the orderliness of the flow of traffic, infringements of separation standards between aircraft, percentage occupancy times of communication channels, delays imposed on traffic by air traffic control instructions, and a multitude of other system measures. These system measures set the scene, quantify the traffic handled, and establish that the task demands are high. The problem of workload is usually posed, and answers to it are expected, in system measures of this kind.

The performance of the controller can also be measured in many ways. These include his usage of controls such as keyboards, his pattern of viewing information displays, the rate at which he discards information, his consultations with his colleagues, and deductions from his actions about problems which he has solved and decisions which he has reached. The quality of his decisions can be assessed, and errors noted. Various forms of activity analysis and time and event recording can be employed as aids to describe the performance of the individual controller. The content and pace of his spoken messages can be analysed. These measures can establish that he is busy and that he may appear to be doing several tasks at once. Some of the most sensitive measures may concern the least important rather than the most important aspects of his tasks. The essential features of his tasks always have to be done, but some peripheral activities may be postponed for a while or omitted altogether: measurements of these may be particularly sensitive indications of high mental workload.

Mental workload can be assessed subjectively, by asking the controller if he is heavily loaded and busy. Suppose he is handling very heavy traffic but doing a task which he is highly familiar with, exercising his skills and knowledge to the full but coping nevertheless. In such circumstances he will report that he is very busy and that at the end of his shift he is tired. He can also indicate that the work was taxing and made great demands on him.

Various physiological indices, associated with high loading, may be measured, including heart rate and variations within it, skin resistance, pupil size, blink rate, breathing rate and volume, and so on. Biochemical measures of endocrine secretions may also point to high workload. Such measures can indicate that the work is being done with great effort and at considerable physiological and biochemical cost. At this point, system measures, performance measures, subjective assessments, and physiological and biochemical indices may all be in substantial agreement that the mental workload is high, and perhaps too high.

But all the evidence has not yet been gathered. Perhaps individual differences are important and one man can handle with ease a situation which another cannot cope with; the whole array of measures therefore should be applied to different individuals and related to individual factors such as age and experience. Biographical data may be needed to appraise the individual's background knowledge and its relevance to workload, and to assess how typical of controllers as a whole the measured controllers are.

I have asked the controller if he is busy. If I ask him whether he likes to be busy and heavily loaded, he normally replies that he does. His professional ability to cope with difficult problems is a main source of challenge, interest, effort, and job satisfaction. It may be influential in the establishment of professional norms and standards among air traffic controllers. High workload provides the controller with opportunities to put his complex skills, which are a matter of professional pride, to practical use, and to demonstrate to his colleagues that he is a worthy and fully competent member of his profession.

Before recommendations to reduce workload are made and implemented, a balance has to be struck. Safety is paramount, and nothing must jeopardize it. However, factors such as job satisfaction, professional status, organizational norms, and the opportunities to exercise highly won skills seem most closely related to high mental workload: clearly if workload is reduced too far, this may precipitate other psychological problems, such as boredom and disillusionment which may prove even more recalcitrant than the problems of high mental workload which inadvertently gave rise to them.

In assessing mental workload, I need to apply my knowledge about human information processing, channel capacity, learning, memory, and serial and parallel information processing. Workload may be increased if the man has to use information which he does not fully trust or has no means of verifying. The introduction of automated aids designed to help the controller may be counter-productive if he does not understand how they are intended to function, what they can and cannot do, how far they should be trusted, and how they could fail. A great deal of disparate information of many kinds from many sources has therefore to be reconciled in order to arrive at the decision on whether the mental workload of the controller is too high and should be reduced. This may then lead to further problems of deciding by how much workload should be reduced and of proving that it has been.

FUTURE PROBLEMS

In looking to the future I must have a broad psychological knowledge and be able to recognize gaps in knowledge which will have to be filled by suitable research in time for the findings to be implemented. I must therefore be able to predict some problems a long time ahead. The more difficult ones may entail not merely the conduct of research but the devising of a research methodology. For example, although boredom can be identified now as a future problem it is not immediately apparent how to study it, although many of the common-sense assumptions about it seem to be wrong (Hopkin, 1979). I have to ensure that the equipment, tasks, functions, and conditions of work which are provided are compatible with human capabilities, limitations, and wishes, and that a man with suitable selection, training, and experience will be able to do the tasks envisaged for him efficiently and safely under the required conditions for the required length of time. He should also enjoy his work, and suffer no adverse effects from it.

Some of these requirements may be difficult to achieve in cockpit environments of advanced aircraft, or where man is crossing many time zones rapidly. Where shift systems are worked and manning for twenty-four hours a day is required, advancing technology tends to aggravate the problems that arise where the man must be present but much of the job is done for him automatically. In an era of complex equipment, the role of the man is ultimately limited by the facilities provided for him, and by his understanding of them.

As far as possible, systems in aviation must never fail. Man when treated as a system component has a reliability much less than that required of the system as a whole. I must find ways of circumventing this problem. Perhaps the man can receive automated assistance so that the machine actually prevents him from making certain mistakes which could be potentially dangerous. Perhaps the machine can draw his attention to any mistakes that he makes. Perhaps the machine could perform the functions, but if the man is assigned a monitoring role he becomes inefficient and dissatisfied. Perhaps the man and machine could perform the same functions in parallel, with cross-checking. Perhaps two men should perform the same functions independently in parallel with some verification of their procedures if they do not agree. I advise on the problems with these various solutions, and on their probable consequences for safety and efficiency.

I look ahead at all the consequences of changes that may be introduced. Speech between pilots and controllers may lead to errors which result from phonetic confusions. Their general nature can be deduced in advance and therefore they can be allowed for. If speech is replaced by information transponded directly from the aircraft to the ground to appear on an air traffic controller's display, then the errors will generally be misreadings of alphanumeric characters which look similar. Again, the particular characters which can be mistaken for each other are largely known so that most of the errors can be predicted in advance and allowed for. In the future it is possible to conceive of automated speech synthesis and recognition but not so easy to predict which errors these might introduce, except that there will be some. I try to predict some of the longer term problems which such a change might introduce. What would it be like to spend a working day talking to a machine which talks back but there is no-one else there? Would some people rather talk to machines than talk to people? Would some people talk to other people as if they were machines, which would be resented? Would the ability to work closely with other people as a member of a team gradually be lost? Would the development of professional norms and standards which are essentially a team function be impaired? It is essential that if such new technology is ever introduced I am not caught by surprise by consequences of this kind, when with thought I can identify them in advance and think through what their effects may be.

The aviation psychologist has to contend with some frustrations. The demand for experienced psychological work in aviation tends to exceed the supply, but opportunities for expansion to meet the demand are severely limited. A few people still treat aviation psychology as a fad, but this attitude is far less common now than it once was. Sometimes psychology may be viewed mistakenly as a panacea, which leads to unrealistically optimistic expectations about what it can achieve. It does not follow that because a question can be defined, and a means of tackling it devised, there must be a satisfactory answer to it, but it can be difficult for others to accept that some human factors problems do not have a solution. Occasionally in the past an aviation psychologist has become tetchy about his status: such an attitude is counter-productive in interdisciplinary work where the psychologist will be accorded by others whatever status his contribution is seen to merit rather than any status he may nominally have.

The aviation psychologist seeks general findings, and would like to interpret his practical conclusions in relation to a theoretical context, but time after time psychological concepts, constructs, theories, and hypotheses prove to be irrelevant, invalid, or wrong when applied to real-life problems, and the aviation psychologist is left to ponder whether these notions, formulated on the basis of data gathered under laboratory conditions, are artifacts of the laboratory setting, or at least are not nearly as universal as they purport to be. Surprisingly few guidelines to the solutions to practical problems can be gleaned from the academic literature. It might be thought, for example, from all the recent work on memory, that recommendations could now be made on the visual coding dimensions which should be chosen if there is a requirement to facilitate the recall of the information portrayed, but relevant evidence is very sparse. Even scarcer is any guidance, from studies of forgetting, on how to depict information to help people to forget it afterwards.

Such problems present a fascinating professional challenge to the aviation psychologist, to find a means of investigating them validly and solve them. They ensure that his work will continue to be stimulating. Technological innovations and increasing demands for aviation provide a never-ending supply of new psychological problems to be solved. I am kept busy, I work hard, I have high job satisfaction, and I enjoy my work very much.

REFERENCES

Dhenin, G. (ed.). (1978). *Aviation Medicine*, London: Tri-Med Books (2 vols).
Hopkin, V. D. (1979). 'Boredom and human reliability: some hypothesised relationships', *Proceedings of Second National Reliability Conference*, 4A/3, 1–7. Also in (1980), *The Controller*, **19**, 1, 6–10.
Hopkin, V. D. (1980). 'The measurement of the air traffic controller', *Human Factors*, **22**, 5, 547–560.
Hopkin, V. D. (1981). 'Integration of navigational information in aircraft', *The Journal of Navigation*, **34**, 2, 240–246.
Hopkin, V. D. and Taylor, R. M. (1979). *Human Factors in the Design and Evaluation of Aviation Maps*, NATO, Neuilly-sur-Seine. AGARDograph No. 225.
Moray, N. (ed.). (1979). *Mental Workload: Its Theory and Measurement*, London: Plenum Press.

Psychology in Practice
Edited by S. Canter and D. Canter
© 1982, John Wiley & Sons, Ltd.

CHAPTER 13

CONSUMER PSYCHOLOGY

Alan Frost and **David Canter**
Alan Frost Associates, London and
Department of Psychology, University of Surrey

INTRODUCTION

To many psychologists the world of market research and consumer psychology may sometimes have an attractive yet promiscuous image. The argument is put forward from time to time that the large budgets and the excitement of being part of active commercial enterprise would be clouded by the feeling that scarce professional talents were being prostituted to the whims of Mammon. There is, as a consequence, often a communication gap between psychologists who are in academic or 'caring' professions and their colleagues who find their way into commerce. Some academics may even give the appearance of being afraid of being tainted with the brush of private enterprise. Communication is not facilitated either by those practitioners in the consumer field who are reticent about their activities, feeling that they may come under attack from psychologists within universities who have the 'high standards' of more leisurely academic researchers.

However, the world of the consumer psychologists is an important one. On occasion they can have a significant impact on commercial development. Furthermore, the prospects which this area of professional activity offers for growth and expansion in the outlets available to psychologists are as yet hardly tapped. For although all major British companies, whether it be British Leyland or ICI, the BBC or Unilever, make use of consumer psychologists, the number of qualified psychologists involved is still in the low hundreds. Further, of the 300 or more market research organizations in Great Britain, only a minority at present employ graduate psychologists. Indeed the American Psychological Association's Division of Consumer Psychology has less than 400 members out of a total membership of well over 50,000.

Beyond this practical significance the techniques which it is necessary to develop in order to respond to the immediacy of the commercial world frequently have some value of a more directly theoretical nature, as illustrated below. There is one other important reason why psychologists should not turn their backs on their commercial colleagues. The general standard of research and psychological advice which is provided in this area is extremely variable. It is therefore essential that psychologists recognize that general standards can be raised to the heights of the best practitioners only if an open dialogue is developed.

However, before a dialogue can be developed there is one other aspect of the world of the consumer psychologist which must be taken into account. As things stand at present, his commitment to the client and to the particular projects on which he is currently working is greater than to any notional contribution to the scientific community. Furthermore there is no strong tradition of training or apprenticeship, so that psychologists involved in commerce do not always have as part of their plan of priorities the making available of accounts of their work for others, although diverse and wide-ranging publication of technical and scientific papers does, of course, occur. There are journals such as the *Journal of the Market Research Society*, *Journal of Marketing Research*, *Journal of Marketing* and overviews of the scientific aspects of the work, such as Worcester's (1978) handbook.

AREAS OF CONSUMER RESEARCH

In order to see how the psychologist may, or may not, have an influence in the world of commerce let us consider a generalized, but typical, sequence of events in which a consumer psychologist would be involved. We will take the most direct involvement, when a new product is being considered, say a new type of chocolate bar, or hair-care equipment. We will note also, in passing, some of the reasons why the great majority of new products fail in the market place.

One common starting point is for a manufacturer to ask the psychologist's organization to help with the development of a new product which is loosely specified. This request can entail a project of some size, which could run from three to six months. It will involve analysis of the way brands compete with each other in the market. It would also involve looking for opportunities for new products for that manufacturer which his competitors are particularly unable to produce. As a result of this work a number of very precise recommendations will be made of the way the product should be: (i) formulated by the manufacturer's laboratory people; (ii) packaged by his packaging people; and (iii) advertised by his advertising people. Until these recommendations are made the client does not actually know whether or not he has a viable new product.

At the stage when the recommendations are made the psychologist is still working directly with the client marketing company. If the work is fruitful and the recommendations are sufficiently encouraging the client will ask his Research and Development Department to examine ways of making the product.

Obstacle one: Research and Development is often a parochial power centre within the organization. They have their own ideas about how things should be planned, based on past experience, prejudice, and a mixture of valid and invalid beliefs. For although Research and Development is, technically speaking, a service centre within the manufacturing company, they usually have a high degree of autonomy based on their expertise and this makes them very hard to control even by senior management. If the product proposals get over this hurdle it then, typically, has to be packaged, physically put in a container of some sort. This packaging has to be designed.

Here is the second obstacle. It is not unknown for the chairman of a manufacturing organization to have regular informal links with the head of a design house with the result that the packaging designers are given such elevated status that for their work to be tested, or in any sense 'evaluated', by consumer research is unthinkable. Therefore, regardless of what the psychologist's research has found the packaging will be developed from the designers' preferences. This is aggravated by the fact that the designers charge enormous fees, so that the thought of redesigning a pack in the light of 'research' is financially frightening.

The third stage of product development may provide the worst obstacle. This is the promotion of the end product to the public by advertising agencies. When a manufacturer has a new product he may go to one of his existing agencies, which is already handling one of his brands, and ask them to prepare some advertising material for the new product, giving them guidelines from the early psychological research. The advertising agency, in that case, would probably read the research and make an honest attempt to fulfil the requirements drawn from the findings in the research. Often, however, the manufacturer will argue that this is a new produce and will go to a new agency. But now he will not go to a single agency. He may go to three. In effect he sets up a competition between various agencies.

Advertising agencies, in the worst cases, may well have a standard response to such an approach. They will take three or four weeks, or five or ten days, or some short time period, to carry out some very rudimentary qualitative research. That is to say, they will hire a psychologist, or use one of their own psychologists to talk to between one and four groups of housewives about the new product concept.

On the basis of this activity they will develop a creative strategy. They will not have been shown the original research because it is a competition and the manufacturer does not want an entrant, whom he may not employ, to benefit from having read the research. So the creative advertising work, which is all-important, is often guided by a very inferior piece of research. Now the client, the manufacturer, will look at the offerings of the three agencies and again typically, but not invariably, he will appoint the agency whose creative work he likes best. At that time he will say, 'right, you have got the job, now here is the research that you should have had before you wrote your winning creative strategy'! It is only to be expected that the agency will not substantially change the creative ideas, which did after all win them the project. The product consequently gets advertised with a treatment that has no parentage in the psychologist's research at all.

So it is possible to end up with a product which is badly formulated, inappropriately packaged, and ineffectively advertised. It will therefore, almost certainly, do what a great many new products do—fail.

We have laboured this point because one of the most embarrassing questions that any psychologist working in new product development has to face is the client who says: 'Please give me a list of your successes'. He can find himself left in the difficult position of saying: 'Well actually I have done a lot of good work but my clients keep messing it up'. The general example here also serves to illustrate the nature of the procedures which the psychologist has to face in his day-to-day work and the frustrations with which any new consumer psychologist must learn to cope. It also illustrates the many other trades and professions with which he may find himself collaborating from time to time. It seems likely that the people attracted to this area of psychology actually enjoy the mixture of personal and intellectual challenge which constitutes the daily experience. They also, of course, get special pleasure out of those projects where it all goes right and the psychological research leaves its mark on the supermarket shelves.

Disengaged from its, perhaps overly pessimistic, tone the above three-stage sequence does provide a useful framework for considering the consumer psychologist's involvement: (i) product development; (ii) packaging; and (iii) promotion. There are many published examples of these different aspects of consumer psychology (cf Worcester, 1978), so for our purposes here we will take some slightly unusual examples with which we have had direct experience. However, as all consumer research has its origins in the development of a product we will look at that first.

PRODUCT DEVELOPMENT

Perhaps one of the major contributions to consumer research which psychologists have made is the notion of a product's 'image'. Cohen (1980) argues that this contribution stems directly, and rather paradoxically, from the work which Watson (the father of 'Behaviourism') carried out when he left university life and joined a marketing company. The ideas of image and 'brand loyalty' have found their way into popular understanding through the writings of people such as Vance Packard (1960) and Daniel Boorstin (1963). What have not percolated so widely are the many systematic developments which have grown out of this perspective.

The starting point of much consumer psychology is that for a product to be recognized, or identified by the consumer at all, it must have a place in a potential purchaser's conceptual framework. The consumer must know about it and have at least a rudimentary understanding of what it is for and how it differs from any other products with which the consumer may associate it. The metaphor which is used to describe these ideas, and which can be taken literally by using advanced statistical procedures, is the reference to a 'product space' in which products which are thought of as similar to each other are clustered together. The writings of Osgood *et al.* (1957) had a major influence on the development of this notion, for they allowed the 'semantic space' which he portrayed, to be transposed to the world of the consumer. The axes of meaning, such as 'evaluation' and 'potency' provided a framework for considering consumer products (for example Downs, 1978). More recently consumer psychologists have developed much more subtle and idiosyncratic vectors for particular product spaces (for an early example see Frost and Braine 1967), taking their impetus from Kelly (1956).

Within this perspective various aspects of product development can be seen as ways of exploring the consumer's conceptual space and of changing the location of products within it. At one extreme this may be product development by *repositioning*. In this case the attempt is made to change an existing product, and/or the consumer's view of it, so that it sits in a different place in the conceptual space, becoming say more 'masculine', more 'appropriate for the kitchen', or 'more prestigious'. A larger change is envisaged when a product is *relaunched*. Here the attempt is to change the way of *thinking* about the product, as when toothpaste started to have fluoride added to it, accompanied by a wave of advertising campaigns emphasizing the prophylactic qualities of toothpaste. Beyond this form of development manufacturers will attempt 'line extension'. Here the existing product is used as a neighbour in the space for launching a related product. A well-known example of this was the introduction of Nescafé's Gold Blend as a sister product to existing Nescafé, or the introduction of floor detergents in addition to washing powders for clothes.

When it comes to *new product* development the idea is to find the equivalent of a hole in the product space which no existing product fills. As Greenlaugh (1978) puts it:

Appropriate multivariate techniques are used to analyse image data and to 'look for gaps'. These gaps are empty spaces in the multi-dimensional attitude space, where no existing product represents a particular set of attitudinal characteristics as seen by a significant segment of the population covered.   (p.384).

If this is a big gap, with no similar products nearby, the product which emerges may even be graced with the marketing label of a *new new product*. Finding successful examples of really new products is difficult, partly because the psychological processes involved are such that in order to understand any product the consumer must find a place for it in his or her conceptual space. But examples which are generally recognized to be new (or new new), which have found their way into the shops in recent years are the J-cloth and those hot hair curlers, known as Carmen rollers.

Having given this overview of product development let us consider an example in the, perhaps unexpected, area of medical prescriptions. This is a project reported by Barnes and Goldsmith (1973) with which one of the authors (AF) was closely involved.

The launch of 'Dixarit'

In 1969, a conversation between two eminent medical research workers sowed seeds which were to germinate into a product which is capable of preventing or decreasing the frequency and/or severity of attacks of migraine. The product became generally available to the medical profession in August 1971 as Dixarit.

The role of the Marketing Research in this instance was to provide the Marketing Department with an assessment of the size and nature of the potential market for the new drug. The first step in this procedure was to make an initial examination of the market into which Dixarit would fall. In a sense this is 'product development', backwards. Not an unusual route for it to follow. We have the product, but where does it fit in the market?

The general approach to answering this question was to spread the net very wide, gain an understanding of the structure of the market, and apply the knowledge acquired to narrowing down the research area to the gathering of information more directly concerned with the real purpose of the work—what was the size and nature of the opportunity presented by this new product?

The initial look

The initial look consisted of a detailed examination of the sales and prescription audits produced by Intercontinental Medical Statistics Limited. The market was defined as the diagnosis of migraine and the products prescribed within it. Trend data of both prescriptions and sales were abstracted back to 1963 and a market profile produced. An examination was made of patient and prescribing data from the prescription index and a study made of promotional literature. Basic data on all the products prescribed for the diagnosis of migraine were compiled.

What emerged was that consultations had remained level at about 1.3 million a year providing a market value of approximately £1m. The market consisted of about half migraine specifics (mainly ergotamine preparations and its derivatives) and the remainder of analgesics, anti-nauseants, tranquillizers, and sedatives. A firm estimate of the prophylactic segment was difficult but it was unlikely to be more than £200,000, most of which was made up of non-specific migraine products.

A subsequent quantitative evaluation of the size of the prophylactic segment suggested an annual total of about 170,000 consultations a year. However, data from epidemiological studies put the number of people in the population suffering from migraine at not less than 3 million. This led us to the hypothesis that the number of consultations might be low because of the inadequacy of existing therapy.

A closer look

Up to this time the research had been carried out by the Marketing Research Department of the manufacturing company, Boehringer Ingelheim Limited. At this point a marketing research agency, AAL Medical Surveys Centre Limited, was called in.

A thorough briefing attended by the marketing personnel and the agency representatives took place at which the results of the research to date and the hypotheses formed were discussed. From it emerged questions that needed to be answered before the fundamental decision on whether or not to introduce Dixarit could be taken.

The questions were recorded as follows:

(1) What market segments exist and what is their size?
(2) Which perceived drug characteristics most influence the way general practitioners discriminate between products for migraine?
(3) What are the general practitioner's perceived attributes of products currently available to him for the treatment of migraine?

For the first stage of the research programme, to answer question (1), 150 general practitioners who were members of a Medical Surveys panel were selected as being representative of the general practitioners' population in terms of geographical location and practice size. A postal questionnaire was mailed to them and an analysis made of the 139 (93 per cent) questionnaires returned.

For questions (2) and (3) a second stage was carried out in which a representative sample of 112 general practitioners was required to complete a questionnaire which had been developed from the research carried out in the first stage. This questionnaire covered three areas in great detail:

(1) Their attitudes towards twelve drugs which were used in the treatment of migraine (these drugs were selected to represent all the main therapeutic classes into which drugs used in the treatment of migraine fall).

(2) Their products needs in the context of treatment of acute attack, abortive treatment, and prophylactic treatment periods (these 'market segments' were ascertained from the first stage).

(3) Their prescription behaviour in the above three contexts.

The analysis of this data consisted of a series of operations in which both the attitudinal (product attribute) and behavioural (prescription) data were processed simultaneously.

The output of the analysis was in the detailed image scores for all the brands studied. The results were made more interpretable by the inclusion of two additions to the analysis. The first of these was the identification at an early stage of those product attributions which were associated with prescription behaviour. This is, in fact, a complex mathematical operation but the concept involved is fairly straightforward. In essence, the analysis is based on the notion that whether or not doctors *say* they require a product with a particular characteristic (for instance—low cost), if they in fact prescribe products which do not have this particular characteristic, then some other product attribute must be crucial to their decision-making. The analysis, by examining the relationship between perceived product attributes and prescription behaviour, is able to identify those characteristics which do appear to influence the doctor's choice.

The second additional analysis involves comparing the doctor's image of the various products with his optimum requirements in particular contexts. In this way, it is possible to say, for instance, not only whether a particular preparation is seen as strong or mild, but whether it was too strong or too mild. These calculations are, of course, only carried out for those product attributes which had been found by the earlier analysis to have an influence on sales. The image scores obtained are reported as deviations from an optimum product specification and the *size* of the deviation reflects its commercial significance.

The findings

As we have briefly mentioned it emerged from these studies that general practitioners consider that there are three different types of treatment for migraine: (i) treatment for an acute attack; (ii) preventative treatment, when the patient thinks an attack is about to occur; and (iii) a course of prophylactic treatment over a period of time. The product-attribute scales which were important for (i) were very similar to those for (ii), but considerably different for the prophylactic treatment, (iii).

When all products were looked at in terms of desired attributes it was found that the products prescribed prophylactically fell short of the ideal. It was also noted that overall the migraine specifics scored less well than the other drugs used. Furthermore, an examination of the desired attributes highlighted the problems associated with ergotamine because it is significant that six out of the nine attributes could be assumed to derive from predictive characteristics of products containing ergotamine.

Because of the weaknesses of existing products it appeared that an estimate of the potential size of the 'prophylactic' segment would largely depend on the efficacy of Dixarit. Clinical studies were continually confirming the power of the product. Thus, although the potential size of the prophylactic market was impossible to estimate with accuracy, judgement based on the evidence of the data and efficacy of the product began to suggest to Marketing that the potential was large enough to justify the introduction of Dixarit.

The next important step was to match the profile of Dixarit against the desired product attributes. It was apparent that Dixarit would satisfy seven of the nine requirements. The two which were debatable were 'the degree to which the brand could be used frequently in pregnancy' and 'the degree to which the brand could be more likely to reduce nervous tension', both of which were scales carrying relatively low importance weights. If nervous tension were a function of the condition, and if Dixarit were efficacious, then a case could be made that Dixarit would satisfy this requirement also.

So, on the basis of these results, a promotion strategy was developed, and as it turned out, a very successful sales campaign followed.

Eighteen months later, 350,000 prescriptions had been written for the product, far more than for any other product in the field, with the exception of one. It had achieved 20 per cent sterling share of a market in which no major changes had taken place for some years prior to its launch.

THE EFFECT OF ADVERTISING

A second example

In our first example the properties of a new product, known from clinical trials, were used as a basis for exploring whether it was worth the manufacturer, while going to the expense of launching that product and, along the way, to identify the best light in which to present the product when it was marketed. Our second example has many similarities but now we are dealing with a product which already exists and which the manufacturer believes should be doing better. The psychologist's role here was to advise on the advertising strategy and monitor the effect of the resulting advertising campaigns.

In order to follow the process which was carried out here it is necessary to understand the notion of 'market segmentation' referred to in passing for our first example. Lunn (1978) summarizes segmentation as an approach to marketing 'whereby products are directed at specific target groups of consumers rather than at a total population' (p.343). In other words, if a manufacturer believes that there are a number of different segments to his market and that he is currently targeting his advertising at a segment which is less than enthusiastic about his product, then redirecting his advertising may be seen to increase his profits. Of course in order to do all this he needs to know what the particular market segments are and how the consumers within those segments differentiate between competing trends.

Our example here concerns a manufacturer in the field of pre-packaged foods who believed his market to be segmented and wished to identify the segment at which he could most profitably aim his brand. A preliminary attitude study we carried out, showed that competitive brands were differentiated by consumers along twelve attitudinal dimensions. These included aspects such as perceived (i) costs, (ii) protein content, (ii) texture, and (iv) 'fatteningness'. These dimensions were found from a survey in which housewives rated the client's brand and two competitors', as well as an 'ideal product', on a number of bi-polar scales. For our purposes, the four in Figure 1, noted above, adequately illustrate our example.

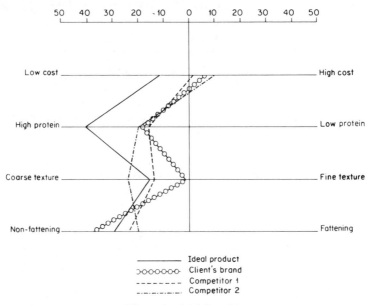

Figure 1   Initial position

Figure 1 shows the initial position at the start of the psychological involvement. It shows what statistical tests supported: (i) that none of the brands is very satisfactory in terms of cost and protein content; and (ii) that the client's brand has too fine a texture and is too non-fattening. Without taking any note of market segmentation these conclusions would normally lead to a promotional strategy which would adjust the brand's image in the obvious directions. However, such a course of action would have been used on the assumption that the 'ideals' were true representations of consumers' requirements. In fact a cluster analysis was carried out which revealed the presence of five distinct market segments. The 'ideals' for these segments were computed individually and three of them are shown in Figure 2.

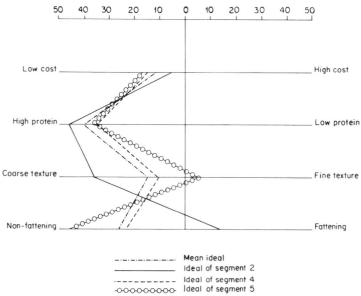

Figure 2   Differential requirements

This analysis revealed the presence of a segment of particular interest, namely segment no. 5. This was a sub-group of housewives with quite deviant requirements in two respects. First, they required a product which was of extremely fine texture and which was definitely non-fattening. Secondly, these were, of course, the very characteristics that had been thought to be faults in the client's brand.

A further check showed that 32 per cent of the client's sales were to members of segment 5, and it was therefore concluded that if the brand's currently perceived properties (namely excessive fineness and non-fattening) could be *exploited* by advertising, then it might become even more attractive to members of segment 5. Consequently, an appropriate advertising campaign was developed, tested, and launched and continuous readings of the brand's image were taken at monthly intervals. Yet after three months it became apparent that whilst the campaign was working in the non-fattening area it was not affecting the perceived texture of the product. Figure 3 shows the changes recorded after three months.

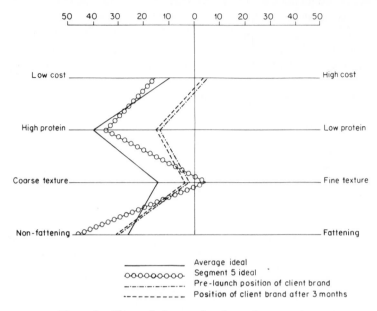

Figure 3   Change in image after 3 months campaign

Attempts to modify subsequent television commercials produced no improvement and it was decided that the textural element could only be effectively tackled by repackaging the product and backing this up with further television exposure. A new pack was developed, tested, and launched together with an appropriate television campaign. This took some time but after a further year image checks showed that the strategy had been most effective, as is shown in Figure 4. This figure shows that the brand's image, although not yet perfect, is much improved for the target population. Other data showed that this improvement was matched by a considerable increase in the brand's share of the market and this increase was largely due to purchasing within the target segment.

An interesting postscript is that the marketing activity after this project caused one competitive brand (No 2 on Figure 1) apparently to panic and adopt a similar approach. This brand was, however, singularly unsuited to such a strategy and would in fact have been well advised to do precisely the opposite and make a play for segment 2. As it was, all this particular competitor was likely to achieve was to improve what was already an attractive new product opportunity for our client.

It should be noted that the research procedures and modes of analysis, briefly mentioned here, have been simplified in the presentation, so that the general framework of the work can be clearly seen.

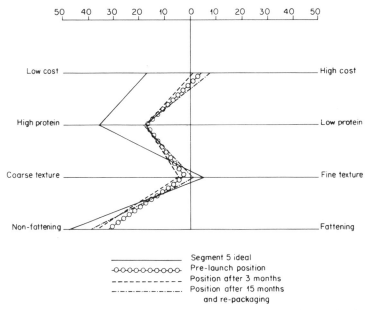

Figure 4   Change in image after 3 months and 15 months (and re-packaging)

COMPANY IMAGE — A THIRD EXAMPLE

In the first two examples we have dealt with rather specific issues and clearly defined products. However, there is an increasing interest in a psychological contribution to more amorphous matters, best summarized as 'corporate' or 'company' image. The generality of this idea can be gauged from Worcester's (1978) definition of it as 'the net result of the interaction of all experiences, impressions, beliefs, feelings and knowledge people have about a company' (p.523).

The study of a company's image may be undertaken for many different reasons, for example when a company is concerned about maintaining brand loyalties in the market place or when it is concerned with its image with the public because of debate, perhaps even in Parliament, about its activities which may have consequences, for instance, for support from its shareholders. Indeed, as we found in one interesting study, one organization was perceived by the workforce as extremely profitable and by the city of London financiers as profligate and inefficient. Such results clearly have major implications for management. In other cases the company image is virtually what it is selling. This is most notable, for example, with banks and building societies where the perceived differences between them are almost totally a function of the 'impressions, beliefs and feelings people have about a company' rather than any distinct differences in the services they offer. However, precisely because of the subtlety of these differences techniques have to be developed which are especially sensitive. For our third example, then, we draw upon the work Alan Frost carried out in conjunction with John Swift, the Market Research Manager of Lloyds Bank Limited.

As we have noted, banks present an almost identical face to the world. Their buildings, both inside and out, are similar and their services are similar. It is the attempts to measure their dissimilarities of image which stem not so much from their physical manifestations but the sum of their presentation to the world which could be described as their 'style', which is the subject of this example.

Previous approaches to banking corporate image

Over a number of years Lloyds Bank had commissioned surveys and participated in Corporate Image Studies in an attempt to locate and track the progress of the image of the bank vis-à-vis its major competitors in the personal market sector. However, these image studies were largely unsuccessful in providing evidence that consumers discriminate to any consistent or significant degree between the four major banks (Lloyds, Barclays, Midlands, and National Westminster).

Nonetheless these studies left the impression that there were underlying differences in the images of the banks which were not being clearly measured by the current techniques. This impression was reinforced by the findings of qualitative research which indicated that in a non-structured research environment, respondents were able to articulate perceived differences in the institutions which pointed in the same direction as the qualitative research, that Barclays was more modern and go-ahead, and Lloyds was rather sedate and old-fashioned. The images of the Midland and the National Westminster were less clearly defined.

It is with this background that at the suggestion of the bank's advertising agency, McCann–Erickson, consideration was given to experimental use of the 'Brand Personality Technique' which the agency had been working on to define the images of the major banks more clearly.

The technique

The technique for measuring brand personality was developed by McCann–Erickson in response to the problem of differentiating between brands in fields where the produce similarities are strong and conventional techniques do not adequately discriminate but where qualitative research suggests that there are underlying differences in the ways in which such brands are perceived by consumers.

The basic principle of the technique is that in order to arrive at the emotional response to the brand or company, the respondent is encouraged to use his or her imagination and to pretend that the subject under investigation is a person with particular physical and personality characteristics. The special value of such an approach to image is that it measures more subtle emotional and possibly deeper-seated reactions. One problem, of course, is that the technique produces substantial quantities of data which need the application of sophisticated data-reduction procedures in order to extract the key relationships.

Alan Frost, as a consultant working with McCann–Erickson, had developed a suite of programmes which provided the means for just such an efficient data reduction. At the same time, he also refined the methodology for the elicitation of the most discriminating personality decriptors.

Questionnaire development

In order to develop a questionnaire for use in a large-scale study two stages were used. The first generates a vocabulary ('trigger sessions'); the second refines the vocabulary by establishing which words or phrases are the most effective discriminators ('charade sessions').

Trigger sessions: The object of this phase is to generate the most comprehensive vocabulary possible of words or phrases which can be deemed to be *relevant* to the subject, that is banks. A small number of groups (three) of relevant consumers were set up, one each in Leeds, Birmingham, and London.

The procedure was as follows:

each respondent was asked to think of their own bank and to think of it as a *person*;

they were requested to write down a series of one- or two-word descriptions of that person;

the first respondent then read out his list whilst the others eliminated words which were on their lists and/ or added additional words which were 'triggered' by the words given;

this process was repeated by the other respondents and then the cycle repeated until no new words were emerging;

the process was repeated with 'user-image' words or phrases, that is the type of people who would use the bank.

This procedure provided us with almost two hundred

personality descriptors and about fifty user images. Clearly far too many for use in a questionnaire. Some would be more relevant and significant than others. Hence the next stage.

Charade sessions: These sessions had as their objective the task of reducing the unmanageable lists developed by the trigger sessions by identifying which words or phrases discriminated most effectively between the banks. Again, three sessions were set up, one each in London, Birmingham, and Leeds, although the number of respondents in each was small (four). A point-scored prize system was incorporated into these actions in order to encourage the maximum effort on the part of its respondents.
The procedure was as follows:

the first person (the transmitter) used words chosen from the list to describe a particular bank, the others (the receivers) tried to guess which bank was being described. Points for receivers were awarded or deducted for correctly or incorrectly identifying the bank and to the transmitter for the speed with which he could delineate the bank;
the process was repeated in a cycle round the group using different words.

The method thus identified those words which most easily described the personality of the banks under study. This phase reduced the longer list to:

sixty-one personality variations;
twenty-one customer stereotypes.

As a result of this 'qualitative' research a questionnaire was constructed in which respondents were asked to describe banks 'as people' using the adjectives derived. They were also asked to use a further list of adjectives to describe 'the sorts of people who might use banks'.

The results

The experiment was successful in that the Brand Personality Study showed conclusively that each of the five banks studied had a clear, concise and significantly different personality from the others and that these personalities were consistent across all the segments investigated. It was also reassuring that in general the personalities described by this research were broadly in line with those smaller scale differences which had emerged in previous research, both qualitative and quantitative.

Even among the banks' own customers, the same personality traits tend to hold true and the overall picture remains remarkably stable. Where there are differences in perspective, these are indicative, as one might expect, given the high level of satisfaction with one's own bank, that other research has indicated, of strong loyalty ties amongst the customers of an individual bank; on the whole, customers do not criticize their own bank and whatever negative attributes are generated by the total sample are not fully acknowledged by each bank's users.

The market-mapping exercise indicated that the banks cluster into three segments:

Lloyds and Barclays;
National Westminster and TSB;
Midland.

This clustering results from a perceived difference in the 'mood' that the banks present to the outside world; National Westminster and the TSB are seen to be outward-going, energetic, and friendly institutions which makes them appropriate for the financially unsophisticated sort of person. The National Westminster personality did surprise us somewhat as previous work had indicated that its image was not particularly clear-cut. It could be that the confusing effects of the major merger of 1970 have at last faded.

The common characteristics that bind Lloyds and Barclays together centre around their financial capability, their professional approach to business matters and the perceived size of their branch network which, taken as a composite picture, makes them attractive to the more middle-class and financially sophisticated sectors of the population.

The Midland's unique characteristics are such that the market as a whole rejects the bank in a fairly positive fashion. It is old and staid, boring and out of date and not at all the sort of bank that people appear to want to be associated with. One gets the impression from the current Midland Bank advertising that they are at present making a determined effort to overcome this very negative personality.

An ideal bank appears to be immediately defined in empathy terms, that is friendly and approachable, helpful and understanding, but nevertheless capable and professional. The ideal bank would therefore fall somewhere between the National Westminster/TSB cluster and the Lloyds/Barclays market position.

IN CONCLUSION — FROM THE MAGICAL
TO THE MUNDANE

The three examples can do little more than indicate the type of activities in which a consumer psychologist may engage. In conclusion, then, it is essential to emphasize that a consumer psychologist's activities are dependent on his own particular interests, motivations and experience. It is possible that in this field of psychological application, perhaps more than in any other, the particular idioxyncrasies of the individual concerned will frame what he actually does and how he does it. Thus a psychologist who has done post-graduate work in developmental psychology may well find himself involved in the study of toy design and the marketing of products for children, possibly drawing upon the techniques pioneered by Piaget. A social psychologist, on the other hand, will possibly find himself much more involved in studies of the impact of particular advertising campaigns and explorations of exactly how particular forms of marketing are likely to change attitudes towards products. In the examples presented Alan Frost's development through a statistically-oriented clinical psychology can be seen to have left its mark on two distinct characteristics of the activities presented. On the one hand, a lot of the work involves development of repertory grid techniques and their use to elaborate the conceptual system which specific segments of the consumer market possess and, secondly, to do this by the use of developments of multivariate, statistical analysis, most notably cluster analysis. Indeed, one of the major services available to offer to a client is the possibility of very rapid and effective repertory grid studies in which the data are collected through the respondent interacting directly with micro-computers.

The use of this technology serves to illustrate the role which careful consideration of cost effectiveness plays in any commercial enterprise. If data capture can be maintained at a moderately precise level, with a reduction in the amount of time it takes and it is further so structured that it leads to immediate computer analysis, the cost savings and hence the competitiveness of a service is greatly increased. This is further illustrated in the effort which is put into the modes of computer analysis and print-out. It is essential, lacking the leisure of the academic researcher to digest and present material, that immediately interpretable and presentable material should be produced from the computer. If histograms will tell the story more clearly than means and standard deviations, then the computer is called upon to compile a histogram. If it is necessary to see profiles of responses to every element of a repertory grid then this will be an immediate option to draw upon for the analysis. The aim is to get the computer to produce material that can be immediately placed into a report, with implications directly obvious from it; indeed, for a client educated in the procedure it is even possible for him to receive a copy of the computer print-out with relatively little need for interpretation by the psychologist.

Of course, not all clients require major data collection and analysis. In some cases, as we suggested earlier, a product might have failed for reasons which are obvious to people outside the company but which their own loyalties hide from them. To take a fictitious but not implausible example, if you are a British subsidiary of a large American chewing gum manufacturer, and your American bosses decide that a new product they have launched in North America should do very well in Britain, then it may be difficult to explain why it is impossible to get people to buy it. If in America the trade name the product has been given is a well-known high-scoring member of a baseball team, the American partners might be prepared to accept that there would be some difficulty in making people aware of the name, but nonetheless feel there is a value in maintaining continuity for the product in keeping the same name. If, as it happens, the only association which people have with that name in Britain is that it is a well-known make of car tyre, then the matter becomes more intricate. However, the nature of within-company rivalries is such that an outside consultant may need to be called in, to demonstrate with his own independent data that what would be obvious to many people outside the company, that you cannot expect to have much impact by naming chewing gum after a car tyre, can actually be demonstrated with real evidence by someone who is not part of the within-company battle.

Nonethless, even within the skills and predelictions of a particular individual the range of clients and concerns can be very great indeed. This makes it especially difficult to provide a coherent, structured account of the activities involved in being a consumer psychologist. No obvious parallels to the divisions apparent in the work of the clinical or educational psychologist, of casework, policy guidance, research and education, can be clearly seen.

A more appropriate pattern for distinguishing consumer psychology activity probably relates to the degree to which the individual is actually concerned with the success of a particular product. For instance, at one end of the continuum are the examples of corporate image which we illustrated in which share of the market and sales are less immediately to the fore. At the other end of the continuum, there is a possibility of monitoring the effect of particular kinds of advertising directly on the sales of a particular product, as in our second example. Somewhere in between these two extremes is the guidance which might be given on new product development. The nature of the contribution is different at these various distances from a precise product, but the similarities of issues and concepts, and above all of tensions and pressures, far outweigh these differences.

IS CONSUMER RESEARCH FRIVOLOUS?

As was discussed at the opening of this chapter, psychologists actively involved in the world of commerce and marketing sometimes receive criticism from colleagues about swimming into the jaws of Mammon. Thus, the excitement and challenge of working outside the usual institutional context common to most psychologists is frequently dulled in the eyes of many students who would aspire to consumer research by their belief that at best the research activity is frivolous and at worst it is morally unjustifiable. Some of the general force of this argument is now being reduced by developments in America (cf. for example Sommer, 1980) in which the psychologist is actually joining groups of consumer activists, using the techniques of the consumer psychologist to tackle the large commercial organizations with their own weapons. But outside this development, what are some of the moral issues involved in carrying out this type of professional activity?

The first question to answer is whether consumer psychology and the associated marketing activities has any real consequence. Certainly, as we have illustrated, there are definitely occasions on which it can have a direct commercial impact. An important question is what proportion of occasions this is. For reasons we have indicated, this is a very difficult question to answer with any precision. The marketing director's standard joke is that half of his budget is wasted and if he could just establish which half he could save a great deal of money. As we have indicated, frequently it is the relationship with the client which makes the difference between a successful contribution and an unsuccessful one.

If the intervention of the consumer psychologist can have an impact the question is then raised of the ethical justification of such an intervention. There are two aspects to this. The first is that in our society, where jobs and the livelihood of the community depends upon the production and selling of goods and services, then any activity which can make that more effective has a place in that society. However, there is one important caveat to this statement, which is the second aspect. It depends on the client. Clearly there are certain clients and certain products which an individual may believe are morally unacceptable. If that individual is a consumer psychologist he can choose not to work for those clients or on those products. A number of agencies, for example, refuse to be involved in the marketing of powdered milk for babies in developing countries if the advertising implies that the powdered milk is better than mother's milk. Another example is the involvement of consumer psychology in the promotion of political parties and ideas. We believe that there is a very large ethical question here because of the way consumer psychology could be abused so as to neutralize the existing democratic procedures associated with the ballot box. But all these examples come back to the psychologist selecting his client rather than inevitably allowing the client always to have the psychologist of his choice. A freedom open to the consumer psychologist, by the way, which is not always so obviously open to psychologists working within large institutions.

In conclusion it is important to emphasize that not all graduate psychologists can stand the pressures or necessarily have the skills, to enjoy a career in consumer psychology. Where undergraduate training is of especial value, in the provision of research skills for instance, it is frequently marred by an emphasis on relatively limited ranges of skills, for example limiting research to laboratory studies, and by not including the appropriate social and professional attitudes in association with those skills. The pressures of time, the seriousness of deadlines and the need for clear and succinct statements are not always part of an undergraduate's experience and are even less part of the world of the PhD student. However, if an individual does wish to be part of actual decision-making activity and enjoys responding to immediate questions with immediate answers then he or she could look forward to a rewarding career in consumer psychology working for someone else's living!

ACKNOWLEDGEMENT

We are grateful to John Barnes, Roger Goldsmith, and John Swift for their assistance in the preparation of this chapter.

REFERENCES

Barnes, J. and Goldsmith, R. (1973). 'Diversification: a case history', paper presented to ESOMAR Seminar on *Communication and Diversification in Pharmaceuticals, Hospital Supplies, and Allied Fields*, Brussels.

Boorstin, D. J. (1963). *The Image*, Harmondsworth: Penguin Books.

Cohen, D. (1980). *J. B. Watson: The Founder of Behaviourism*, London: Routledge & Kegan Paul.

Downs, P. E. (1978). 'Testing the upgraded semantic differential', *Journal of the Market Research Society*, **20** (2), 99–103.

Frost, W. A. K. and Braine, R. L. (1967). 'The application of repertory grid technique to problems in market research', *Commentary*, **9** (3).

Greenlaugh, C. (1978). 'Research for new product development', in Worcester and Downham (eds), pp. 377–411.

Kelly, G. A. (1956). *The Psychology of Personal Constructs*, New York: Norton.

Lunn, T. (1978). 'Segmenting and constructing markets', in Worcester and Downham (eds), pp. 343–376.

Osgood, C. E., Suci, G. J., and Tannenbaum, P. H. (1957). *The Measurement of Meaning*, Urbana: University of Illinois Press.

Packard, V. (1960). *The Hidden Persuaders*, Harmondsworth: Penguin Books.

Sommer, R. (1980). *Farmers' Markets of America: A Renaissance*, Santa Barbara: Capra Press.

Swift, J. (1981). *The Personalisation of the Institution in Order to Establish the Images of the Major British Banks*, London: Lloyds Bank Ltd (internal report).

Worcester, R. M. (1978). 'Corporate image research', in Worcester and Downham (eds), pp.521–536.

Worcester, R. M. and Downham, J. (Eds). (1978). *Consumer Market Research Handbook*, New York: Van Nostrand.

Psychology in Practice
Edited by S. Canter and D. Canter
© 1982, John Wiley & Sons, Ltd.

CHAPTER 14

PSYCHOLOGY AND COMMUNICATION TECHNOLOGY

Bruce Christie*
ITT Europe, Harlow, Essex

INTRODUCTION

We are standing at the threshold of a new era, a new society. We have moved on from a society dependent upon an agricultural economy, and lived through our industrial society. Now we are entering our information society, which will be characterized by an emphasis on information and communication. We humans are unique in the animal kingdom for our powers of communication. We alone amongst animals on this planet have developed true languages. Many other animals have developed primitive systems of communication based on limited repertoires of signals, but these systems lack the flexibility and richness of human language, and they lack the technology which we humans have developed to facilitate our communication and handling of information. It is this emerging technology of communication and information that is enabling us to take our first steps into our information society.

The field can be an exciting one for the psychologist who is interested in applying theory and methods to problems that have practical significance and in influencing the shape of things to come. In this chapter we shall look at what is involved in doing psychological work in this area, to give a feel for what the activity is like rather than a more distant account of research and its results.

AN OVERVIEW OF THE TECHNOLOGY

Developments in this area tend to be technology-driven and no psychologist can work effectively in the area without some understanding of the range of

---

*The views expressed are those of the author. They do not necessarily reflect those of any other organization or person.

systems involved. Examples of the main types of systems are summarized in Figure 1. The main distinction is between Type A systems—alternatives to face-to-face meetings—and Type B systems—alternatives to paper.

Type A systems are concerned with immediate ('real time') interactive interpersonal communication. The telephone is the most familiar system but even this is changing. The old electro-magnetic exchanges are being replaced by computers whose electronic intelligence allows for new possibilities. For example, you can tell the computer to reroute any calls for you to any other telephone on the same exchange so you need never be out of touch. To give another example, the telephone can act as a secretary, repeatedly calling a line that is engaged until the line is free, and then calling you to let you know. In addition to this kind of 'enhanced telephony', as it is called, there are other possibilities: the video telephone, for example, so that people can see one another as well as talk to one another, and teleconferencing, where people in two or more locations hold a 'meeting' using audio systems or audio-video systems. Audio systems include telephones with loudspeakers as well as more sophisticated systems such as the Remote Meeting Table (RMT) which uses several loudspeakers and switches sound between them according to who is speaking. Audio-video systems may be based on standard television equipment, 'slow scan video' (which gives still pictures), or video telephones. A lot of research on psychological aspects of electronic Type A communication was done by the Communications Studies Group at University College, London, and other groups around the world during the 1970s. Most of this has been written up for those who are interested in a book by Short et al. (1976).

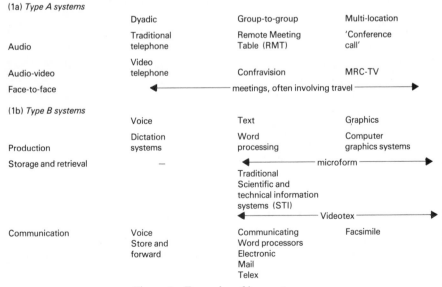

Figure 1   Examples of key systems

Type B systems are concerned with electronic equivalents of written communications. These are recent developments which generally make use of microprocessor technology and are already proving to be an essential ingredient in the 'office of tomorrow', the 'automated office', or 'electronic office', as it is variously called. Although based on modern computer technology they differ from traditional computer systems in many ways, for example:

(1) They are tailored to the office environment, for example producing high-quality typing on A4 sheets (rather than, say, line printer output).
(2) They are 'user friendly', as the parlance has it, and do not require computer personnel to operate them. They can be used by typists with word-processing training, managers, and other office workers.
(3) They are small and can be used in the typical office environment rather than requiring special air-conditioned rooms of their own.

These systems can be regarded in many ways as a logical technological extension to typewriters, filing cabinets, and other traditional office furniture. They deal with all aspects of information handling, including: the production of documents (for example word processors); storage and retrieval (for example microform systems, Prestel and other videotex systems, and large word-processing systems); and communication (for example communicating word processors, electronic mail, and facsimile). Psychological aspects of electronic Type B systems are discussed in a book by the author (Christie, 1981).

The systems listed in Figure 1 are just examples of a whole range of systems that are helping to produce major changes in the human environment. They should be of great interest to psychologists; after all, it is a fundamental assumption of psychology that behaviour is a function of an interaction between a person (or animal) and an environment. If this assumption is true, significant changes in the human environment should result in changes in behaviour. Our environment is changing markedly under the impacts of the emerging technology, and any psychologist with even the slightest concern for the ecological validity of psychological theory and method should be interested in the technology and its effects.

ROLES FOR THE PSYCHOLOGIST

The role of the psychologist in relation to the new technology need not be restricted to a passive understanding of the area, and it would be disappointing if psychologists were to accept such a limited, reactive role. If psychology is a true science psychologists should be able to use it to help influence the direction in which the technology—and society—moves, not simply to conduct retrospective analyses.

Whether the psychologist takes a relatively passive or active role, and what (s)he does within these broad approaches, is influenced a great deal by the clients for whom (s)he chooses to work. For example, if the work is done for The Social Science Research Council it is likely to fall within the broad category of 'passive understanding' because that client is more concerned with the methodological rigour of work done and its contribution to established theory than to its practical significance. This kind of work may be regarded as more fundamental than the work done for some other clients, say an equipment manufacturer interested in developing new system concepts, but the main difference is that it is likely to be reactive—attempting to understanding developments that have already been made—whereas the latter is more proactive—attempting to influence the shape of things to come. The distinction is rarely this clear-cut but it may be useful to bear it in mind when considering the range of clients apart from the research councils for whom the psychologist may choose to work.

There is another important difference between working for the research councils and for some other clients such as equipment suppliers or organizations that are interested in using the new technology. Psychologists working for the research councils may enjoy a degree of academic freedom that others do not but they may also find it difficult to gain access to real organizations for their projects and they are unlikely to be privy to information about new system concepts that are just around the corner. Psychologists working for suppliers and for user organizations necessarily often find themselves working in real organizations and are often privy to information about systems that are under development or alternative system concepts that are being evaluated before being marketed or abandoned, but this can be at the price of having to focus on practical issues rather than more remote, more academic problems.

The main types of clients in this area, apart from the research councils, are the PTTs (British Telecom in the UK), equipment manufacturers, user organizations, government departments, and individuals.

The PTTs are interested in developing telecommunications systems for the countries they serve and often have to take a long-term view, say twenty or thirty years into the future. This can result in fairly fundamental research and in this respect they are like the government departments who may be interested in fundamental impacts on education, employment, transportation, or other areas of government responsibility. Much of the fundamental research done on Type A communication during the 1970s was funded by the Post Office (now British Telecom) (see Short et al. 1976), and the Departments of Environment and Transport recently funded a basic review and theoretical analysis of Type B communication from the psychological point of view (see Christie, 1981).

Equipment manufacturers generally have a shorter time horizon, say up to about five years into the future. Even so, work of general interest can be done.

For example, the recent work of Engel *et al.* (1979)—an IBM team—makes a significant contribution to our understanding of how people filling different roles in the office environment (such as managers, secretaries) spend their time.

User organizations have the shortest time horizon, typically about six months to two years. The potential role for the psychologist is often restricted to applying established knowledge and methods but can sometimes include more basic work. For example, the author and his colleagues recently conducted an assignment for the Commission of the European Communities in Brussels and Luxembourg which included a factor-analytic study of the structure of office activities and of attitudes towards elements of the information environment. One aspect of the study suggested the intriguing possibility of a 'first law' of information behaviour analogous to Guttman's first laws of intelligence and attitude (see Shye, 1978, for a discussion of the first laws of intelligence and attitude, and Christie, 1981, for the possible information behaviour analogy).

Individual clients have rather different requirements, and usually want results very quickly. They may be seeking advice in regard to opportunities they may wish to exploit, jobs they may wish to apply for, or training in new skills. An increasingly important role is concerned with occupational stress. As we move into the information society of the 1980s and beyond the pattern of occupational stresses is changing, and individuals can often benefit from personal counselling. In performing this emerging role, the occupational psychologist may at times use methods such as Rogerian counselling, rational-emotive therapy, and hypnosis which are also used by clinical psychologists and psychotherapists but the area is properly one for the occupational rather than the clinical psychologist because it is concerned with dealing with normal stresses on normal people—before they become 'clinical' cases.

This brief overview of the types of clients for whom the psychologist may work illustrates the wide variety of work done in this area. The author has been fortunate enough to work for all of the types of clients listed above at one time or another and from this experience the following main types of roles have become apparent. Other psychologists working in different contexts may well find other distinctions to be more salient but the following seem convenient for present purposes. In any case, the roles described are ill-defined, are not mutually exclusive in practical situations, and can provide only a rough perspective, but that said the following broad categories seem to account for much of the work done.

The psychologist as researcher

There is plenty of scope for psychological research in relation to the emerging technology, for example:

(1) Ergonomics of visual displays (for example: Do visual displays really cause psychophysiological problems for some people and if so under what circumstances?)

(2) More general ergonomics of workstations and other aspects of the physical environment (for example: Can optimal configurations of keyboards, screens, printers and other equipment be defined?)

(3) Social psychological aspects of the automated office (for example: Do some personality types — perhaps sizothymic individuals — take to word processing better than others? How does the relationship between manager and secretary change?)

(4) The 'consumer psychology' of automated office products and services (for example: In Fishbein's terms — see Fishbein and Ajzen, 1975 — is disposition to acquire new systems influenced more by Aact or NB?)

(5) The communications psychology of the emerging technology (for example: How does the availability of the new media influence use of existing media? How can communication between the human and the electronic system be improved?)

Some good examples of psychological research on the emerging technology of Type A communication are provided by the work of The Communications Studies Group (CSG) of University College London during the 1970s. This work was reported in detail in a large number of research papers which are available for inspection by those who are seriously interested at British Telecom Headquarters, 88 Hills Road, Cambridge. Much of the work is available more readily in the book by Short *et al.* (1976). The following is just one example to give a flavour of what can be done.

The work of the CSG was guided by the Telecommunications Impact Model (TIM) developed jointly by Alex Reid, later to take a very senior position at British Telecom, and Brian Champness, later to take a more academic position at Plymouth Polytechnic. The model was developed to forecast the extent and kinds of possible impacts (especially on office location) of developments in Type A communications technology. The model had several stages and required inputs from specialists in several different disciplines, including psychology. The work to be described here was concerned with the first stage of the model, the 'amount' stage.

The purpose of the amount stage was to count the number of business and government meetings that fell into various categories. A review of the psychological and other literature revealed that no suitable scheme for classifying meetings existed, and such a scheme was necessary before any representative sample survey work could be undertaken. The CSG, led by its psychologists therefore undertook a study of its own to develop a suitable classification scheme. This study, called the DACOM (Description And Classification Of Meetings) study is described in detail by Short *et al.* (1976). Briefly, it was as follows.

The aim was to develop a classification scheme based on the verbal descriptors which managers actually use to describe their meetings. Three main aspects of meetings were considered: their purposes or functions (for example negotiation); the types of interactions involved (for example information exchange); and the atmosphere of the meetings (for example friendly or hostile). The first step was to conduct a series of 65 open-ended interviews to elicit the words and phrases used to describe these three aspects of meetings. The interviewees were drawn from a range of different offices in Greater London. Based on these interviews, a standard questionnaire was developed which contained 104 seven-point rating scales. Three hundred and eleven personnel in various business organizations returned completed questionnaires, in each case describing the respondent's most recent meeting. The 311 descriptions of meetings were then factor-analysed to establish the basic dimensions of the taxonomy. The results of the analysis are summarized in Figure 2, and further details are given in Short *et al.* (1976).

Aspect I: Main dimensions of purpose
1. To allocate tasks
2. To give information
3. To dismiss an employee
4. To present a report
5. To discuss a problem
6. To appraise another department's or organization's services
7. To review a subordinate's work
8. To make tactical or policy decisions
9. To give advice

Aspect II: Main dimensions of interaction
1. Conflict
2. Gathering background information
3. Problem-solving
4. Bargaining
5. Work-related gossip
6. Generating ideas

Aspect III: Main dimensions of atmosphere
1. Anger
2. Constructiveness
3. Caution
4. Informality

Figure 2   Dimensions of face-to-face meetings (results of the CSG's DACOM study)

The results of the DACOM study were used in two related ways. First, they were used to define categories of meetings that could be counted in representative sample survey work (this necessitated further analysis beyond that in Figure 2, including cluster analysis). Secondly, the dimensions defined provided a means of relating psychological experiments on media effects to the sample survey work.

The psychological experiments provide another example of psychological work in this area. The CSG experiments were aimed at testing a whole range of hypotheses concerning the effectiveness and acceptability of electronic Type A communications systems. To this end, the CSG set up psychological laboratories in London and in Sunningdale which allowed small groups of managers in business and government to use two-way audio and audio-video systems for experimental tasks. The experiments were conducted according to the usual principles of experimental design to examine differences between various kinds of audio and audio-video systems in regard to objective measures of task performance and in regard to various measures of attitude towards the systems.

It turned out to be quite difficult to demonstrate any important differences between audio and audio-video systems, even under the highly controlled conditions of the CSG experiments. Even when statistically significant differences were found they were generally small and of doubtful practical significance. This was definitely counter-intuitive at the time and counter to many predictions based on then current psychological theory but it was supported by case studies based on setting up systems to be based for real meetings. The general conclusion seemed clear enough: including a visual channel in an electronic Type A system would usually make the system only marginally if at all more effective or acceptable. This was an important conclusion because the costs of including a visual channel are extremely high. (Cost is very roughly proportional to bandwidth, measured in hertz, or Hz. An ordinary telephone conversation takes about 3500 to 4000 Hz, depending on how it is assessed. In contrast, the American 'Picturephone' video telephone takes one million Hz, and a group-to-group video conferencing system such as the British Confravision' system takes about five to six million Hz.)

It was largely on the basis of this evidence that the various PTTs around the world gradually abandoned ideas of setting up extensive networks of audio-video systems during the 1970s and 1980s. The mass production of the 'Picturephone', which was started in the 1960s, was terminated by the mid-1970s. Televerket—the Swedish PTT—which had even been experimenting with international video conferencing asked the CSG to evaluate various prototype audio-conferencing systems and on the basis of the CSG findings as well as other work decided to put their marketing effort into audio rather than audio-video systems.

The author and his colleagues at PACTEL have continued this tradition of psychological experimentation and the work provides some interesting illustrations in regard to Type B systems, for example videotex. Britain pioneered videotex, and Prestel—the British Telecom service based on the British viewdata videotex system—was the first public videotex system in the world. Many other countries followed suit, often (as in the case of Germany) adopting the British system or a variant of it. Other countries, especially France, Canada, and Japan, have developed alternative systems all of which offer more detailed graphics than does viewdata (although it must be added that British Telecom's 'Picture Prestel' will once again take the lead in this respect during the mid-1980s).

A question which arose early on in regard to videotex was how important detailed graphics were compared with providing a colour as opposed to a monochrome display. Many people felt that detailed graphics were essential but colour of no real value, just a gimmick. The question was important because improving the graphics quality of basic viewdata was an expensive proposition but colour was already a technical option. Experimental work done by PACTEL for The Commission of The European Communities suggested that adding colour to basic monochrome viewdata was worth as much or possibly more psychologically as adding very detailed graphics. What effect this work had on general opinion is difficult to assess but certainly colour is now generally regarded as a 'must' for videotex systems.

Another question which arose concerning videotex was whether it should be seen as a very general purpose information system, or whether its marketing should focus on specific application areas, such as the travel industry. Experimental work by the author and his colleagues, again conducted for The Commission of The European Communities, suggested that at least for people in the home the use of videotex in relation to other information media already used (such as books, radio, telephone, asking a neighbour) would probably depend significantly upon the application area. Again it is difficult to assess the degree to which this work influenced thinking, and certainly other factors were involved as well, but in this country British Telecom has moved away from marketing Prestel as a general information service to putting most effort into marketing it in particular application areas, such as the travel industry; and The Commission of The European Communities has been investigating ways of setting up international videotex systems in particular application areas such as agriculture and energy-saving.

These examples illustrate that psychological research in this area can have a meaningful even if often small influence on the shape of things to come.

The psychologist as information resource

Very often in the real world people prefer to be given a factual response rather than the offer of research. This is not too surprising. A person is most likely to turn to a psychologist when there is a problem to be addressed, some uncertainty that needs to be resolved before progress can be made. The correct facts reduce the uncertainty and are therefore welcomed. A method for discovering the facts is not welcomed so much — it is bad news because it means that uncertainty will remain high for some time, progress must wait, and money must be expended to conduct the required research.

The psychologist can act as an information resource in several ways, of which the following are drawn from the author's own experience:

(1) As adviser (for example giving advice to colleagues on survey design, statistical analysis, and other aspects of research).

(2) As provider of specific facts (for example factual information in ergonomics to colleagues involved in designing terminals).

(3) As a gateway to other sources of information (for example computer-aided searches of the psychological literature, contacts with the research councils, commercial consultancies, university researchers, and other sources of information).

An example of the latter type of case arose in connection with the work on videotex mentioned above. The thrust of that particular assignment was on defining general display requirements for videotex and on forecasting the potential growth of videotex systems throughout Europe during the 1980s and 1990s but some limited effort was also put into understanding its detailed impacts in one or two particular areas, of which education was chosen as a key example. In this case it was not felt appropriate to attempt an analysis of this area in-house when people more knowledgeable about education existed in the universities and could be invited to contribute. The role of the author as psychologist in this instance was simply to find a suitable person (who turned out to be a professor of education), demonstrate videotex to him, explain its general principles and how it might develop, explain the purpose of the study and the educational contribution, and take whatever steps turned out to be necessary to ensure that the contribution was useful and in an appropriate format for the main study. In this case the person concerned, Professor Wragg, did an excellent job and the author's task was very easy.

Another way in which the psychologist can act as an information resource is as a tutor to clients. An example of this is an assignment the author conducted for Embratel. Embratel is the authority responsible for long-lines tele-communications services in Brazil, and Embratel commissioned PACTEL to assess the scope for new telecommunications services in Brazil over the coming ten years. The assignment was multidisciplinary and the author's role included, amongst other things, flying out to Brazil to explain to key client personnel the principles of attitude theory and measurement, and how these could be used to develop an understanding of the 'consumer psychology' of possible new services being contemplated. This involved both tutorials and structured workshops.

The psychologist as change agent

A third main role for the psychologist is that of change agent, both by helping at the organizational level with the introduction of new systems, and at the level of the individual by helping individual clients adapt to the new demands of the electronic environment. The range of methods that may be used is wide, covering:

(1) ergonomics and broader human factors work to help to design effective and acceptable systems;
(2) design, monitoring, and evaluation of pilot trials of systems to iron out bugs at all levels from the human–machine interface to broader organizational aspects;
(3) organizational development methods;
(4) educational and training programmes at all levels of the organization;
(5) work with individual clients, using a variety of techniques including: counselling, role playing, hypnosis, and other techniques;
(6) and other relevant methods according to the needs of the particular project.

All of the above are important in facilitating change but often the most important is promoting awareness of and a positive attitude toward the technology. The author and his colleagues have developed a workshop technique called the PATH (People And Technology Heuristic) workshop which has proved useful in this regard at the organizational level.

The PATH workshop, based on the more general method of the focus group interview (see Calder, 1977) developed partly out of work done for an equipment supplier. In that work, the author was responsible for organizing a series of qualitative market research group interviews in the UK and France to gain an understanding of likely attitudes toward possible future system concepts. At the end of this work the author was left with the strong impression that no matter how 'objectively' the system concepts had been presented, one side-effect of holding the workshops at all was to shift awareness of and attitude toward the general technology being discussed. A further series of workshops held for another client in the UK, France, Germany, and Holland added further weight to this view. Since then, efforts have been made to modify the structure of the workshop deliberately to amplify the effect and make it useful for facilitating the introduction of new systems into organizations.

The group dynamics involved in workshops of this kind are complex but it seems to the author that much of what goes on can be understood in terms of the Fishbein expectancy-value equation (see Fishbein and Ajzen, 1975), especially in terms of shifts in salient beliefs. What workshops can help to do is change the items which are salient in regard to the concepts being presented. For example, some people focus very narrowly on cost reduction possibilities associated with new technology but the workshops can help to improve awareness of (make more salient) other factors such as occupational stress, quality of work done, organizational stability, and so on. Workshops can also change other factors in the Fishbein equation, such as normative belief; it can often be quite interesting—sometimes even amusing—to watch the reactions of a senior manager who comes to realize (s)he is out of step with the others (of equal seniority) in the group. This can be a powerful factor in shifting attitudes towards the concepts being presented.

Once one starts to contemplate deliberately and systematically shifting variables in the Fishbein equation it is not too far a leap to start thinking about some of the techniques used by Erickson (see Erickson and Rossi, 1979) for influencing people's perceptions and beliefs. Some of these techniques, especially those concerned with indirect suggestion, have been used successfully by the author from time to time in group situations, especially where the object has been to break down limiting belief frameworks and lead the group to explore new avenues. This can often be more successful than a more logical argument which can easily be rejected by questioning the assumptions on which it is based, or even rejected on grounds which may appear to be totally non-rational.

An example of the use of quasi-hypnotic techniques in group situations is provided by an assignment the author was recently asked to conduct for a company which was moving more and more into office automation products and services but whose sales people seemed to lack confidence in their own ability to sell the products and services effectively. It was generally held that their lack of confidence was unjustified but was related to a feeling they had of not being sufficiently familiar with the technology involved. The author was considered a suitable person to try and help because he could combine an adequate, if limited, understanding of the technology with the necessary psychological skills to facilitate the necessary changes in the sales people concerned. In such a situation it is clearly not feasible to use formal hypnotic trance induction procedures but it is perfectly feasible to use Erickson-type hypnotic techniques to help the sales people concerned to see the technology and themselves in a new light.

More formal hypnotic techniques can be useful in regard to individual clients, for example in relation to occupational stress (both in examining sources of stress and in helping the person concerned to develop more effective coping patterns). Effective use of these techniques may often depend, however, on an adequate understanding of the occupational environment in which the client finds himself or herself, including changes in that environment related to the emerging technology of information and communication systems. Although some clinical psychologists are skilled in the use of hypnosis it would not be appropriate for them to use it, or other techniques, in this kind of case without an understanding of the occupational context; more properly it is an area for the occupational psychologist. Behaviour is a function of the person and the environment and the occupational psychologist better than anyone else can understand the environment as it affects the person's behaviour and attempts to cope with technological change. The occupational psychologist can help managers and others to develop effective coping strategies *before* those people become 'clinical' cases.

Methods

It should be clear from what has been said above that the psychologist may need to draw on a wide range of methods, depending upon the particular context. The methods that will be appropriate in any given context will depend upon who the client is, what resources (time, money, people, and other resources) are available, and what type of output is required. The method chosen will usually be an optimal method, taking account of all of these factors, and not necessarily the most rigorous one could imagine given no practical constraints. Often a range of different techniques will be used in combination, and there will frequently be close links with work done on other aspects of the project concerned by professionals in other disciplines.

Many projects on which the psychologist is likely to work are essentially multidisciplinary in nature. The inputs which any one of the professionals including the psychologist can make only become useful in combination with the inputs from the other professionals involved. The key disciplines involved are likely to include engineers, computer specialists, information scientists, management scientists, and other specialists (sociologists, graphic designers and others) as the occasion demands.

RELATIONSHIPS WITH CLIENTS AND
OTHER PROFESSIONALS

The psychologist can play many roles in relation to the emerging technology and it is unfortunate that few of them are likely to be identified as being 'psychological'. There is a strong tendency for clients and other professionals to use terms such as 'ergonomics', 'human factors', 'behavioural science', 'specialist in the human aspects', and so on—rarely 'psychology' or 'psychologist'. This may well be because psychology has somehow got itself a very clinical image. Many non-psychologists still confuse psychology with psychiatry. It is a problem that was recognized and discussed by the SSRC Psychology Committee some years ago—that psychologists working in industry run a serious danger of losing their identity as psychologists even if they spend all their time doing psychological work—and the problem remains. The solution to this problem must lie with we psychologists ourselves.

If we take care to identify ourselves as psychologists and explain what that means then the image of psychology will stand a better chance of becoming clearer and more accurate than if we go along too readily with whatever terms others may use in initial interactions.

A related difficulty is that many clients and other professionals who take 'human factors' and other such specialisms seriously often look upon psychology as something of a curiosity. It seems to conjure up a mixture of different images, according to the particular person, of couches and rats, of esoteric psychosexual theory on the one hand and trivial laboratory games on the other. It can take quite some time to teach even one's most immediate colleagues that psychology has more to offer.

A more serious difficulty still is that clients are often not in a position properly to evaluate what a psychologist can offer. In many companies the market research department, for example, is run by people who have come from being sales people. They usually know quite a lot about the particular products and services concerned, and have had practical experience in selling them. What they often do not have an even rudimentary grasp of is psychology.

They are often quite incapable of evaluating the relative strengths and weaknesses of two different methods proposed for examining some aspect of the consumer psychology of concern. The result is that they rely on the 'track record' of the company whose (psychological) services they are considering using. As track records boil down (without too much exaggeration) to a list of clients for whom the company has done similar work before (and who also make judgements on 'track record'), the system is self-perpetuating. The onus is on psychologists to educate clients but this needs to be done by the profession as a whole as well as individual psychologists who are not usually in a position to spend the time required with every client.

The poor understanding of psychology which many clients have also means that the psychologist must learn how to communicate with clients in terms they will understand. This means putting a lot of emphasis on explaining clearly in very simple terms that will be delivered to the client (for example data tapes in such a form, a report of so long specifying such and such, a management summary of such a length—all specified in detail), what it will cost, and how the client will be able to use the outputs. Undergraduate psychologist courses normally do not equip the psychologist well for this kind of communication.

Any student of psychology contemplating working in industry, especially in management consultancy, or where there is a similar need for a flexible response to the needs of different clients, could do worse than become acquainted with Milton H. Erickson's concepts of 'utilization', 'frames of reference' and other concepts relating to the establishment of effective communication—see the introductory chapter in Erickson and Rossi (1979).

THE RELEVANCE OF UNDERGRADUATE PSYCHOLOGY

There is no simple way of describing the relevance of undergraduate psychology because it depends so much on the particular role the psychologist chooses to play and the nature of the particular undergraduate course. The author's impressions are that the following points may be true fairly generally.

Undergraduate psychology equips the student fairly well to do empirical research. This is probably more true for experimental work than for survey and 'qualitative' research, although there seems to be a larger market for the latter than the former. The way research is taught is often, roughly speaking, as follows. Hypotheses are derived from some existing psychological theories. A situation (for example laboratory experiment) is defined in which these hypotheses can be tested. The results of the tests are evaluated for statistical significance, null hypotheses are rejected or not as the case may be, and conclusions are drawn concerning the theory that was being tested. Practical work in relation to emerging electronic technology (and no doubt other topics) proceeds somewhat differently. It starts typically not from theory but from a practical problem — for example which kind of people in which kinds of organizations will be likely to use electronic mail during the next five years, how much will companies be prepared to pay for such systems, and what features should the systems offer? There is nothing explicit about psychological theory here, although the question obviously concerns human behaviour of several different kinds and the prediction of that behaviour in various circumstances. The next step is to define a precise logic for answering the questions posed which includes defining what needs to be measured. What needs to be measured, and often the logic itself, will depend on the more general model one uses. The 'model' will in turn be influenced by one's psychological theories concerning the factors involved. What is done within this framework will then be constrained by the resources (including time) available. Time is often the major constraint as clients generally want results much faster than is typical of 'pure' university research. Where experiments do need to be done, there is likely to be more interest in the variance accounted for by different factors, the confidence intervals involved, and other measures of precision and magnitude of effect, than on the simple criterion of statistical significance or non-significance. The research methods and theories of behaviour taught to undergraduates are certainly relevant but perhaps more could be done to help students apply these tools in practical situations, including help in planning optimal methods to use taking account of the time, money, and other resources available.

Clients and colleagues in other professions often expect psychologists to be good 'practical psychologists', that is 'good with people'. It may be that undergraduate courses could equip students better for the world outside by complementing the teaching of research and theory with some special 'social skills training' to help students manage individuals and groups better. It may be that some undergraduate courses incorporate this kind of 'applied psychology' training but it seems to the author to be more characteristic of management-training courses.

Undergraduate training normally will need to be supplemented by other training, either on the job or on other courses. Some of the topics that might be relevant, according to circumstances, include: counselling skills; practical use of psychological tests; forecasting techniques (such as Delphi, sensitivity analysis) that may not be taught to undergraduate psychologists; and other topics relating to (in this case) emerging electronic technology, including a rudimentary understanding of the technology itself so that one can communicate with colleagues and clients.

ETHICAL AND MORAL ISSUES

There are a number of specific ethical and more general moral issues which the psychologist must deal with either implicitly or explicitly, apart from the obvious ethical considerations of client confidentiality and so forth. Whatever issues are salient will depend on the particular person but they might include the following.

Some psychologists may wish to be careful about which companies they work for, perhaps declining to do work for companies that deal in death or make profit out of people's weaknesses to their eventual detriment.

Others may be concerned about which systems they help to introduce into organizations. In taking steps to smooth the introduction of new systems into an organization the psychologist is influencing people's attitudes and behaviour in the direction of their accepting certain concepts, for example automation, which they might not have accepted as well if left to themselves. Some psychologists in this type of situation might wish to satisfy themselves that the ideas they are helping to introduce are the 'right' ones. The question of what is 'right' in this context in turn raises many other issues.

The ethical and moral issues involved, whatever they may be for the individual psychologist, can be ignored but they are always there. They cannot be avoided by doing 'pure' research, because the decision to do that kind of work is a decision in its own right and means that the person concerned has chosen not to make a positive contribution (at least to the same extent) in other, more applied, areas, that is (s)he has chosen to deprive those other areas — that may badly need psychological inputs — of his or her knowledge and skills. The matter is less pressing the less effective the psychologist is because, by definition, an ineffective psychologist does not influence the situation one way or another. Conversely, the more knowledgeable and skilled the psychologist concerned, the more important it becomes for him or her to contribute in the right way. It also depends on the general area being considered. Presumably if the area itself is relatively trivial then it does not matter what the psychologist chooses to do because the consequences — whether good or bad — are not going to be very great in any case.

CONCLUSION

The emerging technology of information and communication defines a broad area in which the consequences of psychological work done can be significant. Hopefully, the examples given in this chapter give some hints at least of the many ways in which the psychologist can contribute to developments in the area and the broad range of psychological expertise that is required. For the psychologist interested in applying his or her training and experience with effect, this area is likely to be one of the most exciting during the 1980s. For a further discussion of the area the reader is referred to Christie (1981).

REFERENCES

Calder, B. J. (1977). 'Focus groups and the nature of qualitative marketing research', *Journal of Marketing Research*, **14**, 353–364.

Christie, B. (1981). *Face to File Communication: A Psychological Approach to Information Systems*, London: Wiley.

Engel, G. H., Groppuso, J., Lowenstein, R. A. and Traub, W. G. (1979). 'An office communication system', *IBM System Journal*, **18** (3), 402–431.

Erickson, M. H. and Rossi, E. L. (1979). *Hypnotherapy: An Exploratory Casebook*, London: Wiley.

Fishbein, M. and Ajzen, I. (1975). *Belief, Attitude, Intention and Behaviour: An Introduction to Theory and Research*, Reading, Mass: Addison-Wesley.

Short, J., Williams, E., and Christie, B. (1976). *The Social Psychology of Telecommunication*, London: Wiley.

Shye, S. (1978). 'On the search for laws in the behavioural science', in S. Shye (ed), *Theory Construction and Data Analysis in the Behavioural Sciences*, San Francisco: Jossey-Bass, pp. 2–24.

Psychology in Practice
Edited by S. Canter and D. Canter
© 1982, John Wiley & Sons, Ltd.

CHAPTER 15

PSYCHOLOGY AND ENVIRONMENTAL DESIGN

David Canter
Reader in Psychology
University of Surrey

THE NATURE OF THE CONTRIBUTION TO DESIGN

When psychologists, or architects for that matter, think of a psychologist contributing to design, they usually imagine someone suggesting what colours the walls might be painted, or at a larger scale, of where schools might be located in a new town. There is a consequent search, when discussing the professional role of the environmental psychologist, for examples of how he has 'influenced a design'. 'Show me a building,' he is instructed, 'which is different because of your intervention.' Yet in my experience such a request for proof of effect is at worst misleading and at best frivolous. In this chapter I will provide examples of the many diverse and subtle ways in which psychologists contribute to design, drawing mainly on my own experiences as a consultant environmental psychologist.

THE GROWTH OF PROFESSIONAL ENVIRONMENTAL PSYCHOLOGY

There is some evidence that psychologists first became actively involved in design in the early decades of this century, when architecture, notably in Europe and the Soviet Union, was undergoing rapid changes in approach and outlook. Niit *et al.* (1981) report that, in the early days of the Soviet state, perception psychologists worked with leading innovators in the architecture of the time. In Western Europe, it seems likely that some of the German Gestalt psychologists lectured at the Bauhaus school, a unique educational establishment, often regarded as the source of much of the intellectual basis of twentieth-century architecture (Itten, 1975). It would seem, although the evidence is scanty, that these great movements in architecture, which so changed the face of our cities, drew upon only limited aspects of perceptual psychology (where they touched psychology at all). Hence the widespread criticism of the social implications of these designs and the consequent, albeit tentative, involvement of psychologists in the design process had to wait for the radical changes in society which followed the Second World War.

In the aftermath both of the destruction of that war, and of the new-found affluence which followed it, a spate of public building programmes ensued. Professional groups such as architects and planners found themselves in new positions of power. Yet the power had an important difference from that granted by benign patronage a hundred or two hundred years earlier. The clients and users of the public buildings being created, whether for housing, schools, hospitals, or offices, could no longer be treated as ignorant masses to be uplifted by the grand works of their masters. They were people who had identifiable needs and requirements which the buildings must go some way to satisfy. Yet the education of designers had included little reference to the users of buildings. Design was taught as a mixture of Art and Craft with a little building science woven in. So that when the question of 'user requirements' was raised some architects and planners felt the need to turn to social scientists and psychologists.

Psychologists, in the main still steeped in the traditions of the laboratory or the consulting room, found it difficult to respond to the requests for help which began to emerge from the design professions. It thus fell to sociologists such as Chapman and Thomas (1944) to take up the challenge. Where questions related more directly to individual experience of heating or lighting, then physiologists such as Bedford (1964) and engineers such as Hopkinson (1963) initially provided the answers until psychologists from the experimental psychology tradition began to play an active part, most notably Langdon (1966) and the workers at the Applied Psychology Unit in Cambridge (such as Broadbent, 1958).

All these contributions, however, were forays out from an academic base, or at least from a research unit. It was not until the late 1960s and early 1970s that psychologists in practice became specifically interested in contributing to a wide range of environmental decisions. It is only in the penultimate decade of the twentieth century that the psychological contribution to the shaping of our surroundings has reached the level where a few people, in different parts of the world, can actually earn a living as 'environmental psychologists'. Furthermore, the range of activities under this heading also now spreads very widely. They range, for example, from a study of the shared meaning of open spaces in public housing schemes, commissioned by the architects of those schemes to assist in their detailed design (Ellis, 1978), to government requests for assistance in the design of towns for remote communities (Bechtel, 1977).

This diversity of professional activities is carried out by no more than a handful of people in Britain and probably less than a hundred worldwide, although it is complemented by applied psychologists from many different backgrounds straying from time to time into environmental pastures (as revealed, for example, by many of the other contributions to this book). Consequently, the environmental psychology carried out by any individual will have qualities unique to that person. In this chapter I will describe my own professional experiences as illustrative of what an environmental psychologist has done, but the reader is warned that these experiences are not likely to be either exhaustive or typical of what the professional role can be or may be in the future. Furthermore, although my own experiences of professional environmental activity have tended to be related to buildings, working with architects and their clients, the activities of environmental psychologists in general are certainly not limited to this area. As Canter and Craik (1981) discuss, the field spreads beyond buildings to cover many aspects of the natural and manmade environments, varying in scale from the furniture in a room to a region of a country.

A FRAMEWORK FOR PROFESSIONAL ACTIVITY

With the intention of providing a framework for the professional activity of the environmental psychologist which will go beyond my own particular experience, I suggest that there are three aspects of professional environmental psychology which, taken together, effectively describe any piece of work in which a person may be involved. They relate to (i) the stage (or stages) in the decision process at which the involvement occurs; (ii) the type of client or clients) for whom the work is actually carried out; and (iii) the role (or roles, vis-à-vis the client and the decision process, which the psychologist is called upon to play. Let us consider each of these in turn.

Stage in design

The design of a building, chair, or national park proceeds through a number of stages, from early outline ideas to detailed working drawings. The psychologist can be called in to help at any stage in the process of design. The commonly considered examples, of advising on window size or wall colour, are decisions which are usually made late on 'during' the design process. By then most of the major decisions about the layout, form, and materials of the building will already have been made.

However, before any designer's pencil touches a sheet of drawing paper there are many policy and priority decisions to be taken. Many of these emerge in the form of a brief (or programme) for the building. This specifies what the building is to house and it may be produced by someone who is not the architect or his client. The professional psychologist can have a very important

impact at these early stages 'before' design. Indeed many of the recommendations in the 'design brief' will derive from government regulations. These, of
course, exist prior to the building being thought of. Any psychological
intervention at this 'early' stage could thus influence a whole generation of
buildings.

The contribution of the psychologist 'after' the design also requires
attention. Once a building, or even a new town, is in use, there is much that
can be learned about using it more effectively. Here the psychologist's skills in
understanding to what use a building is actually being put may be of great
value (as Heimsath, 1977, shows in great detail).

Type of client

The environmental psychologist usually responds to a request from another
professional, be it architect, engineer, or planner, or from an organization. It
is rare, although not without precedent, for the users of the environment, the
ultimate 'clients', to call in the psychologist directly. It is thus also rare for the
psychologist to be in a position to initiate and control the consequences of his
own recommendations. They are almost always translated through the actions
and interpretations of the other professionals to whom he reports.

Even within the limitation of being always at least one stage removed from
the day-to-day experience of the environment there are diverse types of clients,
each making their own special kind of demands on the psychologist. There is
also a tendency for the stage in the design process at which the psychologist is
called in to be a function of the type of client who approaches him.

As I have mentioned, before any particular design exists the chances are that
government regulations, or general policies, exist covering many aspects of the
design possibilities. Central government in Britain formulates many design
guidelines on many aspects of both public and private buildings. Local
government also formulates its own bye-laws and interprets those it is
instructed to follow by central government. Psychologists have thus found
themselves guiding policy-making, or indeed defending local government
disagreement with central government proposals, such as in public enquiries
into the development of airports. Here, then, typically, the setting for the
psychologist is the committee room and the outcome of his work is an official
report.

During design it is typically the architect who approaches an environmental
psychologist for help. Although an encouraging development is the way in
which clients (who employ architects) now sometimes approach psychologists
directly. In this context the environmental psychologist may be helping the
architect to understand his client's wishes, for example, or more often, to
identify the requirements of frequently anonymous users. The setting here is
the architects' office or leaning over the design drawings with the client and

other professionals. The outcome, or influence, of the activity is produced through discussion and summary notes, or even the wry smile and illustrative anecdote.

Once a building is built it sometimes happens that those responsible for its administration and management *after* it is occupied will call on psychological services. In some extreme cases this has been to help people to cope with an otherwise unacceptable building. Here the psychologist is most likely to spend his time in the building itself discussing it with those who use it, observing it in use, and preparing a brief report on how it can more appropriately be made use of.

It must be emphasized that the links I have indicated between the stage in design and the types of client should be thought of only as a broad trend. Central government, for example, may commission a study of the suitability for the handicapped of their existing buildings, with the intention of modifying those buildings. Or a commercial client may ask for help in preparing general guidelines for the managers of their buildings, for instance in the provision of design for security. This range of possibilities is illustrated in Table 1, where a further consequence of who the psychologist is working for and when, is illustrated.

Table 1   Design questions open to answers from professional psychologists

Phase of Design	Client		
	Politician	*Architect*	*Administrator*
Before	What are the priorities?	What is to be facilitated?	What is to be accommodated?
During	What are the conflicts?	What is to be incorporated?	How will it be utilized?
After	What are the implications?	How is it to be interpreted?	What are its values?

In Table 1 the combination of 'client type' and 'phase in design' is used to summarize nine questions which the environmental psychologist may be called upon to answer. These nine questions serve to illustrate the range of possibilities there are for psychological involvement in design. But rather than discuss each of these questions in isolation and thus imply that they occur independently of each other, I will elaborate some of them in the framework of particular cases, drawn to cover the range of professional environmental psychology involvement I have experienced. However, before doing that I need to discuss one further facet of the psychologist's involvement in design, the types of *role* he may play.

Roles

Cutting across the stages and clients are a great variety of activities in which the environmental psychologist can be engaged. I have, for example, run seminars for clients on aspects of the work they have commissioned from me, taking on a role not dissimilar from university teaching. In a quite different context I have found myself acting virtually as a non-directive counsellor, listening to an architect's anxieties and concerns about his colleagues and client, and attempting to help him find ways of dealing with those anxieties.

Sometimes I have even found that the most useful thing I can do is to provide a way for people to communicate with each other, such as workforce with management, or building users with the financial backer. This may not be the intention of those initially asking for help, but it may be the most valuable contribution the psychologist makes. Furthermore, as we shall see repeatedly in the following examples, the roles the psychologist is able to perform are always constrained by the context in which he is operating.

The different activities and the consultancy roles associated with them do, of course, merge into one another. Some environmental psychologists favour one mode of involvement to all others, but the important point to bear in mind is that the psychologist is certainly not limited to any conventional research role vis-à-vis design. Research activity is the easiest activity about which to write directly, but as I will try to show in the following examples, the collection and analysis of data, or the testing of hypothesis, is only one small part of the environmental psychologist's task.

Example 1 — Building regulations

The context for the consultancy

My first example is rather lengthy because I believe that it illustrates rather well many of the points I have already made. It also happens to be one of those rare, but very welcome, pieces of consultancy in which our immediate client is not only acting directly on recommendations we have made but has actually come back for more. A third reason for going into this example at some length is that it deals with the intriguing questions of what people do when they find themselves in a building on fire.

The work described illustrates the following general points about environmental consultancy:

(1) It relates to a typical combination of aspects of consultancy being indirectly commissioned by government formulators as a contribution to the regulations which influence building design.

(2) The central questions, as a consequence of the policy orientation,

are not about the details of design but about priorities and emphases. (3) The example also serves to illustrate the necessity of understanding the context of any consultancy activity and its cross-disciplinary nature. This in turn throws light on the constraints which serve to structure the professional activity.

In order to understand the psychological questions, how they evolved and how we went about answering them, we must start with a brief consideration of the control which government exerts on the design of buildings.

Central government exerts its influence over planning and architecture through a large and frequently complex set of guidelines, acts of parliament and recommendations, usually referred to as buildings regulations. Of particular relevance here, are a subset of these regulations which are concerned with ensuring that, in the event of a fire, people will be able to leave the building 'by their own unaided effort' (Langdon-Thomas, 1972). Even a casual examination of these guidelines for 'means of escape' reveals that they are replete with assumptions about human behaviour in fires (Canter and Matthews, 1976). For example, many of the recommendations imply that if certain aspects are not included in the design, such as availability of an exit within less than 100 feet, then people are likely to panic if a fire were to happen.

It came as a surprise to me to learn that whilst many of the engineering components, the materials and fire safety systems, have been subject to detailed scrutiny, the assumptions about human behaviour had never had any systematic, scientific test. As discussed in detail by Canter and Matthews (1976) the regulations have arisen out of informed opinion and commissions of enquiry into major fire tragedies. Furthermore, as buildings become more complex and the functions they serve become more various it is becoming increasingly difficult to rely upon the experience of senior fire officers, and somewhat immoral to wait for a new building form to be tested by an actual fire before new regulations are developed. As a consequence, the people who are responsible for framing the regulations and those who have the job of advising them have started to look for help from psychologists. It is in this context that I have been carrying out work for the Fire Research Station.

In this case, then, the environmental psychological activity is prior to any designing at all. The clients for the work are ultimately civil servants, responsible for framing regulations, and their political masters. This distance from any immediate, day-to-day decision-making gives the consultancy work an abstract, almost academic feel to it. However, such a sensation is misleading because the clients are not at all interested in the evolution of psychological theories or the refinements of research methods. They want to know what people typically do in a building on fire and how building regulations can lead to their behaviour being safer. It is true that the research managers at the government Research Station do appreciate that models of behaviour need to be developed and empirically verified, but their aim is still to influence the way in which buildings (or the hardware which goes into them) are designed.

An examination of this context for psychological activity reveals a number of curious constraints on the enterprise, constraints which are most readily described in terms of the properties expected of any results of studies carried out. Consider for example, an aspect of this work which I have always found especially frustrating. We were commissioned, as I mentioned, by the Department of the Environment. They are responsible for building regulations. Thus any consequences of psychological research which had direct implications for public education would be of only marginal interest to my clients. Fire education is a responsibility of the Home Office! This particular constraint has major implications for the direction our studies took. We kept clear of any general attitudinal studies, looking at how people in general feel, think, and behave in relation to the possibility of fires. Such studies, whilst possibly being useful as a basis for television advertisements, would not obviously lead to building-related consequences. The work we do thus has clear organizational constraints imposed by the decision-making system of which we are a part.

Another, more positive constraint, was (and indeed still is) that the research managers do not consider the utility of our work in isolation. They are simultaneously following a number of other approaches to the problems as they see them. In particular, they are developing models of how smoke and flames move around buildings and how microcomputer technology can be harnessed to improve the effectiveness of fire detector and fire alarm systems. What they need from us is information on how the human component fits into the systems they are developing. Our activities are thus essentially cross-disciplinary. We need to keep abreast of what the engineers and physicists are doing if our work is to be, quite literally, relevant.

One further aspect of the process to which we are contributing needs to be understood in order fully to appreciate the nature of the psychological studies in which we have been involved. This is the fact that our results will only be considered if they can be digested by a complex communication network. At one end are the people to whom we have direct access. These are scientists and technologists who have made a profession of managing research, albeit frequently in spheres beyond their own training. Their reports eventually find their way to the desks of civil servants who have often made a craft of not understanding the finer technical details but of perceiving the general consequences of 'research'. They, in turn, report to ministers who are elected politicians who will consider any conclusions with an eye to their general political implications and public acceptability.

This range of implicit clients has some curiously conflicting effects on the psychologist's activities. On the one hand, it is essential that his work be seen to be of very high scientific calibre in a very obvious sense. In a psychologist of senior and established reputation, large numbers of subjects, computer analysis, and a reasonable amount of conceptual sophistication are all expected, whether or not the questions being asked really demand all this. For how else can a senior civil servant judge the validity of the research programme? On the other hand, the message, or conclusions, of the research must be direct and immediately comprehensible and they must be supported by easily recognizable 'evidence'. Such support most typically takes the form of one or two clear and strong illustrations of the conclusions in operation. Thus whilst the request from the client was initially couched in terms of very specific information, such as 'What's the maximum safe distance for a person to travel from a fire to an exit?', it eventually emerged that a much more general question was really being asked. This might be paraphrased as 'what role does the provision of special escape routes play in building evacuations?'. In other words we were, in effect, being asked to indicate the relative priorities of various aspects of design in contributing to safety in fires: the 'what are the priorities?' question in Table 1.

The psychological enterprise

This lengthy introduction to the context of our activities serves a number of purposes. First it illustrates the type of unravelling of what was being asked of me which I found essential before I could decide what I needed to do. Secondly it shows why, although the initial request for help seemed simple enough, the project became a very large one, extending over five years. Thirdly the background shows why it was necessary both to carry out detailed examinations of a few selected fires in order to build up a model of behaviour in fires and, at the same time, to collect strong clear examples as illustrations of the model, and also to do large-scale surveys to provide statistical backing to these models.

However, the strongest consequence of the context in which we were operating, and perhaps the most paradoxical, was that what we needed to develop in order to be of any use was a good 'theory' of behaviour in fires. The model, referred to above, was actually an account of what people typically did in fires together with an explanation of why they did it. Such a theory, backed up by strong illustrations and supported by statistical analyses, provided it is expressed in a direct and clear way, has a much better chance of finding its way through the communication system and of being used by the variety of people who constitute the clients. Even so, any formulation put forward would only be accepted if it accorded with other developments in which the clients were involved. Here the professional is in the lap of the gods. If he honestly develops the theoretical formulations he believes to be appropriate it is quite possible that they will be at odds with other trends to which his theory must relate. As it happens, in this context we were lucky (I think). The other trends happened to fit rather well with the theory which emerged.

Human behaviour in fires

The starting point for examining behaviour in fires was difficult to find. This was for two reasons. First, there are many public accounts of human actions in fires reported, especially in newspapers. These reports find their way into other representations of fires such as films and novels. Thus despite the rarity of the occurrence of fires there has built up a popular belief of what actually happens. In the case of fires this would seem to be an idea that people behave wildly and irrationally and cannot, as a consequence, give any clear description of what they have experienced. Thus our clients started by asking why people behave so irrationally and what can be done to stop 'panic'. Thus, in opposition to a systematic, scientific exploration a firm conclusion is assumed and the psychologist is asked to explain it. Clearly, our task was to see what evidence there was for this conclusion.

The second difficulty in knowing where to begin also derives from the two points above, that is the rarity of fires and the potentially distorted public accounts of them which exist. If we have such a distant contact with our topic, on what basis can we create laboratory simulations for study, or even develop questions to ask of the general population? The experiment and the social survey are the psychologist's stock in trade, yet here they are virtually ruled out from square one. True there have been some experimental studies which have been recognized as 'classic' by social psychologists, such as those in which Schachter pumped smoke under a waiting room door (1959). But no fire officer or senior civil servant, let alone a Member of Parliament, would quote such frivolous studies as evidence for changing legislation! Somehow or other we had to talk to people who had been in fires and find out, as best we could, what they actually did. We had to approach this problem with as open a mind as possible and allow people to express their experiences in their own words.

From these preliminary considerations there emerged two related methodological issues. One was that much of the writing on 'account gathering' (Harré and Secord, 1972) provided useful guidance on this type of exploration. The other was the awareness that non-psychologists, in a variety of situations, are faced with problems similar to those with which we are faced in studying behaviour in fires. Most notably, policemen when taking statements from witnesses have to be careful to record an account in the witnesses' own words of what happened. They then corroborate evidence by comparing statements in order to ascertain accuracy and authenticity. There are, indeed, 'Judges' Rules' (HMSO, 1964) which specify how this should be done.

Thus, taking these approaches together it was possible to develop an interview procedure which would get us as close as possible to an unbiased record of what actually happened in any given fire (Canter and Brown, 1981; Brown and Sime, 1980). The next stage was to find people who had experienced fires. This was when our contact with the fire brigades began to become very important. They informed us of fires that had happened, or gave us details of fires we learnt about through the newspapers. We then followed up as many of the people involved as possible. The results of much of this work and of similar studies carried out for the US Bureau of Standards is reported in Canter (1980). These detailed case studies helped us establish a general framework and from this we developed a questionnaire which we used to survey fire victims in order to obtain further evidence from larger numbers. For our purposes here I will summarize the results briefly.

The general pattern of behaviour in fires to emerge from these studies is illustrated in Figure 1. There it can be seen that in the early stages there is frequently misinterpretation and ignoring of the early warning cues. Once these cues are recognized as indicating a fire then actions are taken which do vary and do not necessarily lead to immediate evacuation of the building. The theoretical formulation which helps best to understand these activities can be summarized by saying that a fire is a complex, rapidly changing situation in which people have to make decisions on very limited information. One further

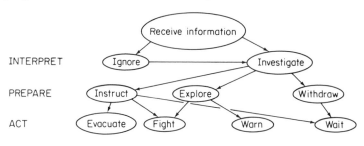

Figure 1

elaboration of this perspective also helps to clarify the nature of the model which emerged. The pattern of activities appears to relate closely to the existing role structure within the building at the time of the fire. Thus, for example, what a nurse would do in a hospital fire is likely to be different to what the same person would do in a fire in her own home, even though of course any training she had had would still be of some relevance.

These 'results' may not seem too surprising to a psychologist. They are also fairly easy to defend and illustrate in a non-technical way. Yet they do carry significant implications for fire precautions and evacuation procedures. Briefly, let us consider two examples. First the conventional fire alarm, then fire training. The conventional fire alarm bell does not really help to resolve the problem of ambiguous early cues and the minimal information on which a person must act. Day-to-day experience, as well as the more formal investigations described above, show that not only do people frequently ignore fire alarms, but that the alarms they hear do not give enough information. People often check with someone else that it is not a false alarm, or that if it is a fire something has been done about it. Clearly, an alarm system which gives information is potentially a more psychologically acceptable alarm. Further, given that fires occur in pre-existing situations, there is a lot to be said for an alarm system which plays a role in the daily life of the individual.

It was as a result of discussions about these considerations that Brian Pigott and his colleagues at the Fire Research Station took advantage of developments in microprocessor technology to design a new type of alarm system. Normally the 'alarm box' shows the date and time. When the alarm system is being tested it tells you so and if there is a fire it not only confirms that the bell actually means there is a fire but it gives you a continuously up-to-date account of where the fire is. The system being developed has other advantages such as much easier maintenance and checking than conventional systems and fewer technically produced false alarms.

A second example relates to training. If the existing organizational structure is so significant in what happens in a fire then the initial selection of any 'fire officers' and the instructions they are given should take account of this. The general way in which fire drills are carried out must pay direct attention to the roles and role relationships which exist within the organization. This means that the tradition of appointing a junior as the 'fire warden', or of putting the central fire warning facility under the aegis of people not trained in its use or significance (practices which have directly contributed to fatalities in major fires), can be clearly shown to constitute dangers. Indeed the idea that a fire drill should take on a function beyond simply 'knowing the drill', to meet the neighbours, for example, or to introduce new members of staff to each other, is an idea which is gaining a little ground.

A number of other examples of the general consequences of this work could be cited, but most of them have the common core of redirecting emphasis away from what might be called the building 'hardware', fire escapes, alarm bells and the like, towards 'software' such as training and more reactive building devices. As indicated above, this redirection happens to coincide with a number of developments quite independent of the psychological studies. One is the dearth of money. For as it happens, software-oriented systems are considerably cheaper than those which depend on 'hardware'. The second is that the new microcomputer-based technologies open up the possibility of more sophisticated systems in a way which was not envisaged when our studies began.

Here then is an example of consultancy which is slowly feeding in to the general way of thinking about the building regulations. Its relationship to any design decision-making is certainly complex. Its influence is also a function of a great range of developments completely outside the researcher's control.

Let us now turn to an example which is closer to an actual design: the preparation of a brief for a building.

Example 2—A design brief

For my second example I move a step down the diagnoal of Table 1. The psychological activity takes place *during* the design. The context here is now the actual design of a specific building, rather than the general building regulations. The clients are the people responsible for commissioning the design and the questions being asked are about the activities to be facilitated and what the design is to incorporate. The context still constrains the psychologist's activities, but in different ways from our first example and the speed of development of the project and its setting require a harnessing of intellectual and physical resource which is far more psychologically demanding on the professionals involved.

This example is drawn from work which I carried out, with my colleague Ian Griffiths, for a major manufacturer of consumer durables. Let us call them National Equipment Ltd. They had been given financing in order to modernize their activities. The financiers had insisted on various conditions including full worker involvement in any decisions. This set the stage for an approach to us because when it was decided that, as part of the modernization, a new building should be produced to house their product designers, it was deemed essential that all the potential users of that building should participate in its design.

National Equipment Ltd. therefore asked us to help them provide a brief for their architects which would draw upon advice from each of their 12000 employees. Here, then, our task was to help senior management inform the architect what the building was to facilitate and what was to be incorporated in the design (cf. Figure 1). It is worth noting also that the brief to us from the management indicated that, somehow or other, every one of the employees associated with the new building had to be involved, at some stage, in the study.

One further set of conditions which had an influence on the impact of the project was that the clients already had a long-standing arrangement with a local architect to design buildings (mainly factories and warehouses) for them. This architect was, in turn, briefed by an 'in-house' architect directly employed, for many years, by National Equipment Ltd. themselves. However, our commission was not from the architect, but from a senior manager in a different section. We were also requested to refrain from communicating directly with the outside architect. We were to present our report to National Equipment Ltd. and they would pass it on, explain it, etc. as they saw fit. This, nonetheless, did not stop the architect from carrying on preparing proposals for the new complex quite independently of our activities. As a consequence a rather curious, almost Byzantine, pattern of communications and potential conflicts was created by our client. A novel could be written around the interviews, surveys, and observations we carried out and the development of the report we produced but, for our purposes here, I will illustrate some key aspects of the work we did.

One of the most instructive reactions to the final report related to a series of 'design exercises' we conducted. For these, groups of people from the same section of the organization were brought together. They were asked to agree, as a group, on a list of the component parts of the organization. They were then asked to indicate the relationship these components bore to each other. In order to do this they wrote the names of the components on cards and then arranged these cards on a large sheet of paper as a way of demonstrating their interrelationships. From a series of these exercises it was possible to prepare an overview of what the building would need to house and the spatial relationships required. A summary of the result of these exercises is shown in Figure 2.

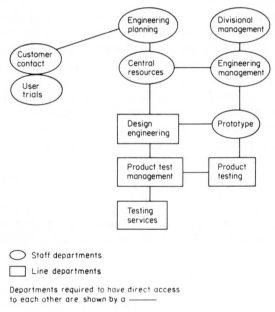

Figure 2

We had assumed that an overview of the organization would have been conducted in some detail by some other group, possibly the architects themselves, but because we were not given access to that we had to do it for ourselves, to give our report at least some coherence. We were therefore surprised to learn that a number of people were not only intrigued to see what to them was a first glimpse of what the proposed building was for, but that the architects had taken such a different approach to the design that they did not even recognize the names of the component parts of the organization which we had learnt from the workforce, let alone comprehend the spatial relationships we had summarized. Thus, almost inadvertently, we found that we had provided a description of the basic layout for the proposed building as well as guidelines for what it should house.

Another illustration of how a psychological contribution can be made to design can be drawn from our exploration of the visual characteristics which the users were looking for in their future building. A representative sample of users were presented with pictures of exteriors and interiors of buildings which had functions similar to the proposed building. They were asked to rate these buildings on a variety of scales, indicating how they would feel about them as places in which to work. From the responses we were able to build up a profile of the appearance required of the future building. From this aspect of the study, for example, it was recommended that the building have 'a neat and pleasant, open frontage with a simple repetitive treatment of elevations, having moderate window sizes'. Internally, the desire was for spaces which were 'clean, efficient, and neat'.

The final report to senior management, as is usually the case, was only the summary of a series of discussions which had taken place throughout the project. Thus the full range of roles for the environmental psychologist, discussed earlier, was drawn upon throughout the project. For example, at one point when the issues of windows, noise level, and climatic control were being discussed it was necessary to run what was virtually a seminar on what was known of the psychological consequences of the architect's current proposals. On another occasion interviews with the technical staff in the product-testing laboratories revealed that they had been coping for many months with an inefficient procedure which could be improved readily if only senior management were to learn about it. We thus found ourselves in the role of diplomats, providing a channel of communication which did not otherwise exist. In all these cases the demands made on our skill in collecting and giving information as well as making sense of the great amount of data we obtained were considerable.

As regards the outcome of our work, there seems to be some larger process which leads to environmental psychology consultants being called into building projects which have a low probability of being completed. Working for National Equipment Ltd. was a strong example of this principle. Soon after our report was presented the people putting up the financing insisted on a reorganization which led to the division we were working for being given less priority and the idea of a new building specifically for them being shelved.

There is one further salutory footnote to this project. About two years after our report had been submitted I was discussing the work with an architect only to discover that his organization had been commissioned to prepare a design for a different division of National Equipment Ltd. He had had many similar problems to us in identifying what they were designing for, but it was only through our chance discussion that he learnt of our earlier study which could have saved him a considerable amount of effort! There are many morals here, but perhaps the most important is that the impact of the psychologist's contribution to design is a function of the network of which he is part. If we are to have any more impact we must find new ways of disseminating ideas throughout the network and possibly, on occasion, find ways of influencing the structure of the network itself.

Example 3 — Remodelling a building

In order to provide an instance that is clearly at a later stage in the design process than the first two examples, my third example deals with our involvement in advising on the use of existing buildings and providing recommendations for their remodelling. Here, then, the buildings were in use and we could examine that use and report back to our client, who had the day-to-day concern of administering those buildings. The strengths and weaknesses of the existing uses and the necessity of creating possibilities for future uses (both questions in the lower right of Table 1) are all examined directly in this project. Again, of course, the context had its own constraints and pitfalls.

Paradoxically, in this case our involvement proved to be much more productive in terms of our relationship with our clients and our contribution to all aspects of the new designs than my previous example. Although one of the constraints, in this case, was that we were expressly forbidden by our client from talking to any of his customers, who were the major building users. However, once again other developments, completely independent of our involvement, led to the building on which we worked and the general principles we evolved being made irrelevant because shortly after our report was submitted the company went out of business.

Our invitation for this work came along possibly one of the most effective channels. The managing director of a recreational industry, Playtime Ltd., was discussing with his architect the conversion of a rather fine old building, which Playtime Ltd. already used, into a new games hall. It seems he asked his architect directly: 'How can you redesign this building without knowing who you are designing for, do you have an environmental psychologist on your staff?' The architect had never heard of such a creature and therefore proposed that he should do a search to find a suitable candidate. That search brought him to interview me. Subsequently he recommended that I and my colleague Ian Griffiths be employed to work with him on the project. Thus from the start we worked closely with the architect and his partners whilst still being directly employed by his client. This arrangement made our role a much more positive one. The architect recognized from the start, in contrast to National Equipment's architects, that it was in his interest to listen to us because our remit was, in effect, to represent the client's requirements. As it turned out there were a few occasions when our interpretation of Playtime Ltd.'s requirements were more in accord with the architect's perspective than with the client's stated view. On these occasions we were able to strengthen the architect's own case.

One example of our coming to the same view as the architect quite independently, but at variance with the established beliefs of Playtime Ltd., was over the matter of background illustrations in the recreational facilities. It was the current practice to have these as neutral as possible, yet one of our findings was that people using the equipment liked to be able to choose different areas with different ambiences to suit their mood. Great variation was disliked because of the focus on the recreational activity itself. It occurred to us that a distinct but subtle difference in ambience could be achieved by the selection of illustrations in any given locale. The architect had proposed a lively scheme on the same theme that had been thrown out by the client but with our reasoned account of what was to be achieved and why the client requested revisions of the proposals to reconsider.

Another interesting feature of our involvement was that, because the facilities had been in use for some time, we were able to gain some very useful information from Playtime Ltd.'s own records and lists of customers. By summarizing their records for them we were able to show them the characteristics of their clientele and what particular facilities they used. The findings which emerged from this analysis of existing information came as a surprise to many of the senior managers involved. They had relied on the summary of experience presented to them by their staff and never thought to check this out against the figures which they kept for quite separate, financial reasons. For example, it was the popular belief within the organization that the majority of their customers lived locally, but by taking a random sample of customers' addresses and preparing bar charts we were able to show that this was just not true.

Another activity we carried out was to observe what people did in the existing recreation centres, using behavioural mapping techniques we had adapted from the work of Proshansky and his colleagues (Ittelson et al., 1970). We found that even during busy times there were areas of the building not in use, although similar equipment in other locations was very crowded and people could not use it properly. By interviewing staff and closely examining what equipment was used where, we were able to point out that the traditional design created areas into which many people did not like to venture, both because of the view from them and the difficulty of moving on to other areas. On this basis we proposed a redesign of both the equipment and its layout.

As mentioned previously, one constraint placed on us by the client was that Playtime Ltd. did not want us to interview any of their customers. We could interview staff, but we could only observe customers unobtrusively. Yet one big question was why people came to these places and what they really got out of being there. We therefore had a detective task of filling in the central piece of the jigsaw from all the other information we could collect. What emerged was a pattern of activities and a type of interaction with the staff, which demanded little social competence being carried out by clients who were often people living away from home. We realized that the recreational facilities provided what might be called a 'club' for people who were not sociable and whose contact with the staff was informal and friendly but totally uninvolved. Thus we were able to build up quite specific recommendations for design and layout which would facilitate the required type of staff–customer interactions and provide the customers with the equipment and atmosphere for which they came. This followed right through from entrance foyer to restaurant to the different recreational areas.

Explaining all the nuances of what was involved entailed educating the architect in what his building was *for* and who would be likely to use it and why. This meant sitting at his drawing board with him and keeping him informed of our ideas as they developed as well as making sure that we ourselves knew which way the design thinking was going and the client's views at the same time. What slowly emerged from these discussions and from our analysis of the staff interview responses, observations of customers, and examination of company records, were a general set of guidelines for a rolling programme of refurbishment of all the buildings owned by Playtime Ltd.

CONTRIBUTING TO DESIGN

In presenting three examples each focusing on a different stage in the process of design, from government regulations through to refurbishing, and different clients (civil servants, brief-makers, and managers) I have tried to illustrate the wide range of roles and activities which now go to make up the professional practice of environmental psychology. We have certainly come a long way from the study of optical illusions or commenting on wall colour. Yet, as I emphasized in the opening sections, the examples I have presented are only a subset of what does go on in this field of application and an even smaller subset of potential applications. The whole area of post-occupancy evaluation has not been touched on, for example, although a recent special issue of the *International Review of Applied Psychology* is devoted to this topic (Canter, 1982).

In emphasizing the context of the psychological activity I have also tended to omit reference to the more direct commercial benefits the work can have. Bechtel (1977) and Heimsath (1977) both explain in some detail the direct commercial advantages of a psychological involvement in design. Deasey (1974) gives the architect's view of his experiences of working with psychologists and also makes the point that there are many direct practical benefits.

However, it might have been discerned from my presentation of my own experiences that I believe that the earlier in the design process that the psychologist is involved the greater is his, or her, potential contribution. This type of contribution requires forms of argument and of activity which are not commonly discussed, let alone taught, on undergraduate courses.

As I have shown in all the examples, the development from the early days of environmental psychology, when tentative forays were made from the laboratories of academe, to the days when requests for help from other professions are treated with serious professional interest, has required that psychologists cope with two related sets of challenges. The first is that any step into 'the field' requires acknowledgement of the constraints imposed there and the development of strategies to deal with them. The second challenge is possibly even more difficult for psychologists to face. This is the need to recognize that other disciplines and professions have skills to contribute and tasks of their own to face. The psychologist thus needs to learn how to work with 'unscientific' professionals such as architects and managers without assuming that because their abilities are in such different areas from his own that they are therefore to be discounted.

THE EMERGENCE OF A DISTINCT AREA OF APPLICATION

Finally I would like to summarize what I see now as typifying environmental psychology as a consultancy activity. In spite of, or perhaps because of, its very recent emergence as an area of professional psychology activity, environmental psychology draws very heavily on the more established applied areas. The theories of organizational and social psychology are combined with techniques which owe a lot to consumer psychology and draw upon the skills which clinical psychologists regard as their stock in trade. Yet out of all this borrowing has grown a distinct set of approaches and methods which mark environmental psychology off from these other activities.

Perhaps the most clear distinction is brought about by the scale and complexity of the building process. This provides both the excitement and the despair of environmental psychology. Buildings usually take months to design and years to build. Unlike a patient whose treatment can be completed in a few weeks or months, the environmental psychologist may have to wait decades to see the consequences of his work, if he ever sees it all. One outcome of this is that long-term involvement with major projects is of considerable importance if he is both to develop professionally and to make a lasting contribution.

Furthermore, environmental psychologists are nothing if not field-based. They consequently have to push the methods and theories of field research to their limits. The use of records, for instance, as in example three, is not simply a novel enrichment of the tool kit, providing 'non-reactive' procedures as advocated by Webb *et al.* (1962). In some cases they may be the only procedures available within the context of the research. It follows that the rituals of the experimental approach (such as the elaboration of control groups, the testing of specific causal hypotheses, the testing of the 'null hypothesis') are irrelevant luxuries when it comes to solving the questions which are presented by the client, or ensuring that such solutions have any impact.

This is not to deny the power of the systematic, scientific approach in environmental psychology. Carefully collected data, intelligently analysed, must provide the evidence for any conclusions and form the basis of any report. Furthermore, as I have illustrated, the closer these conclusions can get to providing an overall model, or theory, the more powerful they are likely to be. But in this scientific activity the language and procedures of undergraduate laboratory experiments are likely to be unhelpful, to put it at its mildest.

The skills of communication also emerge as of especial value. Any procedures which facilitate the comprehension of psychological results by the non-psychologists who must act on them are well worth exploration, whether these be the forms of data collection or of analysis, or the language in which the models and results are expressed. Here again a certain humility is a prerequisite and an acceptance that other disciplines may have cleared a path before.

What about the broader moral questions? Certainly the questions of who is the client and what is the ultimate goal of the enquiry need to be carefully considered. For example, any fire research, which had a hidden aim of saving property at the expense of human lives, I would personally have no involvement in. The position that the psychologist finds himself in in the power structure of a complex communication network also needs careful consideration. Is his work being so constrained, for example, that the results can only support some established standpoint? This is often the case, for instance, when researchers are only permitted to evaluate 'good' buildings. Because of the scale of the undertaking there is also the direct question of whether the product will justify the expenditure.

Certainly there are always likely to be implicit as well as explicit requests from the client. I do not think that it is an accident that in two of my three examples the building came to nothing. I think that it is quite likely that it is in just those situations where the success of the venture is at risk that a psychologist might be brought in to increase its viability. Although frequently, of course, he is given too limited resources too late. It should not be ignored either that the physical environment is a party political issue. A professional environmental psychologist may sometimes have to come to terms with the fact that his research may go directly against his own firmly held political views. Of course, the power of environmental psychology to have any influence at all is still greatly restricted. Yet I am still surprised to see what an impact can be made with the tools and theories at our command at present.

Coming so late to the applied psychology scene we can perhaps be more conscious of the many cul-de-sacs in which we could lose ourselves. We can certainly learn from our colleagues in the more established areas of application such as clinical and educational psychology. We do not need to follow the route of assessment (paralleled in 'building evaluations'), and one-to-one 'therapy' as they did. We do have the opportunity, from the start, of thinking about the whole design decision process and the most appropriate place for our involvement in it.

REFERENCES

Bechtel, R. B. (1977). *Enclosing Behavior*, Stroudsberg: Dowden, Hutchinson & Ross.
Bedford, T. A. (1964). *Basic Principles of Ventilation and Heating*, London: H. K. Lewis.
Broadbent, D. E. (1958). *Perception and Communication*, Oxford: Pergamon.
Brown, J. and Sime, J. (1980). 'A methodology for accounts', in M. Brenner (ed.), *Social Methods and Social Life*, London: Academic Press, pp.157–188.
Canter, D. (ed.) (1980). *Fires and Human Behaviour*, London: Wiley.
Canter, D. (ed.) (1982). 'Environmental Evaluation', special issue of *International Review of Applied Psychology*, April.
Canter, D. and Brown, J. (1981). 'Explanatory roles', in C. Antaki (ed.). *The Psychology of Ordinary Explanations of Social Behaviour*, London: Academic Press, pp.222–242.
Canter, D. and Craik, K. H. (1981). 'Environmental psychology', *Journal of Environmental Psychology* **1** (1), 1–11.
Canter, D. and Matthews, R. (1976). *The Behaviour of People in Fire Situations*, Borehamwood: Building Research Establishment Current Paper CP 11/76.
Chapman, D. and Thomas, G. (1944). 'Lighting in dwellings', *The Lighting of Buildings, Post War Building Studies*, No. 12, Appendix VI, London: HMSO.
Deasy, C. M. (1974). *Design for Human Affairs*, New York: Wiley.
Ellis, P. (1978). 'Social science, user research and the design process', *Architects' Journal*, **167** (6), 248.
Harré, R. and Secord, P. (1972). *The Explanation of Social Behaviour*, Oxford: Blackwell.
Heimsath, C. (1977). *Behavioural Architecture*, New York: McGraw-Hill.
Home Office (1964). *Judges' Rules and Administrative Directions to the Police*, London: HMSO.
Hopkinson, R. G. (1963). *Architectural Physics — Lighting*, London: HMSO.
Ittelson, W. H., Rivlin, L. G., and Proshansky, H. M. (1970). 'The use of behavioral maps in environmental psychology', in H. M. Proshansky, W. H. Ittelson, and L. G. Rivlin (eds.), *Environmental Psychology: Man and his physical setting*, New York: Holt, Rinehart & Winston, pp.658–668.
Itten, J. (1975). *Design and Form: The Basic Course at the Bauhaus*, London: Thames & Hudson.
Langdon, F. J. (1966). *Modern Offices: A User Survey*, London: HMSO.
Langdon-Thomas, G. J. (1972). *Fire Safety in Buildings*, London: Black.

Niit, T., Kruusvall, J., and Heidmets, M. (1981). 'Environmental psychology in the Soviet Union', *Journal of Environmental Psychology*, **1** (2), 157–178.

Schachter, S. (1959). *The Psychology of Affiliation*, Stanford: Stanford University Press.

Sommer, R. (1981). 'Psychologists in court' (personal communication).

Webb, E. J., Campbell, D. T., Schwartz, R. D., and Seechrest, L. (1962). *Unobtrusive Measures: Nonreactive Research in the Social Sciences*, Chicago: Rand McNally.

Psychology in Practice
Edited by S. Canter and D. Canter
© 1982, John Wiley & Sons, Ltd.

CHAPTER 16

PSYCHOLOGY AND WRITTEN INSTRUCTION

James Hartley
Reader in Psychology
University of Keele

INTRODUCTION

In his 1969 Presidential Address to the American Psychological Association, George Miller departed from the usual practice of summarizing his own research and chose instead to express more personal opinions about the current state of psychology at that time. In his address Miller coined a now famous phrase. He concluded:

> For myself, however, I could imagine nothing we could do that would be more relevant to human welfare, and nothing that could pose a greater challenge to the next generation of psychologists than to discover how best to give psychology away. (Miller, 1969)

In this chapter I am not concerned with the social issues that Miller addressed himself to (Miller, 1969, 1980), but I do want to consider some of the problems of giving psychology away in the context of what I have termed the psychology of written instruction. I want to use this context to make the following three general points:

(1) The contribution that psychology can make to practical topics cannot be considered in isolation: it is first necessary to appreciate the difficulties of workers in other areas before assessing the part that psychology can play.

(2) Psychology should be *shared* rather than given away.

(3) Sharing psychology with others benefits psychology itself.

311

I maintain that written instruction provides an example of a situation where sharing knowledge and expertise benefits both psychologists and workers in the field. In this chapter I hope to amplify the three points made above by presenting a series of illustrations based on my own research.

The psychology of written instruction is a large topic, and here I can comment on only a small part of it. I have written elsewhere on the acquisition of reading and writing skills, the production of readable writing, the publication process, and the effects of advances of computer technology on all of these issues (Hartley, 1980a). In this chapter I want to concentrate on two problems: (i) the effects of typography; and (ii) the effects of readability on understanding instructional text.

DESIGNING INSTRUCTIONAL TEXT

Typographic considerations

Instructional text is usually (but not always) more complex — both structurally and typographically — than straightforward prose. Figure 1 provides a typical example of text of this kind — text from which the reader is supposed to learn something or to carry out some action. As this figure shows, such text provides problems — for writers, designers, printers, and users — in addition to those posed by linear prose.

Peter Burnhill — a gifted typographic designer — and I have collaborated for several years in trying to develop and evaluate a set of principles concerned with how best to design such complex text. Working with a typographic designer was (and still is) an eye-opening experience for a psychologist. It becomes immediately clear why much of the previous psychological research on typography (which spans many years) is unhelpful to editors, printers, and practitioners. Much of this early research was (i) conducted with especially constructed prose-like materials; (ii) set in traditional ways; (iii) produced by psychologists who seemed to be unaware of the practical constraints that can determine layout; and (iv) tested — with limited techniques and populations — in laboratory situations. Once one worked with a typographic designer and looked at the decision-making processes of designers working with real-life problems, then the psychological literature became largely irrelevant — at least for certain issues.

Page-size and column widths

When one examines what typographic designers actually do when they are confronted with a typescript, we find that what is of prime importance is determining how the document is to be used when it is printed. Note that this is not as easy as it sounds. Many documents are multipurpose; sometimes the

THE BRITISH PSYCHOLOGICAL SOCIETY

(Incorporated by Royal Charter)

NOTICE IS HEREBY GIVEN that a Special General Meeting of the Society with be held in the Small Meeting House, Friends House, Euston Road, London NW1 on Saturday 26 October 1974 at 10.30 o'clock in the forenoon, when the following business will be transacted.

(1) To consider, and if thought fit, to approve the following SPECIAL RESOLUTIONS subject to obtaining the formal approval of the Privy Council:

A. That the Statutes of the Society be amended in the manner following, namely, by deleting the existing Statutes 4 and 8 and substituting the following new Statutes:

4. GRADUATE MEMBERS

(1) All persons who were elected Graduate Members of the old Institution and all persons who are elected as hereinafter provided shall be Graduate Members.

(2) A candidate for election as a Graduate Memeber:

    (a) shall satisfy the Council that he has one of the following qualifications and such higher qualifications as may be provided in the Rules: —

        (i) a university degree for which psychology has been taken as a main subject;

        or

        (ii) a postgraduate qualification in psychology awarded by an authority recognised by the Council;

        or

        (iii) such other qualification in psychology as the Council shall accept as not less than the foregoing;

        or

    (b) shall pass to the satisfaction of the Council such of the Society's examinations as may be required by the Rules.

(3) The Council may elect such eligible candidates to be Graduate Members as it thinks fit.

8. SUBSCRIBERS

(1) All persons who were elected Subscribers of the old Institution and who are elected as hereinafter provided shall be Subscribers.

(2) No technical qualification shall be required of a candidate for election as a Subscriber.

(3) A Subscriber shall be proposed in accordance with the provisions of the Rules.

Figure 1   An example of instructional text. (Figure reproduced courtesy of the British Psychological Society)

designers will not know how the document will be used; sometimes they will be informed about particular constraints. Nonetheless, the major purpose of the document determines the first main decision of the designer — that of deciding on *what size page* the final document will be printed.

Once this decision has been made, then the nature of the content of the text determines a whole set of interrelated issues that are constrained by the initial decision about page-size. (For example contrast the layout of a pocket dictionary with that of an instructional manual.) Thus, depending on the kind of content and the page-size one might decide whether or not to use one column of print or two, what typefaces and typesizes to use (from the ones available), what interline spaces to employ, where to place tables and figures and their captions, and even where to position the page numbers.

To take a practical illustration let us consider the book *Designing Instructional Text* (Hartley, 1978). Here, because I wished to compare and contrast full-size illustrations, I needed a large page-size. The typographical research typically suggests that one should use a two-column structure with large page-sizes. Tinker (1965) for instance, suggests that lines over 140 mm long go beyond what he calls the 'margin of safety'. It is argued that long line lengths make it difficult to find the beginning of the next line when returning from the end of the preceding one. Our own research, however, has suggested that large illustrations cause difficulties for readers when they cut across two-column structures: readers have to jump over, or sidestep the illustrations. We found, in fact, that readers did better with longer lines (a single column setting of 175 mm) in this case (Burnhill *et al.*, 1976). To resolve these contradictions we chose an A4 page-size (210 × 297 mm) and used the two-column structure depicted schematically in Figure 2. The narrow column (55 mm) was to be used for chapter summaries, figure captions, notes, etc., and the wide column (115 mm) for the main body of the text. Illustrations could range from the left-hand margin of either column — depending on their size.

This example has been quoted at some length because such discussion about the relationship of the content of the text to the page-size and line-length does not loom large in the research writings of psychologists before 1970. As noted earlier, most of the research on optimum line-lengths and typesizes has not been carried out in practical contexts. Tinker's research was done in the laboratory using short paragraphs taken from reading tests, and no mention was made of the page-sizes on which the material was printed. Tinker's advice therefore, was given without taking into account the nature of the text and the appropriate page-size. So, to return for a moment to my more general theme, this example indicates that it is naïve to expect psychologists to provide research findings of practical value when they work in isolation from other experts in the field. And, I would add, this is particularly the case when their advice is supposed to benefit these same experts.

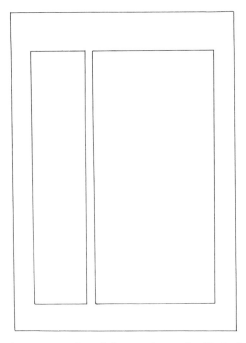

Figure 2   A schematic representation of the page layout for *Designing Instructional Text*

Guidelines for spacing text

Given that a particular page-size is called for, the next concern is how to aid the comprehension of the content. Our research has led Peter Burnhill and I to believe that what affects comprehension most is the use that is made of the 'white-space' — rather than typographic variations, such as italic, boldface, and changes in typeface or typesize.

What we propose is that, given a standard size page (for example A4), one can manipulate the spatial arrangement of the text on that page to enhance comprehension. Our main consideration is that the vertical and the horizontal spacing of instructional text should be regular and consistent. Cognitive psychology (for example see Haber, 1978) suggests that regular spacing helps readers in three ways:

(1) it helps them to perceive redundancies in the text (and thus read faster);
(2) it helps them to perceive more easily those things that they wish to see (and thus focus on what is personally important);
(3) and most importantly, it helps them to perceive the organization of the document as a whole (and thus grasp its structure).

```
2.     Introduction

2.0   Background

2.0.1    The purpose of this report is to comment on the questions
raised by R. Seward (Manager, Standards, Control and Research, I.C.L.,
Education and Training) in his letter of 8th March, 1979, to Dr. J. R.
Hegarty (Lecturer in Psychology, University of Keele).

2.1   Methodological difficulties in evaluating tape-slide teaching.

2.1.1    The majority of the questions posed by I.C.L. either (a) seek
information on Teaching Method A vs. Teaching Method B comparisons or
(b) look at the relevant interactions of the media with the individual
differences of the student and consider the effects of such interactions
upon learning.  Whereas it is possible to make tentative generalisations
for questions falling into the latter category, it is seldom possible to
provide satisfactory answers to questions of a comparative nature.  The
hunt for a "best" method of teaching is not realistic, particularly when
considering minutiae of presentation.   What is best for one student at
any one time may not be best for another student, or even for the same
student at another time.

2.1.2.    The absence of any broad philosophic or theoretical framework
in media research causes such research to be of limited value in ascribing
or assigning rationale for using its products and answering specific
questions.  Difficulties arise because of the complex three-way inter-
action involving (i) the physical characteristics of the audiovisual
presentation, (ii) the content and presentation of the material and,
(iii) the individual differences of the students.  To control for other
variables whilst comparing, for example, the use of 30 slides versus the
use of 35 slides with a taped lecture presents almost insurmountable
problems for the experimenter.
```

Figure 3a   An extract from a report written in the psychology department at Keele.
(Figure courtesy Stephen Lawson)

What is meant by regular and consistent spacing? Let me give some examples. The spacing of text can be considered both from a vertical and a horizontal point of view.

Taking *vertical spacing* first, our argument is that units of line space can be used to separate sentences, paragraphs, and headings in text. These units can be used in proportion (for example 1 : 2 : 4 : 8) to indicate the status of the elements between them but other proportional systems can be used (see Burnhill, 1970; Hartley, 1978, p.25). In addition, certain typographic variations can be used to take the place of space (for example capital letters in typescript, see Figures 3a and 3b), but we work first with space, and then we consider typographic cueing.

Thus vertical spacing can be used appropriately to group and separate related parts of the text. Figure 4a is an extract from a textbook used in schools in Staffordshire. Figure 4b shows a revised version where the text has been clarified (i) by regrouping the parts, and (ii) by respacing them in a proportional way.

2 INTRODUCTION

2.1 Background

2.1.1 The purpose of this report is to comment on the questions raised by R. Seward (Manager, Standards, Control and Research, I.C.L., Education and Training) in his letter of 8th March, 1979, to Dr. J. R. Hegarty (Lecturer in Psychology, University of Keele).

2.2 Methodological difficulties in evaluating tape-slide teaching.

2.2.1 The majority of the questions posed by I.C.L. either (a) seek information on Teaching Method A vs. Teaching Method B comparisons or (b) look at the relevant interactions of the media with the individual differences of the student and consider the effects of such interactions upon learning. Whereas it is possible to make tentative generalisations for questions falling into the latter category, it is seldom possible to provide satisfactory answers to questions of a comparative nature. The hunt for a "best" method of teaching is not realistic, particularly when considering minutiae of presentation. What is best for one student at any one time may not be best for another student, or even for the same student at another time.

2.2.2 The absence of any broad philosophic or theoretical framework in media research causes such research to be of limited value in ascribing or assigning rationale for using its products and answering specific questions. Difficulties arise because of the complex three-way interaction involving (i) the physical characteristics of the audiovisual presentation, (ii) the content and presentation of the material and, (iii) the individual differences of the students. To control for other variables whilst comparing, for example, the use of 30 slides versus the use of 35 slides with a taped lecture presents almost insurmountable problems for the experimenter.

Figure 3b   In this version the text is typed single-spaced, there is one carriage return between paragraphs, two before, and one below each subheading. In addition the line length has been reduced, and the numbering system clarified. (A useful discussion of such numbering systems in text is provided by Waller, 1977)

In passing it should be noted that using consistent vertical spacing can cause difficulties for designers and printers, particularly those who are wedded (as most are) to the convention that there should be a fixed baseline for each page (that is that the text should always stop at the same place on each page, regardless of content). To achieve consistent vertical spacing, either the author has to specify to the typesetter what is required, or computer-assisted rules for vertical spacing need to be built into the production process. In either case there is no need to stop the text at the same point on every page. The length of the text on the page should be determined by content.

```
.... Between Australasia and Africa is the
Indian Ocean.
     These are the oceans in the middle parts
of the earth.   Round the north of the world,
in the very cold areas, there is the Arctic
Ocean.
     It is mostly frozen up, and the North Pole
is in it.   Round the southern parts of the
world, around Antarctica, is the Southern
Ocean ....
```

Figure 4a   The original text


```
.... Between Australasia and Africa is the
Indian Ocean.
These are the oceans in the middle parts of the earth.

Round the north of the world, in the very cold areas,
there is the Arctic Ocean.
It is mostly frozen up, and the North Pole is in it.

Round the southern parts of the world, around Antarctica,
is the Southern Ocean ....
```

Figure 4b   The same text — regrouped and re-spaced in a proportional way

Horizontal spacing can similarly be used consistently to group functionally related parts. Regular word spacing produces what is called 'unjustified text' — that is text with a ragged right-hand edge. (Typescript provides a typical example.) This form of text is now becoming common — largely one suspects for economic reasons. It is cheaper to set than 'justified text' (when traditional printing methods are employed) and it is easier to reset proof-corrections. The more conventional justified text (text with straight right- and left-hand edges) is achieved by varying the space between the words (and sometimes the letters) and by occasionally breaking words (hyphenation). With unjustified text, however, the space between words is consistent, word-breaks can be avoided, and so too can breaks between clauses if this is deemed necessary. Unjustified text is thus more flexible. It is possible to specify, for example, that no line should end with the first word of a new sentence, or that if the next to the last word of a line is followed by any punctuation mark, then the last word can be carried over to the next line. Such a specification allows the content of the text to determine where the line should end, as well as the column width.

Figures 5a and 5b show the effects of this in practice. Figure 5a shows a section of text as it was originally printed. Figure 5b shows a redesigned version where my concern has been primarily with the content rather than with making the text fit a particular line-length. Again, procedures such as these cause difficulties for printers. One can hardly expect typesetters to make

```
. . . . . type-face does not specify the actual
size of the printed image (Hartley et al, 1975).  In
general, however, a good all purpose size is 10-
point type on a 12-point line to line feed:  8-point
in 10-point is possibly about as small as one
would want to go in the design of instructional
materials.
```

Figure 5a   The original text

```
. . . . . type-face does not specify the actual
size of the printed image (Hartley et al, 1975).
In general, however, a good all purpose size is
10-point type on a 12-point line to line feed:
8-point on 10-point is possibly about as small as
one would want to go in the design of instructional
materials.
```

Figure 5b   The same text with line endings determined by syntactic considerations

decisions about the meaning of each line of text in deciding where to end it. However, there are techniques which can help in this respect. For example:

(1) Authors can type their manuscript line for line as they wish, and the manuscript can be photographed. One advantage of preparing camera-ready copy is that it allows authors almost complete control over the preparation of their text.

(2) Authors can type their manuscript line for line and ask the printer to follow it. This can present some difficulties as letter-spacing in typescript is regular, whereas in print it is proportional, but one can get a good estimate of what the final product will look like.

(3) Developments in computer-assisted typesetting will allow one to use grammatical constraints as determinants for line-endings. Figures 6a and 6b show advances in this respect. Figure 6a shows a piece of text set in the standard form: Figure 6b is the same text 'chunked' by computer.

Of course it is artificial to discuss vertical and horizontal spacing separately. I have done so here simply to clarify the argument. *Designing Instructional Text* provides an example of our approach applied to vertical and horizontal spacing simultaneously. However, it should be clear from these examples that our approach is fundamentally opposed to the traditional methods of balancing

A useful theory of design would combine general principles with specific task requirements. It would also be explicit about the means of doing this, that is, describe precisely how a particular design problem might be solved. Our current work on documentation problems contributes to a design theory of this type. The work is motivated by the following assumption. If we can take a text, create a multitude of rational design variations, evaluate them according to different text and reader skill assumptions and deliver up the best design option, then all of these activities together would constitute a workable theory of design.

Figure 6a   The original text

A useful theory of design
would combine general principles
with specific task requirements.
It would also be explicit about the means of doing this,
that is, describe precisely
how a particular design problem might be solved.
Our current work on documentation problems contributes
to a design theory of this type.
The work is motivated
by the following assumption.
If we can take a text,
create a multitude of rational design variations,
evaluate them according to different text
and reader skill assumptions
and deliver up the best design option,
then all of these activities together
would constitute a workable theory of design.

Figure 6b   Text 'chunked' by computer into meaningful segments. The computer program used to produce the text shown was developed by N. J. Macdonald, and is one of a group of programs that constitute the Writer's Workbench facility at Bell Telephone Laboratories. This facility provides a variety of formating and editing functions. (Figure courtesy of Larry Frase and Bell Telephone Laboratories)

the text either horizontally or vertically about a central axis. We start from the top left, and work down and across. We do not fill the page—either vertically or horizontally—just because the space is there.

Sharing psychology

So far all that I have said may seem to be commonsense and to be lacking any 'psychology'. However, I am not convinced of this. The discipline of psychology leads one to consider both problems and processes. It emphasizes the point of view of the total system (writing — editing — designing — printing — reading — comprehending) and it particularly directs attention to the latter end of the chain. Furthermore, treating ideas as hypotheses to be tested is also part of the discipline of psychology — a view which is not shared by many outsiders.

Testing hypotheses, of course, leads to a consideration of methodology and experimental design. The psychologist can help the typographer here by designing experiments to test out the validity of the typographer's hunches. Thus the mock battles fought between designers (for example whether or not one should use unjustified text) can be subject to experimental test. Psychologists stress comparison and evaluation because they are well aware that things do not always happen in the way individuals think they do — they can go sadly wrong. Let me cite two recent personal examples. In one experiment I changed the sequence of illustrations in a text, but thought this would make little difference to students' perceptions of it. However, nineteen out of twenty students preferred the revised version. In another experiment I spent several days revising four pages of a piece of prose. I was sure my version was much clearer and would be preferred by my students. However, ten out of twenty students preferred the original. Research is necessary, therefore, to test the intuitions of both psychologists and designers.

Testing hypotheses, of course, presents the psychologist with methodological difficulties and problems of measurement. Over the last ten years or so we have used a variety of measures (and combinations of them) to test our ideas. Table 1 tries to encapsulate some of the strengths and limitations of these measures, which are divided into four main groups: oral reading, search and retrieval, silent reading, and comprehension. Opposite these four blocks are my estimates of the reliability of these measures and some comments about them. Inspection of the table shows that some measures are more reliable than others, and commonsense indicates that some measures are more suitable than others for different purposes. Thus oral reading measures give detailed information about specific reading difficulties, search and retrieval tasks are appropriate for evaluating the layout of highly structured text, and compre-hension measures are more appropriate for evaluating the effectiveness of continuous prose.

In addition to the traditional psychological measures described in Table 1, consideration must also be given to the costs of different ways of printing text. In our experiments we have sometimes shown reductions in cost without any loss of comprehension and sometimes great improvement in comprehension

Table 1 Methods Used in Typographic Research, and their Reliability

Method	Estimated reliability	Test-retest correlations obtained in our studies	Comments on the method
Reading aloud (with the text upside down)	Highest	0.87 to 0.99	Slows reading down: larger spread of scores with males than females
Reading aloud (normal text)	High	0.78 to 0.95	Insensitive to differences in layouts: readers proceed at same speed regardless of layout
Searching for particular words/items in technical materials	High	0.75 to 0.91	Good for technical materials: sensitive
Searching for particular words/items in prose (with items relatively close to each other)	Moderate	0.49 to 0.68	Moderately useful and sensitive
Searching for particular words/items in prose (with items further apart)	Low	0.36 to 0.83	Poor: searchers 'get lost'
Silent reading speed (with test to follow)	Fairly high	0.70 to 0.82	Knowledge of forthcoming test slows readers down markedly
Silent reading speed (without test)	Fairly high	0.53 to 0.96	The researcher does not know what has been read
Comprehension (cloze test[a])	Fairly high	0.55 to 0.95	Useful for assessing relative difficulty
Comprehension (recall questions)	Low	0.46 to 0.73	Too specific to make comparisons with if different materials are used
Preferences	Fairly high	0.70	Useful for additional information but preferences may be based on uninformed judgement

[a]The cloze test involves the reader filling in, say, every seventh word.

for a slight increase in cost (see for example Hartley and Burnhill, 1976, 1977). Results such as these, we would suggest, point in particular to the hidden costs of poor-quality materials.

THE EFFECTS OF READABILITY

The role of language

The figures in this paper have illustrated an obvious point. The layout of text might hinder comprehension (Figures 1, 3a, 4a, 5a, 6a, 6b) or help it (Figures 3b, 4b, 5b) but in all cases comprehension might be further improved if one paid more attention to the language in which these texts were written.

In this section I want to make three points about language in instructional text. These are: (i) it is relatively easy to obtain a measure of difficulty of prose; (ii) it is not so easy to make prose simple; and (iii) 'simple' text in itself is not always easy to understand.

Measuring text difficulty

One can measure the difficulty of a piece of prose—albeit rather crudely— with one of a number of readability formulae. These formulae typically combine two main measures: average sentence length, and average word length (usually considered in terms of the number of syllables). Other measures add only marginally to their predictive power (see Klare, 1963, 1974–5). The aim of such formulae—of which there are many (see Klare, 1974–5)—is to predict suitable 'grade-levels' or reading ages for the text.

An example of a simple-readability formula is provided by McGlaughlin (1974). He suggests the following procedures: (i) take a sample of thirty sentences; (ii) count the number of words with three or more syllables; (iii) find the square root of this number; (iv) add three. The result is the predicted American reading grade-level. You need to add five to find the British equivalent expressed in years (if you accept that American and British educational systems are similar!). Applying these procedures to the first thirty sentences of this chapter suggests that this chapter is suitable for under- graduates, but that is rather more difficult than the author intended.

As noted above the aim of such formulae is to predict suitable 'grade-levels' or reading ages for the text. In this respect the formulae have run into some difficulties, and many formulae, while they intercorrelate well, predict reading ages rather differently. There are, of course, a number of other objections to readability formulae. Some short words or sentences are difficult to understand (for example God is grace). Some long words are quite familiar (for example communication). Neither word order nor sentence order is taken into account, and nor are the effects of other aids like illustrations, headings, numbering systems, and indeed, typographical layout.

Nonetheless, despite these difficulties, a readability formula can be a useful tool for comparing the relative difficulty of different pieces of text, especially if one is interested in comparing a revised version with its original. Here there have been some clear and practical results. It has been shown that making text more readable can have a marked effect upon the comprehension of school textbooks (Hartley, 1980), examination questions (Johnstone and Cassels, 1978), correspondence texts (Klare and Smart, 1973), car insurance policies (Kincaid and Gamble, 1977), medical instructions (Ley, 1979), scientific

Table 2   The Percentage of Correct Responses to Original and Revised Questions (from Johnstone and Cassels, 1978: reproduced with permission)

Original questions	Percentage correct	Simplified questions	Percentage correct
Which one of the following requires a non-aqueous solvent to dissolve it? A Salt B Sugar C Sodium nitrate D Sulphur	34	Which one of the following requires a liquid other than water to dissolve it? A Salt B Sugar C Sodium nitrate D Sulphur	49
The atomic weight of chlorine is usually quoted as 35.5. It is not a whole number despite the fact that protons and neutrons have very closely integral atomic weights because A Ions are present B Impurities are present C Unequal numbers of protons and neutrons are present D Isotopes are present	66	The atomic weight of chlorine is 35.5. Why is it not a whole number? A Ions are present B Impurities are present C Unequal numbers of protons are present D Isotopes are present	78
An element has only three isotopes of mass numbers 14, 16 and 17. Which one of the following could *not* be the atomic weight of the element? A 14.2 B 15.4 C 16.3 D 17.1	50	An element has only three isotopes of mass numbers 14, 16, 17. Which one of the following could be the atomic weight of the element? A 11.7 B 13.9 C 15.1 D 17.2	62

papers (Turk, 1978), and legal jargon (Charrow, 1979). The work of Johnstone and Cassels with examination questions may be of particular interest to the reader. Table 2 (based on their report) illustrates the kinds of differences found in the percentage of correct answers to original and simplified questions asked in a pre-O level chemistry examination given to approximately 6000 pupils.

Readability formulae would thus appear to be useful tools which psychologists could give away. To some extent this is true, but like most of the tools of psychologists, they are better used with expert guidance. Psychologists are more sensitive to the limitations and qualifications that preclude making general statements. Although it would appear from the experiments just cited that more readable text will be read with better understanding, the issue is not quite that simple. Psychologists have skilfully disentangled those factors which are likely to lead to positive findings and those which are not. It appears that if readers are able and/or highly motivated, and if their prior knowledge about the subject matter is high, and if, in these experiments, the testing time is short, then it is *unlikely* that making the text more readable will have any marked effects. However, if these conditions are reversed, that is if readers are less able and/or less motivated, if the material is relatively novel, and if the testing time is ample, then the more readable material is likely to lead to improved test scores (Klare, 1976).

Kincaid and Gamble's (1977) experiment indicated this kind of finding. They found that (i) high-ability readers could understand both the easy and the difficult versions of passages from a car insurance policy; (ii) average-ability readers could understand the easy but not the difficult versions; and (iii) low-ability readers could not understand either.

Making prose simple

Several guidelines have been written about how to present prose clearly (for example see Tichy, 1966; Klare, 1975; Hartley, 1981) and there are also guidelines which illustrate how to revise text to make it easier to understand (for example see Kern *et al.*, 1975; Hartley *et al.*, 1980). However, there are no firm rules, accepted by all, and routinely applicable. The general procedures that I currently advocate for rewriting text can be considered under three inter-related headings.

Textual

(1) Use the active voice.
(2) Use simpler wording.
(3) Either shorten sentences, or expand them into two or three simpler sentences.

(4) Divide long paragraphs into short ones.

(5) List actions and procedures (and put them in temporal sequence).

(6) When in difficulty think of how you would explain to a friend what you are trying to write, or actually explain it to one.

(7) Write down what you say, and then polish it.

Typographical

(1) Decide on the line-length, typesize, and number of characters per line that there will be in the final printed version. Type the manuscript with a corresponding number of characters per line.

(2) Use units of line-space in proportion so as to separate out and to group units of text. (For example separate headings from the text by using half a line-space below the heading and one line-space above it: separate paragraphs from each other by half a line-space: start new sentences on a new line.)

(3) Type the text unjustified (as in normal typescript).

(4) End each line at a sensible place syntactically (for example at the ends of clauses). Avoid word breaks (hyphenation) at line ends.

(5) End each page at a sensible place (for example do not have the first line of a new paragraph as the last line of the page, or the last line of a paragraph as the first line of a new page).

(6) In print use bold lower-case type (not capitals) for main headings.

Procedural

(1) Leave each revised draft for at least twelve hours.

(2) Revise and simplify revised drafts.

(3) Do not look back at the original text (except afterwards to check on ambiguities or points of meaning).

(4) Ask colleagues to help simplify the revised draft (either by simplifying it themselves, or by pointing out where they might expect difficulties to occur).

(5) Repeat as often as time allows.

As stated above, these are guidelines, not firm suggestions. There are, however, some data to support them (see Hartley *et al.*, 1980). Thus much can be achieved provided our limited knowledge is applied sensibly. If one follows the procedures advocated in this and in the earlier section of this chapter, there will be some startling changes to text. Figures 7a and 7b provide (hopefully) an example.

IMPORTANT INFORMATION FOR OUR PASSENGERS

Even though you may be an experienced air traveler, there are certain
features of this airplane with which you may not be familiar.

AUTOMATIC OXYGEN SYSTEM

>The higher altitudes at which this aircraft operates
>require the prompt use of the automatic oxygen system in
>case of any sudden change in cabin pressure. Should a
>decompression occur, oxygen masks will drop down. Take
>nearest mask and promptly place over nose and mouth.
>BREATHE NORMALLY (NO SMOKING PLEASE).

SEAT BELTS

>Even if the "SEAT BELT" sign is turned off in flight, it
>is recommended that you keep your seat belt fastened,
>whenever you are in your seat.

FLOTATION SEAT CUSHIONS

>The cushion on which you are sitting is designed to keep
>you afloat. In the event of a water landing, grasp the
>cushion at the rear, pull it forward and take it with you.

EMERGENCY EXITS

>There are nine exits provided for your use. The chart below
>will show you the one closest to your seat. The exits over
>the wings are removable windows. For easy access to the
>window, push seat back ahead of the window forward. The two
>exits at each end of the cabin are doors equipped with fast
>operating evacuation slides. There is also a door in the
>rear of passenger cabin. REAR CABIN EXIT (STAIR). (If
>usable, will be opened by a crew member).

Figure 7a   The original text

IMPORTANT!

This aircraft has special safety features.
Read this card carefully.

AUTOMATIC OXYGEN

If, during the flight, there is a sudden change
in cabin pressure, oxygen masks will drop down
automatically.
If this happens
    - take the nearest mask
    - put it quickly over your nose and mouth
    - breathe normally
    - put out all cigarettes

EMERGENCY EXITS

There are nine emergency exits.

The chart on the back of this card shows
the exit nearest to your seat.

The two exit doors at the end of the cabin
are fitted with chutes for sliding down.

To get out over the wings you have to
take out the windows.
To make this easier, put the seat-back down
when you are trying to get to the window.

The door at the back of the cabin is labelled
REAR CABIN EXIT (STAIR).
This door will be opened by a crew member.

FLOATING SEAT CUSHIONS

Your seat cushion will keep you afloat if we
make an emergency landing in the sea.
Get hold of the cushion at the back, pull it
forward, and take it with you.

SEAT BELTS

We suggest that you keep your seat belt
fastened when you are seated - even when the
SEAT BELT sign is turned off.

Figure 7b   The same text revised and respaced according to the recommendations
made in this chapter

Simple text can be difficult

Although simplifying text might be our aim, it is important to note, as I said earlier, that simple text is not always easy to understand. Let me give you three examples:

(1) In a job application form regularly used at Keele, the applicant has to answer the simple request 'Give previous experience with dates'. One applicant for a lectureship in our department wrote 'Moderately successful in the past, but I am now happily married!' The addition of a comma 'Give previous experience, with dates' would lessen this ambiguity.

(2) Consider the final wording of a form as issued by a car insurance company
    •Name..
    •Age ....
    •Address...

This seems clear enough, but at this point the insurance company actually needed to know the age of the *car*, and not the age of the applicant.

(3) Finally consider the following notice observed by Chapanis (1965).

> PLEASE
> WALK UP ONE FLOOR
> WALK DOWN TWO FLOORS
> FOR IMPROVED ELEVATOR SERVICE

People interpret this notice as meaning 'to get on the elevator I must either walk up one floor, or go down two floors' or even 'to get on the elevator I must first walk up one floor and then down two floors'! When they have done this, they find the same notice confronting them. What this notice means, in effect, is 'Please, don't use the elevator if you are only going a short distance'.

I have ended this section with this illustration from Chapanis because his article provides many illustrations to show that short simple directives are often unintelligible and are frequently dangerous. Simple text is often difficult to understand because it is: (i) too telegrammatic, too abbreviated, too brief; (ii) badly sequenced, ambiguous or obscure; (iii) based on the writer's preconceptions and frame of reference rather than the reader's. The moral of all this, with respect to written communication, is that instructions need to be *evaluated in context*. To do this, psychologists must share their knowledge with practitioners.

CONCLUDING REMARKS

Hopefully this chapter has illustrated that psychologists have something useful to contribute to the problems of written instruction. Clearly our approach to designing instructional text has implications for authors. We are suggesting that authors should take more care and control in the preparation of their text. Manuscripts can be marked up in such a way that the required spacing can be followed by a typist or a printer. We would maintain that it is not difficult to use consistent spacing rules and indeed that there are benefits from what might seem an additional burden. It is our belief that consistent spacing helps the writer to clarify his own thoughts and ideas. We have found when we have respaced previously published text that we have often had to rewrite it in order to overcome inherent ambiguities in what was being said. We believe that clarifying layout helps to clarify content because it requires clarity of thought.

More practically, perhaps, we believe that our approach has implications for both students and teachers in higher education. When writing essays, or preparing notices and lecture handouts, space can be used to convey the structure of the content. Students (in psychology) can be encouraged to leave line-spaces between paragraphs and to use headings and subheadings (with proportional spacing) in the presentation of their written work. Lecturers can be encouraged to leave sufficient amounts of space for students to write their notes on lecture handouts. (Research in this context has indicated that students tend to write between the lines on a handout, even when space for notetaking is provided in a left- or right-hand column; see Hartley, 1976.)

Our approach also has implications for the development of computer-assisted writing. Already there is an increase in the ways that computers are being used to aid the writing of instructional text. At Bell Laboratories in the USA for instance, computer programs have been written which will detect spelling errors, indicate poor usage and style, compute the readability of text, flag overly complex sentences, and space complex text. At present these programs (and others) are run after the original text has been written, but it is anticipated that they will soon be incorporated into the production process itself.

One of our concerns here, however, is that in producing such computer aids to composition we shall see the replication of traditional printing practices. The computer will be used to duplicate what is currently done by humans, without first considering whether or not it is ideal or what would be optimum from the point of view of improved communication. Already, for instance, some word processors boast multiple typefaces and programs for justification and hyphenation, and people are spending a lot of time doing what some of us would consider to be unnecessary.

To write a computer program to match some current composition routine in printing requires a great deal of effort: programs have to be meticulously conceived in order to match the capabilities of highly skilled craftsmen. Yet many of us would question whether *all* of this work and ingenuity is necessary. Do we need to write programs in order to hyphenate words, or justify text vertically and horizontally? Would the effort not be better spent in trying to discover effective layouts for different kinds of text?

Furthermore, we fear that the spacing of computer-assisted text will be done page by page, using light pens and the aesthetic judgement of keyboard operators, rather than planned rationally from the outset. Such inconsistent planning methods will produce text that will present readers with the same difficulties that they already find in conventionally printed text.

To carry out effective research in the field of written communication using modern technology, psychologists will have to widen their horizons. Few psychologists seem to know much about current technologies and how they impinge upon the production of text, let alone new ones. Much prior research on typography can be rightly criticized on the grounds that psychologists remained in relative isolation from production problems. To be of help in designing, using, and evaluating new technologies psychologists will have to immerse themselves in new and different disciplines, they cannot go on working in isolation.

In the world of publishing psychologists will discover that textbooks, journals, magazines, and newspapers all differ in their requirements, and that writers, journalists, typographers, editors, designers, publishers, and printers each have their own technology, language, and mystique. An additional problem is that people in these different disciplines do not distinguish between types of psychologist (such as pure/applied, behavioural/analytical). Psychologists are all one to them. They do not know what psychologists do, nor what contribution psychologists can make.

The reasons why psychology must be *shared* in these applied situations rather than *given* away are twofold. First, to use psychology in any of these cases requires that it be tailored to fit particular demands and communicated in a way that specific practitioners can grasp. Such practitioners need convincing that psychology can be relevant and helpful and that it will improve their output over what they are (usually) already satisfied with. The second, related reason why we must share psychology, is that our psychological knowledge and understanding is not so advanced in this area that we can immediately provide straightforward rules for action. Psychologists are needed to interpret and adapt the knowledge that they have and to advise on its applications and limitations. Indeed, where necessary, specific investigations may have to be carried out to supplement existing knowledge. Sometimes these investigations will have to be done mainly to satisfy the practitioner: sometimes (more rarely) the psychologist.

It is here that the true benefit for psychology arises. I am arguing that it is from practical work of this kind that there will be a gain in theoretical knowledge. This is the third theme of this chapter and it is perhaps the hardest to sustain. I maintain, nonetheless, that working with Peter Burnhill on *specific* practical problems has produced a *general* approach to design—an approach which is theoretically useful in the limited area of instructional text. Although much more needs to be done, our work with instructional text has demonstrated that giving psychology away has led to an expansion of psychology at home.

ACKNOWLEDGEMENTS

I am grateful to Alan Branthwaite, Peter Burnhill, Colin Byrne, David Canter, Sandra Canter, Linda Norton, and Mark Trueman for helpful comments on earlier drafts of this paper. I am also grateful to Alice Slaney for typing its several versions.

REFERENCES

Burnhill, P. (1970). 'Typographic education: headings in text', *Journal of Typographic Research*, **4**, 353–365.

Burnhill, P., Hartley, J., and Young, M. (1976). 'Tables in text', *Applied Ergonomics*, **7**, 13–18.

Chapanis, A. (1965). 'Words, words, words', *Human Factors*, **7**, 1, 1–17.

Charrow, V. R. (1979). 'Legal language: policy issues and practical implications'. Paper to the American Psychological Association Annual Convention, New York. (Copies available from the author, American Institutes for Research, Washington, DC.)

Haber, R. N. (1978). 'Visual perception', *Annual Review of Psychology*, **29**, 31–59.

Hartley, J. (1976). 'Lecture handouts and student notetaking', *Programmed Learning and Educational Technology*, **13**, 2, 58–64. (Corrections to printer's errors given in 13, (3).

Hartley, J. (1978). *Designing Instructional Text*, London: Kogan Page; New York: Nichols.

Hartley, J. (ed.) (1980a). *The Psychology of Written Communication: Selected Readings*, London: Kogan Page; New York: Nichols.

Hartley, J. (1980b). 'Space and structure in instructional text', in J. Hartley (ed.), *The Psychology of Written Communication: Selected Readings*, London: Kogan Page; New York: Nichols.

Hartley J. (1981). 'Eighty ways of improving instructional text', *IEEE Transactions on Professional Communication*, PC-24, 1, 17–27.

Hartley, J. and Burnhill, P. (1976). 'Explorations in space: a critique of the typography of BPS publications'. *Bulletin of the British Psychological Society*, **29**, 97–107.

Hartley, J. and Burnhill, P. (1977). 'Space revisited: or the BPS does it again!', *Bulletin of the British Psychological Society*, **30**, 253–256.

Hartley, J., Trueman, M., and Burnhill, P. (1980). 'Some observations on producing and measuring readable writing', *Programmed Learning and Educational Technology*, **17**, 164–174.

Johnstone, A. and Cassels, J. (1978). 'What's in a word?', *New Scientist*, **78**, 1103, 18 May.

Kern, R. P., Sticht, T. G., Welty, D., and Hauke, R. N. (1975). *Guidebook for the Development of Army Training Literature*, Arlington, Virginia: US Army Research Institute for the Behavioural and Social Sciences.

Kincaid, J. P. and Gamble, L. G. (1977). 'Ease of comprehension of standard and readable automobile insurance policies as a function of reading ability', *Journal of Reading Behavior*, **IX**, 1, 85-87.

Klare, G. R. (1963). *The Measurement of Readability*, Ames: Iowa State University Press.

Klare, G. R. (1974-5). 'Assessing readability', *Reading Research Quarterly*, **10**, 62-102.

Klare, G. R. (1975). *A Manual for Readable Writing*, REM Company, 119a Roesler Road, Glen Burie, M. D. 21061, USA.

Klare, G. R. (1976). 'A second look at the validity of readability formulas', *Journal of Reading Behavior*, **8**, 129-152.

Klare, G. R. and Smart, K. L. (1973). 'Analysis of the readability levels of selected USAF instructional manuals', *Journal of Educational Research*, **67**, 4, 176.

Ley, P. (1979). 'Memory for medical information', *British Journal of Social and Clinical Psychology*, **18**, 2, 245-256.

McGlaughlin, G. H. (1974). 'Temptations of the Flesch', *Instructional Science*, **2**, 4, 367-383.

Miller, G. A. (1969). 'Psychology as a means of promoting human welfare', *American Psychologist*, **24**, 1063-1075.

Miller, G. A. (1980). 'Giving away psychology in the 80s', *Psychology Today*, **13**, 38-50, 97-98.

Tichy, H. J. (1966). *Effective Writing for Engineers, Managers and Scientists*, New York: Wiley.

Tinker, M. A. (1965). *Bases for Effective Reading*, Minneapolis: University of Minnesota Press.

Turk, C. (1978). 'Do you write impressively?', *Bulletin of the British Ecological Society*, **IX**, 3, 5-10.

Waller, R. H. (1977). 'Numbering systems in text. Notes on transforming No. 4', Open University. Reprinted in J. Hartley (ed.) (1980) *The Psychology of Written Communication: Selected Readings*, London: Kogan Page; New York: Nichols.

Psychology in Practice
Edited by S. Canter and D. Canter
© 1982, John Wiley & Sons, Ltd.

CHAPTER 17

CAN EXPERIMENTAL PSYCHOLOGY BE APPLIED PSYCHOLOGY?

Ray Bull
Senior Lecturer,
North East London Polytechnic

INTRODUCTION

One of the reasons why the editors of this book requested that I provide a chapter on the relationship between experimental psychology and attempts to reduce behavioural or psychological problems in the real world may have been that they are aware that I am unable to work out what sort of psychologist I am.

My first seven publications in psychological journals were concerned with psychophysiology. Specifically, I conducted laboratory-based studies, using undergraduates as subjects, of the skin conductance response. Following that I worked full-time at Exeter University for two years on memory performance in policemen and on their attitudes toward certain information-dissemination practices. In recent years I have been researching on two applied, 'real-world' topics which are full of interacting and confounding variables. One of these areas is that of eyewitness memory where, together with Brian Clifford, I have conducted a number of studies, and in our book (Clifford and Bull, 1978) we have attempted to relate knowledge gained over the decades by experimental psychologists to the topic of person identification.

My second major research data is that of facial deformity. Here, with the assistance of Julia Stevens and Nichola Rumsey (Bull, 1979; Bull and Stevens, 1981) I have been investigating the effects of having a disfigured face on people deformed in this way. We are employing a two-pronged attack on this problem and we hope that the two approaches we are using are complementary to one another. Largely with the help of several hospitals we have gathered information from people who have been facially deformed from birth or who have become facially disfigured through a traumatic incident such as a car crash. We have also undertaken many field studies, out in the street so to speak, in which we have examined the reactions of the general public to people with a facial deformity. This latter investigatory approach may best be described as experimental social psychology.

Because of this chequered history the editors considered that I might be in a position to see the 'pure' versus 'applied' debate from both sides at one and the same time. Whether, in fact, I can do this is for the reader to decide.

The present chapter will be concerned with the following topics. Firstly, I shall mention psychological statistics and the null hypothesis. Then I shall consider the public relations problems caused by experimental psychologists being seen as spending most of their time saying how wrong their colleagues have been, instead of making non-psychologists aware of those points that most experimental psychologists do, in fact, agree upon. Then to paraphrase one of Eunice Belbin's (1979) points from her 1978 Myers Lecture, I shall suggest that we should view attempts to *apply* experimental psychology as the art, or perhaps the science, of the possible as opposed to the perfect. Then I shall make some comments on our current training of both undergraduate and post-graduate research students in psychology. Finally, I shall suggest that experimental psychologists should not constantly and consciously avoid the media (because the media are thought simplistically to report only sensational psychology?), but that we should attempt to overcome the problems in this area in order that our work can actually be of prompt and direct benefit to society.

I shall attempt, in part, to be a little provocative and so if some of the things you are about to read lead to argument, then at least I will have achieved something.

PSYCHOLOGY AND STATISTICS

Outside the laboratory, experimental psychologists researching in, for example, a large industrial or commercial concern often would like to hold certain variables constant whilst permitting others to vary. In this way they can bring their investigative powers to bear on real-life problems. In attempting to do this, however, the researcher usually has to obtain permission to hold these variables constant (that is, to disrupt normal practice). In trying to obtain such agreement the researcher is often required to outline his experimental design and to say how the data he will thus gather will hopefully lead to a meaningful conclusion. However, when a non-psychologist and/or someone unfamiliar with inferential statistics asks a psychologist to tell him about the basic procedures used in psychological statistics, such a questioner is likely to be dismayed to hear that we have a hypothesis (which is suggested to us by commonsense or by a theory, or by previous research) that we then proceed to state the converse of this 'expected' result (that is to form the null hypothesis), and that we then try to reject or disprove this opposite of what we really expected anyway. No wonder many non-psychologists (and first-year psychology undergraduates) are prone to suggest that this peculiar procedure seems to be drawn from *Alice in Wonderland*.

Greenwald (1975), among others, has attempted to highlight the problems brought about by null-hypothesis testing. He was concerned more with the problems this caused within the discipline of psychology than with the public relations aspect of psychologists frequently being judged as using difficult-to-comprehend statistical procedures. Greenwald, as have others, pointed out that there seem to be few publications in psychological journals in which the null hypothesis was found to be supported and he noted that journal editors (quite rightly given present statistical procedures in psychology) were loth to publish papers in which the null hypothesis had not been rejected. Consequently, one should not be surprised if the inquisitive non-psychologist claims that most psychological knowledge has been gained by us disproving or rejecting what we appeared not to believe in anyway.

Greenwald points out that in *Webster's Dictionary* the word 'null' is defined as, 'invalid; amounting to nought; of no value, effect or consequence'. He suggests that psychologists' beliefs about the null hypothesis (which I suggest their own undergraduate training may have indoctrinated them into accepting) may be summarized as follows:

(1) Given the characteristics of current procedures in psychological statistics, failure to reject the null hypothesis is only a basis for uncertainty.
(2) Psychologists, he says, believe that little or no knowledge can be gained by finding that a variable has no effect. (In my opinion this second belief can sometimes be misleading since in the real world it may often be of value to know that a possible disruptive variable may, in fact, have no effect.)
(3) 'If statistically significant effects are obtained in an experiment, it is fairly certain that the experiment was done properly.' Greenwald points out that this belief would have greater veracity if work which failed to reject the null hypothesis had an equal likelihood of being published as that which found statistically significant effects.
(4) It is inadvisable to introduce real-world practices on the basis of results which supported a null hypothesis because there are a great number of ways (including incompetence of the researcher) in which the null hypothesis may incorrectly be accepted.

This fourth belief is, of course, well-founded, but it leads me on to my next point which is that in my opinion (and in those of many non-psychologists) psychology spends too much time 'washing its dirty linen in public'. However, before turning to that point I would like to conclude my comments on null-hypothesis testing by saying that although the inferential statistical procedures currently used by experimental psychologists may from within psychology be judged as very efficient, such procedures can and I submit *do*, lead to psychology being seen in a bad light by non-psychologists.

Though from the philosophical cost/efficiency point of view Popper's views about disproving hypotheses may seem desirable, and even though it may be a feather in psychology's cap to note that we have for decades been doing what he suggested, nevertheless I suggest that such procedures help confirm, for those people who believe experimental psychology to be a waste of time, that we do not really know what we are doing.

CONSENSUS AMONGST EXPERIMENTAL PSYCHOLOGISTS

What also leads to psychology being seen in a bad light is the way in which we constantly attempt to show how wrong our colleagues within psychology have been. The 'publish in order to be promoted' pressure which exists (perhaps quite rightly) in most academic psychology departments is one reason why it seems perfectly acceptable, even desirable, for us to criticize heavily the work of other psychologists. *Within* psychology this may not produce too many problems but from the point of view of the real world outside I suggest that it is of great importance. Those psychologists whose research rarely, if ever, interfaces with the real world may not have experienced the strength of feeling which exists that if experimental psychologists conducting apparently scientific experiments cannot be seen to arrive at an agreed answer, then why should the real world have any use for experimental psychologists?

A link between this part of the present chapter and the previous section on statistics is made by Gordon Westland's (1978) point that many psychologists (and others) claim that other psychologists misuse statistics. Westland cites McHugh's (1969) paper from the *BPS Bulletin* in which McHugh, in summarizing his work as a reviewer for a psychological journal commented that he 'found that computational errors, inappropriate choices of statistical tests, and misinterpretations of test results were disturbingly common'. Westland points out that if the criticisms within psychology of other psychologist's statistics have foundation then psychology has a problem here; and if the critics are wrong then, since they themselves are psychologists, psychology still has a problem here. What are we to do about this? We (whoever the 'we' are who are good at statistics) could make the teaching of statistics more effective, or perhaps we could attempt to discover what are the consequences of the 'inappropriate choices of statistical tests and misinterpretations of test results' that McHugh complained of. Were they major errors, in the sense that they led to absurdly false conclusions, or were they minor errors (like putting three-star petrol in a car which should have four-star)? Psychologists should criticize each others' work but perhaps pedantic criticism is too costly for us from the public relations point of view.

My personal belief is that psychologists do not devote enough thought, time, and effort in their writings, lectures, talks, etc., to pointing out the areas of *agreement* within psychology. One drawback of learning more and more psychology is that one tends to forget how much of what seems obvious and widely accepted to a psychologist may not be obvious to or even contemplated by a non-psychologist or to someone embarking upon the study of psychology. Basic key concepts like the effects of reinforcement, and of viewing man as a limited information processor, are *not* widely known in the real world.

Over the last seven years I have worked as a consultant psychologist for several police forces, the greater part of my work here being concerned with memory. One question I have been concerned with is how one can most efficiently pass on operational information to police officers who are about to go out from the police station on their tour of patrol duty. I have repeatedly found in various parts of different police forces that the most effective way to increase (in absolute terms) the amount of information remembered by the policemen is to give them *less* initially. What was happening was that in the ten minutes allotted at the beginning of each shift for men to be prepared for duty they were given a great wealth of information almost all of which they did not retain. When I suggested that the men be given less information, this was received with scepticism. The men in charge of the briefing procedures had *not* considered whether they were attempting to impart too much information. They viewed the memories of their men as being like tape-recorders, and sometimes viewed the men's inability to remember information as merely being a sign of lack of motivation. Now we (that is, psychologists) all know that motivation can affect learning and remembering, but that was not the crucial point in this applied work. The important point I am trying to make here is that although what one might loosely term 'processing capacity' or 'memory overload' may be an obvious factor to experimental psychologists it had not been considered by these laymen (that is the police).

The editors of this book asked the authors to draw upon their personal experience, more so than upon the results of their empirical research. At the risk of totally losing my credibility with 'pure' experimental psychologists I now admit that together with a lecturer in hairdressing and two psychologists (one being Denis Gahagan, the other wishing to remain anonymous) I have, in recent years, conducted weekend residential courses entitled 'Psychology in Hairdressing', and have acted as an adviser to a number of hairdressing companies. I hope that most readers' initial reaction to this confession will be one of surprise, as it was at the 'Potential Uses and Current Abuses of Psychology' symposium held at Surrey University in November 1979. There, when I made this revelation, a sudden murmur of comment arose from the audience and much shuffling of chairs occurred. Such reactions serve to underline the point that many 'academic' psychologists, *and* graduating students, seem unprepared to venture out into the commercial and industrial world. There are many reasons for this, one important factor being that it is often frowned upon as 'not being the done thing'. One trusts, however, that such short-sighted reactions are on the wane. If psychologists are not prepared to advertise their skills, then society will not be aware of its need for psychologists.

The editors of this book have asked me to present details of what we tell hairdressers that psychology has to offer them. I hope your reaction to the word 'hairdressing' included some aspect of amazement or disbelief because such reactions may make clearer to you the fact that although here is a very large concern in terms of financial turnover, staff employed, etc., initially you may have wondered how an experimental psychologist could make any useful contribution here, or indeed would want to. I am happy to undertake such ventures not only because I receive some financial reward for doing so but also because a number of most interesting areas for the application of psychological knowledge have become available. Knowledge of social and occupational psychology is obviously of relevance here, but experimental psychology also has a place. For example, most senior people in hairdressing, including those in charge of training, had given little, or more frequently, no thought to such important skill-training topics as: (i) massed vs. spaced practice; (ii) whole vs. part learning; (iii) the role of feedback; and (iv) transfer of training. Further, those hairdressers who attempted to style and cut hair to suit the client's face and headshape knew little or nothing about the psychology of illusions. Many hairdressers told us that they worried about the interpersonal behaviour problems which occurred between staff and clients or among the staff, yet they were ignorant of how psychology could help them there. Many managers complained that they did not know how to conduct interviews successfully and admitted that they knew little about organizational theory and practice. They were uninformed about the psychology of decision-making and frequently felt unable adequately to motivate or counsel their staff. I hope that the reader will readily agree that psychology has something to offer on all these topics, and should not be too frightened of doing so.

PSYCHOLOGY AND THE 'LEAST WORST SOLUTION'

Applying knowledge drawn from experimental psychology or using experimental psychology's techniques in real-world settings is, in my opinion, the greatest challenge an experimental psychologist can face. Here, however, one important rearrangement of approach and assessment is necessary. One has to realize that perfect solutions to applied problems *do not* exist. Perfect cure is not possible, it is a myth. What one is attempting to do is to *reduce* the problem as much as possible.

One of the major strains placed upon applied psychology is that it is usually only called in when things are going wrong. As a psychologist attempting to apply psychological knowledge to the real world one has to accept that one is frequently called in too late in the sense that the problem the organization (or whatever) is experiencing is now considerable, even extreme. It is a comment on psychology that it is often called in as a last resort. So, one is faced with an organization experiencing a problem and one is usually required to deal with this problem in a very short time-scale. In such situations (and perhaps in all situations) psychology can never come up with the 'real answer', the perfect solution. We should rearrange our views and see psychology as attempting to arrive at what I call the 'least worst solution'. Even in areas of life in which psychologists' errors may be of substantially greater importance than in hairdressing it would be well for this dictum to be observed.

As I stated earlier, one of my own areas of research is that of eyewitness memory. Here errors made in the judicial system based on identification (both of people possibly being convicted on unsafe grounds, and of the real culprits not being convicted) can be of great significance to those involved. Even here, in this area, I have noted (Bull and Clifford, 1979) Samuel Butler's comment that, 'Life is the art of drawing sufficient conclusions from insufficient data'. Perhaps a good psychology finals exam question would be: 'Psychology is the science of drawing sufficient conclusions from insufficient data. Discuss'. If this view were more widely adopted by experimental psychologists then more uses would be found for psychology in the real world.

When this perspective is adopted the worries which experimental psychologists have about not being able to arrive at safe conclusions are modified. They still remain genuine, important worries but these must be set against the outcome of doing nothing at all and therefore letting the problem remain. This dilemma is well highlighted in clinical psychology. Here the patients have problems. Is it better to attempt no therapy because the outcome of any therapy is never certain, or is it better to take a calculated risk and attempt one of the currently available therapies fully in the knowledge that such a procedure could, in fact, result in the patient actually getting worse? Such dilemmas are faced every day by clinical psychologists, and experimental psychologists should not constantly avoid such situations merely because the 'pure science' approach is not directly applicable. Westland (1978) cites Kaplan (1964) as making this point by saying that: 'The work of the behavioural scientist might well become methodologically sounder if only he did not try so hard to be scientific!' James Deese (1969), for so long a researcher on the topic of 'pure learning', has stated that: 'The model of experimenting taken from the physical sciences is useful as an aid in psychological research, but I have reached the conclusion that it no longer belongs in the centre of psychology'.

Here is not the place to discuss whether psychology is, in fact, a science. In my opinion it definitely is so. Most debates on this topic take the definition of science as read and then discuss whether psychology is the same thing. I would like to suggest that the definition of 'science' should not be assumed and that what constitutes 'science' in the real world should be debated before one discusses whether psychology is similar to it or not.

One of the important reasons why we believe psychology needs to be seen as a science relates to the funding of research. During this century science has been viewed as being of great value, of making significant practical advances, and to science has gone (and still goes) most research funding. Psychologists want, quite rightly, to receive part of the cake. However, in our attempt to mirror the investigatory approach of the 'pure' sciences we have *lost* funding because what many experimental psychologists do has been judged by the real world as having produced few, if any, useful advances. The more the science of psychology attempts to imitate the pure sciences the more it will lose. The more it attempts to be an applied science the better for all of us.

TRAINING IN PSYCHOLOGY

Our training in psychology both of undergraduates and post-graduates should bear this in mind. In my own department I urge all students who write essays or experimental reports for me to include in their introduction statements which answer the question: 'From the point of view of real-world situations and problems, what is the value of this topic?' Once the students become used to this apparently *strange* request they often find something to say on this point.

Alan Baddeley (1979) has recently fired the debate concerning what PhD training in psychology should consist of, and in response the Scientific Affairs Board of the BPS has set up a working party on this topic. Baddeley, rightly in my view, complained about the narrowness of most PhDs, and of their using a restricted range of investigatory procedures to examine a single topic in depth. He pointed out, as we are no doubt all aware, that the question of choice of topic is crucial. Perhaps I could suggest that if more psychology PhDs were based on research at the interface between psychology and the real world then the complexity of most real-world problems might force the research student to adopt more than one single investigatory approach. The PhD work of Nichola Rumsey, described in the third paragraph of this chapter, in my opinion exemplifies this.

Baddeley also mentioned the limited nature of most psychology PhDs when the authors of these theses are attempting to gain employment. The typical psychology PhD may have some (though perhaps limited) predictive validity with regard to lectureships in psychology, but many employers in the real world complain that the possession (or expected possession) of a psychology PhD tells them very little about the qualities they need from a successful applicant. Sometimes employers have told me that they are biased *against* psychology PhDs because they believe this tells them something undesirable about the applicant.

Baddeley suggested that: 'The implicit model underlying PhD training appears to be that of the nineteenth-century scholar who is able to immerse himself in the topic of his choice until such time as he produces a substantive monograph on the subject'. This gentleman-scholar model may still be appropriate in certain disciplines, but Baddeley argued that psychology is not one of them since he saw most subsequent occupations of psychologists as being, 'likely to involve interacting with other people, writing in such a way as to interest and influence them, and meeting reasonably short deadlines'. Baddeley believes, and so do I, that the psychology PhD student is rarely given either training or experience in any of these.

For the good of psychology I believe that post-graduate and undergraduate training in psychology should devote some effort to enabling the student to become reasonably proficient at communicating meaningfully about psychology to non-psychologists.

EXPERIMENTAL PSYCHOLOGY AND THE MEDIA

Eunice Belbin (1979) has expressed her view that psychologists need to be able 'to communicate in the vernacular' with non-psychologists. Experimental psychologists, however 'pure' they are, should consciously attempt to spread the knowledge gained by their research not only through learned psychological journals but also through the more popular media. We should rid ourselves of the idea that communicating with the outside world must result in a loss of academic standing or status. Society pays us and we ought actively to try to tell society that we have found out so far. Westland (1978) makes the point that 'Psychology needs to be *seen* to be believed', and although this statement can be taken more than one way, it is worth bearing in mind. Of course, psychology and psychologists are often misrepresented by the media, but why should this be? Is it their fault or ours? It is easy for experimental psychologists to say that reporters are too stupid to understand, or that they have to appear stupid because their readers are. But this does not really get us anywhere. It is sometimes possible even in the most popular press for complex psychological ideas to be put over in an understandable way. Psychologists need to develop this. It will take some time and, as in any marriage, there will be some bad moments.

I remember one of the radio interviews I had in 1979 following the publication of our *The Psychology of Person Identification* which was for the *Newsbeat* programme on BBC Radio One. I was asked the question: 'Do men or women make better witnesses?' From the experimental psychologist's point of view an answer to this imprecise question might take ten minutes. I was required to reply with one sentence. I attempted to describe an interactive effect by saying that if the criminal incident involved much emotion then men were likely to have more accurate recall than women, but if the incident involved little emotion then women might be better. The interview was being taped to be broadcast later in the day and so the interviewer asked if we could go over the question again. I thought that perhaps I had attempted to convey too much by my reply! But instead of saying my reply had been too long-winded for her listeners, the interviewer asked if this time I would not use the 'difficult word "emotion" '! She suggested that I used the word 'stress' instead. I complied with her request. As Belbin (1979) suggested, applicable psychology needs people who can be flexible.

Before I conclude this chapter I would like to mention briefly the relationship between psychology and commonsense. Most psychologists will be familiar with the view held by many members of the general public that the majority of psychology is totally divorced from reality and that the remainder of psychology is only commonsense anyway. It is true that most of the suggestions psychology has made for real-world situations are thought merely to agree with intuitive commonsense. (A number of counter-intuitive points come to mind, for example, cognitive dissonance, but they are in the minority.) But one should ask from where this commonsense arises. The findings of psychologists are sometimes so readily adopted by society that few realize the debt owed to psychology (for example many modern child-rearing practices owe a lot to psychology). The important point about the relationship between psychology and commonsense is that it is desirable, often imperative, to have a fair degree of confidence in what one proposes. Psychology does (or can do) a good job by giving support, and often a fairly firm foundation, for practices, therapies, and changes which tie in with commonsense.

CONCLUSION

I would like to conclude this chapter by reiterating that we need to consider what harm null-hypothesis testing does to psychology, and we need to attempt to be creative and increase the development, understanding, and usage of alternative methods of making inferences from data. We need to accentuate and publicize the agreements within psychology concerning the many crucial points that we do in fact agree upon. We should also consider the public relations effects of the constant public bickering between ourselves that we seem to go out of our way to create.

Further, if psychologists admitted publicly the extent of the problems they face in attempting to study the workings of the most complex things in the world (that is humans) then we would not be so readily criticized for failing to achieve what initially we already knew was impossible to achieve anyway. The ultimate question to ask of psychology is *not* whether psychologists can answer *perfectly* questions about human behaviour, but whether anybody else can produce *better* answers and solutions than those provided by psychologists. Are their 'least worst solutions' any better than ours? I doubt it. I hope that I have not been too pessimistic in this chapter. Believe it or not I do believe that modern psychology is the greatest thing since sliced brains.

Given that psychology (and for that matter any other discipline) will never completely solve any of life's problems, we have made a reasonable start. However, especially in today's economic climate, we cannot afford to be complacent. We need to get out there and do it!

REFERENCES

Baddeley, A. (1979). 'Is the British PhD. system obsolete?', *Bulletin of the British Psychological Society*, 32, 129–131.

Belbin, E. (1979). 'Applicable psychology, and some national problems: a synopsis of the 1978 Myers Lecture', *Bulletin of the British Psychological Society*, 32, 241–244.

Bull, R. (1979). 'The psychological significance of facial deformity', in *Love and Attraction*, M. Cook and G. Wilson (eds.), Oxford: Pergamon.

Bull, R. and Clifford, B. (1979). 'Eyewitness memory', Chapter 6 in *Applied Problems in Memory*, M. Gruneberg and P. Morris (eds.), London: Academic Press.

Bull, R. and Stevens, J. (1981). 'The effect of facial deformity on helping behaviour' *Italian Journal of Psychology*, 8, 1, 25–33.

Clifford, B. and Bull, R. (1978). *The Psychology of Person Identification*, London: Routledge & Kegan Paul.

Deese, J. (1969). 'Behavior and fact', *American Psychologist*, 24, 515–522.

Grenwald, A. (1975). 'Consequences of prejudice against the null hypothesis', *Psychological Bulletin*, 82, 1–20.

Kaplan, M. (1964). *The Conduct of Inquiry*, San Francisco: Chandler.

McHugh, M. F. (1969). 'Lies, damned lies, and statistics', *Bulletin of the British Psychological Society*, 22, 143.

Westland, G. (1978). *Current Crises of Psychology*, London: Heinemann.

SUBJECT INDEX

AAL Medical Surveys Centre Limited, 255
Academic psychologists, work in commercial and industrial fields, 339–340
Actuarial evidence, impact on law enforcement, 99–101
Adolescence and childbearing, adult education classes, 153
Adult education, aims, 152
    class composition, 155
    model for psychotherapy, 158
    role of psychologists, 151–163
Adult education classes, advertising, 154
    psychology teaching, 9
    research pool, 161–162
Adult learning, basic principles, 196
    theory, 11–16
Advertising, 251, 257–261
Advisory role, psychologists in communication technology, 279
Air traffic control systems, measurement of input, 244
Air traffic controllers, performance measurement, 244–245
Aircraft cockpits, effect on map use, 242–243
Altimeter design, role of aviation psychologists, 237–238
American Adaptive Behaviour Scale, assessment of social competence of mentally handicapped people, 68
American Psychological Association, 20
American Psychological Association, Division of Consumer Psychology, 249
Amnesia, use of hypnosis in court cases, 96–98

Analgesic requests, effect of pre-operative information and counselling, 51
Andragogy, in adult education, 155–156
Applied psychology, 2
Architects, co-operation with environmental psychologists, 304–305
    collaboration with psychologists, 9
Armed forces, role of psychologists, 4
Art therapy, mentally handicapped people, 72
Assessment, role of clinical psychologists, 28–30
    role of educational psychologists, 128–131
Assessment schedules, clinical psychologists, 29
Association for all Speech Impaired Children, 140
Association for the Teaching of Psychology, 156
Attitude studies, competing products, 258
Attitudinal data market analysis, 246
Audio communications systems, measurement of differences from audio-video communication systems, 278
Authoritarian bureaucracies, contribution to poor work environments, 222
Authoritarian leadership forms, evaluation of efficiency, 209
Autonomous working group, approach to work design, 172
Aviation, international and interdisciplinary aspects, 234–235
Aviation cartography, role of aviation psychologists, 9, 240–243

347

Aviation psychologists, qualification and types of employment, 233–234
Aviation psychology, 233–248
reliance on social psychological methods, 15
Aviation technology, in relation to personnel, 247

Banks, customer stereotypes, 264–265
perceived differences, 261–263
personality variations, 264–265
Barclays Bank, personality, 265
Behaviour, duration of changes after in-service training for teachers, 136
Behaviour disturbance, in mentally handicapped people, intervention by psychologists, 71–72
Behaviour modification, by techniques of organization psychology, 207
prisoners, 111–112
Behaviour patterns, effect on coronary heart disease, 53
in fires, 299
Behaviour therapy, ethics of use on prisoners, 113–115
value to clinical psychology, 26–28
Behavioural contracts, in curriculum planning and class organization, 159–160
Behavioural data, market analysis, 284
Behavioural psychotherapy, courses for nurses, 30
Biochemical indices, of mental work load of air traffic controllers, 245
Biographical data, in assessment of mental work load of air traffic controllers, 245
Blood pressure monitoring, effect of educational programmes, 54–55
Boehringer Ingelheim Limited, 255
Boredom, possible effects in aviation, 246
Brain-washing techniques, Korean war, 215
Brand loyalty, 252
Brand Personality Technology, 262–263
British Association of Behavioural Psychotherapy, membership, 30–31
British Psychological Society, 4, 9–11, 19, 157, 206
membership as an indicator of growth of profession, 9–12

professional affairs board, 11
British Psychological Society Bulletin, 338
Bronchitis, involvement of faulty behaviour, 53
Building design, for increased safety during fires, 296
psychological input, 301
Building management, services of environmental psychologists, 293
Building regulations, means of escape from fire, involvement of environmental psychologists, 294–301
Building remodelling, advice from environmental psychologists, 304–306
Building societies, perceived differences, 261
Buildings, post occupancy evaluation by environmental psychologists, 306–307
Bureaucratic structure, of organizations, 216–217
Burt, Cyril, 125, 170

Campaign for the Mentally Handicapped (1972), 70
(1978), 81
Cancers, involvement of faulty behaviour, 53
Cardiovascular disorders, involvement of faulty behaviour, 52–53
Career opportunities, 11
Career structure, for clinical psychologists in National Health Service, 24–26
Careers counselling, occupational psychologists, 173, 178, 182, 188–191
Caring professions, need for inclusion of mental handicap in training, 79–81
Change agents, organizational psychology, 215
role of psychologist at organizational and individual level, 280–283
Change within organizations, approaches to, 214–215
method of introduction, 205–206, 217–221, 228
reactions to, 205
Charade sessions, questionnaire development, 264
Child abuse, role of behaviour therapy, 31
Child Guidance Clinics, 125
Children, attitudes to mental handicap, 81–83

Cirrhosis of liver, involvement of faulty behaviour, 53
Class organization, adult education, 159–160
Classification scheme for meetings, development, 276–277
Client identification, organization psychology, 207, 210–214, 228
Client orientation, 4–5
Client type, environmental psychologists, 292–293
Clinical psychologists, activities, 28–36
  co-operation with educational psychologists in care of mentally handicapped people, 63–64
  co-operation with health visitors to improve parentcraft classes, 35–36
  membership of British Psychological Society, 11–12
  need to understand day-to-day running of hospitals, 78
  qualifications for employment in National Health Service, 23–24
  relationships with families of handicapped members, 75
  teaching role in courses relevant to mental handicap, 77
Clinical psychology, 2, 23–38
  adult education classes, 154
  as part of undergraduate education, 15–16
  changing role in National Health Service, 24, 26
  effect on aviation, consumer and environmental psychology and communication technology, 15
  future developments, 36–38
  value of behaviour therapy, 26–28
Clinical psychology services, organization, 25–26
Clothing losses, investigation by prison psychologists, 110
Codes of practice, professional psychologists, 20–21
Cognition, in undergraduate teaching, 14
Colour, evaluation in relation to videotex systems, 279
Column widths, effect on text design, 312–314
Commercial development, effect of consumer psychology, 249

Commonsense, in relation to psychology, 344
Communication between health care professionals, effect on length of stay in hospital, 51–52
Communication channels, diplomatic role for environmental psychologists, 303–304
Communication of ideas to layman, 339
Communication of solutions by occupational psychologists, 179–180
Communication psychologists, 6
Communication skills, as part of undergraduate education, 17
  importance to environmental psychologists, 308
Communication technology, and psychology, 271–287
  opportunities for psychologists, 274–275
  reliance on social and organizational psychological methods, 15
Communication with other professionals, 7–9
Communications, in aviation, investigation by psychologists, 247
'Communications between Doctors, Nurses and Patients' (1963), 34
Communications Studies Group, London University, psychological research on emerging technology, 276–278
Community, involvement in treatment begun in prison, 112
Company image, investigation by psychologists, 261–265
Computer-assisted writing, implications of psychological approach to text design, 330
Computer-typesetting, facilitating instructional text design, 319
Computers, role in production of psychological data, 266
Consumer psychological techniques, use in environmental psychology, 307
Consumer psychologists, ethics, 268
  relationship between interests and activities, 266
  required qualities, 269
  role, 267
Consumer psychology, 249–269
  commercial impact, 268
  justification, 268

of automated office products and services, 276

reliance on social and organizational psychological methods, 15

Consumer research, 250–252

Copyright infringement, role of forensic psychologists in determination, 94

Cost effectiveness, consideration in commercial enterprise, 266

Costs, of wrong employee selection techniques, 185–186

Counselling, role occupation psychologists, 183

Counselling skills, supplement to undergraduate psychology courses, 285

Course content, undergraduate psychology training, 18

Course planning, role of education psychologists in adult education, 152–153

Court activities, investigation psychologists, 92

Criminal mind, investigation by hypnosis, 98

Criminal offences, role for forensic psychologists, 94–95

Critical role, organization psychologists, 204

Curriculum planning, student involvement, 158–159

Customer observation, recreation centres, use of behavioural mapping techniques, 305

Democratic leadership forms, efficiency, 209

Demonstration job-redesign projects, 211, 213

Department of Education and Science, organization of adult education classes, 151

Design process, instructional text, 312–320
role of environmental psychologists, 291

Design psychologists, 6

Designing Instructional Text, 314, 319

Deskilling of jobs, World War I, 208

Diagnosis, of organization's requirements for selection or training, 180, 193–198

Direct-care staff, mentally handicapped people, assistance of psychologists, 76–78

Disagreement with rules, effect on

compliance by health care professionals, 49

Disaster victims, psychology, 4

Disordered behaviour, medical or psychological view, 114

'Dixarit', launching, 254–257

'Doctor–patient' model, use in Shell project, 216

Doctors, relationship with psychologists, 27–28, 115

Document use, importance of design of instructional text, 312–313

Dominant group, effect on aims and goals of organizations, 216

Drama therapy, mentally handicapped people, 72

Drug education programmes, adverse effects, 53

Eating habits, aggravation of physical disorders, 53

Eating patterns, effect of education programmes, 54–55

Education, evaluation of role of videotex, 280
layman, 8–9
of clients in understanding consumer psychology, 280
part in preparation for employment, 182
role of psychologists, 7

Education policy formation, role of educational psychologists, 144–146

Educational and child psychologists, membership of British Psychological Society, 11–12

Educational and training programmes, for introduction of new systems, 281

Educational psychologists, 2, 6
co-operation with clinical psychologists in care of the mentally handicapped, 63–64
training, 147–148

Education psychology, 125–148
future developments, 147
growth, 125

Effective performance, identification of qualities for, 186–187

Efficiency, improvement through scientific management methods, 167–168
measurement by aviation psychologists, 234

Electronic communication systems, effectiveness and acceptability testing, 277–278

Electronic technology, courses to promote understanding among psychologists, 286

Emotional problems, counselling from psychologists for families with mentally handicapped children, 73

Emphysema, involvement of faulty behaviour, 53

Empirical research, as part of undergraduate psychology, 285

Employee participation, psychological input to building design, 301

Employee selection, a case study, 192–195

Employment flowchart, 180–181

Emotions, interpretation by psychologists in mentally handicapped people, 70–71

Encounter groups, in borstal, evaluation, 109–121

Energy conservation, psychology, 4

Environmental design, role of psychologists, 289–309

Environmental psychologists, constraints in relationship with clients on building design projects, 301
constraints on activities, 296
relationship with other professionals, 307

Environmental psychology, growth of the profession, 289–291
recognition, 290–291
reliance on social and organizational methods, 15
scientific approach, 308

Epilepsy, and violence, assessment by forensic psychologists, 96–97

Equipment manufacturers, role for psychologists in communication technology, 274

Ergonomics, 167
development, 209
of visual displays, 276
of work stations and physical environment, 276

Ergonomics Research Society, 170

Erikson-type hypnotic technique, use in group situations by psychologists, 282

Ethical issues, 286
clinical psychology, 341
consumer psychology, 268
methods of obtaining informed consent, 46–48
treatment of prisoners, 113–115
use of hypnosis by forensic psychologists, 94

Ethogenic approach, to strategies of research, 16

Evaluation, adult education courses, 160–161

Examination questions, effect of making questions more readable, 324–325

Exercise, effect of lack on physical disorders, 53

Experimental psychologists, consensus of opinion, 338–340

Experimental psychology, in relation to behavioural and psychological problems in real world, 335
in relation to the media, 343–344

Experiments, design for outside laboratory use, 336

Extra-mural education, psychology, 151

Eyewitness memory, investigation, 335, 341, 343

Facial deformity, effect on general public and people concerned, 335–336

Fact provision, role of psychologists, 280

Families of mentally handicapped people, work of psychologists, 66, 72–75

Family support groups, 74

Fascistic leadership forms, evaluation of efficiency, 209

Field studies, as part of undergraduate education, 16

Fighting machines, involvement of organizational psychologist in design, 209

Fire, human behaviour, 295–301

Fire alarms, lack of response to, 299–300
need for new designs, 300

Fire officers, selection with attention to role and role relationships in the organization, 300

Fire Research Service, 295

Fire safety, design priorities, 297

Fires, model of behaviour, 297–299
training for fire drill, 300

Fishbein, expectancy-value equation, effect of shifting of variables on perceptions and beliefs, 281–282
Flesch Reading Ease Formula, 34
Football violence, psychology, 4
Forecasting techniques, training to supplement undergraduate courses, 285
Forensic psychologists, actuarial role, 99–101
    advisory role, 101
    clinical role, 95–99
    experimental role, 93–95
Fraud cases, psychological assessment of the accused, 96
Freud, Sigmund, 15, 208
Frightening information, effects on patients, 49
Fry Readability Chart, 34

General awareness, occupational psychologists, 174–175
General medical practice, role of clinical psychologists, 36–38
General practitioners, referrals to clinical psychologists, 37
General public, attitudes to mental handicap, 81
    involvement in care of the mentally handicapped, 81
Germany, Gestalt psychologists at Bauhaus School, 289
    work reform projects, 224
Government departments, role for psychologists in communication technology, 274
Graylingwell booklet, investigation of comprehensibility by clinical psychology, 34
Graylingwell Hospital, assessment techniques, 28–30
    investigation into problems of self-referring patients by Psychology Department, 32–33
    Nurse Behaviour Therapy Course, 30
Group behaviour, method of exploration, 216
Group dynamics, of workshops, 281

Habit disorders, effectiveness of behaviour therapy, 27
Hairdressing, psychology of, 339–340

Head teacher, attitude to educational psychologists, 127–128, 137–139
Health and safety at work, legislation, 221–222
Health care professionals, changing behaviour to improve care, 43
    non-compliance with advice, 48
Health education programmes, effectiveness in preventing undesirable behaviours, 53–55
    role of psychologists, 53
Health psychologists, 6
Health-related written documents, understandability, 45–46
Health visitors, co-operation with clinical psychologists to improve parentcraft classes, 35–36
HM Borstal, Bullwood Hall, evaluation of encounter groups, 109, 121
HM Prison Grendon, psychology, 106, 108
HM Prison Holloway, attitudes to psychologists, 108–109
Home Office, effect on British professional psychology, 20
'Homework', in adult education for psychology, 160
Horizontal spacing, design of instructional text, 318–320
Human behaviour in fires, 295–301
Human Factor, 169
Human factors, in industry, 169–170
Human relations, 209
Human relations movement, 171
Humanistic psychology movement, 171
Hypnosis, application in forensic psychology, 97–99
    ethical issues for forensic psychologists, 99
    examination of amnesia, 97
    use with individuals in relation to occupational stress and coping patterns, 282
Hypnotherapy, in adult education psychology courses, 154

Ignorance, effect on compliance by health care professionals, 49
In-patients, numbers in relation to out-patients, 36
In-service training, psychological courses for teachers, 127

role of educational psychologists, 133–136

In-service training for teachers, evaluation, 135–136

Independence, improved levels for mentally handicapped people, 65–66

Individual casework, education psychologists, 126–133

Individual clients, facilitation of change by psychological methods, 281

Individual workers, help from occupation psychologists, 173, 177–178
preparation for job choices, 182

Individuals, positive response to training for understanding stress, 199

Induction, in new job, role of psychologists, 183

Industrial efficiency, textbook, 166

Industrial Fatigue Research Board, 169

Industrial Health Research Board, 169

Industrial organizational psychology, 167

Industrial psychologists, 6

Industrial psychology, history, 165–166

Industrial social psychology, development, 170–172

Information, production for decision making in prisons, 109

Information, psychological research into types for videotex systems, 279

Information dissemination practices, investigation in policemen, 335

Information for management decisions, 178

Information handling, psychological aspects, 273

Information resource, role of psychologists, 279–280

Informed consent, role of the psychologist in problems, 43
ethics of compliance induction attempts, 46–48

Institutional management, effect of prison psychologists research, 121–122

Instructional text, evaluation in context, 329
role of psychologist in design, 312–317

Intellectual functioning, mentally handicapped people, assessment, 76

Intelligence quotient testing, mentally handicapped people, 68

Intelligence testing, mentally handicapped people, 67
in selection of employees, 184–185, 187

Intercontinental Medical Statistics Limited, 254

Interactive interpersonal communication, psychological aspects, 272

Interdisciplinary skills, as part of undergraduate education, 17

Intermediary role, psychologists in communication technology, 280

International Review of Applied Psychology, 306

Interpersonal and social skills, acquisition by occupational psychologists, 174

Interpersonal behaviour, methods of exploration, 216
relevance to hairdressing, 340

Interpersonal communication, adult education classes, 154
adult education courses, 17

Interprofessional relationships, 7–9, 27–28, 115

Interview procedure, for people who experience fires, 299

Interview schedules, 187

Interview training, for job candidates, 182

Interviewing procedure, alteration for improved selection of employees, 193–194

Interviews, in development of classification scheme for face-to-face meetings, 277

Job advertisements, 182

Job choice, help from occupational psychologists, 182

Job definition, role of aviation psychologists, 234

Job design, in organizational context, 217
principles, 172
role for organizational psychologists, 204–205

'Job fit' model, occupational psychology, 166

Job specifications, 181

Joint Board of Clinical Nursing Studies courses, 27–28, 30–31

Journal of Occupational Psychology, 169

Jury selection, use of hypnosis, 97

Justification, effect on comprehension and cost of instructional text, 318

Kelly, George, 15

Language, role in readability, 323
Language handicap, local special units, 140
Law, and psychology, 89–93, 101–103
relevance of organizational psychology, 222
Learning, in undergraduate teaching, 14
scientific theories, 155–156
'Least worst solution' application of experimental psychology to real world problems, 340–341, 345
Legal psychologists, 6
Legislation, as method of preventing undesirable behaviours, 53
Lesions, location by psychological testing, 29
Life skill programmes, relationship between staff training, treatment and institutional management issues, 116–117
Lifestyle changes, economic and social implications, 56
Lifestyles, role of psychologists in changing undesirable behaviours, 53
Line extension, product development, 253
Line length, ease of reading, 314
Lloyds Bank, personality study, 262–265
Local Education Authorities, in-service training by psychologists, 133–136
organization of adult education classes, 151
Local issues, national relevance to prison service, 110

'Maladjusted' children, special schools, 131–132
Man, in relation to aviation technology, 247
Man specifications, 181
Management, aids to efficiency from organizational psychologists, 206
effect of retention of control on production methods, 220
role of psychologists, 7
Management orientated research, HM Prison Grendon, 110
Management skills, as part of undergraduate education, 17
Management structure, role of psy-

chologists in services for the mentally handicapped, 83–84
Management training, for improved selection of employees, 194–195
Managers, participation in change, 211
relationship with occupational psychologists, 166
Manpower planning, 181
Map production, collaboration between cartographers and aviation psychologists, 243
Marbe, Karl, 92–93
Marital relationships, effect of behaviour therapy in treatment of child abuse, 31
Market assessment, methods, 254–257
Market research, effect on attitudes to future communication systems, 281
Market research agencies, 255
Market research departments, value of understanding of psychology, 284
Market segmentation, 256–257
Maslow, Abraham, 171
Mass media, effects on attitudes and opinions of general public, 83
McGregor, Douglas, 171
Mechanized production, introduction of standardization of work methods, 168
Media, need for understandable approach by psychologists, 343–344
Medical information, improvement of communication to patients, 46–48
methods for improving transmission, 47
methods for understanding and recall, 47–48
Medical witnesses, role of clinical psychologists, 95
Medical Research Council, Applied Psychology Unit, 169
contribution to design, 290
Medicine, application of psychology, 41–56
Medico-legalism, in relation to clinical psychologists, 91
Meetings, development of a classification scheme, 276–277
Memory, effect of enhancing techniques on recall of medical information, 48
in undergraduate teaching, 14
investigation of performance in policeman, 335, 339

Mens rea, mental subnormality as a legal defence, 96
Mental disorders, prevention, 52
Mental handicap, attitudes of children, 82–83
  attitudes of general public, role of the psychologist, 81–83
  contribution of psychologists, 63–85
  manpower needs, 64
  need for inclusion in training programmes for caring professions, 79–81
  rights of individuals and in the community, 65
Mental state, of the accused, assessment by forensic psychologists, 96
Mental workload, measurement in air traffic controllers, 243–245
Microelectronic technology, psychological consequences, 204
Midland Bank personality, 265
Migraine, prophylactic drug, launching, 254–257
Moral issues, 286
  clinical psychology, 341
  environmental psychology, 308
Moral judgements, educational psychology, 146
Motivation, factors governing, 223
Munitions factories, beginning of industrial psychology, 169–170
Munsterberg, Hugo, 93, 166–167, 170
Music therapy, mentally handicapped people, 72
Myths, testing by psychologists in prison service, 109–110

National Development Group for the Mentally Handicapped (1978), 64
National Health Service, 26, 32–33
  effect on British professional psychology, 20
  status of clinical psychology, 32–36
National Institute of Industrial Psychology, 169
National Westminster Bank, personality, 265
Nature of knowledge, claims of psychologists, 224–227, 228
Need identification, publishing psychology, 331

Neurologists, psychological testing referrals, 29
New new products, launching, 254–257
Non-accidental injury to children, use of behaviour therapy techniques, 35–36
Non-clinical approach to health care, application of psychology, 41–44
Non-compliance with advice, reduction by psychological methods, 44–46
Non-compliance with rules of good practice, health care professionals, 49–50
'Normalization', for mentally handicapped people, role of the psychologists, 71–72
Normative-re-educative approach to change, 215
Northern Ireland Public Service Training Committee, 195
Norway, work environmental legislation, development, 224–227
Null hypothesis testing, problems, 336–338, 344
Nurse Education Centres, teaching role of psychologists in relation to mental handicap, 77
Nurses, education in clinical psychology, 30

Obsessive compulsive behaviour, effectiveness of behaviour therapy, 27
Occupational psychologists, membership of British Psychological Society, 11–12
  modes of operation, 177–200
  qualification and experience, 179
  reasons for being employed, 174–175
  roles, 6, 214–217
  use of hypnotic techniques in attempt to cope with technological change, 282
Occupational psychology, development, 165–176
  historical origins, 165–172
Officer selection, involvement of organizational psychologists, 209
Operational research, prison service, 119
Organization development methods, introduction by psychologists, 281
Organization issues, role of education psychologists, 136–139

Organizational components, effects of relationships on building design, 302
Organizational problems, relevance of psychological concepts, models and theories, 207
Organizational psychological techniques, use in environmental psychology, 307
Organizational psychologists, 2
  overview of work, 227–229
  role, 215
Organizational psychology, 203–229
  development, 170–172, 207–209
  history and development, 206
  influence on aviation, consumer and environmental psychology and communication technology, 15
  relevance to law, 222
  undergraduate education, 145–146
Organizational theory and practice, relevance to hairdressing, 340
Organizations, business planning, 180–182
  effect on the individual, 203
  help from occupational psychologists, 177–178
  lack of effect of training staff to understand stress, 199–200
  study by occupational psychologists, 172
Out-patients, numbers in relation to in-patients, 36
Oversimplification, effect on understandability of text, 328–329

Packaging, 250–251
Page size, effect on text design, 312–314
Parentcraft classes, assessment of effectiveness by psychologists and health classes, 35–36
Parents, relationship with educational psychologists, 131–132, 139–141
Patients, changing behaviour to improve health care, 42–43
  non-compliance with advice, reduction by psychological methods, 44–46
Peggy Jay Report (DHSS, 1979), 79
People and Technology Heuristic Workshop, development of techniques, 281–282
Perceived properties, exploitation by advertising, 269
Perception, in undergraduate teaching, 14

Perception psychologists, collaboration with architects in Soviet Union, 289
Perceptions and beliefs, alteration by workshops, 28–32
Performance, measurement in air traffic controllers, 244–245
'Person–environment fit' model, occupational psychology, 166
Personal Construct Theory, 16
  in career guidance, 189–191
Personality theories, 207–208
Personnel psychology, 165, 167
  development, 170
Personnel selection, role of psychologists, 182, 192–195
Personnel selection and appraisal, occupational psychology, 166
Personnel selection and training, role of aviation psychologists, 234
PhD training, in psychology, 14, 342–343
Phobic disorders, effectiveness of behaviour therapy, 27
Physical disorders, role of psychology in prevention, 52–55
Physiological indices, of mental work load of air traffic controllers, 245
Pilot requirement, altimeter design, 237
Pilot trials, design and evaluation by psychologists, 281
Police, involvement of psychologists in training, 92
  study of memory performance, 335, 339
Policy issues, interest of organization psychologists, 223
Policy making role of environmental psychologists, 292
Pornography, assessment of effect by forensic psychologists, 93
  psychologists as expert witnesses in court cases, 95
Portage Home Teaching Programme, 74
Post graduate training, in psychology, 342–343
'Potential Uses and Current Abuses of Psychology', Surrey University (1979), 1
Power-coercive approach to change, 214
Practical problems, of families with mentally handicapped members, advice from psychologists, 74

Pre-operative communication, effect on patient pain and length of recovery period, 50–52
Pre-release training, role of prison officers, 116–117
Prevention of disease, role of psychologists, 52–55
Primary care level, involvement of clinical psychologists with general practitioners, 35
role of clinical psychologists, 36–37
Printing methods, costs, 321
traditional versus computer assisted, 330
Prison culture, effect on treatment programmes, 113
Prison management, involvement of prison psychologists, 107–111
Prison officer–inmate relationship, 112–113
Prison officers, training programmes, 108
Prison populations, selection for non-custodial dispersals, 110
Prison psychologists, 2, 105, 23
education of other professionals, 9
research, 92
Prison regimes, evaluation, 120–122
Prison security, in relation to psychological treatment at HM Prison Grendon, 108
Prison service, role of psychologists, 105–123
Prison Service College, Wakefield, 116
Prison staff, training, involvement of prison psychologists, 115–118
training for pre-release courses for prisoners, 117–118
Prisons, involvement in overall management, 111
Problem identification, role of aviation psychologists, 246
undergraduate education, 16–17
Problem-oriented approach, occupational psychology, 173
Problem solving, 5, 7
exercises in adult education, 160
Product, effect on selection of employees, 192
Product changes, effectiveness in preventing undesirable behaviours, 53
Product development, 250, 252–257
Product image, 252

effect of altered advertising and re-packaging on sales, 259–261
Product names, role of psychologists in generation, 267
Product profile, in relation to desired product attributes, 257
Product recognition, 253
Production engineers, 168–169
Productivity, in relation to psychological well-being in organizations, 205
Productivity deals, planning by participative joint parties, 211
Procedural methods of prose simplification, 328
Professional ethics, 20–21
Professional psychology, development, 1–21
Progress Assessment Chart, 29
Projective techniques, in adult education, 160
Prose simplification, methods, 325–329
Psychiatrists, psychological testing referrals, 29
Psychiatry, in relation to the law, 89
Psycho-legal education, 91–92
Psycho-social factors, contribution to poor work environments, 22
Psychodynamic therapy, 32
Psychological assessment, mentally handicapped children need for communication with parents and relatives, 75
Psychological functions, testing of effects of lesions, 30
Psychological statistics, 336–338
Psychological testing, assessment of mental state of accused criminals, 96
mentally handicapped people, 67–68
teaching of practical aspects to supplement undergraduate courses, 285
World War I, 208
Psychologist–doctor relationship, prisons, 115
Psychologists, choice of methods, 283
collaboration with typographic designer on text design, 312
co-operation with professionals in publishing industry, 331
establishment of professional image, 283–284
future role, 19–21

need for involvement in new disciplines, 330–331
relationship with doctors, 27–28
research into communication technology, 275
training in mental handicap, 80
Psychology and the law, 89–93, 101–103
applications to medicine, 41–56
broadening of activities and roles, 6–7
changes in practice, 4–6
definition, 341–342
promotion of understanding in adult education, 153–154
relevance of adult education courses, 156–157
sharing knowledge and expertise, 311–312
teaching methods, 158–160
theory and practice in adult education, 152
Psychology graduates, work opportunities, 1–3
Psychology of illusions, relevance to hairdressing, 340
Psychology of Person Identification, 343
Psychotherapy, calculated risks, 341
role of clinical psychologists, 31–32
links with adult education, 157–158
Publishing, co-operation between psychologists and professionals, 331

'Quality of working life' movement, development, 172
Quasi-hypnotic techniques, use in group situations by psychologists, 282
Questionnaires, development for brand personality measurement, 263–264
in development for face-to-face meetings, 277
role in product development, 255–256

Rational–empirical approach to change, 215
Readability, effect on design of instructional texts, 323–329
measurement, 323–324
Readers, effect of ability to read on ability to comprehend material, 325
Reading age, formulae for estimation, 323
Records, use for identifying characteristics of clientele, 305

Recovery speed, effect of pre-operative information and counselling, 51
Recreation centres, part in life of customers, 306
Redundancy counselling, 178
Relaunching, product development, 253
Remedial teaching, assessment of effectiveness, 142–143
Repackaging, effect on product sales, 260
Repertory Grid, career guidance, 188–191
consumer psychology, 266
Repositioning, product development, 253
Research, educational psychology, 141–144
in relation to decision making, 6–7
into contribution of adult education, 161–162
role of clinical psychologists, in National Health Service, 32–33
studies in operation problems and institutional processes in prisons, 119
Research methods, application to clinical issues, 32
in adult education, 160
Research psychologists, in communication technology, 275–279
Residential schools, for 'maladjusted' children, 131–132
Resources, advice from occupational psychologists on best use, 178–179
Responsible body courses, organization and administration, 151–155
Retirement, role of occupational psychologists in preparation, 183
Rodger, Alec, 170
Rogers, Carl, 5, 158, 208
Role structure, in building at time of fire, effect on behaviour, 299

Salesmen, recruitment for insurance broking industry, diagnosis of company needs, 184–188
School achievement, effect of socioeconomic variables, 143–144
School children, effect on in-service training for teachers, 136
School organization, consultant role for educational psychologist, 137–139
Scientific management, effect on productivity, 167–169
Sculpting, in adult education, 160

Self-care skills, reaching to mentally handicapped people, 70
Self-referring patients, investigation of problem by psychologists, 32–33
Sexual disturbances, effectiveness of behaviour therapy, 27
Shell, new philosophy of management, a case study, 210–214
Shift systems, effects in aviation, 246
Skills transmission, as part of undergraduate education, 17–18
training of other professions, 37–38
SMOG grading, 34
Smoking, cause or aggravation of physical disorders, 53
effect of educational programmes, 54–55
Social anxieties, effectiveness of behaviour therapy, 27
Social auditing, 224
Social behaviour, explanation by social psychologists, 223
Social competence, measurement in mentally handicapped people, 68, 76–77
Social pressures, effect on compliance by health care professionals, 49–50
Social psychological techniques, use in environmental psychology, 307
Social psychologists, membership of British Psychological Society, 11–12
Social psychology, in undergraduate education, 14–15
influence on aviation, consumer and environmental psychology and communication technology, 15
of automated office, 276
Social Science Research Council, employment of psychologists, 274
reviewing work of organizational psychologists, 209
Social sciences, understanding behaviour, 204
Social service departments, role for clinical psychologists, 37
Social skills programmes, relationship between staff training, treatment and institutional management issues, 116–117
Social skills training, possible inclusion in undergraduate psychology courses, 285

prison officers, 118
prisons, 11–12
Social workers, training in behaviour therapy, 30
Society for research into Higher Education, 161
Socio-economic variables, effect on school achievement, 143–144
Sociotechnical systems, application at Shell, 210–214
development by Tavistock Institute of Human Relations, 172
Soviet Union, collaboration of perception psychologists with architects, 289
Spacing, effect on understandability of instructional texts, 315, 329–330
Specialized helper, role of organization psychologists, 207
Standing Conference for University Teaching and Research in the Education of Adults, 152
Static assembly unit, investigation at Volvo truck division, 218–221
Statistical analysis, markets, 254–255
Statistical procedures, psychology, 337–338
Stimulation, programmes to combat the effects of institutionalization on the mentally handicapped, 70
Stress in work, training in understanding, 196–200
Suicide, effect of phone-in services, 52
Sweden, laws regarding ownership of large companies, 223
Syntax, effect on design of instructional text, 318–319
System design, use of ergonomics, 281

Target groups, of consumers, direction of advertising, 258
Task analysis, in teaching new skills to mentally handicapped people, 70
Tavistock Institute of Human Relations, 172, 209, 210
Teaching, role of clinical psychologists, 30–31
Technological innovation, effects on personnel in aviation, 246
in fire safety in relation to psychological studies, 300
reconciliation with human capabilities, role of aviation psychologists, 234

relationship of psychologist with other professionals, 283–284
Telecommunication services, role of psychologist in assessment of scope in Brazil, 280
Telecommunications Impact Model, 276
Textual methods of prose simplification, 325–326
Theories of personality, 207–208
Time-study experts, 168
Tourism, role of psychologists, 4
Training for psychologists, 4
Training, professional psychologists, 13–19
role of psychologists, 7
role for psychologists in hairdressing, 340
undergraduate psychology, 336
Training and development, role of occupational psychologists, 183, 195–200
Training programmes, for families with handicapped children, 72–74
for mentally handicapped people, 69
promotion by psychologists, 281
Treatment, function of psychologists in Prison Department, 111–115
Trethowan Report, 23, 24, 27
Trial evaluation, role of psychologist in altimeter design, 238
Trigger sessions, questionnaire development, 263
TSB personality, 265
Tutor support, adult education classes, 155
Type A behaviours, modification in reducing risks of heart disease, 55
Type A communication systems, 272
Type B communication systems, 272
Typographic research, psychological methods and their reliability, 321–322
Typographical methods of prose simplification, 326–328
Typography, in relation to aviation cartography, 242

Undergraduate psychology, relevance to professional psychology, 284–285
Undergraduate teaching, 13, 14–19, 285, 336, 342–343
Universities Council for Adult Education, 162
University adult education departments, 151

User organizations, role for psychologists in communication technology, 274
User requirements, building design, involvement of social scientists and psychologists, 290

Values, role in occupational psychology, 174–175
Vertical spacing, design of instructional text, 316–317
Victims, contribution to crime, 90–91
treatment of amnesia by hypnosis, 98
Videotex, evaluation of impact in education, 280
psychological investigation, 278–279
Visual characteristics of buildings, psychological contribution to design, 303
Visual information, coding and display, in relation to aviation maps, 242
Vocabulary generation, questionnaire development, 263
Vocational guidance, 166
Volvo truck division, methods of assembling trucks, 218–221
Voice of Reason, 32, 34

Wechsler Adult Intelligence Scale, 67
'White space', effect on comprehension of text, 315
Witnesses, treatment of nervousness by hypnosis, 97–99
Work, and psychology, 165–176
organizational context, occupational psychology, 166
Work environment, psychological consequences of architects proposals, 303
identification of faults by social research, 222
Work equipment, design and development, 166
Work methods, design and development, 166
Work reform projects, West Germany, 224
Workers' Educational Association, organization of courses, 151
Working conditions, arrangement, 199
Workspace design, air traffic control systems, role of psychologists, 238–240

aviation psychology, 234
role for psychologist in hairdressing, 340
World War II, origins of aviation psychology, 234

Written communications, electronic equivalents, psychological aspects, 273
Written instruction, and psychology, 311–331
Wundt, Wilhelm, 92, 165